D1453786

CONTEMPORARY NATIVE AMERICAN AUTHORS

CONTEMPORARY NATIVE AMERICAN AUTHORS

A Biographical Dictionary

Kay Juricek
Kelly J. Morgan

Fulcrum Publishing
Golden, Colorado

Copyright © 1997 Kay Juricek and Kelly J. Morgan

Book design by Bill Spahr

Library of Congress Cataloging-in-Publication Data

Juricek, Kay.
      Contemporary Native American authors : a biographical dictionary / Kay Juricek, Kelly J. Morgan.
         p.   cm.
      Includes bibliographical references.
      ISBN 1-55591-917-0 (hardcover)
      1. American literature—Indian authors—Bio-bibliography—Dictionaries. 2. American literature—20th century—Bio-bibliography—Dictionaries. 3. Indians of North America—Biography—Dictionaries. 4. Indian authors—Biography—Dictionaries. I. Morgan, Kelly J. II. Title.
      PS153.I52J87   1997
      810.9'897'09045
      [B]—DC20
                                        96-36309
                                          CIP

Printed in the United States of America

0 9 8 7 6 5 4 3 2 1

Fulcrum Publishing
350 Indiana Street, Suite 350
Golden, Colorado 80401-5093
(800) 992-2908 • (303) 277-1623

CONTENTS

Alphabetical Listing of Authors

I

J

K

L

M

INTRODUCTION

BY KAY JURICEK

In 1991 I was approached by Shirley Lambert to write a book for Fulcrum Publishing, with the assistance of Kelly Morgan. This book was to be a collection of biographies of Native American writers, in response to the growing interest in Native American literature and the recognized lack of biographical information about these individuals. As a researcher and librarian with a lifelong interest in Native peoples, their lives, politics, history and arts, my interest was immediately captured. Shirley, Kelly and I had originally chosen to limit the authors to those who had work published during the period from 1961 to 1991, believing that with a thirty-year span we would cover what one could loosely term "modern" writers; though, the reader will soon notice that many writers of more recent publications are included in the book, as compiling the works and biographies of individuals is a difficult juggernaut to stop once it is started.

Combining Shirley's valuable contacts among writers and publishers, Kelly's knowledge and friendships with many of the writers and my research, writing and analysis experience, we set out upon what became a long and fulfilling journey.

I began to compile a master list of mid-twentieth-century writers with at least three of each writer's citations. This search took me to the Denver Public Library's general collection, its Western History Department and into cyberspace, searching for materials in computerized library systems, which enabled me to examine the published works by the authors and browse through the holdings of research libraries throughout the United States. I had gleaned authors' names from anthologies, historical writings, journals, newsletters, collected works and bibliographies, and Kelly provided recommendations and insights to our growing list of writers. We also chose to limit our search to Native writers of the United States and Canada. I cross-referenced the writers' names from the list with the numerous titles of the books used in locating their names and works, noting who appeared in which anthologies, collections, etc. Out of this work came a list of writers, each with a list of the works their writings were found in, and the number of works found in each publication, or the title of their separate works, novels, etc. (Note that the following abbreviations were used as necessary in the bibliographic material: "s.l." [sine loco], meaning the location of a publisher was not present in a book; "s.n." [sine nominae], meaning the publisher's name was not present in a book and n.d. [no date], meaning no date of publication was present in the book.)

I now had gathered together a list of several hundred names. Before proceeding with the research, we chose to further reduce the list by selecting writers who had either published three works (this could be three poems, a book and two essays, etc.) or a work of special noteworthiness between the years 1961 and 1991. From this we selected the names of authors we wanted to include in this reference book. And from this list we mailed out three rounds of questionnaires to the chosen writers to gain additional biographical information.

Gathering the biographical information was a challenge. We sent the questionnaires to Native American authors living in the United States or Canada. Numerous gracious and generous individuals chose to fill out our questionnaires and return them, many with follow-up calls and letters. To those of you who answered the questionnaire, I wish to extend my heartfelt thanks and gratitude; your responses and narratives will remain with me the rest of my days. Many writers had moved or our address information was not current, so we were unable to get questionnaires out to all those we would have liked to reach. In these cases I gleaned information about the authors from biographical write-ups in other reference works, anthologies, journal articles and the like.

There were, however, many, many individuals who we would have liked to include, but we were unable to obtain much information about them. These authors (for which there are no biographical entries) are listed at the end of the book. To those who should have been included in the text but were not, I apologize and hope you will contact Fulcrum Publishing.

Some writers were quite forthcoming about their lives while others were not. Some needed more room to answer questions, others needed less. Looking back now I wish I had asked more questions, spent more time with people and made the precious time I spent with them last a little longer. These brief offerings are given to the reader with the hopes that some information will be better than none and that it may serve to spark greater interest in these creative, diligent and gifted writers.

The publication highlights are meant to be just that—highlights that provide the reader a sample of the works by these individuals. This list is intentionally not exhaustive in this area, because the focus of this publication is meant to be on the biographical data. Some entries are in-depth; others include only the most basic facts. Great care was taken to provide the reader with as much information as possible. If the information is in error or a misrepresentation, I sincerely apologize. As the principal author and writer of this book my intention was to only have the writers speak for themselves, with their own voices, whenever possible. If this has not been accomplished, I again apologize and am solely responsible.

Many of the difficult questions we have had to deal with are these: Is this writer Native? When does one consider oneself an Indian? Is it merely a question of fractions? If an individual has a quarter or more Indian blood in their veins are they recognized as Native? Perhaps an individual's lifestyle, point of view and approach to life are more indicative of their heritage. How does a biographer with scant information about a writer discern if a person is of Native descent? How are the tribes making this decision? The ramifications are endless. These questions were posed time and again in the course of this project. We finally chose to be inclusive and not exclusive in who gets mentioned in the book, either in a full biographical write-up or in the list at the end of the text.

Without the generous help of so many people, this project would not have come together. I want to thank Shirley Lambert from Fulcrum Publishing, whose knowledge, enthusiasm and kindness were a wonderful source of strength. Her sense of humor was just the boost I needed on this long path, and I also wish to thank past Fulcrum Publishing marketing coordinator, Elizabeth Hawkes, as well as Sam Scinta and Alison Auch for assistance in this project.

Many other individuals gave freely of their time and knowledge. They are Geary Hobson, Joseph Bruchac and Don Birchfield—three men who were wellsprings of enthusiasm, kindness and generous assistance—also Joel Monture, Lisa Harjo, Karen Harvey and Marilou Awiakta. I want to thank Laura Amundson from the Institute of Alaska Native Arts, Inc., for the information she provided on Alaskan writers.

I also wish to extend my thanks and appreciation to the editorial board, which was brought together by Fulcrum Publishing: Joseph Bruchac, writer, publisher and editor;

Lisa Mitten, president of the American Indian Library Association and bibliographer at the University of Pittsburgh Libraries and Norbert S. Hill Jr., executive director of the American Indian Science and Engineering Society. They provided valuable and insightful comments, which helped to make this a better book. I wish to thank the helpful, courteous and professional staff of the Ross University Hills branch of the Denver Public Library, and the library's Western History Department.

I wish to thank my family, my parents, Franklin and Dolores Juricek, and my brother, John Juricek. They taught me to be strong, to work hard, to show compassion and to take pride in myself and in what I do. I would like to dedicate this book to my husband, Jerry Lyons; without his support and inspiration this and many other projects would not have begun or finished.

In closing, I often think of Grace Slwooko and her haunting magical image of creativity "... songs float up on you from the bottom of the sea. [If] there is one that float[s] up on me, I just sing it out." Thank you Grace Slwooko, and all the gifted Native people to whom such songs come and for singing them out.

INTRODUCTION:
A PERSONAL MANIFESTO

BY KELLY J. MORGAN

American Indian literatures are a diverse and complex subject. Within the past several years the field has grown enormously. There are many reasons why this has occurred. Primarily, there has been a continued effort on the part of Native American authors to get published. It is not coincidental that this has happened in unison with the continuing struggle for survival by Native peoples in the Western Hemisphere. Thanks to the actions of individuals such as Joseph Bruchac and Geary Hobson (to name only two), the realization of a dream has come true. For too long Native writers from the various Nations everywhere had wanted to gather. I am proud to say that I was directly involved with Returning the Gift: A Festival of North American Authors (1992). As a staff member and panel participant in The Gift, I can say that I have never seen a more diverse and complicated group of Native Americans. Ranging in every shape, size and color, they personify not only their own individual idiosyncrasies, but they also bring to the forefront something Native peoples everywhere have known for some time. That is, that we are a reflection of our Native communities and, ultimately, we exist as a window to the world, representing our peoples to the outside world.

From that conference held in Norman, Oklahoma, on the University of Oklahoma campus, a literal explosion of publications by Native American authors has occurred.[1] Thankfully, some major presses have come to realize that there is a demand for Native American literatures, and that there is a place for Native American literatures in Academe. I personally came away from the conference exhausted, yet fully proud to have met and worked with such beautiful people. It has been the most rewarding experience of my professional life.

Kay Juricek and I found the 1992 conference an excellent place to interview some of the writers we have included in this volume. Kay interviewed as many people as possible who had the time and were willing to give biographical information and specific quotes on their own personal upbringing and lifestyles. This information makes this text unique. The quality of the "Narrative" sections and other biographical information were determined by what writers themselves contributed to this project. If we found no biographical information on individual writers, we were limited in making the narrative complete. Some individuals are apprehensive to give such information as date and place of birth, personal histories, etc. With this in mind, as a writer, it is inevitable that there will be misinterpretations and misrepresentations throughout one's career. I sincerely hope that this is something that Kay and I have avoided. Certainly, there will be additions and/or corrections that will be needed in the event that this volume gets republished.[2] Anyone finding mistakes or additional material can send that information to Fulcrum Publishing. Kay gave power to the writers themselves by utilizing time spent at the conference to collect information directly from them. They gave their own thoughts on their lives and those aspects of their writing that are most significant to them as writers and Native Americans.

American Indian literatures are distinguishable from American literature. This distinction will eventually become defined more clearly with time through the writings of those American Indian writers who are now obscure or less published. American Indian literatures should not be subsumed under American literature. The two are only related in that some American writers have focused their works on American Indians. Many of these early- and late-American literary works are considered racist, ethnocentric and patronizing by American Indians. Therefore, this is why most Native scholars consider most writing by non-Natives to be outside of the American Indian literary canon. Of course, as always, there are a few exceptions to every rule. The well-known "as told-to" autobiographies are in this genre. The best example of this is *Black Elk Speaks: Being the Life Story of a Holy Man of the Oglala Sioux, As Told to John G. Neihardt* (1932). Scholars of Native American literatures, Native and non-Native alike, usually categorize these "as-told-to" stories as autobiographical. Thus, they would be included in the American Indian literary canon.

American Indian literatures have always been a canon. American Indian literatures have their roots buried deep within the psyche of the American Indian mind. The literature is as diverse and complex as the American Indian cultures and societies that it describes. There is much American ignorance about American Indians and American Indian literatures in the past and especially today. This does not exclude those individuals in Academe. In fact, the notion of American Indian literatures as being part of the American canon of literature has been generated by those in Academe.

There are many reasons American Indian literatures are a separate canon. The primary reasons are: (1) A large enough corpus of literature exists to constitute a "body of knowledge," and (2) This "body of knowledge" originates primarily from an oral culture—unlike American literature, which originates from a written culture.

American Indian literature is secondarily a written literature. Although this has changed gradually over the past two centuries (and has changed dramatically in the past few decades), many Native people still continue to rely principally on orality. There has, however, been a rapid increase in the number of written publications by Native Americans since N. Scott Momaday released *House Made of Dawn* (1968). This is where some of the problems arise.[3] Many so-called scholars of American Indian literatures believe that American Indian literatures begin with Momaday's Pulitzer Prize–winning novel (1969). This could not be further from the truth. Instead, scholars should more accurately state that Momaday's novel begins what is known as the American Indian literary "renascence," as Geary Hobson calls it in *The Remembered Earth: An Anthology of Contemporary Native American Literature* (1979).

As the first "American" literature, American Indian literatures have several differences that set them apart and make them distinct from American literature. American Indian literatures are written by American Indians. This would appear to be self-evident, yet it has been misconstrued by many people. American Indian literatures are *not* works done by non-Indians *on* American Indians. American Indian literatures are *not* works done by "wannabees" or "pseudoIndians" such as Jamakie Highwater or Lynn C. Andrews (Hobson, 1979). These individuals have exploited American Indians and values for their own personal and financial gain. This is one of the reasons such a text as this is needed. Students and teachers who are interested in studying American Indian literatures need to be able to find important biographical data on Native writers.

American Indian literatures, the various tribal groups represented by them and the individual American Indians who speak about them in the oral and written word—this is what constitutes the canon of American Indian literatures. It should be recognized and respected as such by those in Academe. Just as American Indians have not fully acculturated into mainstream American society, neither have the literatures, oral and written, of the numerous American Indian Nations assimilated into the canon of American literature.

The distinction of American Indian literatures into its own canon has been around for quite some time now, but it has been hard to convince certain enclaves in Academe as to its relevance. One question arising from many scholars, both Native and non-Native, has been: "Who is an American Indian?" For years scholars and Native peoples have grappled with this notion. If there is an "Indian problem," it resides in the fact that many individuals refuse to accept people for who they are, as products of their societies. Those individuals, whether enrollees or non-enrollees, rural or urban, who propagate the dogma surrounding whether or not specific writers should be considered American Indian, are only dragging us all down and making Native Americans in general look bad to outsiders.

Inevitably, it is necessary to give tribal background information in order that validity be lent to this text. As much as it grates against my every principle in the profession, I must agree that if an individual cannot or will not provide the appropriate tribal information, they must be excluded from being considered American Indian writers. An American Indian litmus test is to sometimes ask upon meeting someone: "What is your tribe?" It is not the intent of this text to scrutinize each writer by degree of blood. If we as writers start to do this, many well-known and highly respected individuals who write and teach American Indian literatures could be called into question.

For example, some writers early on in their careers may have written poetry or essays that could be construed by today's standards as not very "Indian," or not Indian at all (whatever that may be!). Yet, as their careers progressed, along with their writing skills and their own knowledge of their own culture(s), some of these writers have become more "intact," culturally speaking. Yes, what many Native writers know about their histories, they learned from books. So what! They are Native people struggling to keep their cultures alive. Does not the Anglo-American group and every cultural group represented in America (and the world) learn about themselves from books? Why is it not sanctioned for American Indians to do so?

At the same time, as I have mentioned before, American Indian literatures are continually being defined by those writers who are more "culturally intact." This is, in part, why some of these questions of "authenticity" have arisen in the first place. Many of the reservation and urban Indians, enrollees and non-enrollees alike, are turning to the written word as a means of expression, yes, but also as a means to stimulate interest in cultural survival.

N. Scott Momaday, in *A Man Made of Words,* refers to being American Indian as:

> an idea a given man has of himself. And it is a moral idea, for it accounts for
> the way in which he reacts to other men and to the world in general. And
> that idea, in order to be realized completely, has to be expressed. (Indian
> Historian Press, 1970)

American Indian men and women, as in other minority cultures, are using the written word to portray their personal and political beliefs. Seen as a form of promoting cultural survival, writers such as Elizabeth Cook-Lynn assert that "stories and songs and poems are fictional, but they are born of a very real and usable past which remains unforgettable. If you do not believe that memory and imagination are components of history" (Cook-Lynn 1983, Dedicatory note to *Then Badger Said This*), then there is no reason for you to be interested in reading American Indian literature.

American Indian literatures are about how American Indians identify with their cultural heritage and knowledge. Yes, as far as I am concerned, being culturally Indian is a necessary component of being an American Indian.[4] It is also a criterion for being considered an American Indian writer, artist, etc. This is an unwritten law that many "wannabees" have violated. Yet this does not require us as American Indian writers to be enrolled members of our tribes. Checking each individual's blood quantum would be racist. Some individuals are not considered to be truly *Indian,* because they do not meet another individual's criteria for who is and who isn't Indian. This is taking it a little too far. We have already seen the ramifications of what this "problem" has done to those American Indian professionals in the fine arts. It would be a mistake for those American Indians in the humanities and journalism to make the mistake of following the guidelines first set out by the federal government, defining who *we* are as individuals and groups. There is a difference between the individual who has been raised culturally Indian versus the individual whose only association to their culture is a number. I think the difference is obvious. It seems clear that many "wannabee" Indians are operating on this question: "What can I get from being Indian?" For the person truly Native at heart, what it means to be Indian is known intrinsically: "How the Earth is sacred and that we must always remember our relatives in some form on a daily basis."

Tribes as national governments should also already be wise to this type of "limiting" on the part of the state and federal governments. It seems unwise that the tribes have gone to such lengths to be exclusionary. There are two sides to every issue. I don't like to make these types of decisions, but it is necessary: the tribes must do what is in the best interest of their people—even if that means some groups require an individual to be considered half, others one-quarter and still others less. Then it is so. But when children are excluded because of a parent's gender or the fact that the mother had the child off reservation, this just doesn't hold water for me. As my mother used to say: "They are cutting the throats of their own grandchildren!" Once again, we should learn from others' past experiences. There have been several tribes in the recent past that have had to deal with this complex issue. Their grief is ample evidence of the damage rendered when a people become factionalized.

I do not have to carry a card to remember who my grandmother, Mary Rose Agard, was and how she impacts my life daily. Frankly, this is all too close to home for me as an American Indian. I am a non-enrollee from Standing Rock Indian Reservation in North and South Dakota. I am just as much a Lakota as any of my relatives. My brothers are all enrolled but my sister and I are not. Does this make us any less Indian? I think not. My mother taught me and my sister to be proud of who we are as individuals. We have tried to get enrolled but it seems that the tribe is more concerned with limiting its membership by following the 1960 cut-off date for enrollment at Standing Rock. I personally want to be a voting member of my tribe but since I live off reservation I once again would be excluded, enrollee or non-enrollee. I herald Gerald Vizenor for seeing Indian identity as:

this idea of the invented Indian. The inventions have become disguises … we're invented from traditional static standards and we are stuck in coins and words like artifacts. So we take up a belief and settle with it, stuck, static. Some upsetting is necessary. (*MELUS 8,* 1981)

Thus it is important to write ourselves and how we identify with the world around us, into existence, into history. In contemporary societies, ideas are forgotten if they are not passed down. The written word is a means to never let our existence cease and to continue passing down the knowledge we have of our histories. It is necessary to repeat ideas in order to reinforce them. This is why it is so imperative that we continue our struggle to define ourselves, in life and, ultimately, in literature. "Cultures are not static, human behavior is not static. We are not what anthropologists say we are and we must not live up to a definition. … We're very complex human beings, all of us, everywhere, but especially in America and especially among tribal groups and especially mixed-bloods" (Gerald Vizenor in *Winged Words: American Indian Writers Speak,* edited by Laura Coltelli, 1990, 172).

The more sophisticated and defined the field of American Indian literatures and the writers it studies gets, the less there will be need for such a drawn out introduction as this, and there will be more expectations by Native writers to develop theories of their own about their own writing. Of course, a certain percentage will throw all caution to the wind and risk their publishing careers by strictly writing poetry, fiction, drama, and not pay any attention to Academe. They are the ones who do not care to deal with Academe. That small percentage who teach at universities, colleges, etc., and write critically of American Indian literatures and Native studies are the ones who are responsible to all others who have come before and after them. Like it or not, those at the top are responsible to all others in the profession. Most scholars of American Indian literatures have done their part to mentor the rest of us. As we all grow in our knowledge and prestige, we are responsible to all the others. To me, that is what being a Native writer and an academic is all about. This book has been accomplished because so many wonderful people shared private aspects of their lives. Hopefully it will enrich your life.

I apologize to anyone who unintentionally may have been left out. A list of writers who we found absolutely no biographical information on, who we know to be Native authors, is included at the end of the text. There are also several names of individuals who are not North American, yet they have been published frequently in the United States. Some writers whose work was published posthumously, such as Ella Cara Deloria (*Waterlily* [1988]), will seem out of place. Yet, any work published by "contemporary" authors for the first time during the years 1961–1995 merits mention in this publication.

I would like to thank my coauthor Kay Juricek for her perseverance throughout the gathering of data, Shirley Lambert for her enthusiasm and commentary and Fulcrum Publishing for giving me the opportunity to do such an important text in Native studies. I would also like to thank Elizabeth Hawkes, past marketing coordinator for Fulcrum Publishing. Her contributions in getting this work finished is duly appreciated. Appreciation is also in order for Alison Auch and the three individuals who reviewed the manuscript. They are Norbert Hill of AISES, Joe Bruchac of the Greenfield Review Press and Lisa Mitten, the current president of the American Indian Library Association.

Finally, I would like to thank several individuals for their comments and/or guidance throughout my academic and professional career. I would not be teaching Native American literature without their continued support and criticism. They are Mary Jane Schneider, Geary Hobson, Morris Foster, Barbara Hillyer, Betty J. Harris and Alan Velie. I also need to thank Maurice Kenny, Frank Parmon and Regina J. Bennett. These are only a few of the many individuals who have inspired me to achieve my goals, to be proud of who I am and what I believe in, both personally and professionally. I would like to add a dedicatory note to my mother, Victoria L. Morgan, may she rest in peace. To the Lakota Oyate, may your children always be present on the Plains, Northern and Southern.

NOTES

1. *Returning the Gift: Poetry and Prose from the First North American Native Writers Festival,* ed. by Joseph Bruchac. (Tucson: University of Arizona Press, 1994). This is one of many publications in the past four years that are directly or indirectly related to the conference held in 1992.

2. The information in this text is inclusive through 1995. Although Kay and I have tried to be exhaustive in our search, some of the data for individual writers will be incomplete. For this my sincerest apologies go to those writers whose information is lacking in any degree.

3. I consider American Indian literature to exist on a continuum, which I visualize as a spectrum of many hues; it exists on several levels. Everything from traditional to contemporary exists.

4. Unfortunately, this is also exclusionary of those individuals and their families who have been displaced by governmental practices in the past, and it is also exclusionary of those individuals who have been adopted into non-Indian families. As I see it, they are genetically Indian, but not culturally. They do not think as we Indians do. Depending on the economic base of the family, they may have grown up Native in this country. Albeit, there are huge differences between reservation and urban Indians, there is a difference between being raised culturally Indian (reservation or urban) and being raised mainstream American. As many of us know, there is also a fine line here. Many of today's young people are being raised simultaneously in both worlds. Believe it or not.

KEY TO ABBREVIATIONS

A   Accounts as told through others

E   Educator

F   Fiction writer

J   Journalist

L   Lecturer

M   Musician

N   Nonfiction, prose writer

P   Poet

PA   Performing artist

PL   Playwright

S   Storyteller

SC   Screenwriter

V   Video, filmmaker

VA   Visual artist

CONTEMPORARY NATIVE AMERICAN AUTHORS

A

NAME   P
Luci Abeita

OTHER NAMES USED
Luci Beach
Luci Cadzow

TRIBAL AFFILIATION
Kutchin

PERSONAL
Born: Alaska, 1953

PUBLICATION HIGHLIGHTS
"Squash Blossom Shit and Heishi Horrors,"
"Honest John's Seven Idols Pawn Shop,"
poems in *The Remembered Earth: An Anthology of Contemporary Native American
Literature,* ed. by Geary Hobson (Albuquerque: Red Earth Press, 1979)

NARRATIVE
Abeita has also had her poems published
in the journals *La Confluencia* and *New
America.*

NAME   P
Roman C. Adrian

TRIBAL AFFILIATION
White Mountain Apache

PERSONAL
Born: Phoenix, Arizona, 1950

PUBLICATION HIGHLIGHTS
"Happening," "Bel Woman," poems in *The
Remembered Earth: An Anthology of Con-
temporary Native American Literature,* ed.
by Geary Hobson (Albuquerque: Red
Earth Press, 1979)

NARRATIVE
Adrian's poems have also been published
in the journals *Sun Tracks, The New Times*
and in the monograph *Do Not Go Gentle,*
published by Blue Moon Press.

NAME   F, N
Libby Alexander

TRIBAL AFFILIATION
Spokane

PUBLICATION HIGHLIGHTS
"A Flight Called Love" in *The American Indian Speaks,* ed. by John R. Milton (Vermillion, S. Dak.: Dakota Press, University of South Dakota, 1969)

Alexander's works are also mentioned in
The American Indian Reader, ed. by
Jeanette Henry (San Francisco: Indian
Historian Press, 1972–1977).

NAME   F, N, P
Sherman J. Alexie Jr.

OTHER NAMES USED
Sherman Joseph Alexie Jr.

TRIBAL AFFILIATION
Spokane and Coeur d'Alene

PERSONAL

Born: October 7, 1966, in Spokane, Washington

Education: Coursework at Gonzaga University, Spokane, Washington, 1985–1987; B.A. from Washington State University, Pullman, 1991

AWARDS, HONORS

Recipient of National Endowment of the Arts Grant, 1992; Poetry fellow of Washington State Arts Commission, 1991

PUBLICATION HIGHLIGHTS

Reservation Blues, first edition (New York: Atlantic Monthly, 1995)

The Lone Ranger and Tonto Fist Fight in Heaven, first edition (New York: Harper-Perennial, 1994, 1993)

First Indian on the Moon (Brooklyn, N.Y.: Hanging Loose Press, 1993)

Old Shirts and New Skins (Los Angeles: American Indian Studies Center, University of California at Los Angeles, 1993)

The Business of Fancydancing: Stories and Poems, first edition (Brooklyn, N.Y.: Hanging Loose Press, 1992)

I Would Steal Horses (Niagara Falls, N.Y.: Slipstream, 1992)

Songs from the Film, Poems and Stories (Brooklyn, N.Y.: Hanging Loose Press, 1991)

"The Business of Fancy Dancing," poem in *The Beloit Poetry Journal* (Beloit, Wisc.: Beloit College, vol. 41, no.1, 1990)

Alexie's works have also appeared in the anthology: *Returning the Gift: Poetry and Prose from the First North American Native Writers' Festival,* ed. by Joseph Bruchac with the support of the Association for the Study of American Indian Literatures (Tucson: University of Arizona, 1994).

NARRATIVE

Alexie now lives on the Spokane Indian Reservation in Washington State. A pro-

lific and highly regarded writer, Alexie's works have appeared in the publications *Caliban, Ploughshares, Callaloo, Esquire, The New York Times Magazine,* the *New York Quarterly, Another Chicago Magazine,* the *Kenyon Review* and the *Journal of Ethnic Studies,* among many others.

NAME   F, N, P

Minerva Allen

TRIBAL AFFILIATION

Assiniboine

PERSONAL

Born: April 24, 1935, in Lodgepole, Montana

Education: Coursework at Northern Montana College, Havre, Montana, 1964–1973; B.S. from Central Michigan University, Mount Pleasant, 1974; coursework at Weber State College, Ogden, Utah, 1975–[?]

PUBLICATION HIGHLIGHTS

Minerva Allen's Indian Cookbook: From Ft. Belknap Reservation Montana (Dallas: Wowapi, 1988)

Bandit, the Raccoon (Hays, Mont.: Hays/Lodgepole Schools, 1988)

School Days at Big Warm, Big Warm Day School (Hays, Mont.: Hays/Lodgepole Schools, 1986)

Stories by Our Elders: The Fort Belknap People (Hays, Mont.: Hays/Lodgepole Title IV Program, 1983)

"Returning from Scouting for Meat," poem in *The Remembered Earth: An Anthology of Contemporary Native American Literature,* ed. by Geary Hobson (Albuquerque: Red Earth Press, 1979)

Father Me Home Winds ([S.l.]: Big Timber, 1976)

Like Spirits of the Past: Trying to Break Out

and Walk to the West (Albuquerque: Wowapi Productions, 1974)

NARRATIVE

Born to a ranching family in Lodgepole, Montana, Allen was married to tribal chair John Allen and together they raised eight children. Allen worked as a teacher's aide in the Lodgepole Public Schools and in the local Headstart program. She later worked as a legal aide specialist, and later became the director of community education at the Ft. Belknap Headstart program in Harlem, Montana. Since 1980 Allen has acted as the bilingual director and federal project coordinator for the Hays/ Lodgepole Public Schools, and also works as a consultant on Indian heritage for various schools and universities. Other titles by Allen published by the Hays/ Lodgepole Schools include *Decoration Day* (1988), *Selling Wood in Lodgepole* (1986), *Chinook Winds* (1986), *Pretty Flower* (1986), *Little Muskrat* (1986) and *Orange Tree in Lodgepole* (198[–?]).

NAME   E, F, N, P

Paula Gunn Allen

TRIBAL AFFILIATION

Laguna Pueblo

PERSONAL

Born: 1939 in Cubero, New Mexico
Education: B.A. in English, University of Oregon, Eugene, 1966; M.F.A. in creative writing, University of Oregon, Eugene, 1968; Ph.D. in American studies, University of New Mexico, Albuquerque, 1975

AWARDS, HONORS

American Book Award for *Spider Woman's Granddaughters,* sponsored by the Before Columbus Foundation, 1990

Susan Koppelman Award for *Spider Woman's Granddaughters,* sponsored by the Women's Caucus of the Popular and American Culture Associations, 1990
Native American Literature Prize, sponsored by the University of California, Santa Cruz, 1990
Nominations for Pushcart Poetry Prize, 1983, 1981 and 1979
Creative Writing Award, National Endowment for the Arts, 1977–1978
Julia Burgess Prize for Poetry, University of Oregon, 1967

PUBLICATION HIGHLIGHTS

Life Is a Fatal Disease: Selected Poems 1964–1994 (Albuquerque: West End Press, 1997)
As Long As the Rivers Flow: The Stories of Nine Native Americans, with Patricia C. Smith (New York: Scholastic, 1996)
Song of the Turtle: Native American Literature, 1974–1994 (New York: Ballantine Books, 1996)
Voice of the Turtle: American Indian Literature 1900–1970 (New York: Random House, 1994)
Grandmothers of the Light: A Medicine Woman's Sourcebook (Boston: Beacon Press, 1991)
Spider Woman's Granddaughters: Traditional Tales and Contemporary Writing by Native American Women, ed. with an introduction by Paula Gunn Allen (Boston: Beacon Press, 1989)
Skins and Bones: Poems 1979–87 (San Francisco/Albuquerque: West End Press, 1988)
The Sacred Hoop: Recovering the Feminine in American Indian Traditions (Boston: Beacon Press, 1986)
The Woman Who Owned the Shadows (San Francisco: Spinsters Ink, 1983)
Shadow Country (Los Angeles: American Indian Studies Center, University of California Press, 1982)

Ms. Gunn Allen's works have also appeared in numerous anthologies, among them:

American Visions: Multicultural Literature for Writers, ed. by Delores La Guardia and Hans P. Guth (Mountain View, Calif.: Mayfield Publishing, 1995)

Yefief One: A Narrative of Culture at the End of the Century, Lucile Adler, et al. (Images for Media, 1994)

Braided Lives: An Anthology of Multicultural American Writing, by the Minnesota Humanities Commission and the MinnesotaCouncil of Teachers of English (St. Paul: The Commission, 1991)

The Remembered Earth: An Anthology of Contemporary Native American Literature, ed. by Geary Hobson (Albuquerque: Red Earth Press, 1979)

Forever There: Race and Gender in Contemporary Native American Fiction, by Elizabeth I. Hanson (New York: P. Lang, 1989)

I Tell You Now: Autobiographical Essays by Native American Writers, ed. by Brian Swann and Arnold Krupat (Lincoln: University of Nebraska Press, 1987)

Survival This Way: Interviews with Native American Poets, by Joseph Bruchac (Tucson: Sun Tracks: University of Arizona Press, 1987)

New and Old Voices of Wah'Kon-Tah, ed. by Robert K. Dodge and Joseph B. McCullugh (New York: International Publishers, 1985)

Coyote Was Here: Essays on Contemporary Native American Literary and Political Mobilization, ed. by Go Scholer (Aarhous, Denmark: SEKLOS, 1984)

That's What She Said: Contemporary Poetry and Fiction by Native American Women, ed. by Rayna Green (Bloomington: Indiana University Press, 1984)

Native American Renaissance, by Kenneth Lincoln (Berkeley: University of California Press, 1983)

Studies in American Indian Literature: Critical Essays and Course Designs, ed. by Paula Gunn Allen (New York: Modern Language Association, c1983)

NARRATIVE

Paula Gunn Allen was born in Cubero, New Mexico, a Spanish land-grant town surrounded by the Laguna and Acoma Reservations. The daughter of a Laguna and Scottish mother and Lebanese American father and sister to writers Carol Lee Sanchez and Lee Francis, Allen's home reverberated with the sounds of Spanish, German, Laguna, English and Arabic languages. She attended a convent school as a young woman and later attended the Universities of Oregon and New Mexico. Allen began her academic career as an instructor at the University of Oregon, Eugene, in 1968 and since then has worked at De Anza Community College, the University of New Mexico, San Diego State University, San Mateo Community College, San Francisco State University, Ft. Lewis College and the University of California at Los Angeles.

Allen received a postdoctoral fellowship from the Institute of American Cultures at UCLA in 1981, and a National Endowment for the Arts Writers Grant in 1978. Since 1990 she has been professor of English at the University of California at Los Angeles. As an educator her areas of specialization include Native American literature, creative poetry and fiction writing, women's literature and culture with special emphasis on American Indian women, American Indian religion, American literature, including Third World literature and criticism.

Poet, lecturer, renowned literary critic and scholar, Allen has had seven books of her poetry published and has had poems, fiction and short reviews published in numerous journals such as *Pembroke, American Poetry Review, South Dakota Review, Journal of American Indian Culture and Research, Suntracks, Shantih, Chicago Review,*

Ms. Magazine, Whole Earth Review, the *American Indian Quarterly, La Confluencia, Dodeca, Southwest Women's Poetry Exchange, Radix* and *Poets Gallery.* Allen is also politically active and has been involved in antiwar, antinuclear and feminist movements. She is the mother of three children.

NAME   P
Alta

TRIBAL AFFILIATION
Mandan

PERSONAL
Born: Reno, Nevada, 1942
Education: A.A. from the University of California

PUBLICATION HIGHLIGHTS
I Am Not a Practicing Angel (Marshall, Minn.: Crossing Press, 1975)
Pauline and the Mysterious Pervert ([S.l.]: Wyrd, 1975)
Momma: A State on All the Untold Stories (Ojai, Calif.: Times Change Press, 1974)
No Visible Means of Support (San Lorenzo, Calif.: Shameless Hussy Press, 1972)
Burn This and Memorize Yourself, Poems for Women (Ojai, Calif.: Times Change Press, 1970)
Song of the Wife, Song of the Mistress (San Lorenzo, Calif.: Shameless Hussy Press, 1970)
Letters to Women (San Lorenzo, Calif.: Shameless Hussy Press, 1970)
Poems and Prose by Alta (Pittsburgh, Pa.: Know, 1970)
Theme and Variations ([S.l.]: Aldebaran, 1975)
Freedom's in Sight ([S.l.]: Noh Directions Press, 1969)

Alta's works have appeared in: *From the Belly of the Shark: A New Anthology of Native Americans,* ed. by Walter Lowenfels (New York: Vintage, 1974); *The Whites of Their Eyes* (Seattle: [s.n.], 1970)

NARRATIVE
Alta founded and published the Shameless Hussy Press in San Lorenzo, California, in 1969 and produced the journal *Shameless Hussy.* She was an instructor of women's poetry at the University of California at Berkeley from 1969 to 1970 and also worked as a television producer.

NAME   E, L, N, P, S
Anne Anderson

OTHER NAMES USED
Dr. Anne Anderson
Anne Anderson-Irvine (nee) Gairdner

TRIBAL AFFILIATION
Plains Cree (Canadian)

PERSONAL
Born: February 3, 1906, in St. Albert, Alberta, Canada
Education: Grade 10, St. Albert, Alberta Canada

AWARDS, HONORS
C.M., Order of Canada Award; Honorary Doctorate of Law, University of Alberta, 1973

PUBLICATION HIGHLIGHTS
Plains Cree Dictionary in the "Y" Dialect (Edmonton, Alberta: A. Anderson, 1975)
The First Metis: A New Nation (Edmonton, Alberta: MarCon, 1985)
Arrangements of Alphabet Cree and Syllabic Symbols (Edmonton, Alberta: Cree Productions, 1972)

NARRATIVE

Anne Anderson-Irvine was born February 3, 1906, in St. Albert, Alberta, Canada, and spent her childhood near the place of her birth, on the outskirts of Edmonton. She attended school until the tenth grade at one of the first settlements in the St. Albert area. When talking about her school years Anderson says, "I've always enjoyed school. As having an illiterate mother, I could help her more by learning." She was also an athlete while in school: "I particularly enjoyed basketball."

Anderson's life and future work as an author and educator was shaped and directed by her late mother, who had a great knowledge and deep regard for her culture and traditions. It is her mother's last wish that Anderson would work to preserve her language, culture and herbal knowledge for future generations. After her mother passed away, Anderson recalled the "appearance of my mother, after her death two years prior in 1965, asking me if I remembered my promise to write the language." Anderson has been fulfilling her mother's dream ever since.

A prolific writer of over ninety books on a wide variety of subjects, Anderson writes about Native and Metis culture, Native herbalism and cooking. She has authored numerous children's books, books about history, language instruction, dictionaries, books on animals and birds and is a storyteller. Anderson has taught classes on education, language and culture over the past twenty years throughout Canada, the United States and Europe, in schools and universities and before public and private organizations. She has translated educational, health and legal materials into Cree, has more than ninety copyrights on Cree-language books for school grades 1–12 and has created educational slide presentations. She is the founder of The Native Puppet Theatre, which operates through the Indian Puppetry Project, and is the director of the Dr. Anne Anderson Native Heritage and Cultural Centre in Edmonton, Alberta, which is a center dedicated to Metis and Indian history. The Centre is a meeting place and school, which has a resource library, a crafts shop and classrooms.

Anderson is currently working on an expanded edition of her previous work, *Plains Cree Dictionary in the "Y" Dialect,* which will include terms common to modern society, such as *computer* and *microwave.* She lives in St. Alberta, which she finds plays a important role in her work and writings because it "was one of the first agricultural area(s with a) settlement and school in the end of the ninteenth century and has a very rich history."

She is working toward the completion of her autobiography, and when she is not teaching, directing her Center or translating, Anderson works on knitting, crocheting, crafts and cooking.

NAME   L, M, P, PA, PL, S

M. Cochise Anderson

TRIBAL AFFILIATION

Chickasaw/ Mississippi Choctaw

PERSONAL

Born: July 20, 1965, in Los Angeles, California

Education: Coursework in theater and philosophy from Portland State University; coursework at the American Musical and Dramatic Academy, New York City

PUBLICATION HIGHLIGHTS

"Old Ones Who Whisper," "Quiet Pride," poems in the journal *Nitassinan Notre Terre* ([S.l.: s.n.], Special 20/21, Spring

1990); "Winter's Dream," "Take Your Nap," poems in *World of Poetry Anthology* (Stockton, Calif.: [s.n.], Winter 1983); *Alter Native Views,* poems ([S.l.: s.n., n.d.])

NARRATIVE

M. Cochise Anderson was born in Los Angeles and lived in Torrance, California, for thirteen years. He then moved to Portland, Oregon, where he lived for nine years before moving to New York City in 1986. "Living as an urban Indian has so many different aspects—it is many books to come. Meeting so many different cultures and peoples is mind-opening ... however, I did meet a lot of other Native Americans while working at the American Indian Community House; it's almost impossible to not be affected [by the geography of the city]."

Anderson was bit by the acting bug while he was a student in high school working on his first acting role. "I knew I wanted to do this for a living. I also loved the plays as well. So poetry and plays and music all came together in my school years." He also enjoyed writing while he was a student: "I remember I used to write song lyrics before I wrote poems, and then in school I took a class of poetry and I loved the form because you could do so much with such a minimal effort."

Through the years Anderson and his friends have served as sources of support and as sounding boards for each other. He counts among them: "My friend Ada Bad Roads Modig, who passed away last year ... supported my poetry and encouraged me to read for my community. ... [She] and Rose Hill, both Native women who took me under their wing—oh I mustn't forget Elizabeth Woody and Vince Wannassay and Ed Edmo who shared their work with me."

Anderson enjoys reading the works of authors Louis Owens, Elizabeth Woody, N. Scott Momaday, James Welch, Gerald Vizenor, William Yellow Robe Jr. "I think just how they tell the story is most influencing. Different images meaning different things. It reveals Native thinking." In his own writings Anderson strives to focus on the continuance of his culture in a contemporary context, adding that the process involves "Searching through the last five hundred years for qualities which have lasted, i.e., songs, languages, ceremonies, elders and youth."

Anderson now works as a storyteller in the New York City schools. "I tell coyote stories and the flute story and the drum story as well as rattle songs, etc." He also works as a musician, playing traditional flute, steel flute and harmonica and sings rock and blues. He is writing a play with four other Native American actors and has two screenplays in the research stage.

NAME   P
John Angaiak

TRIBAL AFFILIATION
Inuit

PERSONAL
Born: Tununak, Alaska, 1941

PUBLICATION HIGHLIGHTS
"My Native Land, the Beautiful," poem in the *Tundra Times* (Fairbanks, Alaska: Tundra Times, n.d.)

Angaiak's poems have appeared in: *From the Belly of the Shark: A New Anthology of Native Americans,* ed. by Walter Lowenfels (New York: Vintage, 1974)

NAME   E, N
Will Antell

TRIBAL AFFILIATION
Chippewa

PERSONAL
Born: October 2, 1935, on the White Earth
Reservation, Minnesota
Education: B.S. from Bemidji State College,
Bemidji, Minnesota; M.S. from Mankato
State College, Mankato Minnesota; Ed.D.
from the University of Minnesota, 1973;
coursework at Northern Michigan Uni-
versity, Marquette; coursework at St.
Cloud State University, St. Cloud, Min-
nesota

AWARDS, HONORS
National Defense Education Act Fellowship from Northern Michigan University,
1965; National Defense Education Act
Fellowship from the University of Minnesota, 1968; Recipient of Bash Foundation Fellowship, 1972

PUBLICATION HIGHLIGHTS
*Beyond Degradation: Urgent Issues in the Edu-
cation of Minorities* (New York: College
Examination Entrance Board, 1978)
*Culture, Psychological Characteristics, and
Socioeconomic Status in Educational Pro-
gram Development for Native Americans*
(Austin: National Educational Laboratory
Publishers, 1974)
William Warren (Minneapolis: Dillon, 1973)
*American Indians: An Annotated Bibliogra-
phy of Selected Library Resources,* ed. by
Will D. Antell (Minneapolis: University
of Minnesota, 1970)

NARRATIVE
Through the years Antell has worked in
the field of education, first as a public
school teacher in the cities of Jamesville

and Stillwater, Minnesota. He later became human relations consultant for the
Minnesota Department of Education, and
then assistant commissioner of education
in 1974. In 1970 Antell was selected to
represent Indian children and youth at the
White House Conference on Children
and Youth. Since 1971 Antell has been a
regent at the Institute of American Indian
Art in Santa Fe, New Mexico, he was the
chair of the Special Committee on Indian
Education of the National Council for
Indian Opportunity from 1970 to 1972
and was a visiting professor of educational
administration at Harvard University
from 1973 to 1974. Antell was also a vice
chair of the National Advisory Council
on Indian Education in 1973 to 1974 and
has acted as chairman of the Council since
1974.

As an educator Antell has taught
courses in Indian culture and history, as
well as social science and human relations
in high schools. He is married and has
three children.

NAME   P, SC
Annette Arkeketa

TRIBAL AFFILIATION
Otoe-Missouria/Creek

PERSONAL
Born: May 27, 1958, in Clinton, Oklahoma
Education: B.A. in business administration,
Central State University, Edmond, Okla-
homa, 1986

PUBLICATION HIGHLIGHTS
"So You Think You Are Crazy Horse," poem
in *Nimrod* (Tulsa: Tulsa Arts and Humani-
ties, 1989)
"The Absence," poem in *Nimrod* (Tulsa,
OK: Tulsa Arts and Humanities, 1989)

"Coyote Brother Song," poem in *That's What She Said* (Bloomington: Indiana University Press, 1984)

Prairie, chapbook of poems (Marvin, S. Dak.: Blue Cloud Quarterly, 1978)

Arkeketa's works have also appeared in the anthology: *Returning the Gift: Poetry and Prose from the First North American Native Writers' Festival,* ed. by Joseph Bruchac with the support of the Association for the Study of American Indian Literatures (Tucson: University of Arizona, 1994)

NARRATIVE

Annette Arkeketa was born May 27, 1958, in Clinton, Oklahoma, and spent many of her early years growing up in the town of Sand Springs, Oklahoma. While she excelled in her studies as a young woman, she also had misgivings about the traditional, Eurocentric slant on her education. She remembers "… just wanting to graduate. … I went to an all-white school with the classic all white education, and I remember hating it. The typical European indoctrination. I did well though. I was in the top 10 percent of my graduating class, which wasn't bad for someone who hated school."

Arkeketa had always enjoyed writing, starting as a child in the second grade. In high school her friends asked her to submit several of her essays for publication in the school newspaper, which was not only an honor but also added to her impetus to write and publish. It was such interest and care shown by her many family members and friends that helped Arkeketa continue writing throughout her life. Of all the individuals and family members who have provided her with such encouragement and support in her career, Arkeketa particularly mentioned three individuals who she felt could be called mentors: Mary McAnally-Knight, Jon West and Lance Henson.

She has worked as a coordinator and instructor of classes in the Muscogee-

Creek language in the Oklahoma City area and at the University of Oklahoma. Arkeketa is the past president of the American Indian Resource and Education Coalition and is currently a board member of the Indian Education Conference. She lives in Texas "where the American consciousness is just about thirty years behind the times as far as civil rights and discrimination are concerned. It's like going back in time. I am learning and adjusting a lot. I am very involved in Indian education in a community where people ask, 'Are there Indians in Texas?.' "

Arkeketa is also writing for the soon-to-be-published Native American children's magazine *Great Promises* and is writing screenplays on various Indian issues and a chapbook. Her works have also appeared in *Nebraska Literary Journal* and *Great Promises Magazine.* Arkeketa says she has felt directed by all Native American writers: "The more I read, the more I learn and all these writers have influence," particularly Joy Harjo, Leslie Marmon Silko, N. Scott Momaday, Louise Erdrich and the European classics. "I understand where their writing influences are derived from, e.g., Homer, Virgil, Erasmus. I enjoy reading the Bible also, so I can understand the Christian thinking better."

When not writing, Arkeketa reads, goes fishing, enjoys being with her family and having conversations about tribal politics, family doings, bowling, tribal functions, both social and ceremonial, and watches film documentaries on Indian issues.

NAME   E, F, P

Jeannette C. Armstrong

OTHER NAMES USED

Jeannette Bonneau

Jeannette Christine Armstrong

TRIBAL AFFILIATION

Okanagan

PERSONAL

Born: Penticton Indian Reservation, British Columbia
Education: Undergraduate degree in fine arts from the University of Victoria, 1979

AWARDS, HONORS

Mungo Martin Award, Helen Pitt Memorial Award, Vancouver Foundation Graduate Award (all for visual art)

PUBLICATION HIGHLIGHTS

Looking at the Words of Our People: An Anthology of First Nation Literary Criticism, ed. by J. Armstrong ([S.l.]: Orca Book Publishers, 1993)
Neekna and Chemai (Penticton, B.C.: Theytus Books, 1984, 1992)
"Trickster Time," in *Voices: Being Native in Canada,* ed. by Drew Hayden Taylor and Linda Jaine ([S.l.]: University of Saskatchewan, 1992)
Native Creative Process: A Collaborative Discourse between Douglas J. Cardinal and Jeannette C. Armstrong (Penticton, B.C.: Theytus, 991)
Slash (Penticton, B.C.: Theytus Books, 1985, 1988, 1990)
"This Is a Story:" in *All My Relations: An Anthology of Contemporary Canadian Native Writing* (Toronto: McLelland and Stewart, 1990)

Armstrong's works have also appeared in a number of anthologies, including:

Returning the Gift: Poetry and Prose from the First North American Native Writers' Festival, ed. by Joseph Bruchac with the support of the Association for the Study of American Indian Literatures (Tucson: University of Arizona, 1994)

Looking at the Words of Our People: An Anthology of First Nation Literary Criticism, ed. by Jeannette Armstrong (Stratford, Ontario: Theytus, 1993)
An Anthology of Canadian Native Literature in English, ed. by Daniel David Moses and Terry Goldie (Toronto: Oxford University Press, 1992)
Four Feathers: Poems and Stories by Canadian Native Authors (Germany: s.n., 1992)
Breath Tracks: A Collection of Poetry, by Williams and Wallace (Stratford, Ontario: Theytus, 1991)
Native Literature in Canada from the Oral Tradition to the Present: A Study of History and Criticism, by Penny Petrone (Toronto: Oxford University Press, 1990)

NARRATIVE

A resident of the Penticton Indian Reservation, Armstrong is a fluent speaker of the Okanagan language. Her poems have been published in numerous journals and periodicals, among them the *Malahat Review: An International Quarterly of Life and Letters, Okanagan Life Magazine, From an Island: A Collective Review of Artists and Writers, Indian World: Native Political Magazine, Women and Words: An Anthology, Kick It Over: Quarterly International* and *Tiger Lily Voices That Dare: A Journal by Women of Colour,* among many others. She has produced three poetry musical works, two videotapes and has appeared on television including a national TV talk show titled *Visual Express.*

Armstrong has recently been appointed to the Council of Listeners in the International Testimonials on Violations to Indigenous Sovereignty. She is a consultant on a wide variety of issues and addresses conferences and assemblies at home and abroad. The titles of her published presentations include "Writing from a Native Women's Perspective," "Traditional Indigenous Education: A

Natural Process," Cultural Robbery: Imperialism Voices of Native Women," "Bridging Cultures," "The Disempowerment of First North American Native Peoples and Empowerment Through Their Writing" and "Real Power: Aboriginal Women—Past, Present and Future." Armstrong is active in educating and guiding young Native writers and is the director of the En'owkin International School of Writing in Penticton, British Columbia.

NAME   E, F, L, N, P
Caroll Arnett

OTHER NAMES USED
Gogisgi

TRIBAL AFFILIATION
Cherokee

PERSONAL
Born: November 9, 1927, in Oklahoma City, Oklahoma
Education: B.A., *magna cum laude*, Beloit College, 1951; graduate hours, University of Oklahoma, 1953–1955; M.A., University of Texas, 1958; graduate hours, University of Texas

AWARDS, HONORS
National Endowment for the Arts Fellowship in Creative Writing, 1974; featured reader, Oklahoma Poets Day, 1988

PUBLICATION HIGHLIGHTS
Spells (S.l.: Bloody Twin Press, 1995)
Night Perimeter: New and Selected Poems 1958–1990 (Greenfield Center, N.Y.: Greenfield Review Press, 1991)
Engine, poems (Norman, Okla.: Point Riders Press, 1988)
Coyote's Journal, ed. by Steven Nemirow,

Peter Blue Cloud, James Koller, Carroll Arnett (Berkeley: Wingbow Press, 1982)
Rounds, poems (Merrick, N.Y.: Cross-Cultural Communications Press, 1982)
South Line, poems (New Rochelle, N.Y.: Elizabeth Press; Kensington, Calif.: Distributed by SBD, [1979])
Tsalagi, poems (New Rochelle, N.Y.: Elizabeth Press, 1976)
Come (New Rochelle, N.Y.: Elizabeth Press, 1973)
Earlier, poems (New Rochelle, N.Y.: Elizabeth Press, [1972])
Through the Woods, poems (New Rochelle, N.Y.: Elizabeth Press, [1971])
Like a Wall, poems (Berkeley/New Rochelle, N.Y.: Elizabeth Press, [c1969])
Then, poems (New Rochelle, N.Y.: Elizabeth Press, 1965, 1969 printing)
Not Only That, poems (New Rochelle, N.Y.: Elizabeth Press, [1967])

Arnett's works have appeared in numerous anthologies, among them:

Returning the Gift: Poetry and Prose from the first North American Native Writers' Festival, ed. by Joseph Bruchac with the support of the Association for the Study of American Indian Literatures (Tucson: University of Arizona, 1994)
Coyote's Journal, Steven Nemirow, et al. ([S.l.]: Wingbow Press, 1982)
The Remembered Earth: An Anthology of Contemporary Native American Literature, ed. by Geary Hobson (Albuquerque: Red Earth, 1979)
Voices of the Rainbow: Contemporary Poetry by American Indians, ed. by Kenneth Rosen (New York: Viking, 1975)

NARRATIVE
Carroll Arnett was born November 29, 1927, in Oklahoma City, Oklahoma, son of Herschel and Ethel Arnett, and is of Cherokee and French ancestry. He was raised and schooled in Oklahoma City,

and spent twenty-one months in the U.S. Marine Corps in 1946–1947. He has taught literature and writing at Wittenberg, Knox and Stephens Colleges and is currently professor of English at Central Michigan University.

Arnett has authored more than nine books, is a contributor of more than three hundred stories and poems to various publications and anthologies and has co-edited a special "Coyote" issue of *Coyote's Journal* (Berkeley: Wingbow Press, 1982) with Peter Blue Cloud. He has given readings at many colleges nationwide. Carroll Arnett is one of the most widely respected writers today, especially in poetry circles. His poems have been translated into many languages such as French, German, Dutch and Hungarian, and have appeared in many anthologies. Arnett acknowledged the substantial help and support his friends and family gave him in his development as a writer, adding that an event of primary importance was his marriage to Claudia Wilson in 1964. Arnett considers his writings to have been shaped a great deal by the poems and essays of writer Ezra Pound, and he regards as his teachers the writers Peter Blue Cloud, Barney Bush, Robert Conley and Joy Harjo, among many others.

When asked if his geographic surroundings play a significant role in his work, he replied "Tremendously so. I've taught for more than twenty years at this ... university where I work solely because it's near the fifty acres of woodland where I live. These fifty acres and their inhabitants are the most important parts of my life, more important than my life." When Arnett isn't writing he's practicing marksmanship with "all manner of small arms." He is of the Deer Clan and is an enrolled member of the Overhill Band of the Cherokee Nation.

❖❖❖

NAME F, L, N, PA, PL
Assiniwi, Bernard

OTHER NAMES USED
Chagnan (on childrens books only)

TRIBAL AFFILIATION
Algonquin and Northern Cree

PERSONAL
Born: July 31, 1945, in Montreal, Quebec
Education: B.A. in agriculture

AWARDS, HONORS
Finalist in the Montreal Literacy Prize in 1971 for *Anish-nah-be*

PUBLICATION HIGHLIGHTS
La medecine des Indiens d'Amerique (Montreal: Guerin Litterature, 1988)
Les Montagnais et Naskapi ([Montreal]: Lemeac, 1979)
Le bras coupe (Montreal: Lemeac, 1976)
Makwa, le petit Algonquin, with John Fadden (Montreal: Lemeac, 1973)
Anish-nah-be: contes adultes du pays Algonkin, with Isabelle Myre (Montreal: Lemeac, 1971)

Assiniwi's works also appear in the anthology: *Returning the Gift: Poetry and Prose from the First North American Native Writers' Festival,* ed. by Joseph Bruchac with the support of the Association for the Study of American Indian Literatures (Tucson: University of Arizona, 1994).

NARRATIVE
Bernard Assiniwi was born in Montreal, Quebec, and grew up three miles from Montreal, at Coteau-Rouge, among the French Canadians. As a student, Assiniwi was active in athletics, particularly boxing, and fought his way up to the finals of the Golden Gloves boxing tournament

where he lost "against another Indian."

Assiniwi recalled that he decided to become a writer because of his three sons. "I wanted them to have no excuses not knowing who they are." He considers himself to be a self-made writer whose works focus primarily on history and culture. He has authored more than twenty books in French. Assiniwi is now working on a book for the Canadian Museum of Civilizations on the history of Indian affairs in Canada and its impact on Native peoples, and is currently the historian for the Canadian Museum of Civilization in Ottawa. He lives in Gatineau, Quebec.

NAME   F, N
Catherine Attla

TRIBAL AFFILIATION
Koyukon

PUBLICATION HIGHLIGHTS
K'etetaalkkaanee, the One Who Paddled Among the People and Animals: The Story of an Ancient Traveler (Nenana, Alaska/ Fairbanks Alaska: Yukon Koyukuk School District, Alaska Native Language Center, College of Liberal Arts, University of Alaska, 1990)

Bakk'aatugh ts'uhuniy (Stories We Live by: Traditional Koyukon Athabaskan Stories) (Nenana, Alaska/Fairbanks, Alaska: Yukon Koyukuk School District ; Alaska Native Language Center, College of Liberal Arts, University of Alaska, 1989)

Sitsiy yugh noholnik ts'in (As My Grandfather Told It: Traditional Stories from the Koyuuk) (Nenan, Alaska/Fairbanks,Alaska: Yukon Koyukuk School District, Alaska Native Language Center, 1983)

NAME   P, L, N
Marilou Awiakta

OTHER NAMES USED
Awiakta

TRIBAL AFFILIATION
Cherokee

PERSONAL
Born: January 24, 1936, 12:20 A.M., Knoxville, Tennessee
Education: B.A. in English and French, University of Tennessee, 1958

AWARDS, HONORS
Outstanding Contribution to Appalachian Literature by the Appalachian Writers Association, 1991; Distinguished Tennessee Writer Award by the Smoky Mountain Writers Conference in conjunction with Whittle Publications, 1989; U.S. Information Agency chose *Abiding Appalachia* and *Rising Fawn and the Fire Mystery* for the global tour of its show "Women in the Contemporary World" 1986

PUBLICATION HIGHLIGHTS
Selu: Seeking the Corn-Mother's Wisdom (Golden, Colo.: Fulcrum Publishing, 1993)

"Baring the Atom's Mother Heart" in *Homewords: A Book of Tennessee Writers* (Knoxville: University of Tennessee Press, 1986)

"Red Clay: Reunion of the Cherokee Councils" in *Southern Exposure, Special Issue: Indians of the South*, vol. xiii, no. 6 (Durham, N.C.: [s.n.], 1985)

Rising Fawn and the Fire Mystery: A Story of Heritage, Family and Courage (Bell Buckle, Tenn.: Iris, 1993, 1983)

Abiding Appalachia: Where Mountain and Atom Meet (Memphis: St. Lukes Press, 1978)

Awiakta's works have also appeared in the anthology: *Returning the Gift: Poetry and Prose from the First North American Native Writers' Festival*, ed. by Joseph Bruchac with the support of the Association for the Study of American Indian Literatures (Tucson: University of Arizona, 1994).

NARRATIVE

Born in Knoxville, Tennessee, Awiakta was raised in the company town of Oak Ridge, Tennessee, during the 1940s and 1950s, when atomic research and the cold war were both in their infancy. Her writings reflect a childhood surrounded by the highly secretive world of an atomic energy research establishment yet was steeped in the heritage and tradition of her Cherokee forbears. Because of her unusual experience living with ancient and modern cultures through her formative years Awiakta's writings often return to the motif that humanity cannot tempt nature that one cannot divorce oneself from nature and that one must treat the atom with reverence and respect.

As a young girl, Awiakta witnessed an event that was to influence her profoundly and gave her an understanding of pain at an early age. At the age of six, while she stood with her mother by the door to their home, she witnessed a man burn alive after a nearby industrial accident. Because of the deadly tragedy Awiakta was moved to respond by the most expressive and eloquent means she could—by writing.

An excellent student as a young woman, Awiakta was fortunate to have an individual who served as her mentor and guide in school, Oak Ridge High School French instructor Madame Zimmerman. She helped Awiakta realize that she could gain entrance into other worlds through the use of language and supported her literary efforts. Because of her academic achievement, Awiakta received a college scholarship to study in France, and later as an adult she returned to France, where she spent three years with her family. Through this experience she came to understand what it meant to be an American of Cherokee and Appalachian descent. She later described this period as the "watershed of [my] work and life." Awiakta came to understand language in another way and recognized that the manner in which a people think and define their existence is through their language.

Awiakta recounted other individuals who have influenced her life as a writer: her mother, Wilma, who was responsible for instilling great confidence in her, and her partner and companion through the years, husband Paul. Writers whose works have influenced Awiakta's literary life include Paula Gunn Allen, Rayna Green, Wilma Mankiller, Colette, Leslie Silko and mentor Joseph Bruchac, who helped guide her career as a writer, and friends Alice Walker and Ethridge Knight.

She sees her work as an act of giving to the people through her literary creations and her activities in communities and schools. Awiakta currently serves on the board of the Tennessee Writers Alliance.

B

NAME F, M, N, P, VA

Lorenzo Baca

OTHER NAMES USED

Lorenzo

TRIBAL AFFILIATION

Isleta/Mescalero

PERSONAL

Born: September 9, 1947, in Morenci, Arizona

Education: A.A. in Commercial Art, Halbor Junior College, Wilmington, California; 1969; B.A. in Art, California State University at Long Beach, 1973; graduate studies at California State University, Turlock, California; M.A. in American Indian Studies with additional coursework in fine arts from the University of California at Los Angeles, 1986

PUBLICATION HIGHLIGHTS

Indian Heroes and Great Chieftains, audio recording, read by Lorenzo Baca (Berkeley: Audio LitErature, 1994)

Songs, Poems and Lies by Lorenzo, audio recording (Sonora, Calif.: Mr. Coyote Man Productions, 1990)

"Untitled Poems" in *Joint Effort II: Escape* (Jamestown, Calif.: Nugget Press; Sierra Correction Center, California Department of Corrections, 1988)

"Untitled Poems" in *The Shadows of Light: Poetry and Photography of the Motherlode and Sierras* (Markleeville, Calif.: Jelm Mountain Publications, 1985)

Baca's works have also appeared in the anthologies: *Returning the Gift: Poetry and Prose from the First North American Native Writers' Festival,* ed. by Joseph Bruchac with the support of the Association for the Study of American Indian Literatures (Tucson: University of Arizona, 1994)

Neon Pow-Wow: New Native American Voices of the Southwest, first edition, ed. by Anna Lee Walters. (Flagstaff: Northland, [1993])

NARRATIVE

Writer and musician Lorenzo Baca was born in Morenci, Arizona, in 1947 and spent his early years near Roswell, New Mexico, later moving to southern California during his teen years. He names his elders, particularly his aunts, as being his greatest teachers during his youth, and that they, in turn have had the greatest bearing on his life and writings. He says that "life's daily spiritual events" are the driving force behind his writings and a constant source of inspiration in all of his works. Lorenzo chose to pursue writing when he read works that didn't "communicate very well," realizing that he had the ability and ambition to clearly express himself in print.

NAME P

Liz Sohappy Bahe

OTHER NAMES USED

Omnama Cheshuts (which means "stopping on a hill and looking down")

TRIBAL AFFILIATION

Yakima

PERSONAL

Born: Toppenish, Washington, in 1947

PUBLICATION HIGHLIGHTS

Bahe's works have appeared in numerous anthologies, among them:

Carriers of the Dream Wheel: Contemporary Native American Poetry, ed. by Duane Niatum (New York: Harper & Row, 1975)
New and Old Voices of Wah'Kon-Tah, ed. by Robert K. Dodge and Joseph B. McCollugh (New York: International Publishers, 1985)
Native American Renaissance, by Kenneth Lincoln (Berkeley: University of California Press, c1983)
The Whispering Wind: Poetry by Young American Indians, ed. by Terry Allen (New York: Doubleday, 1972)

NARRATIVE

Born in Toppenish, Washington, Liz Sohappy Bahe was also raised in the state of Washington but attended high school at the Institute of American Indian Arts in Santa Fe. Her additional studies include a postgraduate workshop in poetry in the summer of 1970 after her graduation, and coursework in art in Portland, Oregon. She has a husband and two sons.

NAME   E, N, P

Charles G. Ballard

TRIBAL AFFILIATION

Quapaw and Cherokee

PERSONAL

Born: June 4, 1930, in Quapaw, Oklahoma
Education: B.A. from Oklahoma State University at Stillwater, 1957; M.A. from Oklahoma State University at Stillwater, 1966; Ed.D. from Oklahoma State University at Stillwater, 1979

AWARDS, HONORS

Fellowship for one year at the American Indian Studies Center, University of California at Los Angeles, 1979–1980

PUBLICATION HIGHLIGHTS

"The Conference" poem in *Platte Valley Review* (Kearney, Nebr.: Kearney State College, 19.1 (1991): 97–98)
"Changing of the Guard," poem in *Voices from Wah'Kon-Tah: Contemporary Poetry of Native Americans,* ed. by Robert K. Dodge and Joseph B. McCullough (New York: International Publishers, 1974)
"During the Pageant at Medicine Lodge," poem in *Nimrod* (Tulsa: University of Tulsa, 16.2 (1972): 12)

Ballard's works have also appeared in anthologies such as:

Dear Christopher, ed. by Darryl Wilson and Barry Joyce (Riverside, Calif.: Native American Studies, 1992)
Contemporary Native American Culture Issues, ed. by Thomas E. Schirer (Sault Ste. Marie, Mich.: Lake Superior State University Press, 1988)
Native American Renaissance, by Kenneth Lincoln (Berkeley: University of California Press, c1983)
The First Skin Around Me: Contemporary American Tribal Poetry, ed. by James L. White (Moorhead, Minn.: Territorial Press, 1976)
Voices of the Rainbow: Contemporary Poetry by American Indians, ed. by Kenneth Rosen (New York: Viking, 1975).

NARRATIVE

Charles Ballard was born in Quapaw, Oklahoma. Though his family moved among three states during his grade school years it was the family home near Quapaw where he was raised that he remembers the best. As a young man growing up in the country, much of his time was spent in solitude: "Being much alone on a farm and having the task of entertaining myself caused me to turn to reading. A larger world filtered in through magazines and books."

In high school Ballard enjoyed reading a variety of American and British works and studied classical music, working hard to become an accomplished pianist. "I seemed in those early years to be in training to be a recluse or a monk. In grade school I remember Jack London and the New England poets; in high school I loved Mark Twain, Hawthorne, George Eliot, Sir Walter Scott and the philosopher Will James. I immersed myself in classical music and in my senior year gave a concert (Tchaikovsky's B-flat Minor Concerto)." Since then he has taught at the Chilocco Indian School for seven years, the Northern Oklahoma College in Tonkawa, Idaho State University and Bacone College. He is currently an associate professor of English at the University of Nebraska, Lincoln, and the interim director of the school's Institute for Ethnic Studies Program, with plans to retire.

Ballard writes poetry—"any topic (that is, I do not limit myself to Indian material)"—nonfiction and conducts research in areas of historical and current Indian studies. As a researcher, his close proximity to the university's large research collection has been quite beneficial to him, though when he writes poetry, he admits his geographic surroundings leave him a bit short on ideas. "As for poetry, I am not inspired at all by the landscape of Nebraska." His works have appeared in the journals *American Indian Culture* and research journal, *Mokakit: Selected Papers, North Dakota Quarterly, MELUS* and *Wicazo Sa Review.*

Many individuals have influenced his work through the years: "My writing has been inspired by many thinkers in the past. Immediate family and friends had little influence at all, unfortunately. I was a recluse." He continues, "Writing simply seemed a way to understand my own world and myself." Ballard is also a voracious reader: "I am a binge reader. Currently I am on a history kick: Paul Kennedy's *The Rise and Fall of the Great Powers* (it was great and very enlightening), Walter Isaacson's *Kissinger* ..., Hoffding's *A History of Modern Philosophy* ... and also Timothy Crusius's *Philosophical Hermeneutics.* Later in the summer I will pick up a few novels." Two works that remain his favorite through the years have been James Welch's works *Winter in the Blood* and *Fool's Crow.* "The first confronts the issue of purpose in the area of cultural consciousness (American Indian world view), and the second idealizes a possible cultural framework from the past."

He is currently working on two writing projects, one is an article for the Smithsonian Press on the Indian's point of view on issues in Native American literature and a book review for Temple University Press. In his spare time Ballard enjoys gardening, playing the piano and wood carving. He is also quite active within the local Lincoln Indian community. "I do volunteer work at the local Indian Center [as] president of the board, head of the executive committee, member of the Housing committee and [am] a member of a current selection committee for a new director of the Center."

NAME　　　　　　F, N, P

Rudy Michael Bantista

OTHER NAMES USED

R. M. Bantista

TRIBAL AFFILIATION

Kiowa

PERSONAL

Born: Lawton, Oklahoma, in 1952

PUBLICATION HIGHLIGHTS

Bantista's works have appeared in numerous anthologies:

Arrows Four: Prose and Poetry by Young American Indians, ed. by T. D. Allen (New York: Washington Square Press, c1979)

The Remembered Earth: An Anthology of Contemporary Native American Literature, ed. by Geary Hobson (Albuquerque: Red Earth Press, c1979)

Zero Makes Me Hungry: A Collection of Poems for Today, compiled by Edward Kyeders and Primus St. John (New York: Lothrop & Shepard, 1976)

American Indian Prose and Poetry: We Wait in Darkness, ed. and introd. by Gloria Levitas [et al.] (New York: Putnam, [1974])

NAME   E, F, N, P

Jim Barnes

TRIBAL AFFILIATION

Choctaw

PERSONAL

Born: December 22, 1933, in Summerfield, Oklahoma

Education: B.A. in English and drama, Southeastern Oklahoma State University, 1964; M.A. in comparative literature, University of Arkansas, 1966; Ph.D. in comparative literature, University of Arkansas, 1972

AWARDS, HONORS

National Endowment for the Arts Fellowship in Poetry, 1978

William Carlos Williams Award, 1979

Translation Award from the Translation Center of Columbia University, for *Summons and Sign: Poems by Dagmar Nick,* 1980

Pushcart Prize for poem *The Chicago Odyssey,* 1980

Rockefeller Foundation Bellagio Fellowship for Translation, 1990

Oklahoma Book Award for *The Sawdust War,* 1993

Senior Fulbright Fellowship to Switzerland, 1993–1994

PUBLICATION HIGHLIGHTS

On Native Ground: Memoirs and Impressions (Norman: University of Oklahoma Press, 1997)

Paris: Poems (Champaign: University of Illinois Press, 1997

The Sawdust War (Urbana: University of Illinois Press, 1992)

Fiction of Malcolm Lowry and Thomas Mann: Structural Tradition ([S.l.]: Thomas Jefferson University Press, 1990)

La Plata Cantata, poems (West Lafayette, Purdue University Press, 1989)

A Season of Loss, poems (West Lafayette: Purdue University Press, 1985)

American Book of the Dead, poems (Urbana: University of Illinois Press, 1982)

Summons and Sign: Poems by Dagmar Nick, translated from the German (Kirksville, Mo.: Chariton Review Press, Northeast Missouri State University, 1980)

This Crazy Land (Temple, Ariz.: Porch Publications, 1980)

The Fish on Poteau Mountain (DeKalb, Ill.: Cedar Creek Press, 1980)

Barnes has had poems appearing in numerous anthologies, among them:

Dancing on the Rim of the World: Contemporary Northwest Native American Writing (Tucson: University of Arizona Press, 1990)

Harper's Anthology of Twentieth Century Native American Poetry (San Francisco: Harper & Row, 1990)

Carriers of the Dream Wheel: Contemporary Native American Poetry (New York: Harper & Row, 1988)

Songs of this Earth on Turtle's Back, first edition, ed. by Joseph Bruchac. (Greenfield Center, N.Y.: Greenfield Review Press, 1983)

The Pushcart Prize V: Best of the Small Presses (S.l.:Pushcart Press, 1980)

NARRATIVE

Writer and educator Jim Barnes was born in Summerfield, Oklahoma, to parents of Choctaw Welsh ancestry and reared in Le Flore County in eastern Oklahoma. He is married and has two children. He moved in 1951 to Oregon, where he worked as a lumberjack for ten years in Oregon's Willamette Valley, and in 1960 he returned to Oklahoma to enroll at Southeastern State College.

Barnes began writing seriously in the mid-1950s and had his first work published in 1968. Now considered to be one of the best in Native American poetry, he is one of the best represented and studied authors in Native American literature. His poems and essays have appeared in numerous literary magazines such as *The Nation, The North American Review, Kenyon Review, Poetry Wales, Chicago Review, Northwest Review, Prairie Schooner, Mundus Artium, Poetry East, Paintbrush, New England Review, Denver Quarterly, TriQuarterly, Southwest Review, Tamaqua,* and others. His works have also been published in more than thirty anthologies, including *The Pushcart Prize, V: Best of the Small Presses* (Pushcart Press, 1980), *After the Storm: Poems on the Persian Gulf War* (Maisonneuve Press, 1992) and *Inheriting the Land* (University of Minnesota Press, 1993). He has had poetry readings in universities throughout the United States and in Europe, at schools such as the University of Nebraska in Lincoln and Omaha, Purdue University, University of Illinois, University of Kansas, University of Nevada at Las Vegas, Pompidou Center (Paris) and La Madeleine (Paris).

Barnes is the founding editor of the Chariton Review Press, is the editor of the Chariton Review and is a professor of comparative literature at Northeast Missouri State University, Kirksville.

Of all the writers he has read, he considers the works of Ernest Hemingway, William Faulkner and Katherine Ann Porter to have had the greatest impact on his own writing. He considers his most significant work-to-date to be *The Sawdust War* because of the uses of memory and the attention to form, organic and practical. Barnes is now working on a manuscript-in-progress of poems titled *Paris.* As he says of his work, "I did not decide to become a writer—I became a writer by writing."

NAME   F, N
Katsi Cook Barreiro

TRIBAL AFFILIATION
Mohawk

PUBLICATION HIGHLIGHTS
"Woman's Thread" in *New Voices from the Longhouse: An Anthology of Contemporary Iroquois Writing,* first edition, ed. by Joseph Bruchac (Greenfield Center, N.Y.: Greenfield Review Press, c1989); "Through the Women's Door" in *Daybreak Magazine* (Highland, Md.: Five Rings Corporation and Eagle Eye Communications Group, vol. 2, issue 1, 1988) and "The Coming of Anontaks" in *Mothering Magazine* (Santa Fe: Mothering Pub., 1985)

NARRATIVE

Cook Barreiro's works have also been published in the Cornell University journal *Indian Studies.*

NAME   F, N, P

John Barsness

TRIBAL AFFILIATION

Tuscarora

PERSONAL

Born: December 1, 1952, in Bozeman, Montana
Education: Coursework at the University of Montana, Missoula

PUBLICATION HIGHLIGHTS

Western Skies (New York: Lyons & Burford, 1994); *Montana Time: The Seasons of a Trout Fisherman* (New York: Lyons & Burford, 1992); *Hunting the Great Plains* (Missoula: Mountain Press, 1979)

Barsness's work has also appeared in: *Four Indian Poets,* ed. by John R. Milton (Vermillion, S. Dak.: Dakota Press, 1974).

NARRATIVE

The grandson of homesteaders, Barsness was born in Bozeman, Montana, and raised in Montana. His father was a professor of English and his mother was a professor of psychology. Through the years he has worked various jobs as a cowboy and a farmhand. Since 1988 Barsness has been a contributing editor to the journal *Field and Stream,* and from 1992 he has been the editor of *Game Journal.*

Barsness's writings reflect his interest in the relationship between humanity and the environment and the lifestyles of people who depend on the land for their own survival, such as farmers, anglers and hunters. His writings also reveal his concern about how the environment affects people and in turn how people affect the environment. Barsness is married and lives in Montana.

NAME   E, F, J, N, S, SC, V

Russell Louis Bates

TRIBAL AFFILIATION

Kiowa and Wichita

PERSONAL

Born: June 6, 1941, in Lawton Oklahoma
Education: Anadarko High School, Anadarko Oklahoma, graduated in 1959; coursework at the following:
University of Kansas at Lawrence
Bacone College, Muskogee, Oklahoma
University of Oklahoma at Norman
Clarion College, Clarion, Pennsylvania
Tulane University, New Orleans, Louisiana
University of Washington at Seattle
Eastern Michigan University, Ypsilanti, Michigan
University of Miami, Coral Gables, Florida
U.S. Air Force Technical School, specialization in Missile Electronics, Lowry Air Force Base, Denver, Colorado, 1964
Caddo-Kiowa V-Tech School, specialization in Computer Operation and Word Processing, F. Cobb, Oklahoma, 1990
University College, London, England
University of Edinburgh, Edinburgh, Scotland
University of Sussex, Brighton, England

AWARDS, HONORS

Academy of Television Arts and Sciences Emmy credential, 1975

Robby Award, TV Film Festival of Monte Carlo

Melies Prize, TV Film Festival of Monte Carlo

Fantasy Film Award, TV Film Festival of Monte Carlo

PUBLICATION HIGHLIGHTS

"Legend of the Kiowas" in INFOJOURNAL magazine (Washington, D.C.: The International Fortean Society, June 1987); "Rite of Encounter" in *The Remembered Earth: An Anthology of Contemporary Native American Literature,* ed. by Geary Hobson (Albuquerque: University of New Mexico Press, 1979); "Wilderness Trek" in *The Written, Spoken and Unspoken Word* (Norman: University of Oklahoma Press, American Indian Institute, 1980)

NARRATIVE

Russell Bates was born in Lawton, Oklahoma, in the Kiowa Indian Hospital. His grandmother visited him and named him Thay-nay-tonh, Bluejay Tailfeathers, after a blue jay pecked at the hospital window and flew away. During World War II his family lived in Los Angeles, then moved back to Anadarko, Oklahoma, in 1948. Bates later reflected on the two distinctly different geographic areas in which he was raised, noting that "The contrast between the two is a mix that I would not trade for anyone else's upbringing." He was encouraged to learn from an early age by his parents: "My mother gets most of the credit because she taught me to read and write at age 3, and by age 5, I was reading her science fiction books and magazines."

In school Bates had two distinctly contrasting teachers: one very good and one bad one. One teacher discouraged him from pushing his creative and intellectual limits, accusing him of plagiarism when he was in the eighth grade. The

other teacher, a ninth grade instructor named Mr. Potts, encouraged Bates to write stories, and on one memorable occasion asked Bates to read his work in front of his fellow classmates. As he continues, "When I finished reading, I looked up and the other students all were captivated and completely taken by the story. There wasn't a sound in the room; then they applauded, and I fled to my seat. Thereafter Mr. Potts did that again and again, until the other students would ask me if I had written any more stories, because they all wanted to hear them. Through high school it continued, and I became capable of performing my material before audiences. Without Mr. Potts I likely would have remained a closet writer."

Bates was interested in science after he graduated from high school and enrolled in college as an aerospace engineering major. As a senior, when aircraft companies were trying to recruit him, he had a change of heart about his chosen field, feeling that he was somewhat directed into the field by his father who was a aerospace inventor. As a result of this uncertainty, Bates dropped out of college and decided to pursue a different career. He was ten days from entering the Federal Marshal Service when he received his draft notice, and he chose to join the U.S. Air Force. Because of his scientific training, he was sent back into the kind of work he left behind in college and was given the duty of becoming a missile electronics technician.

Before he was to be sent to Thailand and the Vietnam War Bates was caught in a violent explosion that wrecked the missile facility on his base, and was one of only three survivors. Bates remained in the hospital for nine months, recovering from his injuries. While healing he turned to writing as a form of therapy and soon realized that this was his true calling. "It took a horrible accident while I was in the U.S. Air Force and a nine-month hospitalization for me to find that I was a writer and always had been. The writing saved me from hospital psychosis and I then healed as I was supposed to. Thereafter, I have rarely spent much time away from my writing."

Since that time Bates has written science fiction screenplays for television, including one titled "How Sharper Than a Serpent's Tooth" for the animated movie *Star Trek* in 1974, and articles and short stories for various journals, newspapers and books. "Science fiction literally can be about any subject—roughly half of my writing is about Native Americans, but the themes and executions rarely are the same." When asked if his present location in some way influences his writing, Bates responds, "Yes, but only as settings. My stories do not depend upon small-town life or even rural environs for their inspirations. When one can imagine (as I have for my movie script, *Intergalactic!*) galaxy-spanning civilizations whose interplay impinges on our solar system by accident, there is nothing provincial about that at all."

Bates considers writer Harlan Ellison to be his mentor: "Harlan Ellison's writings had the most affect on my career because he wrote so freely, so evocatively, and so completely. He writes SF [science fiction] as a personal vehicle, and I aspire to that myself." He adds the names of other writers who have shaped his style and goals: "Gene L. Coon and Dorothy C. Fontana share credit for most of my ability to write TV and film scripts. Among my teachers, I count Robin Scott Wilson, Robert Silverberg, Paul Nagel and Bob Duncan as those truly affecting my course of pursuit in my career."

Bates enjoys the works of "Most '30s, '40s, '50s, '60s and '70s SF writers. Past that time, the field turned to experimental forms that mostly were nonsense. Today's SF concentrates too heavily on series novels to really be that interesting.

The short story currently is in retreat, and that's mainly my interest. Again, my favorite writers are Harlan Ellison, Robert Silverberg, Frank Herbert, Fritz Leiber, Damon Knight, Kate Wilhelm, Samuel R. Delany, Joanna Russ, Ursula K. LeGuin, Vonda McIntyre, Ed Bryant, Robin Scott Wilson, Glen Cook, Gustav Hasford, Octavia Estelle Butler, among others."

He is currently working on screenplays and "treatments with Thomas McKelvey Cleaver, a caucasian writer based in Los Angeles. Novel treatments of those screenplays also are in development. Currently, Milton Paddlety and I are marketing a TV-series concept titled 'Freelance,' which would chronicle the adventures and misadventures of a three-man freelance videography team. As if that concept were being brought to life, Lowell Keith Russell, Milton Paddlety and I are projected to be accomplishing a two-hour PBS documentary on Native American religions and religious practices within the next year." Bates also works at home as a writer for hire: "I do word processing for various people on an IBM-compatible computer. I have generally acted as a writing/teaching consultant on prose and teleplays. I also do income tax returns in season. I have edited other people's writings and I am a master proofreader."

When he is not working on his writing, Bates is busy hunting down rare and unusual books to add to his extensive science fiction collection. "I am an avid book collector, specializing in older SF paperbacks, and have a valuable collection of some ten thousand. I search each city I visit like a hunter of rare treasures. From my old USAF electronics days, I still tinker with TVs, VCRs, and other electronic gadgets. I collect movies and TV shows on videotape and have some three thousand films captured so far, mostly science fiction. I work on keeping fit and also on keeping my weight down by walking a 100-pound Siberian husky to exercise us both."

Bates is also an amateur meteorologist and is known to regional television viewers for his current Anadarko temperature reports.

NAME   E, N
Gail Bear

TRIBAL AFFILIATION
Cree

PUBLICATION HIGHLIGHTS
Saskatchewan Indian Cultural Calendar 1983 (Saskatoon: Saskatchewan Indian Cultural College, 1982)
Ki-ihkin (coloring book for children) (Saskatoon: Saskatchewan Indian Cultural College, 1980)
Learning about the Indian Reserve (Saskatoon: Saskatchewan Indian Cultural College, Curriculum Studies and Research, 1974)
The Indian Family, revised edition (Saskatoon: Saskatchewan Indian Cultural College, Curriculum Studies and Research, Federation of Saskatchewan Indians, 1973, 1976)

NARRATIVE
Bear's title *The Indian Family* is an Indian culture supplement to elementary social studies curriculum materials and includes a handbook and lesson plans for teachers.

NAME   E, F, N
Denton R. Bedford

TRIBAL AFFILIATION
Minsi

PERSONAL
Born: 1907

Education: B.S. in history from Lafayette College, Easton, Pennsylvania; M.S. in history from Lafayette College, Easton, Pennsylvania; graduate coursework from Columbia University, New York, New York

PUBLICATION HIGHLIGHTS
The Foxes and Lumpwoods (New York: Vantage, 1977); Tsali (San Francisco: Indian Historian Press, 1972)

Bedford's works have also appeared in *American Indian Fiction,* by Charles R. Larson, first edition (Albuquerque: University of New Mexico Press, c1978).

NARRATIVE
An educator in high schools and college for more than twenty years, Bedford is descended paternally from Chief Wapalanewa, a famous pro-British raider during the American Revolution. Bedford is now deceased.

NAME   F
Betty Louise Bell

TRIBAL AFFILIATION
Cherokee

PERSONAL
Born: 1949

PUBLICATION HIGHLIGHTS
Faces of the Moon (Norman: University of Oklahoma Press, 1994)

NAME   J, N, P, V
Kathryn Kemler Bell

TRIBAL AFFILIATION
Cheyenne

PERSONAL

Born: January 1, 1948, in Clinton, Oklahoma
Education: B.A. in art and journalism

PUBLICATION HIGHLIGHTS

"Robbie McMurty" in *Intertribal: Serving Oklahoma's Indian Country,* ed. by Kathy Bell (Okmulgee, Okla.: American Indian Media Services, July 1990); "Cordee, Ok, 1950," poem in *Piecework: A Magazine of Poetry by Women* (Oklahoma City: Red Dirt Press, Fall, 1986); "Ester," poem in *The Phoenix Oklahoma Poets,* vol. ix (Tahlequah, Okla.: Northeastern State University, 1986)

NARRATIVE

Kathryn Kemler Bell was born in western Oklahoma and grew up in the northeastern portion of the state. As a child in school she recalled, "My third grade teacher, who told a very painfully shy and introverted and alone child (me) that 'one day you will be a writer.' I've never forgotten those words ... my elementary school teachers were, for the most part, encouraging and supportive of my interest in writing." Bell's work focuses on her identity as an Indian woman and on a variety of life experiences. She describes her poetry as stream-of-consciousness writing. While she credits her family and friends for having had the greatest influence on her, she also regards the Cheyenne poet Lance Henson as her mentor, adding that he served as her literary guide "by relating to me what it means to be Cheyenne and then encouraging me to put it in writing." Among the many authors Bell reads, she particularly enjoys Faulkner, Hemingway, Ayn Rand and N. Scott Momaday. She is currently working on a film documentary about the Sand Creek Massacre of Cheyenne Indians in 1864, which is presently in the production stage.

When asked about her other activities Bell says, "I don't do anything else! I've made a career of writing (fifteen years as a reporter, editor on Indian newspapers, plus script writing, technical and proposal writing) and I write poetry in any 'spare' time I have on vacation or while traveling." An individual with a close tie to the land she says that "it [Oklahoma] is the heart of my existence and 'home base' and no matter where I go, I always return to Oklahoma's red earth and red spirit—for it is home to many Indian people. It is infused with our history and traditions."

She currently conducts research and writes legislation as a legislative research specialist for the National Council (legislative branch) of the Muscogee (Creek) Nation of Okmulgee, Oklahoma, which is the tribal headquarters.

NAME   F, N

Salli Benedict

TRIBAL AFFILIATION

Akwesasne Mohawk

PERSONAL

Born: January 5, 1954
Education: B.S. in visual arts and Native studies, State University of New York, Platsburg, 1981; B.A. in fine arts, State University of New York, Potsdam, 1986

PUBLICATION HIGHLIGHTS

Kanerokwakonha anoware sanerokwa [by Arthur Caswell Parker and Salli Benedict] (Fort Covington, N.Y.: Mohawk Language Consortium, 1980)

Benedict has had works published in *New Voices from the Longhouse: An Anthology of Contemporary Iroquois Writing,* first edition, ed. by Joseph Bruchac (Greenfield

Center, N.Y.: Greenfield Review Press, c1989); *A Gathering of Spirit: A Collection by North American Indian Women,* ed. by Beth Brant (Ithaca, N.Y.: Firebrand Books, 1988, c1984); *Earth Power Coming: Short Fiction in Native American Literature,* ed. by Simon J. Ortiz (Tsaile, Ariz.: Navajo Community College Press, c1983)

NARRATIVE

Benedict has served as the director of the Akwesasne Museum in Hogansburg, New York.

❖❖❖

NAME   M, N, VA

Kay C. Bennett

OTHER NAMES USED

Kaibah Bennett

TRIBAL AFFILIATION

Navajo

PERSONAL

Born: 1922 at Sheepsprings Trading Post, New Mexico

PUBLICATION HIGHLIGHTS

A Navajo Saga, by Kay C. Bennett with Russ Bennett (San Antonio: Naylor, [1969]); *Kaibah: Recollection of a Navajo Girlhood,* autobiography (Los Angeles: Westernlore Press, 1964)

Bennett's works have also appeared in: *Native American Renaissance,* by Kenneth Lincoln (Berkeley: University of California Press, c1983); *The American Indian Speaks,* ed. by John R. Milton (Vermillion, S. Dak.: Dakota Press, University of South Dakota, 1969)

NARRATIVE

Kay Bennett was born in a hogan at the Sheepsprings Trading Post in Sheep-springs, New Mexico. Given the name Kaibah, she has shortened it to Kay. As a young woman Bennett attended the Toadlena Boarding school in Toadlena, New Mexico, for five years, and after World War II she became a teacher and an interpreter at the Phoenix Indian School, where she stayed for seven years. In 1951 she began singing in public and has since entertained at numerous events and has recorded a variety of Navajo songs. Later, Bennett moved to Afghanistan, where she lived from 1958–1960 and during this period in her life traveled in the Middle and Far East and throughout Europe. In 1969 she was appointed to the Arizona Commission on Human Rights by the governor. Bennett is also known for her Navajo dress designs and the Navajo dolls she makes, and she also illustrates her own books. She lives with her husband, Russ Bennett, near Gallup, New Mexico.

❖❖❖

NAME   N, P, PA, PL

Diane Lxeis Benson

OTHER NAMES USED

Diane E. Benson

TRIBAL AFFILIATION

Tlingit

PERSONAL

Born: October 17, 1954, in Yakima, Washington

Education: B.A. in theater, University of Alaska, with a minor in justice (Indian law) and journalism, 1985; coursework in acting and screenwriting at the American Film Institute, Washington, D.C., 1989

AWARDS, HONORS

University of Alaska Outstanding Alumni, 1990; Best Actress Award, Epsilon Zeta Alpha Psi Omega, 1985

PUBLICATION HIGHLIGHTS

"Potlatch Ducks" in *Callaloo*, vol. 77 (1) (Winter 135, 1)

"Sister Warrior," play in *Raven Tells Stories: An Anthology of Alaskan Native Writing*, ed. by Joseph Bruchac (Greenfield Center, N.Y.: Greenfield Review Press, 1991)

"Of Value," poem in *Sovereign Indigenous Women of the Arctic Newsletter* ([S.l.: s.n.], No. 1, November 1986)

"Eskimo Man," poem in: *The Al-Esk-Ind* ([S.l.: s.n.], Summer–Fall 1978)

Benson's works have also appeared in: *Returning the Gift: Poetry and Prose from the First North American Native Writers' Festival*, ed. by Joseph Bruchac with the support of the Association for the Study of American Indian Literatures (Tucson: University of Arizona, 1994).

NARRATIVE

Diane Lxeis Benson was born in Yakima, Washington, and grew up in southeastern Alaska, primarily in the areas of Ketchikan and Sitka. Her traditional lineage is of the Raven and the Sea Tern Clan, and she comes from the Snail House of Sitka. "I lived my childhood and youth on the ocean. At one time literally, considering house boats and fishing boats. I also lived in Metlakatla, one of the few actual Indian reserves in Alaska, and Juneau, and time outside of Hoonah, where the elder whom I was named after came from." Of her schooling, she says, "I didn't win any awards in school, had very few friends and was not particularly athletic. I recall very few teachers, and the ones I do, I only remember as white, abrasive and ignorant about my tribe. They could very

well appear different to me now. But there was a couple from Indiana teaching at Mt. Edgecumbe Indian Boarding School in Sitka while my brother and I were there. They published a poem that I wrote about our people someday getting back our land. They actually taught creative writing. My first clue that I could write more than the detailed complaints to my father." Benson spent many years of her youth being shuttled about among various foster homes. In order for her to cope with these continuing changes, she turned to writing. "I wrote as a child to keep my sanity. I removed myself from my abusive environment by writing about anything. Sometimes I wrote to myself about my environment." She enrolled at the University of Alaska, where she had a journalism mentor named Howard Rock who was an Inuit and publisher of the *Tundra Times* newspaper: "unfortunately, that was brief, and he has since passed to the spirit world." He inspired and corrected Benson, who was a young, formidable college student on her first newspaper job.

Benson's writing are concerned with Native American social issues, tribal issues that are legal, social, spiritual in nature "or on a very personal level, our relationship to the world around us, as per my own experience and the experiences of others that I have witnessed. I often use the theatre to express my words." She considers one of her most successful works to be an analysis of a tribal dispute and the ensuing "inflammatory media coverage by non-Native local papers" unofficially titled *Tyonek and the Media*. As she explains, "I am not totally satisfied, as I never sent the manuscript out for publishing. Another favorite piece is a poem I wrote titled 'Potlatch Ducks' hopefully to be published [soon]. I am fond of this poem because it is unlike anything else I have written. It is simple, soft and a statement of culture alive and well today. Since much of what

I write can be 'raw,' as I'm told, and hard punching, I am pleased to see myself write something still effective without the anger (although I like very much to write with emotion).

"I never saw myself as a writer. I basically wrote to stay alive. The question for me is: What made me choose to share my writing? I always kept my writings to myself. I still have a problem with that. I was inspired to share my writing and think of myself as a writer with my university script-writing class, out of which was born my play 'Sister Warrior.' This play gave me the local attention as a writer that I had never had before, and I realized then, the power of the written word, and that it knows no bounds. ... I write about pain and recovery, I suppose, more than anything. I want to move people, cause them to experience sadness and then hope. Sometimes to laugh in the midst of despair. No matter what hope is the outcome. I borrow from my life when I write more than anything ... briefly, I have written all my life ... since I could first hold a pencil and make letters. Growing up in numerous foster homes and such situations breeding abuse, I escaped into writing. I was never the greatest at grammar, curiously enough, but I have always been aware of the rhythms of speech. Although today I am an actress, I was a very shy child. So instead of talking, I listened."

In 1985 Benson created Alaska's first contemporary theater and performance group. The six-member group was called Kokeena Inprov, though they were not an inprovisational company. Benson created pieces for the group on various subjects such as land claims, corporate ethics and its damage to tribal identity, alcohol abuse and death and comedic situations about money and tribal decisions. She is the founder of the newly formed Ya-haan Circle of Native Writers.

Benson enjoys reading the works of authors Vine Deloria Jr., N. Scott Momaday, Simon Ortiz and Paula Gunn Allen. "They have not so much had an influence on my work as much as they have influenced my life. I am strongly concerned with justice, and that is what they also address in their writings in one form or another. I first read Vine Deloria Jr. in 1970. He taught me much, and still does."

"I'd have to say that my current surroundings play a part in my not writing as much as I should. I now have eleven dogs that require a great deal of care. I am currently reducing my possessions and my space to something more manageable. But alas, I am still keeping the dogs. I have numerous projects that I am working on. Many things are started. I have two scripts in the works, and I have a series of poems which I have been focusing on, and I am turning more to prose and fiction and nonfiction—feeling a desire to write in many genres and styles. I am also turning 'Sister Warrior' from a one-act play to a full length play." Benson's works have appeared in the special Native American issue of the journal *Callaloo*.

Benson is currently a performing artist and talent agent, representing talent for film, radio and stage, and also contract to cast, floor direct, stage direct and train individuals. As a performing artist she is primarily a stage actress, though she had a small role in the Walt Disney movie *White Fang*. She is the mother of one son who "motivates me by his very existence." In her off hours Benson relaxes with cooking, reading and running her dog sled team. She also enjoys teaching and performance work. Benson is also a member of the Alaska Press Women, the Alaska Film Group, the Chugiak/Eagle River Chamber of Commerce and the Chugiak Dog Mushers.

NAME P
Clifford Bernie

OTHER NAMES USED
Storm Horse

TRIBAL AFFILIATION
Yankton Dakota

PERSONAL
Education: Coursework at Yankton College, Yankton, South Dakota, 1983–1984; Dakota Plains Institute of Learning, Marty, South Dakota, 1983; Standing Rock Community College, Fort Yates, South Dakota, 1981–1982.

PUBLICATION HIGHLIGHTS
"A Primitive Journey," poem in *The Blue Cloud Quarterly* (Marvin, S. Dak.: Blue Cloud Quarterly, 1988); "Along the Whiteman's Road," "Promise," "Calling of Relatives," poems in *Riverrun* (Yankton, S. Dak.: Yankton College, 1983); "The Eagles Word," "Calling of Relatives," "Homecoming," poems in *Horizons: An Anthology of South Dakota Writers* (Hermosa, S. Dak.: Lame Johnny Press, 1983)

NARRATIVE
Clifford Bernie graduated from the Marty South Dakota High School in 1971. He worked as an editor both at the Denver Native Americans United and for the publication *The Yankton Sioux Messenger.* He was a writer and reporter for the journal *Dakota Sun,* which was published at the Standing Rock Community College in Fort Yates North Dakota, he worked as a tutor at the Dakota Plains Institute of Learning in Marty, South Dakota, and he worked as a counselor and teacher's aide at Yankton College in Yankton, South Dakota. Bernie has studied sociology at Yankton College, and he has taken general education classes from the Dakota Plains Institute of Learning and from Standing Rock Community College.

Bernie has given readings of his poems at the Dakota Plains Institute of Learning, the Marty Indian School, the Springfield Correctional Facility in Springfield South Dakota, at Yankton College and at the University of South Dakota. He is now a writer and teacher's aide in writing skills.

NAME P
Ted Berrigan

OTHER NAMES USED
Edmund Joseph Michael Berrigan Jr.

TRIBAL AFFILIATION
Choctaw

PERSONAL
Born: November 15, 1934, in Providence, Rhode Island; died July 1983.
Education: B.A. from University of Tulsa, Tulsa, Oklahoma, 1959; M.A. from University of Tulsa, Tulsa, Oklahoma, 1962

AWARDS, HONORS
Poetry Foundation Award for *The Sonnets,* 1964

PUBLICATION HIGHLIGHTS
Selected Poems (New York: Penguin, 1994)
Talking with Tranquillity: Interviews with Ted Berrigan, ed. by Stephen Ratcliffe and Leslie Scalapino (Bolinas, Calif.: Avenue B/O Books, c1991)
A Certain Slant of Sunlight (Oakland, Calif.: O Books, c1988)
Carrying a Torch ([S.l.: s.n.], 1980)
So Going Around Cities: New and Selected

Poems, 1958–1979 [first edition] (Berkeley: Blue Wind Press, 1980)

In the Early Morning Rain (New York: Cape Goliard Press, [1971, c1970])

The Sonnets (New York: Grove Press, 1967)

Berrigan's work has also appeared in the anthologies:

Voices from Wah' kon-tah, ed. by Robert K. Dodge and Joseph B. McCullough. (New York: International, 1974)

Sparklers (New York: Random House, 1969)

Young American Poets, ed. by Paul Carroll (Chicago: Follett, 1968)

The American Literary Anthology I (New York: Farrar, Straus Giroux, 1968)

NARRATIVE

Born in Providence, Rhode Island, of Irish and Choctaw heritage, Berrigan received his B.A. and M.A. degrees from the University of Tulsa and served in the U.S. Army from 1954 to 1957. He had worked as an editorial assistant for the publication *Art News* and was editor and publisher of the journals *"C" Press* and *C Magazine.* Berrigan also worked as a poetry workshop instructor at St. Mark's Art Project in New York City, he was a visiting lecturer for the Writer's Workshop at the University of Iowa in Iowa City from 1968 to 1969 and he taught at numerous colleges and universities such as Yale University, the Kerouac School in Boulder, Colorado, Essex University in Essex, England and at the University of Michigan. He was poet in residence at Northeastern Illinois University from 1969 to 1976 and was poet in residence at the City College of the City University of New York.

The author and coauthor of over twenty-five books, Berrigan was also an active editor and contributor to numerous anthologies. His work has also appeared in the journals *Art News, Art and Literature, Angel Hair, Poetry* and *World.*

He was married twice and had four children. He died on July 4, 1983.

NAME F, P, VA

Duane Big Eagle

TRIBAL AFFILIATION

Osage

PERSONAL

Born: May 20, 1946, Claremore, Oklahoma

Education: B.A. from the University of California at Berkeley, 1970

AWARDS, HONORS

Artist in Residence at the Headlands Center for the Arts, 1992; California Arts Counci Artist in Residence, 1987–1990; Sonoma County Community Foundation Literary Fellowship, 1990

PUBLICATION HIGHLIGHTS

"Birthplace," poem in *Songs From This Earth On Turtle's Back* (Greenfield Station, N.Y.: Greenfield Review Press, 1983)

"The Journey," fiction in *Earth Power Coming* (Tsaile, Ariz.: Navajo Community College Press, 1983)

Bidato: Ten Mile River Poems (Berkeley: Workingman's Press, 1975)

NARRATIVE

Duane Big Eagle was born in Claremore, Oklahoma, and was raised in two places: as a small child, in Claremore with his grandparents and in Hominy, Oklahoma, his father's hometown. He later attended high school in Oklahoma City and attended the University of California at Berkeley during the "turbulent '60s," which was "a shock for an Oklahoma kid, but I loved it." He also worked at the UC library while he was a student.

Currently Big Eagle is an artist in residence at the Headlands Center for the Arts in Marin, California. "You might say I'm being paid to sit in a national park by the ocean and be a writer. I've been lucky to travel a lot in my life, but the Oklahoma landscape seems most familiar to my imagination." Big Eagle admits that it's a paradox that he lives in California, but he adds that he also enjoys the Southwest too.

There were many people who inspired him throughout his life and work, among them are his parents, by their way of looking at the world, and by watching them get through life and enjoy it. He also includes his friends, writers Barry Gifford and Bill Bradd, many European writers, Dylan Thomas, the Japanese writer Kenji Miyazawa, W. C. Williams, the Beats in America and Indian writers Simon Ortiz, Leslie Silko, James Welch, Scott Momaday, Coeur D'Alene, Sherman Alexie and Peruvian Indian writer Cesar Vallejo. In the area of fiction he notes two memorable stories: *To the River's Edge* by Elizabeth Cook-Lynn and *Ghost Singer* by Anna Lee Walters. Big Eagle also reads Dostoyevsky. His works have appeared in the special Native American issue of the journal *Callaloo.*

Big Eagle is also a visual artist who paints in oil and watercolors. He has felt the influence of many artists throughout history, particularly the works of the Japanese artist Hiroshige, the French impressionists and Indian artists Harrison Begay, Jerone Tiger, T. C. Cannon, Jaune Quick-to-See-Smith. Big Eagle is presently working on a poetry manuscript, which he is illustrating with his paintings.

NAME   E, F, L, N, P, PL
Fred Bigjim

OTHER NAMES USED
Fred Seagayuk Bigjim

TRIBAL AFFILIATION
Inupiat/Eskimo

PERSONAL
Born: July 20, 1941, in Nome, Alaska
Education: B.A. in secondary education and social sciences, University of Alaska, 1972; M.A. in educational administration, Harvard University, 1973; C.A.S. in social policy, Harvard University, 1978

AWARDS, HONORS
Outstanding Teacher at Sheldon Jackson College, Sitka, Alaska, 1963; Outstanding Teacher at the University of Alaska, 1965

PUBLICATION HIGHLIGHTS
Walk the Wind (Portland, Oreg.: Press-22, 1987)
We Talk, You Yawn: A Discourse on Education in Alaska (Portland Oreg.: Press-22, 1985)
Sinrock (Portland, Oreg.: Press-22, 1983)
Letters to Howard: An Interpretation of the Alaska Native Land Claims, with James Ito-Adler (Anchorage: Alaska Methodist University Press, 1974)

NARRATIVE
Fred Bigjim was born and raised in Nome, Alaska, and in the Bering Sea coastal area, where as a young child he spent five years in an evangelical church children's home and where some his most vivid memories come from. Bigjim's works focus on the Eskimos and Natives of Alaska and the Alaskan tundra. He writes fiction, nonfiction, poetry and is a playwright as well as an educator and lecturer. Individuals who were significant in Bigjim's artistic development were Bill Vaudrin, a college English and literature instructor, who is of Chippewa heritage, and members of his family as well as friend Eben Hopson. Bigjim also recalled with pleasure the time

he spent as the tour guide for author James Michener while he was conducting research for his novel *Alaska*. He enjoys reading the works of Native American poets as well as the works of poet Wilford Owen and other early twentieth-century English poets. He is currently working on a novel and employed as an educator in the Auburn school district, Auburn, Washington.

NAME   F, J, N, P
D. L. Birchfield

OTHER NAMES USED
Isuba Hanta Holitopa
Don Birchfield

TRIBAL AFFILIATION
Chickasaw and Choctaw

PERSONAL
Born: July 10, 1948, in Blackjack, Oklahoma
Education: A.A. degree in history, Mesa College, Grand Junction, Colorado, 1968
Coursework at the University of Colorado, Boulder, 1967
Coursework at the University of Denver, Denver, Colorado, 1968–1969
Military science credits, United States Marine Corps Officer Candidate School, Quantico, Virginia, 1969
B.A. double major in history and political science, Western State College of Colorado, Gunnison, 1971
Graduate studies in history, University of Oklahoma, Norman, 1971–1973
Juris doctor, University of Oklahoma College of Law, Norman, 1975

AWARDS, HONORS
Student body president, Mesa College, Grand Junction, Colorado, 1967–1968; Hazel Butler Garms United States History Scholarship from the Daughters of the American Revolution, 1967–1968

PUBLICATION HIGHLIGHTS
Animal Lore and Legend—Rabbit: American Indian Legends (New York: Scholastic, 1996)
Jim Thorpe, World's Greatest Athlete (Morristown, N.J.: Modern Curriculum Press, 1995)
Tecumseh, Leader (Morristown, N.J.: Modern Curriculum Press, 1995)
Durable Breath: Contemporary Native American Poetry, ed. by John E. Smelcer and D. L. Birchfield (Anchorage: Salmon Run, [1994])
"Lop a loi soi," poem in *Bishinik*, vol. 3, no. 9 (Durant, Okla.: Choctaw Nation of Oklahoma, , March 198?)
"Ode to Rich Mountain," in *Absolute* (Oklahoma City: Oklahoma City Community College, Spring 198[?])
"First Reader," fiction in *The Final Draft* (Phoenix: [s.n.], March 1990)
"The OKC Camp Crier," history in *Native Press Research Journal*, no. 8, Summer (Little Rock, Ark.: American Indian and Alaska Native Periodicals Research Clearinghouse, 1988)

Birchfield's works have also appeared in *Looking at the Words of Our People: First Nations Analysis of Literature,* ed. by Jeannette Armstrong (Penticton, B.C.: Theytus Books, 1993)

NARRATIVE
Don Birchfield was born in rural Atoka County, Oklahoma, near the community of Blackjack in the farmhouse of his maternal grandparent's, and raised there until he was old enough to start kindergarten. At this time his family moved to Oklahoma City, though he and his family went back to his grandparents home regularly for five years after their move.

Birchfield's parents played an important role in his intellectual and creative developments. "Without question, my parents have been the central influence in my writing life. At a parent-teacher conference at the beginning of the fourth grade, my parents were informed that I had only a second grade reading level. My idyllic reverie came to a sudden end, as my mother forced me to read, beginning with *The Hardy Boys,* and my father saw to it that I took up violin in the elementary school orchestra program (I think he had in mind that I would learn Bob Wills and the Texas Playboys kind of stuff, where I eventually came to love Mendelssohn). ... My mother and her mother and my paternal grandmother were all extremely talkative storytellers in my youth. My father and my uncles told stories at every gathering. ... My father placed great store in formal education, especially on my learning Choctaw history, as he had only a fourth grade formal education, [he] actually taught himself how to read in the CCC [California Conservation Corps] camps, and did not learn any Choctaw history at all until he was in New Zealand in the marine corps, where a professor ... had a personal interest in Indian history, it was from him that my father first learned such things as the forced removal of the Choctaws in the 1830s and my father was determined that I should not have to go overseas to learn Choctaw history."

Birchfield was ten when missionaries convinced his parents to take the family to church six nights a week with only whirlwind trips back home. "At the age of 14, maybe 15, but probably along about the spring of 1963, I read Anna Lewis's biography of Pushmataha and other things, among them the *Treaty of Dancing Rabbit Creek,* and I became infuriated at the right-wing fundamentalist

Christian world in which I had been immersed for five years, blaming its mentality, which I knew excellently by then, for what had been done to my paternal grandmother's people, the Choctaws; at the same time I was disgusted with the Choctaws for not having resisted forced removal with violence."

Because Birchfield disagreed with his parents' views he distanced himself from them during this period and completely severed his ties with the church. To busy himself he worked several jobs during high school and became very active in high school activities, competing in sports and participating in numerous high school functions and committees.

As a high school student Birchfield had an unusual instructor who expanded his students' horizons and taught his class as a college freshman lecture course. Teacher Gary Lower's knowledge and enthusiasm for the subject of world history would fire an interest in history in Birchfield and influence his future course of studies. After graduation from high school, Birchfield attended Mesa College in Grand Junction, Colorado, where he received his associate of arts degree in history in 1968.

Active in the democratic party during Robert Kennedy's presidential campaign, Birchfield was devastated by his assassination in 1968. He switched to the Rockefeller campaign, but abandoned his activities in six months and thus ended his political activities. "I was so sick of it I eventually transferred to a small college campus in the high mountain country to get away from it all. That loss of interest has been total and permanent."

Birchfield later took courses at the University of Colorado at Boulder and at the University of Denver. In 1969 he earned military science credits from the U.S. Marine Corps Officer Candidate

School in Quantico, Virginia. At this time he received a high draft lottery number and dropped out of the program and school for a half year to take his exposure to the draft. He worked at the Climax Molybdenum Company mine on the continental divide in Leadville, Colorado, and on the construction crew who built lodges at the bottom and top of mountains of the Keystone Mountain Ski Area near Lake Dillon, Colorado, a dangerous job where coworkers of his who were old friends were either seriously injured or killed at the job sites.

He returned to school at Western State College of Colorado at Gunnison, earned his bachelor of arts degree and began studying for a doctoral degree at the University of Oklahoma, specializing in seventeenth-century Apache Spanish relations. After learning that an influential professor in his degree program would be retiring because of medical reasons and would not be able to see him through to the end of his Ph.D., Birchfield switched to law school and earned his juris doctorate degree from the University of Oklahoma College of Law in 1975. In 1987–1988 he was the director of the publication *Camp Crier* with coeditor Sammy Tonekei White, which emanated from the Oklahoma City Native American Center. Birchfield had been an active member of many college activities and associations as a student in his college career. He has always been an avid chess player and has written articles for national publications on the sport and has been an active member and officeholder of the Oklahoma Chess Association. He has also served as the chair of the board of directors of the Oklahoma Choctaw Tribal Alliance, Inc.

A writer of fiction, nonfiction, poetry and articles for newspapers and chess publications, Birchfield enjoys reading about subjects that he is working on at the time. "I can barely stand to read anything anymore that isn't directly related to something I'm researching. If I happen to be looking into it for some project, then whatever it is, whether a subject or an author or whatever, I cannot get enough of it. But on the whole, writers who I enjoyed reading years ago no longer hold my interest. Occasionally I can lose myself in some work of popular fiction, such as Thomas Harris's *The Silence of the Lambs* ... but I do less pleasure reading now than at any earlier period of my life."

Birchfield actively works on short-term projects such as short stories, poems, articles, profiles and essays for small circulation periodicals such as chess journals and Native American newspapers. He is also working on four large projects: a historical work titled *The Critical Century in Choctaw History, 1729–1828; Blood Promise,* a three-act musical comedy based on the history of Western State College of Colorado; *Quiet Retreat—the Autobiography of a Junior College Student Body President* and a satirical novel titled *The Little Choctaws.* Birchfield has recently been appointed the general editor of the ten-volume *Encyclopedia of American Indians,* to be published in 1996 by Marshall Cavendish, and he was the guest coeditor of the 1994 Native literatures issue of *Callaloo.* Birchfield is also the book review editor of the newspaper *News from Indian country.*

When asked about some of his strongest works, he responds, "I consider my best work to be *The Legend of the Little Bitty Bragger,* a children's theater production in my novel-in-progress *The Little Choctaws,* because it embodies the earthy humor and irreverent attitude toward institutions and established authority that I find at the core of Choctaw life and thought."

NAME   N, P

Gloria Bird

TRIBAL AFFILIATION

Spokane

PERSONAL

Education: B.A. in English from Lewis and Clark College, Portland, Oregon; M.A. from the University of Arizona, Tucson

AWARDS, HONORS

Writers Grant from the Oregon Institute of Literary Arts, for poetry, 1988

PUBLICATION HIGHLIGHTS

Families and Intimate Relationships, Gloria Bird and Keith Melville (New York: McGraw-Hill, 1994); *Full Moon on the Reservation* (Greenfield Center, N.Y.: Greenfield Review Press, 1993); *A Filmography for American Indian Education* [Carroll Warner Williams and Gloria Bird] (Santa Fe: Zia Cine, 1973)

Some of Bird's works have appeared in the following anthologies: *Returning the Gift: Poetry and Prose from the First North American Native Writers' Festival,* ed. by Joseph Bruchac with the support of the Association for the Study of American Indian Languages (Tucson: University of Arizona, 1994); *Talking Leaves: Contemporary Native American Short Stories, an Anthology,* ed. by Craig Lesley (New York: Laurel, Dell, 1991); *Dancing on the Rim of the World: An Anthology of Contemporary Northwest Native American Writing,* ed. by Andrea Lerner (Tucson: Sun Tracks, University of Arizona Press, c1990)

NARRATIVE

Bird was raised on the Spokane and Colville Indian Reservations in Washington state. She attended the Institute of American Indian Arts in Santa Fe, New

Mexico, before she went on to earn her B.A. and M.A.

Bird is one of the founding members of the Northwest Native American Writers Association, and her works have appeared in numerous publications such as *Mr. Cogito: American Indian Issue* (1988), the *NWNAW Broadsides Collections,* (1988, 1990) and journals such as *Caylx, High Plains Literary Review* and *Tamaqua.*

She has taught at Pima Community College in Tucson and is currently working on a series of poems based on the Nez Perce War of 1877.

NAME   F, N

Kimberly M. Blaeser

TRIBAL AFFILIATION

Anishinabe (Minnesota Chippewa from White Earth)

PERSONAL

Education: Degree from the College of St. Benedict, Minnesota; Ph.D. candidate at the University of Notre Dame, Notre Dame, Indiana

AWARDS, HONORS

Francis C. Allen Fellowship recipient

PUBLICATION HIGHLIGHTS

Trailing You (Greenfield Center, N.Y.: Greenfield Review Literary Center, 1994)
Looking at the World of Our People: First Nations Analysis of Literature, ed. by Jeannette Armstron (Penticton, B.C.: Theytus Books, 1993)
"The Multiple Traditions of Gerald Vizenor's Haiku Poetry" in *New Voices in Native American Literary Criticism* (Washington, D.C.: Smithsonian Institution, 1993)
"Living History," "On the Way to the

Chicago Pow-Wow," "Asphalt, the Odd Perfume of Summer" and "Alaskan Mountain Stories, Transfiguration," poems in *Loonfeather* (Bemidji, Minn.: Loonfeather Magazine, Fall/Winter, vol. 12, no. 2, 1991)

Blaeser's work have also appeared in the following anthologies: *Returning the Gift: Poetry and Prose from the First North American Native Writers' Festival*, ed. by Joseph Bruchac with the support of the Association for the Study of American Indian Literatures (Tucson: University of Arizona, 1994); *Narrative Chance: Postmodern Discourse on Native American Indian Literatures*, ed. by Gerald Vizenor (Albuquerque: University of New Mexico Press, 1989)

NARRATIVE

A graduate from the College of St. Benedict in Minnesota, Blaeser is now a Ph.D. candidate at the University of Notre Dame. She studied at the Newberry Library's D'Arcy McNickle Center for the History of the American Indian and is currently a lecturer in Native American literatures at the University of Wisconsin at Milwaukee. Her written works have also appeared in the University of Notre Dame publication *Notre Dame Magazine, The American Indian Quarterly* and the special Native American issue of *Callaloo.*

NAME　　　E, P

Lew Blockcolski

OTHER NAMES USED

Short Feathers

TRIBAL AFFILIATION

Cherokee and Choctaw

PERSONAL

Born: 1943 in Enid, Oklahoma

PUBLICATION HIGHLIGHTS

Blockcolski's works have appeared in: *Voices of the Rainbow: Contemporary Poetry by American Indians*, ed. by Kenneth Rosen (New York: Viking, 1975); *Come to Power: Eleven Contemporary American Indian Poets* (Trumansburg, N.Y.: The Crossing Press, 1974); *From the Belly of the Shark: A New Anthology of Native Americans*, ed. by Walter Lowenfels (New York: Vintage, 1974)

NARRATIVE

Born in Enid, Oklahoma, Blockcolski is the son of Polish and Cherokee/Choctaw parents. He has worked at Emporia State College as an Indian education specialist and is married and the father of two girls. His works have also appeared in numerous journals and publications such as *The Galley Sail Review, Steelhead* and *Akwesasne Notes.*

NAME　　　F, J, P

Peter Blue Cloud

OTHER NAMES USED

Aroniawenrate

TRIBAL AFFILIATION

Mohawk Nation at Kahnawake

PERSONAL

Born: June 10, 1933, at Kahnawake, Quebec, Canada
Education: Eighth grade

AWARDS, HONORS

American Book Award from the Before Columbus Foundation, 1981

PUBLICATION HIGHLIGHTS

I Am Turtle (Ich bin Schildkröte) (Osnabrück: VC-Verlagscooperative, 1991)

The Other Side of Nowhere: Contemporary Coyote Tales (Freedonia, N.Y.: White Pine Press, 1990)

Sketches in Winter, with Crows (New York: Strawberry Press, 1984)

A Gentle Earthquake (for Mt. St. Helens) (Brunswick, Maine: Blackberry Press, 1983[?])

Elderberry Flute Song: Contemporary Coyote Tales (Trumansburg, N.Y.: Crossing Press, 1982)

The Paranoid Foothills: A Work of Fiction (Brunswick, Maine: Blackberry Press, 1981)

Alcatraz Is Not an Island, audio recording (Rooseveltown, N.Y.: Akwesasne Notes, Mohawk Nation, 1980)

White Corn Sister (New York: Strawberry Press, 1979 [1978?])

Back Then Tomorrow (Brunswick, Maine: Blackberry Press, 1978)

Reflections on Milkweed (New York,: Strawberry Press, 1977)

Coyote and Friends (Brunswick, Maine: Blackberry Press, 1976)

Turtle, Bear and Wolf (Rooseveltown, N.Y.: Akwesasne Notes, 1976)

Blue Cloud's works have also appeared in these anthologies:

American Indian Literatures: An Introduction, Bibliographic Review and Selected Bibliography, by A. LaVonne Brown Ruoff (New York: Modern Language Association, 1990)

Circle of Motion: Arizona Anthology of Contemporary American Indian Literature, ed. by Kathleen Mullen Sands (Tempe, Ariz.: Arizona Historical Foundation, 1990)

Native American Reader: Stories, Speeches and Poems, ed. by Jerry D. Blanche (Juneau: Denali Press, 1990)

New Voices from the Longhouse: An Anthology of Contemporary Iroquois Writing, ed. by Joseph Bruchac (Greenfield Center, N.Y.: Greenfield Review Press, 1989)

Survival This Way: Interviews with Native American Poets, by Joseph Bruchac (Tucson: Sun Tracks, University of Arizona Press, 1987)

Earth Power Coming: Short Fiction in Native American Literature, ed. by Simon J. Ortiz (Tsaile, Ariz.: Navajo Community College Press, 1983)

A Nation Within: Contemporary Native American Writing, selected by Ralph Salisbury (Hamilton, New Zealand: Outrigger Publishers, 1983)

Native American Renaissance, by Kenneth Lincoln (Berkeley: University of California Press, 1983)

Voices of the Rainbow, ed. by Kenneth Rosen (New York: Viking, 1975)

From the Belly of the Shark, ed. by Walter Lowenfels (New York: Vantage, 1974)

NARRATIVE

Peter Blue Cloud was born in Kahnaqake, Quebec, and raised in Kahnawake, Brooklyn and Buffalo, New York. He is a member of the Turtle Clan of the Mohawk Nation. Blue Cloud worked as an ironworker in New York City, where he helped build many of the skyscrapers that form Manhattan's skyline. In the 1960s he participated in the occupation of the island of Alcatraz and also worked as a coeditor for the publication *Coyote's Journal.* Although officially retired, Blue Cloud actively works as a woodcarver and newspaper columnist and enjoys doing hide paintings and reading. "I devour books." He is also putting together a collection of his poems for publication. He currently lives in Kahnawake, Quebec, Canada.

NAME   F, N, P, S

Tracey Kim Bonneau

TRIBAL AFFILIATION

Okanagan

PERSONAL

Born: August 7, 1967, in Penticton, British Columbia

Education: Certificate in business, British Columbia Institute of Technology, 1989; coursework at the Enowkin International School of Writing, 1990–1992

AWARDS, HONORS

Bursary for Excellence in G.P.A. from Parliament Buildings Victoria First Citizens Fund, 1991

PUBLICATION HIGHLIGHTS

"For Ola," poem in *Matriart: Special Issue on Native Women Artists* (journal) (Toronto, Ontario: *Womens Feminist Journal,* 1991)

"My Name Is Lucy," "For Ola," poems in *Gatherings* (journal) (Penticton, B.C.: Theytus, 1991)

"Concrete City," "Stranded on an Island," "Doorway," poems in *Gatherings* (journal) (Penticton, B.C.: Theytus, 1990)

"Mourning," "White Magic," "Recovery," poems in *Seventh Generation* (Penticton, B.C.: Theytus, 1989)

Bonneau's works have also appeared in: *Returning the Gift: Poetry and Prose from the First North American Native Writers' Festival,* ed. by Joseph Bruchac with the support of the Association for the Study of American Indian Literatures (Tucson: University of Arizona, 1994).

NARRATIVE

Tracey Kim Bonneau was born in Penticton, British Columbia, and raised on the Penticton Indian Reserve with her grandparents Lillian and William Armstrong "... on a small ranch in a rural area without electricity. Chopping wood, packing water!" As a young woman in school Bonneau had a principal who encouraged the Native children to be proud of their heritage and who named the school sports teams after the animal clans. She was encouraged by her mother, writer Jeanette Armstrong, to treasure the written word and value her own uniqueness. "She encouraged me never to be voiceless and always believe in my literature. My style is my own." As she continues, "My mother saw my chicken scratch on an old piece of paper and told me, 'Tracey you are an excellent writer go to school, let your voice be heard.'" Bonneau fondly remembers a book she had read that had impressed her as a young woman, *In Search of April Raintree* by Canadian novelist Beatrice Culleton. An admirer of Culleton, Bonneau considered her to be a mentor to her own career. "That book changed my life." Bonneau writes about colonization and its effect on North American Natives, Native spirituality and the environment. She also reflects upon on current world politics and most recently has written about the effects of the Gulf War and Oka Crisis in Canada. She considers her strongest works to be her poems "because I write using metaphor." She enjoys the works of Joy Harjo: "She still blows my mind!" Chrystos, because her work is "honest, caring and gutsy," and Jack Forbes, because he "made me understand being Indian in a university setting."

Bonneau is writing a half-hour drama script for a Canadian Broadcasting Company (CBC) Native anthology series for television in Canada and writes freelance for a television program in Canada titled *Kia-huw-ya.* She currently works for the Penticton Indian Band selling aggregate products, where she is responsible for the payroll, invoicing, government remittances and customer service. In her spare hours, Bonneau participates in activities within her community: "I enjoy cultural events within my Native community that enhances awareness and promotes Indian pride! I live in a community, the Penticton Reserve, that are all one. We have a strong sense of identity."

NAME A, E, F, L, N, P, S
DuWayne "Duce" Bowen

OTHER NAMES USED
DuWayne Leslie Bowen
DuWayne L. Bowen

TRIBAL AFFILIATION
Seneca Nation of Indians, Salamanca, New York

PERSONAL
Born: July 7, 1946, in Salamanca, New York
Education: Robinson Run School, Allegany Indian Reservation, New York; Red House Indian School, Red House, New York; Salamanca Junior/Senior High School, Salamanca New York; Vale Technical Institute, Blairsville, Pennsylvania; Jamestown Community College, Olean, New York

AWARDS, HONORS
Participant, presenter on PBS/P.O.V. (Point of View) national television documentary "Honorable Nations," 1991; Emmy Award for Best Documentary of the Year, 1991

PUBLICATION HIGHLIGHTS
One More Story: Contemporary Seneca Tales of the Supernatural (Greenfield, N.Y.: Greenfield Review Press, 1991)

Bowen's works have appeared *New Voices from the Longhouse: An Anthology of Contemporary Iroquois Writing,* first edition, ed. by Joseph Bruchac (Greenfield Center, N.Y.: Greenfield Review Press, c1989).

NARRATIVE
DuWayne "Duce" Bowen was born in Salamanca, New York, and raised on the Allegany Indian Reservation in the Cold Spring/Quaker Bridge area. He writes about Seneca history and subjects and is currently working on a collection of ghost stories. He is also working on the development of an Iroquois adventurer character for use in his future stories. He enjoys writings that deal with the supernatural; Peter Straub inspired him to finish his work on his collection of supernatural stories. He also enjoys the stories of Stephen King and Chuck Swindoll. Bowen has also contributed to the anthology *A Quaker Promise Kept* (Eugene: Spencer Butte Press, 1990).

People who have had an impact on his life include his wife, Janis, his grandmother Mary Halftown and publisher Joseph Bruchac. He also notes that an event that had a momentous effect on his life and work was the forced removal of his people during the 1960s by the U.S. Government, in order to build the Allegheny (Kinzua) Dam.

Bowen is now a manager at the Seneca-Iroquois National Museum at Salamanca, New York.

NAME F, N
Beth Brant

TRIBAL AFFILIATION
Mohawk of the Bay of Quinte, Tyendinaga Mohawk Territory

PERSONAL
Born: May 6, 1941, at the Mohawk Nation

AWARDS, HONORS

The Canadian Council Award, 1992; National Endowment for the Arts Literature Fellowship, 1991; Michigan Council for the Arts Grant, 1984 and 1986

PUBLICATION HIGHLIGHTS

Writing as Witness: Essays and Talk (Toronto: Women's Press, 1994)

"Swimming Upstream" in *Talking Leaves: Contemporary Native American Short Stories, an Anthology,* ed. by Craig Lesley (New York: Laurel, Dell, 1991)

A Gathering of Spirit: A Collection by North American Indian Women, ed. by Beth Brant (Ithaca: Firebrand, 1988, 1984)

Food and Spirits: Stories (Ithaca: Firebrand Books, 1985)

Mohawk Trail (Ithaca: Firebrand Books, 1985)

Brant's works have also appeared in: *Returning the Gift: Poetry and Prose from the First North American Native Writers' Festival,* ed. by Joseph Bruchac with the support of the Association for the Study of American Indian Literatures (Tucson: University of Arizona, 1994).

NARRATIVE

Beth Brant was born in 1941 in the Tyendinaga Mohawk Territory in Ontario, Canada, and grew up in Canada and Detroit, Michigan. Brant says that her father has been a significant positive influence in her life, as is her partner, Denise Dorsz. Brant considers Michelle Cliff and Gloria Anzaldua to be her literary mentors because they "encouraged me to keep writing and they understood what I was saying." She enjoys the works of Linda Hogan, James Welch, James Baldwin, Michelle Cliff, Janice Gould and Margaret Laurence. Brant is working on a book of essays on land and spirit, a book about her father and a number of short stories.

"Turtle Gal" and "Swimming Upstream" are two pieces that Brant considers to be her finest to date because they transcend space and time. Other works by Brant have appeared in the journals *The Kenyon Review, Signs* and the special Native American issue of *Callaloo.*

NAME   E, F

Charles Brashear

OTHER NAMES USED

Howard Charles Brashers

TRIBAL AFFILIATION

Cherokee

PERSONAL

Born: December 11, 1930, in Martin County, Texas

Education: B.A. in creative writing, University of California, Berkeley, 1956; M.A. in creative writing, San Francisco State University, San Francisco, California, 1960; Ph.D. in English, University of Denver, Denver, Colorado, 1962

AWARDS, HONORS

Fulbright Teaching Grant for Study at the English Institute of the University of Stockholm, Stockholm, Sweden, 1962–1965; Outstanding Faculty Award, College of Arts and Letters from San Diego State University, 1980

PUBLICATION HIGHLIGHTS

A Writer's Toolkit: Essays, Poems, and Stories (La Mesa, Calif.: Associated Creative Writers, 1991)

Contemporary Insanities, Short Fiction Stories (Arroyo Grande, Calif.: The Press of MacDonald & Reinecke, 1990)

Creative Writing Handbook (La Mesa, Calif.: Associated Creative Writers, 1984)

A Snug Little Purchase: How Richard Henderson Bought Kaintuckee from the Cherokees (La Mesa, Calif.: Associated Creative Writers, 1979)

Creative Writing: Fiction, Drama, Poetry and the Essay (New York: American Book, 1968)

Creative Writing for High School Students (Ann Arbor: University of Michigan Bureau of School Services, 1968)

An Introduction to American Literature for European Students, with Vincent Petti and Dennis Gotobed (Stockholm: Svenska Bokforlaget, 1965)

The Life of America (Stockholm: Natur och Kultur, 1965)

The Other Side of Love (Denver: Alan Swallow, 1963)

Brashear's works have also appeared in the anthology: *Returning the Gift: Poetry and Prose from the First North American Native Writers' Festival,* ed. by Joseph Bruchac with the support of the Association for the Study of American Indian Literatures (Tucson: University of Arizona, 1994).

NARRATIVE

Howard Charles Brashear was born in Martin County near the town of Knott, Texas. Brashear has worked as an educator for many years, starting as a teacher at Maxwell Union High School in Maxwell California, and later as a graduate teaching fellow at the University of Denver. Upon the receipt of his Fulbright Scholarship, he became a lecturer in American studies at the Royal University of Stockholm, in Stockholm, Sweden.

After he returned to the United States, Brashear worked as an assistant professor of English at the University of Michigan, and currently he holds the position of professor of English at San Diego State University, where he has been since 1968. In 1989 Brashear became an adjunct faculty member in the area of American Indian studies at San Diego State University. Married and divorced, Brashear has three sons.

NAME   E, N, P

Jeane Coburn Breinig

TRIBAL AFFILIATION
Haida

PERSONAL
Born: July 5, 1955, in Ketchikan, Alaska

Education: B.A. in English; M.A. in English; currently enrolled in Ph.D. program in Native American literature at the University of Washington

PUBLICATION HIGHLIGHTS
"Mood Music," poem in *Bellowing Ark,* vol. 4, no. 4 ([S.l.: s.n.] 1988); "Raven Tells Stories: An Anthology of Alaskan Native Writing," "The Light on the Tent Wall," book reviews in *Studies in American Indian Literatures: Newsletter of the Association for Study of American Indian Literatures* (New York: The Association, [n.d.])

NARRATIVE
Jeane Coburn Breinig was born July 5, 1955, in Ketchikan, Alaska, and grew up in Kasaan and Ketchikan. She is a Ph.D. candidate in American Indian literature at the University of Washington. She notes that as a student the "focus of my literary studies has been oral narratives, contemporary Native American writers and Haida storytelling, mythology and narrative analysis." Breinig enjoys the works of writers Mary Tall Mountain, Mora Davenhauer, Robert Davis, Louise Erdrich, Gerald Vizenor and Beth Brant.

After finishing her degree, Breinig hopes to begin a university teaching career back in her native Alaska and plans on spending more time writing poetry.

NAME   E, P, F, N

Silvester J. Brito

TRIBAL AFFILIATION

Comanche and Tarascan

PUBLICATION HIGHLIGHTS

The Way of a Peyote Roadman (New York: Peter Lang, 1989)

"Intermountain Messages," poem in *Wicazo Sa Review,* vol. iv, no.2 (Cheney, Wash.: Indian Studies Department, Eastern Washington University, 1988)

Red Cedar Warrior, poems (Laramie, Wyo.: Jelm Mountain Press, 1986)

Looking Through a Squared Off Circle, poems (Marvin, S. Dak.: The Blue Cloud Quarterly Press, 1985)

Man from a Rainbow, poems (Marvid, S. Dak.: The Blue Cloud Quarterly Press, 1983)

Spirit Shadows (Milwaukee: Tarascan Press, 1981)

The Development and Change of the Peyote Ceremony Through Time and Space, thesis (Ann Arbor: University Microfilms, 1975)

Brito's works have also appeared in: *Returning the Gift: Poetry and Prose from the First North American Native Writers' Festival,* ed. by Joseph Bruchac with the support of the Association for the Study of American Indian Literatures (Tucson: University of Arizona, 1994).

NARRATIVE

Brito is a member of the English Department of the University of Wyoming at Laramie. His works have also appeared in the journals *American Indian Quarterly* and the special Native American issue of *Callaloo.*

NAME   N

Emily Ivanoff Brown

TRIBAL AFFILIATION

Inupiat

PUBLICATION HIGHLIGHTS

The Roots of Tecasuk: An Eskimo Woman's Family Story, revised edition (Anchorage: Northwest, 1981); *Grandfather of Unalakleet, the Lineage of Alluyagnak,* second edition (Fairbanks, Alaska: Eskimo Aleut Printing, 1974)

NAME   E, F, J, L, P, PL, S, SC

Vee F. Browne

OTHER NAMES USED

Elvita

TRIBAL AFFILIATION

Navajo Nation of Arizona Central Agency, Chinle

PERSONAL

Born: September 4, 1956, in Ganado, Arizona

Education: B.S. in education; M.A. in counseling

AWARDS, HONORS

Best Juvenile Book Award for *Monster Slayer,* Western Heritage Award, National Cowboy Hall of Fame, 1991; The Buddy Joe Bojack Nationwide Award for Humanitarian Childrens Books, 1992; Beta-Phi-Ganna National

Honorary Co-Educational Journalistic Sorority, 1977

PUBLICATION HIGHLIGHTS

Maria Tallchief ([S.l.]: Simon & Schuster, 1995)

Monster Slayer (Flagstaff: Northland Publishers, 1991)

"Wanted Man," short story in *Writing across Curriculum* [?] (Tucson: University of Arizona Press, 1987)

Owl Book ([S.l.]: Scholastic, [n.d.])

Monster Bird (Flagstaff: Northland, [n.d.])

Browne's works have also appeared in the anthology: *Neon Pow-Wow: New Native American Voices of the Southwest,* first edition, by Anna Lee Walters. 1st ed. (Flagstaff: Northland, [1993]).

NARRATIVE

Vee Browne was born in Ganado, Arizona, as a member of the Bitter Water and Water Flows Together clans. She was raised in foster homes across the state. "I grew up at Holbrook Dormitory from third to sixth grade, seventh through tenth grade in Mesa, Arizona, and eleventh grade in Gilbert, Arizona, and half of [my] senior year I enrolled at Holbrook Arizona High School." Lonely and far from her family, she turned to books to fill the void in her life. "When I was in a foster home, yearning for my parents and friends I spent my free time in the library next to the Native American literature section. I cried with the books and characters." While in school she had a memorable journalism teacher Janice Quinton, who encouraged her students explore their own culture's mythology by assigning them to do projects on Navajo mythology such as skinwalkers. "Janice Quinton did encourage me to write for our high school sports articles; I was the sports editor."

Browne writes about the Southwest, the Diné and her stories are often written for young audiences. She considers these stories to be some of her best work. "I enjoy writing for Indigenous people's children. We have an oral language, and I feel it is time to write for the little ones, open a whole new [area] in Native literacy." She continues, "because we have a rich tradition in storytelling and our children need Native writers. But, being lonely for my tribe had a major impact on my writing, when I was in a foster home."

Browne enjoys reading works by authors such as Beatrice Culleton, V. C. Andrews, indigenous poets, Eve Bunting ("I like Eve Bunting as a mentor for children's literature"), Edward Dolch, Dee Brown and many more. She is now working on a children's play and coyote tales, two more children's books, poetry and four short stories. When she is not teaching and writing, Browne enjoys gardening, sewing, doing crafts, driving through historical parks and conceptualizing her next book or film project. Browne is currently working as a journalist for the *Observer,* a Navajo-Hopi newspaper and is an educator and presenter.

She now lives at Cottonwood/Tselani, Arizona, a place whose great beauty she draws upon as she writes. "[As] I sit here next to me is a view of the most beautiful mountain called 'Fish Point.'" I have to see it every morning and during the time I'm writing."

NAME F, N, P, S

Joseph Bruchac

OTHER NAMES USED

Joseph Edward Bruchac III

TRIBAL AFFILIATION

Abenaki (St. Francis/Sokoki, Mississquoi Nation)

PERSONAL

Born: October 16, 1942, in Saratoga Springs, New York

Education:

Saratoga Springs High School

B.A. in English with zoology minor, Cornell University, 1965

M.A. in literature and creative writing, Syracuse University, 1966

Earned graduate hours in literature at SUNY, Albany, 1970–1973

Ph.D. in comparative literature, Union Graduate School, 1975

AWARDS, HONORS

Notable Books for Young Adults mention for *Dawn Land,* American Library Association, 1994

The Hope S. Dean Memorial Award, 1993

New York State Council on the Arts Editors Fellowship, 1986

The Cherokee Nation Award for Prose, 1986

Yaddo Residency Fellowships, 1984, 1985

American Book Award for *Breaking Silence,* 1984

NEA/PEN Syndicated Fiction Award, 1983

New York State CAPS Poetry Fellowships, 1982, 1973

Rockefeller Humanities Fellowship, 1982

CCLM Editors Fellowship, 1980

NEA Writing Fellowship for Poetry, 1974

Skidmore Faculty Development Grants, 1969–1972

Syracuse Writing Fellowship, 1965

PUBLICATION HIGHLIGHTS

Bowman's Stone: A Journey to Myself (New York: Penguin/Dial Books, 1997)

Eagle Song (New York: Penguin/Dial Books, 1997)

Makiawisug: The Gift of the Little People, with Melissa J. Fawcett (Uncasville, Conn.: Little People Publications, 1997)

The Man Who Loved Buffalo (San Diego: Harcourt, Brace, 1997)

Tell Me a Tale: A Book About Storytelling (San Diego: Harcourt, Brace, 1997)

Children of the Longhouse (New York: Dial Books for Young Readers, 1996)

The Circle of Thanks (Mahwah, N.J.: Bridge Water Books, 1996)

Roots of Survival: Native American Storytelling and the Sacred (Golden, Colo.: Fulcrum Publishing, 1996)

Between Earth and Sky: Legends of Native American Sacred Places (Orlando: Harcourt Brace & Company, 1996)

Four Ancestors, ed. by Joseph Bruchac ([S.l.]: Bridgewater Books, 1996)

The Boy Who Lived with the Bears: and Other Iroquois Stories (New York: HarperCollins, 1995)

The Dirt Road Home (Willimantic, Conn.: Curbstone Press, 1995)

Dog People: Native Dog Stories (Golden, Colo.: Fulcrum Publishing, 1995)

The Earth Under Sky Bear's Feet (New York: Putnam Publishing Group, 1995)

Gluskabe and the Four Wishes, retold by Joseph Bruchac (New York: Dutton Children's Books, 1995)

Long River: A Novel (Golden, Colo.: Fulcrum Publishing, 1995)

Native Plant Stories, with Michael Caduto. As told by Joseph Bruchac. (Golden, Colo.: Fulcrum Publishing, 1995)

The Story of the Milky Way: A Cherokee Tale, Joseph Bruchac and Gayle Ross (New York: Dial Books for Young Readers, 1995)

A Boy Called Slow (New York: Putnam Publishing Group, 1994)

The Girl Who Married the Moon: Tales from Native North America, Joseph Bruchac and Gayle Ross (Mahwah, N.J.: BridgeWater Books, 1994)

The Great Ball Game: A Muskogee Story (New York: Dial Books for Young Readers, 1994)

Keepers of Life: Discovering Plants Through Native American Stories and Earth Activities for Children, with Michael Caduto

(Golden, Colo.: Fulcrum Publishing, 1994)

Keepers of the Night: Native American Stories and Nocturnal Activities for Children, with Michael Caduto (Golden, Colo.: Fulcrum Publishing, 1994)

Dawn Land (Golden, Colo.: Fulcrum Publishing, 1993)

The Native American Sweat Lodge: History and Legends (Freedom, Calif.: The Crossing Press, 1993)

The First Strawberries: A Cherokee Story (New York: Dial Books for Young Readers, 1993)

Flying with Eagle, Racing the Great Bear: Stories from Native North America, as told by Joseph Bruchac (Mahwah, N.J.: BridgeWater Books, 1993)

Fox Song (New York: Philomel Books, 1993)

Native American Animal Stories, with Michael Caduto. As told by Joseph Bruchac (Golden, Colo.: Fulcrum Publishing, 1992)

Thirteen Moons on Turtle's Back: A Native American Year of Moons, retold by Joseph Bruchac, ed. by Jonathan London (New York: Putnam Publishing Group, 1992)

Turtle Meat and Other Stories (Duluth, Minn.: Holy Cow! Press, 1992)

Keepers of the Animals: Native American Stories and Wildlife Activities for Children, with Michael J. Caduto (Golden, Colo.: Fulcrum, 1991)

Native American Writers, ed. by Stanley Barkan and Joseph Bruchac (Merrick, N.Y.: Cross-Cultural Comunications, 1991)

Native American Stories, with Michael Caduto. As told by Joseph Bruchac (Golden, Colo.: Fulcrum, 1991)

Return of the Sun: Native American Tales from the Northeast Woodlands (Freedom, Calif.: The Crossing Press, 1989)

Talking Book Box B: Multiethnic, poetry (Native American, African Interest, Latin American) Joseph Bruchac, Arthur Dobrin, Jose Kozer, ed. by Stanley Barkan (Merrick, N.Y.: Cross-Cultural Communications, 1989)

The Faithful Hunter: Abenaki Stories (Greenfield Center, N.Y.: Greenfield Review Press, 1988)

Keepers of the Earth Teacher's Guide, with Michael J. Caduto (Golden, Colo.: Fulcrum Publishing, 1988)

Keepers of the Earth: Native American Stories and Environmental Activities for Children, with Michael J. Caduto (Golden, Colo.: Fulcrum, 1988)

Survival This Way: Interviews with American Indian Poets (Tucson: Sun Tracks: University of Arizona, 1987)

Iroquois Stories: Heroes and Heroines, Monsters and Magic (Freedom, Calif.: The Crossing Press, 1985)

The Wind Eagle and Other Abenaki Folk Stories (Greenfield Center, N.Y.: Greenfield Review Literary Center, 1985)

Translator's Son (Merrick, N.Y.: Cross Cultural Communications, 1980)

The Good Message of Handsome Lake (Greensboro, N.C.: Unicorn Press, 1979)

There Are No Trees Inside Prison ([S.l.]: Blackberry Press, 1978)

This Earth Is a Drum: Poetry (Austin: Cold Mountain Press, 1976)

Flow (Austin: Cold Mountain Press, 1975)

The Last Stop, ed. by Joseph Bruchac (Greenfield Center, N.Y.: Greenfield Review Literary Center, 1974)

Bruchac has edited numerous anthologies, among them are:

Between Earth and Sky: Legends of Native American Sacred Places (New York, NY: Harcourt Brace & Company, 1996)

Four Ancestors (Mahwah, N.J.: BridgeWater Books, 1996)

Aniyunwiya, Real Human Beings: Contemporary Cherokee Indian Fiction (Greenfield Center, N.Y.: Greenfield Review Literary Center, 1995)

The Boy Who Lived with the Bears: And Other Iroquois Stories (New York: HarperCollins Children's Books, 1995)

Dog People: Native Dog Stories (Golden, Colo.: Fulcrum Publishing, 1995)

The Earth Under Sky Bear's Feet (Putnam Publishing Group, 1995)

Long River: A Novel (Golden, Colo.: Fulcrum Publishing, 1995)

Smoke Rising: The Native North American Literary Companion, ed. by Joseph Bruchac, Janet Witalec and Sharon Malinowski (Detroit, Mich.: Visible Ink Press, 1995)

Native Wisdom, ed. by Joseph Bruchac (San Francisco: Harper San Francisco, 1994)

Returning the Gift: Poetry and Prose from the First North American Native Writers' Festival, ed. by Joseph Bruchac with the support of the Association for the Study of American Indian Literatures (Tucson: University of Arizona, 1994)

Raven Tells Stories: An Anthology of Alaskan Native Writing (Greenfield Center, N.Y.: Greenfield Review Press, 1991)

New Voices from the Longhouse: An Anthology of Contemporary Iroquois Writing (Greenfield Center, N.Y.: Greenfield Review Press, 1989)

North Country: Writing from the Upper Hudson Valley and the Adirondacks, ed. by Joseph Bruchac, Alice Gilborn, Craig Hancock and Jean Rikhoff (Greenfield Center, N.Y.: Greenfield Review Press, 1986)

The Light from Another Country: Poetry from American Prisons (Greenfield Center, N.Y.: Greenfield Review Press, 1984)

Songs from This Earth on Turtle's Back: Contemporary American Indian Poetry (Greenfield Center, N.Y.: Greenfield Review Press, 1983)

Bruchac's works have appeared in numerous anthologies, including:

Talking Leaves: Contemporary Native American Short Stories, An Anthology, ed. by Craig Lesley (New York: Laurel, Dell, 1991)

American Indian Literatures: An Introduction, Bibliographic Review and Selected Bibliography, by A. LaVonne Brown Ruoff (New York: Modern Language Association, 1990)

Circle of Motion: Arizona Anthology of Contemporary American Indian Literature, ed. by Kathleen Mullen Sands (Tempe: Arizona Historical Foundation, 1990)

I Tell You Now: Autobiographical Essays by Native American Writers, ed. by Brian Swann and Arnold Krupat (Lincoln: University of Nebraska Press, 1987)

The Sacred Hoop: Recovering the Feminine in American Indian Traditions, by Paula Gunn Allen (Boston: Beacon Press, 1986)

Native American Literature, by Andrew Wiget (Boston: Twayne, 1985)

New and Old Voices of Wah'Kon-Tah, ed. by Robert K. Dodge and Joseph B. McCollugh (New York: International Publishers, 1985)

Coyote Was Here: Essays on Contemporary Native American Literary and Political Mobilization, ed. by Bo Scholar (Aarhaus, Denmark: SEKLOS, 1984)

Earth Power Coming: Short Fiction in Native American Literature, ed. by Simon Ortiz (Tsaile, Ariz.: Navajo Community College Press, 1983)

A Nation Within: Contemporary Native American Writing, selected by Ralph Salisbury (Hamilton, New Zealand: Outrigger, 1983)

The Remembered Earth: An Anthology of Contemporary Native American Literature, ed. by Geary Hobson (Albuquerque: Red Earth Press, 1979)

Carriers of the Dream Wheel: Contemporary Native American Poetry, ed. by Duane Niatum (New York: Harper & Row, 1975)

From the Belly of the Shark, ed. by Walter Lowenfels (New York: Vantage, 1974)

NARRATIVE

Born in Saratoga Springs, New York, Joseph Bruchac was raised "In the same house where I still live, my grandparents' house on the corner of Route 9N and Middle Grove Road in Greenfield Center, New York. Just a bit north of Saratoga Springs and a bit south of the beginning of the Adirondack Mountains of northern New York," where his great-grandfather used to sell his handmade ash splint baskets to the tourists. "I am very much a part of this land and no matter how far I travel, I will always come back here. This area and the Northeast, in general, figure in most of my writing and in my storytelling."

The son of a Slovakian immigrant, Bruchac was raised by his maternal grandparents. His grandfather was St. Francis Abenaki, a fact which was not revealed until after his death. Earlier, while still a young man living with his grandparents, his grandmother passed away. "The death of my grandmother when I was 16 left me alone with my grandfather and having to take care of myself and really look at my own life from a different perspective affected me deeply while making me draw closer to my grandfather's Indian identity. For that matter, being raised not by my parents but by my grandparents was a major factor in my being who I am now. My grandmother [was responsible] for instilling a love of books, my grandfather for taking me into the woods and teaching me to listen. From my teenage years on I've been influenced by a series of adopted grandparents, including Maurice Dennis whose Abenaki name was Mdawelasis (Little Loon), Swift Eagle who was a Pueblo/Apache storyteller and musician and my fourth grade teacher, Miss Dorothea McTygue, who gave me a sapling maple that I planted in my back yard when I was 10 and today that tree is forty feet tall. Like that tree, her belief in me when I was an undersized and out of place child helped me to grow. I will never forget her."

Bruchac also recalls one particularly memorable summer while he was still a student in high school. "In high school I grew six inches the summer between my junior year and my senior year and went from being known as a 'brain' (nerds did not yet exist) to being a jock. I'd never done any sports, but became a varsity football lineman, a track athlete and a heavyweight wrestler, winning first place in the conference. It was an amazing transition and all occurred after my grandmother's death."

After high school Bruchac continued his studies at Cornell University, where he earned his bachelors degree in 1965. As an undergraduate Bruchac had an influential instructor by the name of David Ray. "I took my second college class in creative writing from David Ray, and he inspired me by telling me I could never write poetry. So that was all I wrote for him from then on, until he capitulated. He later wrote a blurb for my first book of poems, *Indian Mountain*."

He has been the director and cofounder, with his wife, of the Greenfield Review Press from 1969 to the present, and he is also the director of the Greenfield Review Literary Center. In 1987–1988 he was an adjunct faculty member at the State University of New York at Albany, served as a January-term faculty member at Hamilton College during the years 1985, 1986 and 1987, he worked as the coordinator for the Skidmore UWW College Program at Great Meadow Correctional Facility during the years 1974–1981, and from 1969–1973 taught English at Skidmore College. Earlier, Bruchac spent three years in Ghana, Africa, as an English teacher and liaison officer in the Teachers for West Africa Program in Ghana, from 1966 to 1969.

Bruchac is presently the coeditor of the Greenfield Review Press, beginning in 1969, and he has been the poetry editor of Studies in American Indian Literature (SAIL) since 1989. He was the editor of The Greenfield Review (1969–1987), was the editor of *The Prison Writing Review* (1976–1985) and has been a member of various editorial and advisory boards for journals such as *Parabola, Obsidian, National Storytelling Journal* and *Melus.*

He has also conducted prison poetry workshops, worked as a writer and storyteller in residence for over seventy schools, libraries and institutes across the United States, has been a featured storyteller at various festivals and has read his poems at numerous colleges and universities and conferences. A prolific author of more than thirty monographs, Bruchac's poems and stories have also been published in over three hundred periodicals and journals, such as *Chicago Review, American Poetry Review, The Ohio Review, The Beloit Poetry Journal, Nimrod, Quarterly West, The Nation Akwesasne Notes* and *Chariton Review,* as well as in more than fifty anthologies.

When asked about some of the influences on his literary career, Bruchac responds: "My most important influence, first reader and best critic has been my wife, Carol. Since we first met in 1963 I have shared every writing project with her, and her advice has been deeply important to me. Connected to that has been the influence of our two sons. I began to write things I had never written before after they were born, and they were the ones who turned me into a storyteller and a writer for children. Jim is now 24 and Jesse 20 as I write this and both of them share my love for the natural world and for storytelling and music."

Bruchac enjoys reading the works of a wide variety of authors. "I've always enjoyed the work of the T'ang dynasty Chinese poets such as Li Po, Tu Fu, Wang Wei and Po Chu-i and the haiku masters Basho and Issa. Until my third year in college I was going to be a naturalist and majored in wildlife conservation, so I always read a great deal of nonfiction about the natural world and still do. I'll never forget a book called *Wild America* by James Fisher and Roger Tory Peterson. Chinua Achebe, the Nigerian novelist was a great influence on my understanding of writing fiction. But I also read just about every kind of writing. I am always reading at least 4 or 5 books. I've read all of Dashell Hammett, Raymond Chandler, Dick Francis, Elmore Leonard, Max Allan Collins. I try to read every book of poetry and every novel or collection of poetry in print by every contemporary Native American writer, as well as anything written by anyone dealing with the Native people of the northeastern woodlands past and present." Bruchac also enjoys reading works by Bruce Chatwin, Redmond O'Hanlon, Barry Lopez, Pater Matthiessen and collections of folklore and storytelling, especially tall tales, ghost stories, tales of his region and Native American traditional stories. "And wherever I travel I always read books which tell me about the stories and the natural history of that part of the world."

A black belt in Pentjak Silat, the martial art of Indonesia, he is also interested in gardening, creating objects with his hands and music. "I enjoy working with my hands, gardening or making things such as birchbark baskets and elm bark rattles. Physical activities such as walking, martial arts and canoeing are always part of every day for me—even if it is only doing tai chi form in the morning. Music is also one of my hobbies and I enjoy playing the guitar—largely as a percussion instrument—and writing songs."

NAME   N
Percy Bullchild

TRIBAL AFFILIATION
Blackfeet

PERSONAL

Born: 1915(?) on the Blackfeet Reservation in Montana

PUBLICATION HIGHLIGHTS

The Sun Came Down: The History of the World As My Blackfeet Elders Told It, first edition (San Francisco: Harper & Row, 1985)

NARRATIVE

Born on the Blackfeet Reservation in Montana, Bullchild spoke only his native language as a youth until the time he began school, which he attended until the sixth grade. He was an artist and musician, traveling with his wife throughout the United States, participating in intertribal pow-wows and events. His book *The Sun Came Down* is an extensive account of the Blackfeet history and tribal myths. Bullchild is now deceased.

NAME   P

Diane Burns

TRIBAL AFFILIATION

Chemchuevi and Ojibwa

PERSONAL

Education: Coursework at the Institute of American Indian Arts, Santa Fe, New Mexico; coursework at Barnard College, New York, New York

AWARDS, HONORS

Recipient of the Congressional Medal of Merit

PUBLICATION HIGHLIGHTS

American Visions: Multicultural Literature for Writers, by Delores La Guardia and Hans P. Guth (Mountain View, Calif.: Mayfield, 1995)

Burns's works have appeared in numerous anthologies, among them:

Braided Lives: An Anthology of Multicultural American Writing, by the Minnesota Humanities Commission and the Minnesota Council of Teachers of English (St. Paul: The Commission, 1991)

Survival This Way: Interviews with Native American Poets, by Joseph Bruchac (Tucson: Sun Tracks, University of Arizona Press, 1987)

The Sacred Hoop: Recovering the Feminine in American Indian Traditions, by Paula Gunn Allen (Boston: Beacon Press, 1986)

Native American Literature, by Andrew Wiget (Boston: Twayne, 1985)

That's What She Said: Contemporary Poetry and Fiction by Native American Women, ed. by Rayna Green (Bloomington: Indiana University Press, 1984)

NARRATIVE

Active in literary groups, Diane Burns is a member of the Poets' Overland Expeditionary Troupe, the Third World Writer's Association and the Feminist Writers' Guild. Her work has appeared in numerous periodicals and journals such as *White Pine Journals,* the *Greenfield Review* and the *Blue Cloud Quarterly.* Burns lives in New York City and has traveled throughout the United States to give readings of her works.

NAME   F, M, P

Barney Bush

TRIBAL AFFILIATION

Shawnee/Cayuga of Oklahoma

PERSONAL

Born: Late summer, Saline County, Illinois, 1946

Education: B.A. in Humanities, Ft. Lewis College, Durango, Colorado, 1972; M.A. in English/fine arts, University of Idaho, Moscow, Idaho, 1980; coursework at the Institute of American Indian Arts, Santa Fe, New Mexico, 1971–1972 and Southeastern Illinois Junior College, Harrisburg, Illinois 1968–1969

AWARDS, HONORS

D'arcy McNickle Fellowship, Newberry Library, Chicago, 1984

Author's Guild Award, New York City, 1983

PEN American Grant, New York City, 1983

National Endowment for the Arts Writing Fellowship, Washington, D.C., 1981

National Park Service, Jackson Hole and Yellowstone District, Wyoming Guest Artist Award, 1980

PUBLICATION HIGHLIGHTS

The Look of Electrum (Chicago: Another Chicago Press, 1993)

The Bronze Serpent (Chicago: ACM Press, 1992)

Left for Dead (Paris: Gerrard Gormel, 1992)

Inherit the Blood: Poetry and Fiction (New York: Thunder's Mouth Press, c1985)

Petroglyphs (Greenfield, N.Y.: Greenfield Review Press, 1982)

My Horse and a Jukebox (Los Angeles: American Indian Studies Center, University of California, 1979)

Bush's works have also appeared in: *Returning the Gift: Poetry and Prose from the First North American Native Writers' Festival,* ed. by Joseph Bruchac with the support of the Association for the Study of American Indian Literatures (Tucson: University of Arizona, 1994).

NARRATIVE

Writer, lecturer and musician, Barney Bush was born near the end of World War II and grew up near the Ohio River in a part of his ancestral homelands. As a child Bush experienced the cruel and heavy hand of racial intolerance. In grade school he was "filled with Southern Baptist indoctrination" and was beaten by his instructors for investigating the so called "savagery" of his ancestors. When he found positive and supportive evidence about his heritage in encyclopedias, he was beaten with razor strops for showing it to his male teacher. He remembered the kindness of one teacher, Miss Jessie Crank, who carefully took the time to show him how to read and how to mix colors for his art projects. Another teacher, his high school freshman English teacher, Miss Bernice Patterson, took the time to vigorously drill him in English grammar as no one had done before.

In recalling memories and people in his past, Bush recalled a painful turn of events in his family's history that took place when attorneys for a strip-mining company persuaded his father to sign away his family land, which was subsequently stripped of its natural beauty in the pursuit of minerals. The land and its spiritual qualities play an important part in his life and in his writings as "the primary spiritual role, second only to our creator."

Bush was moved to express himself through writing for many reasons, especially his need to respond to the writings of other authors. "I just couldn't tolerate the lies, and perhaps innocent misrepresentations, even in the religion. After reading the Bible for myself, I found they even lied about that, taught it to insure their self image of superiority," and that Vine Deloria was the first Indian Bush ever read who had "the guts to tell it like it is."

Bush's leisure reading consists of a variety of works by black, white, Native and Asian writers, including authors Haley, Kosinski and Louis Oliver. He is now working on a novel about a church in east Tennessee and has been working as a musician in Europe.

C

NAME   E, N, P
Jeanetta L. Calhoun

TRIBAL AFFILIATION
Western Delaware

PERSONAL
Born: February 25, 1961, in Hobart, Oklahoma

Education: Coursework at the University of Houston, Tulsa Oklahoma Junior College, Seminore Junior College, Vermont College of Norwich University

PUBLICATION HIGHLIGHTS
"Decision," "Museum Pieces," poems in *Studies in American Indian Literatures,* vol. 2, no. 2 (New York: Association for Study of American Indian Literatures, 1990)

"Lance Henson: Evolution of a Poet," essay in *Greenfield Review Newsletter,* vol. ix, no. 1 (Greenfield Center, N.Y.: Greenfield Review, 1990)

"After Dark" in *Jules Magazine,* vol. I, issues 1, 2, 3 (Oklahoma City: [s.n.], 1988)

"Author's Forward," poem in *Piecework,* vol. 11, no. 2 (Oklahoma City: [s.n.], 1988)

"Untitled," poem in *Mensokie,* vol. I, issue 11 (Oklahoma City: [s.n.], November 1984)

Calhoun's works also appear in: *Returning the Gift: Poetry and Prose from the First North American Native Writers' Festival,* ed. by Joseph Bruchac with the support of the Association for the Study of American Indian Literatures (Tucson: University of Arizona, 1994).

NARRATIVE
Calhoun was born in Hobart, Oklahoma, and raised in Wewoka, Oklahoma, capital of the Seminole Indian Nation. She was surrounded by creative family members as she grew, reaping the benefits of their experiences. "My grandmother Jeanette Sanderson always encouraged my writing. Her grandmother, Ellen Rogers, was a published poet and my grandmother had been a professional dancer and singer when she was young. Also, my mother, Myrna Sanderson Teague, always encouraged me to read extensively and to question the answers (a good trait in a writer!)"

In grade school Calhoun was fortunate to have two supportive instructors who acted as mentors: "My first mentor was Valerie Carolina, my second grade teacher. When I wrote a small poem about my dog, she made sure it was hung on the wall for open house. My second mentor was Mr. Dedmon, my sixth grade teacher. He and his wife convinced me to send a story I'd written to *Highlights* for *Children Magazine.* It was kindly rejected, but they kept encouraging, criticizing and praising my writing for ten years."

As an adult, Calhoun has twice experienced a trauma not many individuals share. "There have been two occasions in which I was declared clinically dead. These two occasions changed my life and my writing. I have also written much more and with much more quality after recovering from drug addiction. My two-year-old son is also a constant inspiration." Reflecting on her experiences and their impact on her writings, she continues, "living as a writer in this world lends itself to writing about many subjects including current affairs, the environment, indigenous rights and the tiny everyday things that make it all worthwhile."

When reading for her own relaxation, Calhoun admits, "I read everything. I recently read *Anna Karenina* for the first time and was totally blown away. As far as poets go, I am highly influenced by James Wright, Lance Henson, Roberta Whiteman, Carroll Arnett (a Native American author who is under appreciated), Simon Ortiz, W. S. Merwin, Rita Dove and many others." She is presently working on two book reviews, performance art pieces and a chapbook of her work. Currently Calhoun is a freelance writer and poet, workshop instructor, mother and literary manager. In her spare time she takes care of her son, Michael, and schedules readings for her husband, Lance Henson, through Badger and Snake Literary Productions. She is currently attending Vermont College of Norwich University's Adult Degree Program to finish her bachelors degree in liberal arts studies.

NAME   N

Maria Campbell

TRIBAL AFFILIATION

Metis

PERSONAL

Born: April, 1940, in Saskatchewan, Canada

PUBLICATION HIGHLIGHTS

Stories of the Road Allowance People (Penticton, B.C.: Theytus, 1994)

Halfbreed (Lincoln: University of Nebraska Press, 1973)

People of the Buffalo: How the Plains Indians Lived, first paperback edition, revised (New York: Douglas & McIntyre, 1976)

Little Badger and the Fire Spirit (Buffalo, N.Y./Toronto: McClelland & Stewart, 1977)

Revolutionary Services and Civil Life of General William Hull, ed. by Maria Campbell (New York: Irvington Publishers, 1972)

NARRATIVE

Campbell has written several radio plays and her work has appeared in newspapers and periodicals such as *Maclean's*. She has also authored the story "The Little Red Dress," which was made into a film released by the National Film Board of Canada in 1977. Campbell is currently an activist working to help the indigenous peoples of Canada.

NAME   F, N

Ramona Carden

TRIBAL AFFILIATION

Colville

PERSONAL

Education: Senior year of high school at the Institute of American Indian Arts, Santa Fe, New Mexico; B.A. from Eastern Washington State College, Cheney, Washington

PUBLICATION HIGHLIGHTS

Carden's works have appeared in these anthologies:

New and Old Voices of Wah'Kon-Tah, ed. by Robert K. Dodge and Joseph B. McCullough (New York: International Publishers, c1985)

Voices from Wah'Kon-Tah, third edition, ed. by Robert K. Dodge and Joseph B. McCullough (New York: International Publishers, 1974)

The Whispering Wind: Poetry by Young American Indians, ed. by Terry Allen (New York: Doubleday, 1972)

The American Indian Speaks, ed. by John R. Milton (Vermillion: Dakota Press, University of South Dakota, 1969)

NARRATIVE

Ramona Carden was raised in Washington state and as a high school student traveled to Santa Fe, New Mexico, where she finished her senior year at the Institute of American Indian Arts. She later returned to Washington State, where she earned her bachelors degree.

NAME   P, PL

Gladys Tiana Cardiff

TRIBAL AFFILIATION

Eastern Band Cherokee

PERSONAL

Born: November 23, 1942, in Browning, Montana
Education: B.A. in English, University of Washington, 1989; M.F.A., University of Washington, 1993

AWARDS, HONORS

Nelson Bentley Award for Poetry, 1989
Louisa Kerns Award for Excellence in Literary Endeavors, University of Washington, 1988
Seattle Arts Commission Literary Contest Winner, 1986 and 1986
Washington Governor's Award for her book *To Frighten a Storm,* 1976
National Endowment for the Arts Fellowship

PUBLICATION HIGHLIGHTS

To Frighten a Storm (Port Townsend, Wash.: Copper Canyon Press, 1967)

Cardiff's poems have appeared in numerous anthologies, among them:

Dancing on the Rim of the World, ed. by Al Lerner (Tucson: University of Arizona Press, 1991)
Elements of Literature (Austin: Holt, Rinehart and Winston, 1991)
Crystal Stair (New York: McGraw Hill School Division Press, 1989)
Harper's Anthology of 20th-Century Native American Poetry, ed. by Duane Niatum (San Francisco: Harper & Row, 1988)
Bumershoot Anthology, ed. by Judith Roche (S.l.: Red Sky Press, 1985)
That's What She Said: An Anthology of Contemporary Native American Women Poets of the Twentieth Century, ed. by Rayna Green, (Bloomington: Indiana University Press, 1984)
Rain in the Forest, Light in the Trees, ed. by Rich Ives (Seattle: Owl Creek Press, 1983)
Songs from This Earth on Turtle's Back, ed. by Joseph Bruchac (Greenfield Center, N.Y.: Greenfield Review Press, 1983)
Wounds Beneath the Flesh, ed. by Maurice Kenny ([Marvin, South Dakota?]: Blue Cloud Quarterly Press, 1983)
The Remembered Earth, ed. by Geary Hobson (Albuquerque: Red Earth Press, 1979)
Carriers of the Dream Wheel, ed. by Duane Niatum (New York: Harper & Row, 1975)
From the Belly of the Shark, ed. by Walter Lowenfels (New York: Vintage Books, 1973)

NARRATIVE

Gladys Tiana Cardiff was born in Browning, Montana, and raised in a white, upper-middle-class neighborhood of Seattle, Washington. Her storytelling abilities began to show at an early age. "I told stories to my mother when I was a toddler which she wrote down for me. I still have one, "How the Pig Got His Curly Tail."

"We were a proud, financially struggling family in a very acquisitive setting. While my older sister and brother suffered some bigotry, neither my appearance nor my family's lifestyle identified me as an Indian. When I became concerned with having a matching sweater sets or flats instead of brown oxfords, my parents would say, 'Remember who you are.' Early on who I was someone different, and someone who was not to be concerned with material competition."

As she was growing up, Cardiff was surrounded by the strength and support of her parents, both of whom taught their children about their Native traditions. "Both parents talked often about what Native American cultural traditions meant to them. My mother was a musician and composer who left her very white and conventional family to teach at an Indian boarding school where she met and married my father. My father, inspired by his mother, earned an M.A. in history through hard work and many struggles."

Cardiff studied with three well-known poets while she was studying for her bachelors degree at the University of Washington: Theodore Roethke, Beth Bentley and Nelson Bentley. "Poet Beth Bentley has been a long-time friend and a keen critic. Theodore Roethke was a fine teacher, a stupendous example as a poet concerned with honest personal investment and craftsmanship [and] Nelson Bentley was also a fine teacher whose faith in his students often gave me the courage to attempt more. Perhaps all of those ... encouraged me, but who knows which came first? Maybe it was the sense instilled at a very early age that writing and telling stories was a worthy pursuit and not a personal achievement—in other words, I have always felt that writing is not an act of the ego or self-enclosed will which saves me from being too avid or too disappointed or too envious, etc., etc. (most of the time)."

The subject of Cardiff's works include the *Cherokee Cosmogonic Stories,* which have "been a long interest, but sub-

ject preference has more to do with what seems to resonate: artworks, personal experience and observation, newspaper articles, any lucky accidents." Her poems have appeared in many anthologies, journals and magazines such as *Poetry East, Seattle Review, Inscape* and *Puget Soundings.* One of her poems, "Combing," has been a favorite of readers for twenty years. "After twenty years I still get requests for it from all over."

As an educator and lecturer, Cardiff has participated in the poetry-in-the-schools programs for Seattle and Edmonds, Washington, school districts in their elementary, junior high and high school classes. She has participated in the Centrum Workshop for Gifted High school students and has been a workshop leader and panel member for various conferences, including the Edmonds Writer's Conference in 1990, Pacific Northwest writers conferences, women's conferences at the University of Washington and the University of Puget Sound. She has given readings of her poems at public school, libraries, the Bumbershoot Arts Festival, the University of Reno, University of Washington, Pacific Lutheran University and, most recently, at Port Angeles Community College in 1991.

Living and working in the Pacific Northwest agrees with Cardiff. "This is beautiful country, lots of water and mountains. We have all four seasons. I like the rain. Having the university campus closeby is a delight. Mount Rainier, which didn't impress me much as a child, has become a significant presence for me. I'm sure where I live plays a role in my writing but the indications probably show up more in an internal landscape that feels well-fed rather than landmark poems or 'nature' poems."

She enjoys reading works by Louise Bogan, James Merrill, John Ashbery, Leslie Marmon Silko, Don DeLillo, Yeats,

Wallace Stevens and Robert Hayden. "I believe everything I read and then return to periodically has influenced my work— this can be a particular essay, or art book, one or two specific poems out of a body of work, etc."

Recently divorced after a twenty-six-year marriage ("While not an event I recommend, it has allowed me to return to school and focus on writing and research intensively"), Cardiff is now a student in the Masters of Fine Arts program at the University of Washington and is writing a poetic drama. She also works as an office manager for a furniture representative for two days a week doing bookkeeping, customer service, clerical work and correspondence.

When she is not studying and writing she practices flower arranging. "I am a sensei in Japanese flower arranging— Sogetsu school. I enjoy all kinds of music, play the piano when I have one, but lately my time is ALL BOOKS. I hope to travel, to ride horses, and I do swim often during the summer."

NAME   P, F, N
Aaron Carr

TRIBAL AFFILIATION
Navajo and Laguna

PERSONAL
Born: 1963 in New Mexico

PUBLICATION HIGHLIGHTS
Eye Killers: A Novel (Norman: University of Oklahoma Press, 1995); untitled poem in *The Remembered Earth: An Anthology of Contemporary Native American Literature,* ed. by Geary Hobson (Albuquerque: Red Earth Press, c1979)

NARRATIVE
Aaron Carr was born and raised in New Mexico. Other works by Carr can be found in the journals *Sun Tracks* and *Planet Quarterly.*

NAME   P
Victor Charlo

TRIBAL AFFILIATION
Bitterroot Salish

PUBLICATION HIGHLIGHTS
Charlo's works have appeared in the anthology *Dancing on the Rim of the World: An Anthology of Contemporary Northwest Native American Writing,* ed. by Andrea Lerner (Tucson: Sun Tracks, University of Arizona Press, c1990).

NARRATIVE
Charlo is currently working as a counselor with the Confederated Salish and Kootenai Tribes at the Kicking Horse Job Corps in Montana.

NAME   P
Bernadette Chato

TRIBAL AFFILIATION
Navajo

PERSONAL
Born: New Mexico
Education: Coursework at the University of New Mexico, Albuquerque

PUBLICATION HIGHLIGHTS
Chato's works have appeared in *The*

Remembered Earth: An Anthology of Contemporary Native American Literature, ed. by Geary Hobson (Albuquerque: Red Earth Press, 1979).

NARRATIVE

Chato has also had her works published in the journal *New America* and now lives with her family in Austin, Texas.

NAME   F, N, P, VA
Dallas Chief Eagle

OTHER NAMES USED
Dallas Chief Eagle Bordeaux

TRIBAL AFFILIATION
Lakota

PERSONAL
Born: August 14, 1925, on the Rosebud Reservation, South Dakota
Education: Coursework at Oklahoma A&M College

PUBLICATION HIGHLIGHTS
Fools Crow, recorded by Thomas E. Mails, assisted by Dallas Chief Eagle (Garden City, N.Y.: Doubleday, 1979); "Blood on the Little Bighorn" (excerpt from *Winter Count*) in *American Indian Authors,* ed. by Natachee Scott Momaday (Boston: Houghton Mifflin, 1972); *Winter Count* (Colorado Springs, Colo.: Dentan-Berkland Printing, 1967)

Dallas Chief Eagle's works also appear in *Native American Literature,* by Andrew Wiget (Boston: Twayne, 1985).

NARRATIVE
Born in a tent on the Rosebud Reservation of South Dakota, Dallas Chief Eagle was orphaned at an early age and raised by the elders of his tribe. A descendant of Red Cloud and Crazy Horse, Chief Eagle learned English from Jesuit missionaries and later continued his studies at the Oklahoma A&M College. He also served in the military as a U.S. marine.

In 1967 Dallas Chief Eagle was named Chief of the Teton Sioux, a title and honor that was last conferred on Red Cloud in 1868. He has also served as the director of tourism for the Development Corporation of the United Sioux Tribes of South Dakota. A writer of poetry and prose, singer and lecturer, Chief Eagle was also a visual artist. He was married to Shirley Bennett and raised six children. Chief Eagle died in 1978.

NAME   P
Martha Chosa

TRIBAL AFFILIATION
Jemez Pueblo

PUBLICATION HIGHLIGHTS
Chosa's works have appeared in the anthologies *The American Indian Speaks,* ed. by John R. Milton (Vermillion: Dakota Press, University of South Dakota, 1969); *New and Old Voices of Wah'Kon-Tah,* ed. by Robert K. Dodge and Joseph B. McCullough [third edition] (New York: International Publishers, c1985) and *Voices from Wah'Kon-Tah,* ed. by Robert K. Dodge and Joseph B. McCullough (New York: International Publishers, 1974).

NARRATIVE
Chosa is from the Jemez Pueblo in New Mexico. Her work has also been published in the journal *The South Dakota Review.*

NAME   F, N, P

Chrystos

TRIBAL AFFILIATION

Menominee

PERSONAL

Born: November 7, 1946, San Francisco, California

Education: High school diploma

AWARDS, HONORS

Audre Lorde Award, 1994

Lannan Foundation Grant, 1991

Fund for Free Expression Human Rights Watch, 1990

National Endowment for the Arts, 1990

Barbara Demming Memorial Award, 1988

PUBLICATION HIGHLIGHTS

Fire Power (Chicago: CPC In Book, 1995)

Fugitive Colors (Cleveland: Cleveland State University, 1995)

In Her I Am (Vancouver, B.C.: Press Gang Publishers, 1993)

Dream On (Vancouver, B.C.: Press Gang Publishers, 1991)

Not Vanishing (Vancouver, B.C.: Press Gang Publishers, 1988)

Fire Power (Vancouver, B.C.: Press Gang Publishers, n.d.)

Chrystos's works have also appeared in the anthologies: *Returning the Gift: Poetry and Prose from the First North American Native Writers' Festival,* ed. by Joseph Bruchac with the support of the Association for the Study of American Indian Literatures (Tucson: University of Arizona, 1994); *Getting Wet: Tales of Lesbian Seductions,* anthologized by Carol Allain and Rosamund Elwin, ed. by Mona Oikawa (Toronto: Womens Press, 1992) and *This Bridge Called My Back: Writings by Radical Women of Color,* ed. by Cherrie Moraga and Gloria Anzaldua (New York: Kitchen Table Press, 1983).

NARRATIVE

Chrystos was born in the San Francisco Bay area to a Lithuanian mother and a Menominee father. Raised in the San Francisco Bay area, Chrystos admits she was not an ideal student in school, but she did enjoy reading. Her father had taught her to read and in doing so passed on to her the love of the printed word. He also encouraged her to think for herself. Chrystos wanted to write from an early age and began writing at the age of 9, later inspired by N. Scott Momaday's "Way to Rainy Mountain." In her adult years, Chrystos struggled with alcoholism, but eventually became sober. She had to face the pain of her childhood and teenage years, a process of emotional healing that had a profound influence on her writings.

Chrystos credits Pat Parker for teaching her how to do readings as performance. Joy Harjo, Janice Gould, Elizabeth Woody, Kitty Tsui, and Dorothy Allison are all good friends who have provided her feedback in her work. She regards several writers as her literary mentors: Audre Lorde, who encouraged her to take her writing seriously, Kate Millet, who encouraged her to publish and Gloria Anzaldua, who is a strong supporter and was her first publisher. Other writers Chrystos regards as influential to her work include Leslie Marmon Silko, Alice Walker, Bell Hooks, Ward Chirchill, Marie Baker, Barbara Cameron, Mary Oliver, Luci Tapahonso, Jewell Gomez, Dionne Brand and Beth Brant. Her work has also appeared in the journal *Ms.*

Current projects include a series of essays on the colonizer culture, a new book of poems and prose, a possible videotape of a long interview piece, a novel about surviving incest and a beadwork army blanket of extinct nations. She is also considering college at some time in the future. Now living in the Pacific Northwest, the region's landscape gives her solace and pleasure "... the mountains and water which surround me ... which I overlook as I write, provide stability and serenity." When not writing, Chrystos works on graphic arts, beadwork and gardening. "I'm a fanatic gardener."

NAME   E, N, P, VA

Ward Churchill

TRIBAL AFFILIATION

Creek/Cherokee

PERSONAL

Born: October 2, 1947, in Urbana, Illinois
Education: M.A. in cross-cultural communications, Sangamon State University, Springfield, Illinois, 1975

AWARDS, HONORS

Doctor of Human Letters, Honoris Causa, Alfred University, 1992; Gustavus Myers Award for Writing on Intolerance in the United States, 1989; President's University Service Award, University of Colorado, 1987

PUBLICATION HIGHLIGHTS

Draconian Measures: A History of FBI Political Repression (Monroe, Maine: Common Courage Press, 1995)
Since Predator Came: Notes from the Struggle for American Indian Liberation (AIGIS Publications, 1995)
Indians Are Us?: Culture and Genocide in Native North America (Monroe, Maine: Common Courage Press, 1994)
Struggle for the Land: Indigenous Resistance to Genocide, Ecocide and Expropriation in Contemporary North America (Monroe, Maine: Common Courage Press, 1993)
Fantasies of the Master Race: Literature, Cinema and the Colonization of the American Indians, ed. by M. Annette Jaimes (Monroe, Maine: Common Courage Press, 1992)
Critical Issues in Native North America, vol. 2, ed. by Ward Churchill (Copenhagen: IWGIA, 1991)
Culture Versus Economism: Essays on Marxism in the Multicultural Arena, second edition revised (Denver: Fourth World Center for the Study of Indigenous Law and Politics, University of Colorado at Denver, 1989)
The COINTELPRO Papers: Documents from the FBI's Secret Wars Against Dissent in the United States, with Jim Vander Wall (Boston: South End Press, 1990)
Agents of Repression: The FBI's Secret Wars Against the Black Panther Party and the Critical Issues in Native North America, ed. by Ward Churchill (Copenhagen: International Working Group for Indigenous Affairs, 1989)
American Indian Movement, with Jim Vander Wall (Boston: South End Press, 1988)
Marxism and Native Americans, ed. by Ward Churchill (Boston: South End Press, 1983)

NARRATIVE

Ward Churchill was raised in downstate Illinois, in Rushville, Peoria and Elmwood. From his parents he learned the love of books. "My mother ... used to read to me continuously when I was a child and ... always rewarded my own reading when I was a bit older." In high school his principal argued with him about what she thought was his "'wasting' myself playing football, drinking beer and aspiring to fast cars," Churchill found her admonitions to be a "covert influence." Churchill served in the Vietnam War, where a friend Joe Stroop, another GI ("who had three years of college to my zero"), read some of his early writings and encouraged him to seriously pursue literature. After he returned home from the war, he met Russell Means, Vine Deloria,

John Trudell and Bob Robideau. Shortly after their meeting, the events at Wounded Knee, South Dakota, in 1973 unfolded, profoundly affecting his perspective and writings. "I was particularly influenced by the writing approaches of Noam Chomsky and Vine Deloria Jr. Tom Hayden (unfortunately) provided a role model for combining writing and activism ... I also have a great fondness for the work of Barbara Tuchman, Richard Drinnon, Lewis Hanke, Dashiell Hammett, William Manchester, Simon Ortiz and Kirk Sale (in no particular order). Eclectic stew, eh?"

A prominent scholar, distinguished among his peers, Churchill has been published extensively in several anthologies and journals. He writes primarily on the subjects of historical and topical American Indian legal and political issues, Indian-focused literary and cinematic criticism. His poetry has appeared in *Shantih, El Nahuatzen, Magnum* and *Akwesasne Notes.* One if his new works is *Fantasies of the Master Race: Literature, Cinema and the Colonization of American Indians* (Monroe, Maine: Common Courage Press, 1992). "This collection allowed me to explore psychological themes of domination impossible in a more straightforward political analysis." Current projects include *Fantasies of the Master Race, Volume II: A Reinterpretation of the Indian Wars,* in collaboration with Vine Deloria Jr. and a collection of sociopolitical history of the American Indian Movement.

Churchill is also a visual artist, working as a painter and printmaker. He is an associate professor of communications and American Indian studies and associate director of the Center for Studies of Ethnicity and Race in America at the University of Colorado at Boulder.

NAME — F, L, N, VA
George Clutesi

TRIBAL AFFILIATION
Nootka Tse-Shaht

PERSONAL
Born: January 1, 1905, at Port Alberni, British Columbia

AWARDS, HONORS
Canada Centennial Medal for Valuable Services to the Nation, 1967; Citation for Contributions to British Columbia, British Columbia Centennial, 1959

PUBLICATION HIGHLIGHTS
Stand Tall, My Son (Victoria, B.C.: Newport Bay Publishing, 1990); *Potlatch,* third edition (Sidney, B.C.: Gray's Publishing, 1973); *Son of Raven, Son of Deer: Fables of the Tse-Shaht People* (Sidney, B.C.: Gray's Publishing, 1967)

Clutesi's works have appeared in: *Harper's Anthology of 20th-Century Native American Poetry* [first edition] (San Francisco: Harper & Row, 1988).

NARRATIVE
George Clutesi attended reservation schools in Port Alberni, British Columbia, the place of his birth. Talented in visual arts, he studied with the artist Emily Carr as a youth. As an adult, Clutesi worked as a pile driver for twenty-one years, until he became involved in an accident that broke his back, leaving him unable to work for seven years. While recovering from his injuries, Clutesi began painting and continued to paint, even after he returned to his demanding work as a pile driver during the summers and as a fish packer in the winters. Since that time Clutesi has had over twelve exhibits of his

paintings. He exhibited his work in the Seattle Worlds Fair in 1962 and was later commissioned to paint a mural for the Expo' '67 in Montreal.

His first book, published in 1967, *Son of Raven, Son of Deer,* has been used as an elementary textbook in Canadian schools. Active in education Clutesi has lectured throughout Canada, taught adult education classes and university classes on Indian culture as a resident member of the University of British Columbia and has appeared on various television documentaries and programs. He also taught Indian dancing under a Canada Council Grant.

He was married and raised six children. He is now deceased.

NAME   E, F, L, N, P, PA, S, VA
Jo Whitehorse Cochran

TRIBAL AFFILIATION
Upper Brule

PERSONAL
Born: September 17, 1958, in Seattle, Washington
Education: M.F.A. in creative writing from the University of Washington, 1985

AWARDS, HONORS
Grayson Award for an Undergraduate Writer, University of Washington, 1984; Edith Draham Scholarship, University of Washington, 1980–1981

PUBLICATION HIGHLIGHTS
"Bearing Witness/Sobreviviendo: An Anthology of Native American/Latina Art and Literature," by Jo Cochran, et al. in *Calyx: A Journal of Art and Literature by Women,* Special Issue (Corvallis, Oregon: Calyx, 8:2 Spring 1984); *Gathering Ground: New Writing and Art by Northwest Women of Color* (Seattle: Seal Press, 1984)

Cochran's works have also appeared in the anthologies: *Dancing on the Rim of the World: An Anthology of Contemporary Northwest Native American Writing,* ed. by Andrea Lerner (Tucson: Sun Tracks, University of Arizona Press, 1990) and *The Sacred Hoop: Recovering the Feminine in American Indian Traditions,* by Paula Gunn Allen (Boston: Beacon Press, 1986).

NARRATIVE
Jo Whitehorse Cochran grew up in the Seattle region. She is of Norwegian and Upper Brule descent. Cochran remembers that she loved school as a young woman, adding that she still "contemplates going on for a Ph.D." She was encouraged to write by "my high school English teachers who kept pushing the kid-who-played-basketball to write." She had a mentor while a young woman—friend, poet, publisher and translator Sam Hamill. "He gave me free access to his huge library; he edited my work and taught me discipline. He encouraged [me] to develop a good ear, good vision and a kind heart." At the age of twenty Cochran made a decision that was to have a powerful and lasting impact on her life and writings. "I came out as a Lesbian and all the pronouns changed in my work—and have been correct ever since."

In her writings Cochran addresses the subjects of spirituality, Native peoples, love, sexuality, "anything that interests me and I am passionate about—racism, sexism, ageism, classism, how hate manifests in shaping our lives." One of her poems has proven to be quite popular with her readers, and it is also one of her personal favorites. "I have this one poem everyone loves and wants to publish; it is titled 'Halfbreed Girl in a City School.' It is my best piece because people get it in their hearts." As a writer who was born and raised in the Pacific Northwest, Cochran feels that her work has taken on the flavor of the region: "... the Northwest has a very specific feel, weather, topography and palate that definitely affects my writing and my visual art. I think who made me decide to be a writer, was/is the Great Spirit that is within each one of us. I say this because I am compelled to write, its in my blood and bones, by all rights I should have been a gym teacher. But the Great Spirit has other plans." Cochran continued in her studies and received her M.F.A. in creative writing from the University of Washington.

Writers whose work Cochran enjoys include Paula Gunn Allen, Ranier Maria Rilke, Adrienne Rich, Louise Erdrich, Leslie M. Silko, Rumi, Denise Leverton, Joy Harjo, Colleen McElroy, Martha Grimes. "These writers have had a great deal of influence on my work because of their varied voices and their expansive vision and attention to detail."

Cochran is coeditor of *Changing Our Power: An Introduction to Women's Studies* ([S.l.]: Kendall-Hunt, 1987). She is a Reiki practioner and Seichim master. Current projects include a science-fiction novel and a new poetry manuscript as yet untitled.

She was formerly working in the Office of Management and Budget for the City of Seattle and is currently the Arts Capital Projects Manager for King County, Washington, and an artist-in-residence within the Washington schools. In her leisure time Cochran enjoys working on visual arts. "I enjoy painting and oil pastel. Right now I am working on a series of paintings on animal bones—it is a new very rich medium for me."

NAME   P
Robin Coffee

TRIBAL AFFILIATION
Cherokee, Creek and Sioux

PERSONAL
Born: October 5, 1953, in Lawrence, Kansas

PUBLICATION HIGHLIGHTS
The Eagle's Path, poems (Tahlequah, Oklahoma: Whitebird Publishing, 1992); *Voices of the Heart,* poems (Tahlequah, Oklahoma: Whitebird Publishing, 1991); *Echoes of Our Being,* poems (Muskogee, Oklahoma: Indian University Press, 1981)

NARRATIVE
Coffee was raised in Tahlequah, Oklahoma, where she now resides. She is presently working on her masters degree in counseling and psychology and is writing poetry.

NAME   P, VA
Grey Cohoe

TRIBAL AFFILIATION
Navajo

PERSONAL
Born: Shiprock, New Mexico
Education: Coursework at the Institute of American Indian Arts, Santa Fe, New Mexico, 1965–1967; coursework at the University of Arizona, Tucson

PUBLICATION HIGHLIGHTS

Cohoe's works have appeared in the following anthologies:

New and Old Voices of Wah'Kon-Tah, ed. by Robert K. Dodge and Joseph B. McCullough [third edition] (New York: International Publishers, c1985)

The Remembered Earth: An Anthology of Contemporary Native American Literature, ed. by Geary Hobson (Albuquerque: Red Earth Press, c1979)

Voices from Wah'Kon-Tah, ed. by Robert K. Dodge and Joseph B. McCullough (New York: International Publishers, 1974)

American Indian Authors, ed. by Natachee Scott Momaday (Boston: Houghton Mifflin, 1972)

The Whispering Wind: Poetry by Young American Indians (New York: Doubleday, 1972)

The American Indian Speaks, ed. by John R. Milton (Vermillion: Dakota Press, University of South Dakota, 1969)

NARRATIVE

Cohoe attended the Phoenix Indian High School and later the Institute of American Indian Arts in Santa Fe, New Mexico, where he became an instructor. He has also taken classes at the University of Arizona. A poet and visual artist, Cohoe's paintings have been exhibited in Oklahoma City, Washington, D.C., and in shows in Africa and South America. His poems have been published in numerous journals and periodicals such as *Pembroke* magazine and *Sun Tracks.* Cohoe is now deceased.

NAME   N, P

Carl Concha

TRIBAL AFFILIATION

Taos Pueblo

PERSONAL

Education: Coursework at the Institute of American Indian Arts, Santa Fe, New Mexico

PUBLICATION HIGHLIGHTS

Concha's works have appeared in: *From the Belly of the Shark: A New Anthology of*

Native Americans, ed. by Walter Lowenfels (New York: Vantage, 1974) and *The American Indian Speaks,* ed. by John R. Milton (Vermillion: Dakota Press, University of South Dakota, 1969).

NARRATIVE

Concha's works have also been published in the journals *The Blue Cloud Quarterly* and *The South Dakota Review.*

NAME   F, L, P, PL, PA, S, VA

Joseph Leonard Concha

OTHER NAMES USED

J. Leonard Concha

TRIBAL AFFILIATION

Taos Pueblo

PERSONAL

Born: October 8, 1954, in Santa Fe, New Mexico

Education: Taos Pueblo Day School, Taos New Mexico, 1960–1968; High school graduate of the Institute of American Indian Arts, Santa Fe, New Mexico, 1969–1973; associate of fine arts, Institute of American Indian Arts, 1989–1990

PUBLICATION HIGHLIGHTS

"Chokecherry Hunters," "August," "Leaf" in *The Remembered Earth,* ed. by Geary Hobson (Albuquerque: University of New Mexico Press, 1979)

Chokecherry Hunters and Other Poems, foreword by Frank Waters. (Santa Fe: Sunstone Press, 1976)

Lonely Deer: Poems by a Pueblo Boy (Taos: Red Willow Society, 1969)

Beyond the Horizon: Poems by a Pueblo Boy (Taos: Taos Pueblo Day School, 1968)

NARRATIVE

Joseph Leonard Concha was raised in Taos Pueblo, which he describes as "... a sacred place, and the mountains are my refuge and inspiration." As a youth he attended the Taos Day School and lived in a close, loving home with his parents. He was deeply influenced by his parents, who both were very creative. His father was a trained artist and his mother a gifted storyteller. Together they encouraged young Concha in his artistic endeavors. While still a youth Concha had an experience that guided him toward a life of creativity. "I had a vision when I was 12 years old and my life as an artist has been the fulfillment of that dream. In a way 'art for life's sake' ... seems to be in my blood. If I don't write, I'm not happy." In high school he studied under the late C. F. Porter, a creative writing teacher "whose lectures I liked, who said 'what we need is more expert Indians, instead of Indian experts.' Mr. Stan Aiello was my junior high teacher and mentor ... [he] inspired and supported me and was instrumental in my career as a poet and artist."

Concha writes about Native American experiences and about nature and geography. He enjoys the writings of poets Simon Ortiz, Robert Frost, Octavio Paz, James Wright and Leslie Marmon Silko and considers one of his best poems to be about the grandmothers he never had: "Grandmother, you flew away, from my open arms, like an aspen leaf, unable to fly."

Concha is also a potter and visual artist; he works on video proposals and story lines and is currently working on a long-term video project. "I also like to work with children telling stories [and] I like to work on creating a written language for my tribe, transcribing the oral histories and preserving them." He is a self-employed advocate for senior citizens and young children.

NAME   E, F, N, P

Robert J. Conley

TRIBAL AFFILIATION

Cherokee (United Keetoowah Band)

PERSONAL

Born: December 29, 1940, Cushing, Oklahoma

Education: B.A. in drama and art, Midwestern University, Wichita Falls, Texas, 1966; M.A. in English, Midwestern University, Wichita Falls, Texas, 1968

AWARDS, HONORS

Spur Award from the Western Writers of American for the Best Short Story of 1988 (*Yellow Bird: An Imaginary Autobiography*)

PUBLICATION HIGHLIGHTS

The Dark Island (New York: Doubleday, 1995)

Mountain Windsong: A Novel of the Trail of Tears (Norman, Okla.: University of Oklahoma Press, 1992, 1995)

The War Trail North (New York: Doubleday, 1995)

White Path (New York: Bantam Books, 1995)

Crazy Snake (New York: Pocket Books, 1994)

Geronimo: Una leyenda Americana (Barcelona: Plaza & James, 1994)

The Long Way Home (New York: Doubleday, 1994)

Nickajack (New York: Bantam Books, 1994)

To Make a Killing (New York: Pocket Books, 1994)

The Way South (Thorndike, Maine: Thorndike Press, 1994)

Zeke Proctor: Cherokee Outlaw (New York: Pocket Books, 1994)

The Dark Way (New York: Bantam Books, 1993, 1994)

Border Line (New York: Pocket Books, 1993)

The Way of the Priests (New York: Bantam Books, 1992, 1994)

Killing Time ([S.l.]: Thorndike Press, 1991)

Ned Christie's War (New York: M. Evans & Company, 1991)

The Witch of Springsnake and Other Stories (Norman, Okla.: University of Oklahoma Press, 1991)

Colfax ([S.l.]: Thorndike Press, 1990)

Go-Ahead Rider (New York: M. Evans & Company, 1990)

Quitting Time (s.l.: Thorndike Press, 1990)

Poems for Comparison and Contrast, by Robert J. Conley and Richard L. Cheny (New York: Macmillan, 1971, 1972)

Conley's works have also appeared in the anthology *Returning the Gift: Poetry and Prose from the First North American Native Writers' Festival,* ed. by Joseph Bruchac with the support of the Association for the Study of American Indian Literatures (Tucson: University of Arizona, 1994).

NARRATIVE

Robert J. Conley was instructor of English at Southwest Missouri State University and at Northern Illinois University, director of Indian Studies at Eastern Montana College and was an associate professor of English at Morningside College. Conley was also the assistant programs manager for the Cherokee Nation of Oklahoma for one year. Although he has written numerous novels, poems and short stories over the years, he considers his best work to be *Mountain Windsong.* He credits his grandparents and parents with having the greatest impact on his life and written works, as well as his marriage to Evelyn Snell (Gwisti Elaqui). He is currently writing western novels for Pocket Books and has developed a series of novels for Bantam, Doubleday and Dell titled *The Real People,* which traces Cherokee history through fiction, beginning in about the year 1500. *The Way of the Priests*

is the first book of this historical fiction series. He began writing about Cherokee history and cultural issues because he was frustrated with what was, or was not, already written about his people.

Two writers he enjoys are William Shakespeare and Max Evens. He lives in Tahlequah, Oklahoma, the historic capital of the Cherokee nation, which he features in his writings.

NAME F, N, P

Elizabeth Cook-Lynn

TRIBAL AFFILIATION

Dakota–Crow Creek Sioux

PERSONAL

Born: November 17, 1930, in Ft. Thompson, South Dakota

Education: Masters degree

PUBLICATION HIGHLIGHTS

Why I Can't Read Wallace Stegner and Other Essays: A Tribal Voice (Madison: University of Wisconsin Press, 1997)

"Wounded Knee 1973: A Personal Account," *A Review Journal of Ethnic Studies,* July 1995 vol. 14 (4) Summer p 82(3)

From the River's Edge (New York: Arcade Publishing, 1991)

The Power of Horses and Other Stories (New York: Arcade Publishing, 1990)

Seek the House of Relatives (Marvin, S. Dak.: Blue Cloud Quarterly Press, 1983)

Then Badger Said This, second edition (Fairfield, Wash.: Ye Galleon Press, 1983)

Cook-Lynn's works have also appeared in numerous anthologies, among them:

Returning the Gift: Poetry and Prose from the First North American Native Writers' Festival, ed. by Joseph Bruchac with the support of the Association for the Study of American Indian Literatures (Tucson: University of Arizona, 1994)

Talking Leaves: Contemporary Native American Short Stories, An Anthology, ed. by Craig Lesley (New York: Laurel, Dell, 1991)

American Indian Literatures: An Introduction, Bibliographic Review and Selected Bibliography, by A. LaVonne Brown Ruoff (New York: Modern Language Association, 1990)

Spider Woman's Granddaughters: Traditional Tales and Contemporary Writing by Native American Women, ed. by Paula Gunn Allen (Boston: Beacon Press, 1989)

I Tell You Now: Autobiographical Essays by Native American Writers, ed. by Brian Swann and Arnold Krupat (Lincoln: University of Nebraska Press, 1987)

Survival This Way: Interviews with Native American Poets, Joseph Bruchac (Tucson: Sun Tracks, University of Arizona Press, 1987)

The Sacred Hoop: Recovering the Feminine in American Indian Traditions, by Paula Gunn Allen (Boston: Beacon Press, 1986)

Earth Power Coming: Short Fiction in Native American Literature, ed. by Simon J. Ortiz (Tsaile, Ariz.: Navajo Community College Press, 1983)

The Remembered Earth: An Anthology of Contemporary Native American Literature, ed. by Geary Hobson (Albuquerque: Red Earth Press, 1979)

NARRATIVE

Elizabeth Cook-Lynn was raised on the Crow Creek Sioux Reservation in South Dakota. She holds a masters degree and has taught courses in the humanities and literature as associate professor of English and Indian Studies at Eastern Washington University in Cheney, Washington.

Cook-Lynn writes about many topics, from problems in Indian education to literary criticism. "I write what I know about. I try to write real stories about realistic characters—believable people." She enjoys reading nonfiction works. "I read very little contemporary fiction, mostly biography and history." She is now working on several projects: a new, second novel, literary criticism and poetry. Cook-Lynn's stories and poems have appeared in numerous journals and periodicals such as the *CCC Journal, Prairie Schooner, Sun Tracks, South Dakota Review,* the *Great Plains Observer, Pembroke, Wicazo Sa Review, Parabola* and the *Greenfield Review* among many others. She was the founding editor of the *Wicazo Sa Review* in Rapid City, South Dakota, where she now works as an editor.

NAME   E, F, L, N, P
Karen Cooper

OTHER NAMES USED
Karen Coody Cooper

TRIBAL AFFILIATION
Cherokee (Oklahoma)

PERSONAL
Born: November 10, 1946, in Tulsa, Oklahoma

Education: B.A. in anthropology and sociology, Western Connecticut State University, Danbury, Connecticut

AWARDS, HONORS
Poetry Award from Western Connecticut State University, 1981

PUBLICATION HIGHLIGHTS
"A Wealth of Spirit" in *Auch Dag Gras ein Leid* (Austria: [s.n.], 1988)

"A Native Woman" in *A Gathering of Spirit: A Collection by North American Indian Women,* ed. by Beth Brant (Ithaca, N.Y.: Firebrand Books, 1988, c1984)

"Through the Eyes of Deer," poem in *Fireweed* ([S.l.: s.n.], issue 2, Winter 1986) "Like the Ticking of a Clock" in *Eagle* (Naugatuck, Conn.: Eagle Wing Press, March 1982)

NARRATIVE

Karen Cooper was raised in Oklahoma, close to her grandparents who lived in a rural setting. "My grandparents' farm was my special place." A writer from an early age, Cooper's poetry was published in her school yearbook, church bulletins and in other local publications. Cooper stayed in the New England region and remained there for twenty years after she graduated from Western Connecticut State University. She notes that her writing was affected by her stay in the Northeast because she was impressed with the woodlands and seasons, though she hastens to add "... my childhood [in] Oklahoma will always be a part of me."

When asked if she'd had a mentor in her career as a writer, Cooper responded "If I'd understood what a mentor was earlier, I'd have had a few. As a freshman at Oklahoma College for Women, one professor encouraged me and another taught me a lot, but I hardly heeded their help. I'm sure it helped, but a decade passed before I began to try to write." While she may not have had a mentor as a student in college, Cooper did have a number of changes and opportunities that fueled her interest in writing later in her life. "Opportunities [such as] working in a museum with a good newsletter. A divorce that gave me time to look into myself and to listen and to write. An Indian newspaper that needed me when I needed it."

Cooper writes about stereotypes and misconceptions, role models, philosophy, history and "revisioning history." As an admirer of a well written piece, Cooper found, to her great satisfaction, that she too could generate such memorable works. "I've always read and always loved beautiful passages. I discovered that I could, at times, capture things in words. Writing felt good." She enjoys reading the works of a variety of authors. "I like Southern and English gothic tales, O. Henry and Maugham, Taylor Caldwell and Michener. I like deep, tactile descriptions, yet I write sparsely. Maybe I studied too much journalism, my original major. I like Momaday's poetry and personal writings." Two contemporary Native writers who have also fueled Cooper's imagination are Beth Brant and Joe Bruchac.

Now working as a museum educator and living in Lawton, Oklahoma, Cooper is also working on her masters degree in museum studies. In her spare time, Cooper enjoys fingerweaving, hiking, reading, having good discussions, listening to music and "dancing passionately."

❖❖❖

NAME N

Rupert Costo

TRIBAL AFFILIATION

Cahuilla of Southern California

PERSONAL

Born: 1906

PUBLICATION HIGHLIGHTS

A Thousand Years of American Indian Storytelling, by Rupert Costo and Jeannette Henry Costo (San Francisco: Indian Historian Press, 1981)

Indian Treaties: Two Centuries of Dishonor, by Rupert Costo and Jeannette Henry Costo (San Francisco: Indian Historian Press, 1977)

The Missions of California: A Legacy of Genocide, by Rupert Costo and Jeannette Henry Costo (San Francisco: Indian Historian Press, 1974)

Contributions and Achievements of the American Indian (San Francisco: Indian Historian Press, 1973)

Redman of the Golden West (San Francisco: Indian Historian Press, 1970)

Textbooks and the American Indian (San Francisco: Indian Historian Press, 1970)

Costo's works have also appeared in *Literature of the American Indians: Views and Interpretations: A Gathering of Indian Memories, Symbolic Contexts and Literary Criticism*, ed. by and with an introduction and notes by Abraham Chapman (New York: New American Library, 1975).

NARRATIVE

Costo was the president of the American Indian Historical Society, an organization based in San Francisco, which was composed of Native artists, scholars, professionals and traditional historians. The Society also published under the imprint The Indian Historian Press and also produced the journal the *Indian Historian*. Costo is now deceased.

NAME

Mary Crow Dog

OTHER NAMES USED

Mary Brave Bird

TRIBAL AFFILIATION

Brule Lakota

PERSONAL

Born: 1953 in the town of He Dog, Rosebud Sioux Reservation, South Dakota

AWARDS, HONORS

American Book Award for *Lakota Woman*, with Richard Erdoes, 1991

PUBLICATION HIGHLIGHTS

Ohitika Woman, by Mary Brave Bird with Richard Erdoes (New York: Grove Weidenfeld, 1993); *Lakota Woman: Ma vie de femme Sioux* (Paris: Albin Michel, 1992); *Lakota Woman,* by Mary Crow Dog with Richard Erdoes (New York: Grove Weidenfeld, 1990)

NARRATIVE

Born Mary Brave Bird on the Rosebud Reservation to a Lakota mother and white father, Crow Dog lived in a world of alcoholism, violence, racism and degradation. Raised by her grandparents, her father left the family when she was young and her relationship with her mother remained stormy. Crow Dog was sent to the mission Catholic school, where her traditional language and beliefs were discouraged by the nuns and priests. She began drinking heavily at ten, was raped as a youth and soon left the reservation with other runaways to live in Rapid City, South Dakota, and Los Angeles. While in Los Angeles and Rapid City, Crow Dog lived among other runaways and youths who fought, drank and took drugs, had casual sex and committed crime.

Crows Dog's life began to change when she became active in the American Indian Movement (AIM) in the 1960s and 1970s, later finding herself in 1973 among the two thousand or so at Wounded Knee, South Dakota, who held out against the National Guard and federal agents for seventy-one days. It was during this time (and at age 17) that she gave birth to her first child. After her experience at Wounded Knee, she met and married medicine man Leonard Crow Dog, AIM's spiritual leader, and began following the teachings of the Native American Church.

Mary is now divorced from Leonard Crow Dog and has remarried. A film was made of the book *Lakota Woman.*

D

NAME   F, J, P
Kateri Damm

TRIBAL AFFILIATION
Ojibway

PERSONAL
Born: February 3, 1965, in Toronto, Ontario, Canada

Education: Completed secondary school at the Owen Sound Collegiate and Vocational Institute; B.A. in English from York University, Toronto, Ontario; M.A. candidate in English at the University of Ottawa, Ottawa, Ontario

AWARDS, HONORS
Graduate Studies Research Scholarship, University of Ottawa, 1992

Founding Member and Interim Vice President, Aboriginal Youth Council of Canada, 1986–1989; Lucille Herbert Memorial Scholarship, York University, 1987

PUBLICATION HIGHLIGHTS
My Heart Is a Stray Bullet (Cape Croker, Ont.: Kegedonce Press, 1993)

"I Lose Track of the Land," "My Secret Tongue and Ears," "Stray Bullets," poems in *Gatherings: The En'owkin Journal of First North American Peoples,* vol. 2 (Penticton, B.C.: Theytus Books, 1991)

"Toronto Transit," poem in *Glide Path Destinations* (Scarborough, Ont.: Prentice-Hall Canada, 1991)

"Suicidal Tendency," poem in *Gatherings: The En'owkin Journal of First North American Peoples,* vol. 1 (Penticton, B.C.: Theytus Books, 1990)

Damm's works have also appeared in the following anthologies:

Returning the Gift: Poetry and Prose from the First North American Native Writers' Festival, ed. by Joseph Bruchac with the support of the Association for the Study of American Indian Literatures (Tucson: University of Arizona, 1994)

Looking at the Words of Our People: First Nations Analysis of Literature, ed. by Jeannette Armstrong (Penticton, B.C.: Theytus, 1993)

Seventh Generation (Benticton, B.C.: Theytus Books, 1989)

Beedaudjimowin ([S.l.]: Beedaudjimowin Publications and Communications, 1991)

NARRATIVE
Kateri Damm was raised in Toronto and the Owen Sound area. She spent her summers at her grandparents' home on the Cape Croker Reserve, a location that she to this day regards as home. As a child, she was engrossed with watching her grandmother write, and as she grew, her interest in writing blossomed. "My grandmother was a role model … . I started writing at a very young age. For me it was just a natural part of life, I didn't think about it much until I was in [the] university." Damm enrolled in creative writing courses and later submitted her work to various publications, many of which were accepted. It was after these affirmations of her work that Damm said, "I started to think that maybe I was a writer or could be a writer."

Surrounded by loving and supportive family members, Damm remembers those who were most influential. "My grandmother Irene Akiwenzie, who was a writer, avid reader, storyteller and a beautiful caring person, was probably the greatest influence on me. My grandfather Joseph Akiwenzie was also very influential. My mother, niece and sister as well. Friends who have had a major impact are Jeannette Armstrong, Greg Younl Ing, Drew Taylor, Allen De Leary ... My Polish-Canadian grandmother also had a huge impact." Sadly, her Polish grandmother, Ojibway grandfather and her Ojibway grandmother passed away, all within a short time of one another.

Damm enjoys teaching, physical activity, traveling and reading the works of many Canadian and indigenous writers, particularly the works of Louise Erdrich, Patricia Grage and Jeanette Armstrong. She is a member of the writing group WIND, which is working on an anthology of writings and is currently a graduate student and teaching assistant at the University of Ottawa. She is also a coordinator of "Beyond Survival," an International Conference of Indigenous Writers, Performing and Visual Artists (which was held April 15–18, 1993 in Ottawa). She is also a freelance writer.

NAME   P

Nora Dauenhauer

TRIBAL AFFILIATION

Tlingit

PERSONAL

Born: May 8, 1927, in Juneau, Alaska

Education: B.A. in anthropology from Alaska Methodist University, 1976; coursework at the Summer Institute of Linguistics, University of Alaska–Fairbanks, 1975; coursework in anthropology, Sheldon Jackson College, Sitka, Alaska, 1974

AWARDS, HONORS

Award for Contribution to Native Literature, Returning the Gift Festival, 1994

Governor's Award for the Arts, 1989

Humanist of the Year by the Alaska Humanities Forum, 1980

First Prize in Short Story and Poetry Categories, Southeast Alaska Native Arts Festival, Sitka, Alaska, 1979

Commissioner, Alaska Historical Commission, 1978–1981

PUBLICATION HIGHLIGHTS

Hau Kusteeyi: Our Culture: Tlingit Life Stories (Seattle: University of Washington Press, 1994)

Haa Tuwun'aagu Y'is, for Healing Our Spirit: Tlingit Oratory, ed. by Nora and Richard Dauenhauer (Seattle: University of Washington Press, 1993, 1990)

The Droning Shaman (Haines, Alaska: The Black Current Press, 1988)

Haa Shuk'a, Our Ancestors: Tlingit Oral Narratives, ed. by Nora Marks Dauenhauer and Richard Dauenhauer (Seattle: University of Washington Press, 1987)

"Alaska Native Writers, Storytellers And Orators," in Special Issue Of *Alaska Quarterly Review,* ed. by Nora Marks Dauenhauer, Richard Dauenhauer and Gary Holthaus (Anchorage: University of Alaska, 1986)

Tlingit Spelling Book, third revised edition, Nora and Richard Dauenhauer (Juneau: Sealaska Heritage Foundation, 1984)

"Because We Cherish You ... ": Sealaska Elders Speak to the Future, ed. by Nora and Richard Dauenhauer (Juneau: Sealaska Heritage Foundation, 1981)

Beginning Tlingit, Nora and Richard Dauenhauer ([S.l.]: Alaska Native Language Center, Alaska Native Education Board and Tlingit Readers, Ind. 1976)

Dauenhauer's works have also appeared in these following anthologies:

Returning the Gift: Poetry and Prose from the First North American Native Writers' Festival, ed. by Joseph Bruchac with the support of the Association for the Study of American Indian Literatures (Tucson: University of Arizona, 1994)

Raven Tells Stories: An Anthology of Alaskan Native Writing, first edition, ed. by Joseph Bruchac (Greenfield Center, N.Y.: Greenfield Review Press, 1991)

New Worlds of Literature, first edition, ed. by Jerome Beaty and Paul J. Hunter (New York: W. W. Norton, 1989)

Harper's Anthology of 20th-Century Native American Poetry, first edition (San Francisco: Harper & Row, 1988)

That's What She Said: Contemporary Poetry and Fiction by Native American Women, ed. by Rayna Green (Bloomington: Indiana University Press, 1984)

Earth Power Coming: Short Fiction in Native American Literature, ed. by Simon J. Ortiz (Tsaile, Ariz.: Navajo Community College Press, c1983)

NARRATIVE

Dauenhauer spent her childhood in Juneau and Hoonah. Born into a family of well-known beadworkers and carvers, her early years were spent in a traditional Tlingit way of life, on the family fishing boat except when her family stopped to visit her relatives or when her family had to stop in Juneau to do business. It was only while they were in Juneau that her family would speak English; otherwise, they spoke their traditional language, Tlingit. Her family lived primarily on game meats and foods purchased in towns where her family stopped to sell their fish and furs or to stock up on fuel and supplies.

Dauenhauer began to learn English when she entered school at the age of 8. She attended school periodically, and at 16 she dropped out. She married at the age of 18 and later raised four children. Dauenhauer returned to the classroom, where she earned her GED and worked as a Tlingit language researcher in 1972–1973 for the University of Alaska's Alaska Native Language Center. After receiving her B.A. in anthropology Dauenhauer spent two years, 1978–1980, as the cultural coordinator for the Cook Inlet Native Association. She has worked as a translator and principal investigator for the Tlingit Text Translation Project, which was funded by a National Endowment for the Humanities Translation Grant, and from 1981 to 1982 she held the position of assistant professor of Alaska Native Studies at the University of Alaska, University Within Walls Program, and also worked as an instructor at the Hiland Mountain Correctional Center in Eagle River, Alaska. She is now the principal researcher in language and cultural studies at the Sealaska Heritage Foundation in Juneau.

Dauenhauer's work has been influenced by her husband and family, who stress the study of traditional Tlingit education, storytelling and expertise in traditional Tlingit technology. She is a teacher of her native language, has translated traditional Tlingit texts and is well known for her scholarship in the field of Tlingit oral literature. She writes Tlingit poetry as well as Tlingit instructional materials. She is also a traditional dancer. Dauenhauer enjoys reading Native American and Asian American literature and some of the classics of western literature. Dauenhauer's works have been published in the journals the *Greenfield Review, Northward Journal, NEEK* and *Raven's Bones Newsletter.*

Her husband is writer and former poet laureate of Alaska, and together they work on media presentations and publications about Native performances and oral arts. They have four children and thirteen grandchildren.

NAME E, P, VA
Robert Davis

OTHER NAMES USED
Robert H. Davis

TRIBAL AFFILIATION
Tlingit

PERSONAL
Born: 1954

PUBLICATION HIGHLIGHTS
Davis' works have appeared in the following anthologies: *Raven Tells Stories: An Anthology of Alaskan Native Writing*, first edition, ed. by Joseph Bruchac (Greenfield Center, N.Y.: Greenfield Review Press, 1991); *Standing on the Rim of the World: An Anthology of Contemporary Northwest Native American Writing*, ed. by Andrea Lerner (Tucson: Sun Tracks, University of Arizona Press, c1990) and *Harper's Anthology of 20th-Century Native American Poetry*, first edition (San Francisco: Harper & Row, 1988).

NARRATIVE
Davis was born in southeast Alaska to parents who both were educators. His father was a Tlingit teacher, and his mother was of European ancestry and in the 1940s left her Michigan farm home for a teaching position in Alaska. Consequently, a portion of Davis's childhood was spent traveling back and forth between the two distinctly different locations and cultures of Kake, Alaska, and Michigan as his family visited both sets of relatives.

In addition to his poetry, Davis currently works as a painter and a woodcarver and gives woodcarving workshops and classes.

NAME F, P
Charlotte DeClue

TRIBAL AFFILIATION
Wa-zha-zhe (Osage)

PERSONAL
Born: July 9, 1948, in Enid, Oklahoma
Education: Oklahoma State University, 1967–1968; University of Missouri, St. Louis, 1970–1972; University of Missouri, Kansas City, 1974–1979

PUBLICATION HIGHLIGHTS
"Ten Good Horses: Visions from the True Tongue" in *Stiletto 2: The Disinherited* (Kansas City: Howling Dog Press, 1991); *Without Warning, Poems* (New York: Strawberry Press, 1985); "The Underside of Trees," "61," "Healing," poems originally published in *Spawning the Medicine River* (Santa Fe: Institute of American Indian Arts), reprinted in *That's What She Said: Contemporary Poetry and Fiction by Native American Women*, ed. by Rayna Green (Bloomington: Indiana University Press, 1984)

DeClue's works have also appeared in *Returning the Gift: Poetry and Prose from the First North American Native Writers' Festival*, ed. by Joseph Bruchac with the support of the Association for the Study of American Indian Literatures (Tucson: University of Arizona, 1994); *Native American Reader: Stories, Speeches and Poems*, ed. by Jerry D. Blanche (Juneau: Denali Press, 1990) and *A Gathering of Spirit: A Collection of North American Indian Women*, ed. by Beth Brant (New York: Firebrand, 1988, c1984).

NARRATIVE
Charlotte DeClue was raised on the plains of northern Oklahoma. "My adopted

family was run out of most counties after my 'pretend-to-be father' ended up in McAlester Prison for embezzlement." Of her childhood, DeClue remembers "I was sick a lot as a child ... I never got a case of anything in the 'mild way.' Usually 'near death' was the point I reached before the fever broke. But once, the fever refused to break and my mind went wild. Sometimes I wonder if that wasn't why I became a writer—so I could release all those stories some demon left in my brain. Whatever it was, it left me with a lazy heart valve and a need to express myself on paper.

"If anything influenced my choice to write, it was all the diaries I kept while growing up. Especially entries that talked about running away (with boys, of course); escape routes (to Montana) and what I would have done if I had been Pochahantas (save my own ass). I threw them all out when I got to high school. Mostly because I was sick of myself. That's when I discovered other people. They had feelings and thoughts and lives very much like my own. And all of them hated school." DeClue started to read all types of drugstore magazines when she was in the third or fourth grade. "Every once in a while I would grab a comic book and read about the adventures of Archie and Veronica, the typical American teenagers. But they never got drunk, ended up in jail or did anything very exciting. So we knew they weren't real. Because they weren't like our brothers or sisters, or really anybody we knew. I used to want to be like the really 'wild girls,' the ones who wore toreador pants and the black leather jackets. Instead I had to wear dumb stuff like wool skirts and sweaters. ... "

While her friends ended up in girls' homes, DeClue ended up in a prep school, where she "could carry books and study sports. Before I could count in American English they made me count beans in a cannery. All because some 'home' hired us orphans out as free labor. Later I found out, when I learned to read law journals, that 'orphan law' was similar to 'illegal citizen law,' especially for Indian kids. Eventually the scholarly Indians would pass the Indian Child Welfare Act. Never again would an Indian child ever have to pick peanuts, pull apart cotton or smell dead pig meat stuffed in cans. At least not for nothin'!

"I had nothing more to read in my life that made any sense but the few lines of poetry I had scratched down here and there. Later, in college, I would read poetry written by Gertrude Stein, Virginia Wolfe, Sylvia Plath—all those depressed and disillusioned women who never fit in. And they taught me how to use words to paint pictures. But it was my native tongue that taught me what 'poetic language' really was. And I had retained enough to know that even the sound for 'bird' (Wa-zhin-kah) made you think of one. And the world my language pictured was ancient, wise and beautiful. And the stories I had learned, throughout my life, and the stories I had been told, throughout my life, were a lot truer than the ones I could make up.

"One day all those elements came together and I started writing. I started sending out my first poems in 1979. Editors would write back and ask 'there is something I need to know about you.' You see, I wanted to make it as a writer, not an Indian writer. But I couldn't explain my use of symbolism without the truth coming out. ... Sometimes I celebrate that label 'Native American writer,' but it is mostly with other Indians. Seldom has it come easy. And practically never has it fit right. It's either awkward or tiring or just doesn't explain the nature of my work. We are a complex people, with differing ways of seeing the world. Hardly ever are we just one person. ... Tokenism is a monstrous horror to overcome. Because it forces a person to speak for everybody. And one person can only speak for their own experiences. ... The difference with Native writers is that we come from a spiritual source that is universal, and our value system is communal. But we are a product of many things, the least of which is assimilation. But we are a product of many things. Our experiences with assimilation, relocation and racism are as important in our work as our cultural orientation. But I found that tokenism places a great deal of emphasis on individuality. And individuality can be a burden for Native people who must accommodate for a traditional world that emphasizes caring for all creatures in the natural world, and love for our Mother Earth. The gulf between the two, the western mind and its need to devour everything around it, and the traditional Indian world, which teaches respect for even the smallest of creatures, became so huge I could no longer stand the pain. I left college at 29 to become a writer. And that process of 'becoming' has healed that pain." When asked by a colleague what made her become a writer, DeClue responded, "I followed my heart one day and it's gotten me in trouble ever since."

DeClue lives in Norman, Oklahoma, where she writes and gives poetry readings.

NAME P
June I. Degnan

TRIBAL AFFILIATION
Yupik and Inupiaq

PUBLICATION HIGHLIGHTS
"Protecting the Seventh Generation," Essay in *KIVIOQ* (Ottawa, Ontario: Baffin Writers' Project, Summer 1990); "Direc-

tions in Silence," poem in *Alaska Native News* (Anchorage: [s.n.], Vol. 4, No. 3, January–February 1986); "Norton Sound Dream," poem in *Back Country Alaska, Alaska Geographic* (Anchorage: [s.n.], Vol. 13, no. 2, 1986)

NAME E, N
Ella Cara Deloria

TRIBAL AFFILIATION
Yankton Dakota

PERSONAL
Born: Wakpala, South Dakota
Education: Coursework at Oberlin College, Oberlin Ohio, 1911–1912; B.A. from the Teachers College, Columbia University, New York, 1914; Special diploma from the Columbia University Teacher's College; Indian Council Fire Achievement Award and honorary life membership

PUBLICATION HIGHLIGHTS
Ella Deloria's The Buffalo People, first edition, by Ella Deloria and Julian Rice (Albuquerque: University of New Mexico, 1994)

Ella Deloria's Iron Hawk, by Ella Deloria and Julian Rice (Albuquerque: University of New Mexico, 1993)

Deer Women and Elk Men: The Lakota Narratives of Ella Deloria, compiled by Julian Rice (Albuquerque: University of New Mexico, 1992)

Speaking of Indians, by Ella Deloria, Agnes Picotte and Paul N. Pavich (Vermillion, S. Dak.: Dakota Books, 1992, 1944)

Waterlily (Lincoln: University of Nebraska Press, 1988)

Dakota Texts, compiled by Ella C. Deloria, edited with introductory notes by Agnes Picotte and Paul N. Pavich (Vermillion, S. Dak.: Dakota Press, 1978, originally published in 1944)

NARRATIVE

Deloria's father was the Reverend Philip Deloria, one of the first Dakotas to receive a college education and to become an ordained Episcopalian minister. He was assigned to St. Elizabeth's mission on Standing Rock Indian Reservation a year after Ella's birth. Ella left St. Elizabeth's at the age of 14. She attended the All Saints High School in Sioux Falls, where she improved her English and also learned French and German. Deloria was awarded a college scholarship at Columbia University, where she studied anthropology, linguistics and ethnology, and was a classmate of Margaret Meade. After she earned her bachelors degree from Columbia University, Deloria worked for a time as an instructor at All Saints High School and also taught physical education, girls' basketball, volleyball and dancing at the Haskall Institute in Lawrence, Kansas, in 1923. She later worked as a national health education secretary for the YWCA.

Deloria later received the appointment as research specialist in Indian ethnology and linguistics in the Department of Anthropology at Columbia University and was a coauthor with Franz Boas of two works on Dakota linguistics. Deloria also worked as principal of the St. Elizabeth's Mission School in Wakpala. She was the sister of Vine Deloria Sr. and aunt of Vine Deloria Jr. She died in 1971.

❖❖❖

NAME   E, L, N

Vine Deloria Jr.

OTHER NAMES USED

Vine (Victor) Deloria Jr.

TRIBAL AFFILIATION

Yankton Dakota

PERSONAL

Born: March 26, 1933, in Martin, South Dakota

Education: B.S. from Iowa State University, Ames, 1958; M.S.Th. (master of theology) from Lutheran School of Theology, Rock Island, Illinois, 1963; J.D. (*juris doctor*—doctor of law) from the University of Colorado at Boulder, 1970

AWARDS, HONORS

DHL from Hamline University, 1979

DHL from Scholastica College, 1976

Indian Achievement Award from the Indian Council Fire, 1972

Anisfield-Wolf Award for *Custer Died for Your Sins,* 1970

National Conference of Christians and Jews Special Citation for *We Talk, You Listen: New Tribes, New Turf,* 1971

D. H. Litt from Augustana College, 1972

Indian Achievement Award, Indian Council Fire, 1972

DHL Northern Michigan University, 1991

Athabasca University Honorary Professorship, 1977

Distinguished Alumni Award from Iowa State University, 1977

Distinguished Alumni Award from the University of Colorado School of Law, 1985

PUBLICATION HIGHLIGHTS

Red Earth, White Lies: Native Americans and the Myth of Scientific Fact (Golden, Colo.: Fulcrum Publishing, 1997 [paperback]; New York: Simon and Schuster, 1995 [hardcover])

Exiled in the Land of the Free: Democracy, Indian Nations and the U.S. Constitution, Oren Lyons, John Mohawk and Vine Deloria Jr. with contributions by Daniel Inouye and Peter Matthiessen (Sante Fe: Clear Light Publishers, 1994)

God Is Red: A Native View of Religion (Golden, Colo.: Fulcrum Publishing, 1994)

Frank Waters: Man and Mystic, ed. by Vine Deloria ([Athens: Swallow Press; University of Ohio Press, 1993?])

Native American Animal Stories (foreword) (Golden, Colo.: Fulcrum Publishing, 1992)

Indian Education in America: Eight Essays by Vine Deloria Jr. (American Indian Science and Engineering Society, 1991)

Custer Died for Your Sins: An Indian Manifesto (Norman: University of Oklahoma Press, 1988)

American Indian Policy in the Twentieth Century (Norman: University of Oklahoma Press, 1985)

The Aggressions of Civilization, ed. with Sandra Cadwalader (Philadelphia: Temple University, 1984)

The Nations Within, with Clifford Lytle (New York: Pantheon Books, 1984)

A Sender of Words (Salt Lake City: The Neihardy Centennial Essays, Howe Brothers, 1984)

American Indians, American Justice, with Clifford Lytle (Austin: University of Texas Press, 1983)

The Metaphysics of Modern Existence (San Francisco: Harper & Row, 1979)

Indians of the Pacific Northwest (New York: Doubleday, 1977)

Behind the Trail of Broken Treaties: An Indian Declaration of Independence (New York: Delacourte, 1974)

The Indian Affair (New York: Friendship Press, 1974)

Of Utmost Good Faith (San Francisco: Straight Arrow Books, 1971)

Red Man in the New World Drama: A Politico-Legal Study with a Pageantry of American Indian History, by Jennings Wise, revised edition with introduction by Vine Deloria Jr. (New York: Macmillan, 1971)

We Talk, You Listen: New Tribes, New Turf (New York: Macmillan, 1970)

Custer Died for Your Sins: An Indian Manifesto (New York: Macmillan, 1969)

NARRATIVE

Born on the Pine Ridge Reservation in South Dakota, where his grandfather, father and aunt lived for many years, Deloria is a member of a family with a history of scholarship and distinction within his tribe and in the church. His father, Reverend Vine Deloria Sr. was an archdeacon in the Episcopal church and a noted clergyman, and his aunt was anthropologist and linguist Ella Deloria. He attended reservation schools as a youth and later left his home in South Dakota to serve in the Marine Corps Reserve from 1954 to 1956. After his military service he attended the Kent School in Connecticut, then went on to Iowa State University. From 1963 to 1964 Deloria served as the executive director of the National Congress of American Indians in Washington, D.C.

Deloria was the chair of the Institute for the Development of Indian Law in Golden, Colorado, from 1970 to 1976. He worked as a lecturer at Western Washington State College from 1970 to 1972, and at the University of California at Los Angeles from 1972 to 1974. In 1978, he joined the faculty of the University of Arizona at Tucson as a professor of political science. From 1979 to 1982 Deloria was the chair of the American Indian studies program at the University of Arizona, Tucson. He is currently on the faculty of the University of Colorado at Boulder in the history department.

Many of Deloria's books have become bestsellers and are some of the most popular and widely read books on Native people. He is also the author of numerous special reports on Native legislation and education and has been a contributor and editor to numerous books.

Deloria has also had numerous articles appear in a wide variety of journals and periodicals such as *Playboy, The New*

York Times Magazine, Defiance Magazine, Civil Rights Digest, Soroptimist Magazine, Forum for Contemporary History, Harvard Medical Bulletin and *American Airlines Magazine,* among others.

NAME   E, N

Frederick J. Dockstader

TRIBAL AFFILIATION

Oneida and Navajo

PERSONAL

Born: 1919 in Los Angeles, California
Education: B.A. from Arizona State College, 1940; M.A. from Arizona State College, 1941; Ph.D. from Western Reserve University, Cleveland, Ohio, 1951

PUBLICATION HIGHLIGHTS

Weaving Arts of the North American Indian, revised edition (New York: Icon Editions, 1993)

Pre-Columbian Art and Later Tribal Arts (New York: Abrams, 1968)

Indian Art in South America: Pre-Columbian and Contemporary Arts and Crafts (Greenwich, Conn.: New York Graphic Society, 1967)

Indian Art in America (Greenwich, Conn.: New York Graphic Society, 1966)

Indian Art in Middle America (Greenwich, Conn.: New York Graphic Society, 1964)

Indian Art in America: The Arts and Crafts of the North American Indian (Greenwich, Conn.: New York Graphic Society, 1962)

The American Indian in Graduate Studies (New York: Museum of the American Indian, Heye Foundation, 1956)

The Kachina and the White Man: The Influences of the White Culture on the Hopi Kachina Cult (Bloomfield Hills, Mich.: Cranbrook Institute of Science, 1954; Al-

buquerque: University of New Mexico Press, c1985 [revised and enlarged edition])

NARRATIVE

Dockstader worked as a teacher in Flagstaff, Arizona, from 1936 to 1941, and in Cranbook, Michigan, from 1942 to 1949. He became an ethnologist at the Cranbrook Institute of Sciences in 1949, and in 1952 joined the faculty of Dartmouth College, where he was also the curator of anthropology. In 1955 Dockstader assumed the role of assistant director of the Museum of the American Indian, Heye Foundation, in New York and in 1960 became the director of the Museum. In addition to his work as an educator, scholar and administrator, Dockstader is known as a visual artist and silversmith. His works have also appeared in the journal *American Indian Quarterly.*

NAME   E, F, N

Michael Dorris

OTHER NAMES USED

Michael Anthony Dorris

TRIBAL AFFILIATION

Modoc

PERSONAL

Born: January 30, 1945, in Dayton, Washington; died: April 1997
Education: B.A. in English and classics from Georgetown University, Washington, D.C., 1967; M.Phil. in Philosophy from Yale University, New Haven, Connecticut, 1971

AWARDS, HONORS

National Book Critics' Circle Award for *The Broken Cord,* 1989

Indian Achievement Award, 1985

Rockefeller Fellowship, 1985

Woodrow Wilson Fellowship, 1967 and 1980

Guggenheim Fellowship, 1978

Spaulding-Potter Program Grant recipient, 1973

National Institute of Mental Health Research Grant recipient, 1971

PUBLICATION HIGHLIGHTS

Cloud Chamber (New York: Simon and Schuster, 1997)

Sees Behind Trees (New York: Hyperion, 1996)

Guests, first edition (New York: Hyperion Books for Children, 1995)

Paper Trail: Essays (New York: Harper Collins, 1995)

A Circle of Nations: Voices and Visions of American Indians, Leslie Silko, Michael Dorris and Joy Harjo, ed. by John Gattuso (Hillsboro, Oreg.: Beyond Words Publishing, 1993)

Rooms in the House of Stone (Minneapolis: Milkweed Editions, 1993)

Working Men: Stories (New York: H. Holt, 1993)

Morning Girl (New York: Hyperion Books for Children, c1992)

The Crown of Columbus, with Louise Erdrich (New York: Harper Collins, c1991)

Route Two, Michael Dorris and Louise Erdrich (Northridge, Calif.: Lord John Press, 1990)

The Broken Cord, Michael Dorris with a foreword by Louise Erdrich (New York: Harper & Row, c1989)

A Yellow Raft in Blue Water (New York: H. Holt, c1987)

Guide to Research on North American Indians, Michael Dorris with Arlene Hirschfelder and Mary Lou Byler (Chicago: American Library Association, 1983)

Native Americans: 500 After (New York: Crowell, [1975])

Dorris's work has appeared in: *Talking Leaves: Contemporary Native American Short Stories, An Anthology,* ed. by Craig Lesley (New York: Laurel; Dell, 1991) and *Winged Words: American Indian Writers Speak,* by Laura Coltelli (Lincoln: University of Nebraska Press, 1990).

NARRATIVE

Dorris was raised in Washington, Idaho, Kentucky and Montana. He began his academic career in 1970 as an assistant professor at the University of Redlands, Redlands, California, and from that post he went on to teach at numerous colleges and universities. In 1971 Dorris taught at Franconia College in Franconia New Hampshire, and in 1972 he joined the faculty of Dartmouth College, where he was an instructor until 1976. He became an assistant professor in 1976, and in 1979 he became an associate professor of anthropology. Dorris was most recently a professor of anthropology and Native American studies at Dartmouth College and chair of the Native American studies department.

Since 1976 Dorris also served as a consultant for the National Endowment for the Humanities, and he worked as a consultant to television stations such as Los Angeles Educational Television and the Toledo Public Broadcast Center.

He had numerous articles published in journals such as American West, Ploughshares and Suntracks and was a member of the editorial board of the *American Indian Culture and Research Journal.*

Dorris was married to writer Louise Erdrich, and together they collaborated on several books through the years. In 1991 Dorris and Erdrich were featured on a public broadcasting television program hosted by Bill Moyers. In the program they discussed the book *The Broken Cord,* the novel about their adopted son who suffered from fetal alcohol syndrome.

Dorris and Erdrich lived in New Hampshire for many years with their six children. He is now deceased.

NAME   E, N
Edward P. Dozier

TRIBAL AFFILIATION
Santa Clara Pueblo

PERSONAL
Born: April 23, 1916, at the Santa Clara Pueblo, New Mexico; died May 2, 1991
Education: B.A. from the University of New Mexico, Albuquerque; M.A. from the University of New Mexico, Albuquerque; Ph.D. from the University of California at Los Angeles

PUBLICATION HIGHLIGHTS
The Pueblo Indians of North America (New York: Holt, Rinehart and Winston, 1970)
The Kalinga of Northern Luzon, Philippines (New York: Holt, Rinehart and Winston, 1967)
Hano: A Tewa Community in Arizona (New York: Holt, Rinehart and Winston, 1966)
Mountain Arbiters: The Changing Life of a Philippine Hill People (Tucson: University of Arizona Press, [1966])
"Two Examples of Linguistic Acculturation: The Yaqui of Sonora and Arizona and the Tewa of New Mexico" in *Language and Culture and Society,* ed. by Dell Hymes (New York: Harper & Row, 1964)
The Hopi-Tewa of Arizona (Berkeley: University of California Press, 1954)

NARRATIVE
Anthropologist and linguistic authority Edward P. Dozier was born and raised at the Santa Clara Pueblo in New Mexico. He served in the U.S. Air Force as a staff sergeant for four and a half years during World War II. After his military service, Dozier decided to pursue the study of anthropology with the assistance of the GI Bill of Rights. He has worked as an educator at the University of Oregon and Northwestern University and was a professor of anthropology at the University of Arizona. Dozier joined the faculty of the University of Minnesota as a professor of American Indian studies and anthropology in 1969 and was later named chair of the Indian studies department. Dozier was married with three children.

NAME   P, VA
Jimmie Durham

TRIBAL AFFILIATION
Cherokee

PERSONAL
Born: 1940 in Nevada County, Arkansas
Education: B.F.A. from the Ecole des Beaux Arts in Geneva, Switzerland

AWARDS, HONORS
Fellowship Grant for Poetry from the New York Foundation for the Arts, 1985

PUBLICATION HIGHLIGHTS
A Certain Lack of Coherence: Writings on Art and Cultural Politics (London: Kala Press, 1993); *Columbus Day: Poems, Drawings and Stories about American Indian Life and Death in the 1970s* (Minneapolis: West End Press, 1983)

Dunham's works have also appeared in anthologies: *Harper's Anthology of 20th-Century Native American Poetry,* first edition (San Francisco: Harper & Row, 1988) and *I Tell You Now: Autobiographical Essays by Native American Writers,* ed. by Brian Swann and Arnold Krupat (Lincoln: University of Nebraska Press, c1987).

NARRATIVE

Durham was founding director of the International Indian Treaty Council of the American Indian Movement and was a member of the Central Council of the American Indian Movement in the 1970s. His work has appeared in the journals *Artforum, Art Journal Ikon,* the *Minnesota Review* and *Parnassus.* Durham was the executive director of the Foundation of the Community of Artists. He is currently the editor of the newspaper *Art and Artists* and is also a sculptor and performance artist.

E

NAME   E, F, L, S
Debra Cecille Magpie Earling

OTHER NAMES USED
Debra Earling

TRIBAL AFFILIATION
Flathead Indian of the Confederated Salish and Kootenai Tribes of Montana

PERSONAL
Born: August 3, 1957, in Spokane, Washington

Education: GED Spokane, Washington; B.A. from the University of Washington, Seattle, 1986; from M.F.A. Cornell University, Ithaca, New York, 1991; Ph.D. coursework in American Literature, Cornell University, Ithaca, New York

AWARDS, HONORS
Edith K. Draham Creative Writing Award, University of Washington, 1983; Ford Foundation Doctoral Fellowship, 1985–1989

PUBLICATION HIGHLIGHTS
"The Old Marriage" in *Talking Leaves: Contemporary Native American Short Stories,* ed. by Craig Lesley (New York: Laurel, 1991); "Winter Keeps," "Summer Humming 1946, " "Montana Burial Wind," "Summer of Bees," in *Dancing on the Rim of the World,* ed. by Andrea Lerner (Tucson: Sun Tracks and the University of Arizona Press, 1990)

NARRATIVE
Debra Cecille Magpie Earling grew up in Spokane, Washington. As she recalls, her school years were painful: "My brother and I were two out of maybe four [minority students]." At the age of fifteen, Earling dropped out of high school, though she remembers one particular instructor with fondness, "I had a teacher named Mrs. Vincent who believed in me as a writer, and even though she knew I intended to leave school she continued to encourage me."

Many people have contributed to her literary development; as she explains, "Every time someone shares a heartfelt story with me I feel it is a major influence on my writing." Three people in particular who have encouraged her are friend Barry Robert Holt, her father, Virgil Atlas Earling, and mother, Florence McDougall Earling, who was a storyteller and a keeper of history. "My mother tells the stories. She holds the memories of many people."

Earling writes about women and the West, though she feels that some of her influences come from both North and South America. "N. Scott Momaday has had a profound effect on the way in which I see things. I'd have to say that the Latin American writers influence my desire to tell a good story, to set not just one hook but many. James Welch has always been inspiring, also Michael Ondaatje." The geography of her surroundings plays an important part in Earlings work: "Sometimes it seems I write better or at least more easily when I am far away from the Flathead. When I am in the middle of the old voices of the land I am often silenced by the drama of living. I am not sure that makes sense. It is enough to say it's difficult to write at home. I'm distracted."

When she is not writing, she is "gathering stories" and "listening." She is currently a visiting assistant professor in Native American studies and English at the University of Montana. Her works have also appeared in the journal *Ploughshares*.

NAME   L, P, PL, S
Ed Edmo

TRIBAL AFFILIATION
Shoshone Bannock, Nez Perce and Yakima

AWARDS, HONORS
One Act Play Festival Award for "Through Coyote's Eyes: A Visit with Ed Edmo" from the Interstate Firehouse Cultural Center, Portland, Oregon, 1984

PUBLICATION HIGHLIGHTS
There Few Words of Mine (Marvin South Dakota: *Blue Cloud Quarterly*, 1985); *Bridge of the Gods, Mountains of Fire* ([San Francisco: Friends of the Earth, 1980?]); *To You Whiteman* (Wishram, Wash.: Edmo, 1972)

Edmo's works have also appeared in the following anthologies:

Returning the Gift: Poetry and Prose from the First North American Native Writers' Festival, ed. by Joseph Bruchac with the support of the Association for the Study of American Indian Literatures (Tucson: University of Arizona, 1994)
Talking Leaves: Contemporary Native American Short Stories, An Anthology, ed. by Craig Lesley (New York: Laurel; Dell, 1991)
A Nation Within: Contemporary Native American Writing, compiled by Ralph Salisbury (Hamilton, New Zealand: Outrigger Publishers, 1983)
From the Belly of the Shark, ed. by Walter Lowenfels (New York: Vantage, 1974)

NARRATIVE
Edmo's works have also appeared in the journals *Akwesasne Notes, Blue Cloud Quarterly* and the *Greenfield Review*. He is a poet, playwright, lecturer and storyteller.

NAME   P
Susan Edwards

TRIBAL AFFILIATION
Colville

PUBLICATION HIGHLIGHTS
Edwards's works have appeared in the anthologies: *American Indian Prose and Poetry: We Wait in the Darkness,* by Gloria Levitas et al. (New York: Putnam, 1974); *Future Directions in Native American Art* (Santa Fe: The Institute of American Indian Arts, [c1973]) and *Arrow IV,* ed. by T.D. Allen ([Washington, D.C.?]: U.S. Bureau of Indian Affairs, Creative Writing Project, 1972).

NAME   F, VA
Larry Emerson

TRIBAL AFFILIATION
Navajo

PERSONAL
Born: near Shiprock, Arizona

PUBLICATION HIGHLIGHTS
Emerson's works have appeared in *Native American Renaissance,* ed. by Kenneth Lincoln (Berkeley: University of California Press, c1983) and *The Remembered Earth: An Anthology of Contemporary Native American Literature,* ed. by Geary Hobson (Albuquerque: Red Earth Press, 1979).

NARRATIVE

In addition to his short story writing, Emerson worked as a journalist, writing a syndicated column titled *Red Dawn,* which appeared in several Indian newspapers. A visual artist, he has exhibited a number of his paintings. His works have also appeared in the journal *Sun Tracks (The Remembered Earth: An Anthology of Contemporary Native American Literature,* 1979).

❖❖❖

NAME   F, L, N, P, S

Anita Endrezze

TRIBAL AFFILIATION

Yaqui

PERSONAL

Born: March 13, 1952, in Long Beach, California

Education: B.A.; M.A. in creative writing, Eastern Washington University; teaching degree

AWARDS, HONORS

Bumbershoot/Weyerhaeuser Award, Seattle Washington, 1992

PUBLICATION HIGHLIGHTS

At the Helm of Twilight (Seattle: Broken Moon Press, 1992); *Burning the Fields* (Lewiston, Idaho: Confluence Press, 1983); *The North People* (Marvin, S. Dak.: Blue Cloud Quarterly Press, 1983)

In addition to several other publications, Endrezze has works appearing in the following anthologies: *Dancing on the Rim of the World* (Tucson: University of Arizona Press, 1990); *Harper and Row's Anthology of 20th-Century Native American Poets* (San Francisco: Harper & Row, 1988); *Carriers of the Dream Wheel* (New York: Harper & Row, 1975).

NARRATIVE

Endrezze was raised in California, Oregon, Hawaii and Washington. Her geographical surroundings in the Pacific Northwest influence her writing because she is "a Yaqui living among other tribes of this mountainous, Pacific region." Writers whose works have inspired her include Neruda, Paz, Mistral, Allende and many Native authors. Of her own works *At the Helm of Twilight* and her writings cited in *Harper's Anthology of 20th-Century Native American Poetry* are what she feels are some of her principal works. A professional storyteller, poet and visual artist for many years, Endrezze has taught classes at high schools, universities and elementary schools. She has also taught at YWCAs and at Washington state's Artist in Residence Program for the city of Spokane. Her works have appeared in the journals *Ploughshares, Callaloo, Ms. Magazine* and the *Kenyon Review.*

❖❖❖

NAME   E, F, L, N, P

Heidi Ellen Erdrich

TRIBAL AFFILIATION

Turtle Mountain Ojibway

PERSONAL

Born: November 26, 1963, in Breckenridge, Minnesota

Education: B.A., Dartmouth College, 1986; M.A., Johns Hopkins University, 1989

AWARDS, HONORS

Writing Seminars Graduate Fellowship from Johns Hopkins University, 1988–1989; Academy of American Poets College Prize, 1983, 1984, 1985, 1986; Senior Fellowship in Creative Writing from Dartmouth University, 1985–1986

PUBLICATION HIGHLIGHTS

Maria Tallchief: Osage Ballerina (Washington, D.C.: Raintree Books, [1991?])

NARRATIVE

Erdrich grew up in Wahpeton, North Dakota, and is the sister of writers Louise and Lise Erdrich. Raised in a family of storytellers, she explains, "My parents tell great stories; my sisters and brothers too. ..." She left her home at the age of fourteen and attended an eastern preparatory and boarding school.

Erdrich worked as a lecturer, teaching classes and seminars in creative writing and literature at Johns Hopkins from 1989 until 1993. She currently is a multicultural admissions counselor at the College of St. Catherine in St. Paul, Minnesota. "I moved to St. Paul so I could spend more time in North Dakota, in the flat lands of the Red River Valley. But I love St. Paul too—the bleak parts, the rusty old urban ruins—I'm writing about that. I always wanted to write and teach writing, but my sisters Louise and Lise have shown me that the writing life is possible, that a woman isn't crazy to want to write. It seems like I've always known I'd be a writer, but I do remember I was in second grade when I first started thinking of myself as a writer-in-training. I still think that way at times."

Topics of her poems and prose include family, landscape, spiritual in daily life, "magic, haunting, personal mystery, parentage and lineage, mixed bloods [and] also the behavior of upper-class East Coast Americans whose culture I did field work [on] for twelve years."

Her poems, prose and short stories have appeared in the *Raven Chronicles,* the *Maryland Poetry Review, Tamaqua,* the *Inquirer and Mirror, Women of the Ivy League, Spawning the Medicine River* and *Redbook.* Erdrich was also the coeditor of *The Hopkins Guide to Baltimore* and has also edited several Dartmouth campus publications.

NAME   F, L, N
Lise Erdrich

OTHER NAMES USED
Lise McCloud

TRIBAL AFFILIATION
Turtle Mountain Chippewa

PERSONAL
Born: 1969 in Breckenridge, Minnesota
Education: B.A. in English from the University of North Dakota, Grand Forks, 1987; M.S. in health science, Mankato State University, Mankato, Minnesota, 1993

AWARDS, HONORS
Best of Class and Best of Show, North Dakota State Fair Writing Contest, 1992
Robert C. Wright Minnesota Writers Scholarship Award, 1992
Region Nine/McNight Individual Artist Grant, 1992
Finalist in the Bush Foundation Artist Fellowship, 1990
John Hove Creative Writing Fellowship, 1989

PUBLICATION HIGHLIGHTS
"Peace Turtles," story in *Sing Heavenly Muse!: Women's Poetry and Prose* (Minneapolis: [s.n.], Winter/Spring 1991)
"Pukkons," story in Tamaqua ([S.l.: s.n.], Winter/Spring 1991)
"Kookum's Journal," "Jolly Boeuf, Metis Legend" in *North Dakota Quarterly* (Grand Forks, N. Dak.: University of North Dakota, Fall 1990)

"Looking for St. Joe," story in *Special Report: Fiction* ([Knoxville, Tenn.: Whittle Communications?], February–April, 1990)

NARRATIVE

Erdrich was raised in a warm and positive family that took an active interest in their children's creative growth. "My grandfather was a writer as well as many other things (tribal chair, entrepreneur, traditional dancer, linguist, hobo, magician, naturalist, hero, etc.) which always encouraged me to keep at it. My mother taught me how to read before I was 2, and my dad is a wonderful storyteller; my sisters are writers and artists, my brothers are very great liars too!"

Erdrich writes about historical and contemporary "Indian stuff," and some of her favorite works are *100 Years of Solitude* by Gabriel Gárcia-Marquez and *Huckleberry Finn* by Mark Twain. "Never get tired of 'em. [I] read them every couple two, three years. Also historical stuff like John Tanner's narrative, etc." Some of Erdrich's other favorite writers include "Joy Harjo—astonishing, Diane Glancy, Louise Erdrich, Ray Young Bear—a genius, Jim Harrison—delightful, Linda Hogan—strong, strong writing, Roberta Hill Whiteman—amazing use of language, Carol Bly, Janis Agee, Jim Welch and Janet Campbell Hale, many more ... ." Currently Erdrich is pursuing a career as a health educator and chemical dependency counselor.

NAME   F, N, E

Louise Erdrich

OTHER NAMES USED

Heidi Louise
Milou North
Karen Louise Erdrich

TRIBAL AFFILIATION

Turtle Mountain Chippewa

PERSONAL

Born: June 7, 1954, in Little Falls, North Dakota

Education: B.A. in English from Dartmouth College, 1976; M.A. from Johns Hopkins University, Baltimore, Maryland, 1979

AWARDS, HONORS

First Prize, O. Henry Awards, 1987

National Magazine Fiction Awards, 1983 and 1987

Guggenheim Fellowship, 1985 to 1986

Publisher's Weekly's Best Books for *The Beet Queen,* 1986

National Book Critics Circle Award for Best Work of Fiction for *Love Medicine,* 1984

Virginia McCormick Scully Prize for Best Book of the Year for *Love Medicine,* 1984

National Endowment for the Arts Fellowship in Fiction, 1983

Pushcart Prize, 1983

Chicago magazine's Nelson Algren Prize for Fiction for "The World's Greatest Fisherman," 1982

PUBLICATION HIGHLIGHTS

Tales of Burning Love (New York: HarperCollins, 1996)

Grandmothers Pigeon, first edition (New York: Hyperion Books for Children, 1996)

The Blue Jay's Dance: A Birth Year (New York: HarperCollins, 1995)

The Granta Book of the Family, Peter Carey et al. ([S.l.: s.n.], 1995)

The Bingo Palace (New York: Harper Collins, c1994)

Best American Short Stories (Boston: Houghton Mifflin, 1993)

Love Medicine (New York: Holt, 1984; expanded edition, 1993)

Crown of Columbus, with Michael Dorris (New York: HarperCollins, 1991)

Route Two, Michael Dorris and Louise Erdrich (Northridge, Calif.: Lord John Press, 1990)

Baptism of Desire, poems (New York: Harper, 1989)

Tracks (New York: Harper, 1988)

The Beet Queen (Boston: G. K. Hall, 1987, c1986)

Jacklight, poems (New York: Holt, 1984)

Erdrich's works have appeared in numerous anthologies:

American Visions: Multicultural Literature for Writers, ed. by Delores La Guardia and Hans P. Guth (Mountain View, Calif.: Mayfield, 1995)

The Lightning Within: An Anthology of Contemporary American Indian Fiction, ed. by Alan Velie (Lincoln: University of Nebraska Press, 1991)

Spider Woman's Granddaughters: Traditional Tales and Contemporary Writing by Native American Women, ed. by Paula Gunn Allen (Boston: Beacon Press, 1989)

Earth Power Coming: Short Fiction in Native American Literature, ed. by Simon J. Ortiz (Tsaile, Ariz.: Navajo Community College Press, c1983)

Writing in a Nuclear Age, ed. by Kim Schley (Hanover, N.H.: University Press of New England, 1983)

NARRATIVE

Erdrich's mother is Turtle Mountain Chippewa and her father is of German descent. She grew up in the town of Wahpeton, North Dakota, and is the sister of writers Lise and Heidi Ellen Erdrich. Erdrich met her husband at Dartmouth, the late writer and anthropologist Michael Dorris, who was the chair of the Native American studies department at that time. They would later marry in 1981 after several years of literary collaboration.

Upon her graduation from Dartmouth, Erdrich returned to North Dakota as a visiting poet in the schools under the North Dakota State Arts Council Poetry in the Schools Program. Returning to the East Coast in 1978, Erdrich enrolled in the creative writing program at Johns Hopkins University in Baltimore, where she also worked as a writing instructor. At the same, time she worked for the Boston Indian Council as the communications director and editor of the journal *Circle.* After earning her masters degree in 1979, Erdrich returned to Dartmouth, where she participated in a writer-in-residence program. She has also worked in a variety of different jobs through the years: as a waitress, lifeguard, poetry instructor in the prisons and beet weeder for a time in North Dakota.

Erdrich's writings have appeared in the journals *Redbook, Ms., North American Review, American Indian Quarterly, New York Times Book Review,* the *New Yorker, Chicago,* the *Atlantic* and *Kenyon Review,* the *Georgia Review, New England Review, Vogue* and *Mother Jones,* among others.

In 1991 Erdrich and Dorris were featured on a Public Broadcasting television program hosted by Bill Moyers. In the program they discussed the book *The Broken Cord,* a novel about their adopted son who suffered from fetal alcohol syndrome. Erdrich lives in New Hampshire.

F

NAME　　　N

Ray Fadden

OTHER NAMES USED

Aren Akweks

TRIBAL AFFILIATION

Mohawk

PUBLICATION HIGHLIGHTS

Costumes of the Iroquois (Ohsweken, Ont.: Iroqcrafts, 1980)
Tales of the Iroquois (Rooseveltown, N.Y.: Akwesasne Notes, 1980)
Migration of the Iroquois (Rooseveltown, N.Y.: White Roots of Peace, 1974)
History of the Oneida Nation (Hogansburg, N.Y.: Akwesasne Mohawk Counselor Organization, n.d.)

Fadden's works have also appeared in: *New Voices from the Longhouse: An Anthology of Contemporary Iroquois Writing*, first edition, ed. by Joseph Bruchac (Greenfield Center, N.Y.: Greenfield Review Press, c1989).

NAME　　　F, N, P

Connie Fife

TRIBAL AFFILIATION

Cree

PUBLICATION HIGHLIGHTS

The Color of Resistance: A Contemporary Collection of Writing by Aboriginal Women, compiled by Connie Fife (Toronto: Sister Vision Press, 1993); *Beneath the Naked Sun: Poetry* (Vancouver: Write-On Press, 1992)

Fife's works have also appeared in: *Returning the Gift: Poetry and Prose from the First North American Native Writers' Festival*, ed. by Joseph Bruchac with the support of the Association for the Study of American Indian Literatures (Tucson: University of Arizona, 1994).

NARRATIVE

Fife's works have appeared in the journals *Fireweed: A Feminist Quarterly* and *Gatherings*.

NAME　　　E, F, P

Jack D. Forbes

TRIBAL AFFILIATION

Powhatoan and Delaware

PERSONAL

Born: January 7, 1934, in Long Beach, California
Education: A.A. from Glendale College, 1953; A.B. from the University of Southern California, 1955; M.A. from the University of Southern California, 1956; Ph.D. from the University of Southern California, 1959

AWARDS, HONORS

Guggenheim Fellowship, 1963–1964
Fulbright-Hays Award, 1981–1982

PUBLICATION HIGHLIGHTS

Only Approved Indians: Stories (Norman: University of Oklahoma, 1995)

Apache, Navajo and Spaniard, second edition (Norman: University of Oklahoma Press, 1994)

Africans and Native Americans: The Language of Race and the Evolution of Red-Black Peoples (Urbana: University of Illinois, 1993)

Columbus and Other Cannibals (New York: Autonomedia, 1991)

Black Africans and Native Americans: Color, Race and Caste in the Evolution of Red-Black Peoples (Oxford, England; New York: Blackwell, 1988)

"Colonialism and Native American Literature" in *Wicazo Sa Review* (Rapid City, S. Dak.: vol. 3, no. 2, Fall 1987)

Aztecas Del Norte: The Chicanos of Aztlan (Greenwich, Conn.: Fawcett, 1973)

Native Americans of California and Nevada, by Jack D. Forbes (Heraldsburg, Calif.: Naturegraph Publishers, 1969)

Afro-Americans in the Far West: A Handbook for Educators (San Francisco: Far West Laboratory for Educational Research and Development, 1968)

Nevada Indians Speak (Reno: University of Nevada Press, 1967)

Frontiers in American History and the Role of the Frontier Historian (Reno: Desert Research Institute, University of Nevada, 1966)

Warriors of the Colorado: The Yumas of the Quechan Nation and Their Neighbors (Norman: University of Oklahoma Press, 1965)

Forbes's works have appeared in many anthologies, among them:

Returning the Gift: Poetry and Prose from the First North American Native Writers' Festival, ed. by Joseph Bruchac with the support of the Association for the Study of American Indian Literatures (Tucson: University of Arizona, 1994)

"The Gulf War: Once Again the Drama of Human Sacrifice" in *Wicazo Sa Review,* vii (1), Spring, 60 (3) (Cheney, Washington: Indian Studies, Eastern Washington University, 1991)

Circle of Motion: Arizona Anthology of Contemporary American Indian Literature, ed. by Kathleen Mullen Sands (Tempe, Ariz.: Arizona Historical Foundation, c1990)

I Tell You Now: Autobiographical Essays by Native American Writers, ed. by Brian Swann and Arnold Krupat (Lincoln: University of Nebraska Press, c1987)

Earth Power Coming: Short Fiction in Native American Literature, ed. by Simon J. Ortiz (Tsaile, Ariz.: Navajo Community College Press, c1983)

NARRATIVE

Forbes was raised on a small farm until he reached the age of nine, when his family moved to northern Los Angeles. As a young man he enjoyed going to museums and libraries in the Los Angeles area, especially the Southwest Museum, where he was able to pursue his study of Native history with the assistance of librarian Ella Robinson and M. R. Harrington, who is part Indian and an authority on Delaware-Lenape people. Forbes was an insatiable reader as a youth and was encouraged to read by his family. While a young man he was taught Native history by his father and aunts, family members who Forbes regards as some of his most influential teachers.

In 1959 Forbes began his long career as an educator by teaching at the University of Southern California. In following years Forbes has taught history and Native American studies at institutions such as Citrus College in Azusa, California; San Fernando Valley State College, the University of Nevada at Reno; the Far West Laboratory for Educational Research and Development at Berkeley, California; and since 1969 he has been a professor of Native American studies at the University of California at Davis.

Throughout his career as an educator, Forbes has been interested in ethnic minorities and working within the area of Native affairs. These interests, coupled with his political inclinations, moved Forbes to help in the establishment of the Native American Movement and the American Indian College Committee. He was instrumental in the founding of the Coalition of Eastern Native Americans, and he has also been active in developing Native American Studies programs and institutions such as D-Q University and the Tecumseh Center at the University of California, Davis. Forbes has also worked as a journalist, editing and publishing the Powhatan newspaper *Attan-Akamik.*

Forbes moved to England in 1979 and lived there for one year, and to the Netherlands for another year. He is married and has two children.

❖❖❖

NAME   E, L, N
Lee Francis

TRIBAL AFFILIATION
Laguna Pueblo

PERSONAL
Born: May 21, 1945, in Albuquerque, New Mexico
Education: B.A. in la raza studies, San Francisco State University, 1983; M.A. in education, San Francisco State University, 1984; Ph.D. in multicultural communication, Western Institute for Social Research, Berkeley, 1991

AWARDS, HONORS
American Indian Student Council, California State University, Long Beach, October 1990
Who's Who in the East, 22nd Edition, Marquis Who's Who, Willamette, Illinois, 1988

Elected Life Member, National Psychiatric Association, Carpenteria, California, 1979
Citation for Eminent Service, Office of the Lieutenant Governor, State of New Mexico, 1967
Honor's Scholar Award, New Mexico State University—Grants, New Mexico, 1967

PUBLICATION HIGHLIGHTS
"Elder Wisdom: A Cause for Cultural Studies" in *English Studies/Cultural Studies: Institutionalizing Change,* ed. by Isaiah Samuelson (Carbondale: Southern Illinois University Press, 1993)
"This Business of Columbus" in *Columbus and Beyond: Views from Native Americans,* ed. by Randolph Jorgen (Tucson: Southwest Parts and Monuments, 1992)
"Restoring the Clans: A Traditional Approach to Retention" in *Western Institute for Social Research* (journal) (Berkeley: The Institute, 1990)
"Situational Dynamics: Revisioning Our Personal Reality" in *Magus Journal of Communication* (Albuquerque: [s.n.], July 1989)
BEST Course: A Cultural Communications Handbook (Washington, D.C.: Meta-Life Pub., 1986)
"Congressional Interest Groups—The Politics of Influence" in *Professional Staff Journal* (Washington, D.C.: s.n. (95-2), 1977)

NARRATIVE
Writer and educator Lee Francis spent the first thirteen years of his life in Cubero, New Mexico. He then lived in Albuquerque for three years and later moved to the communities of San Fidel and Grants New Mexico. Francis recalls his childhood school experiences, the advice his dominant-culture teachers gave him, urging him to learn some vocational skills, even to attend a vocational school because he was "clever with his hands." After graduating from high school, Francis chose a different path.

Francis is a member of a family of exceptional writers, which includes his sisters, Carol Lee Sanchez and Paula Gunn Allen, and great uncle, Vine Deloria Jr. Their mother, Tdu-u wetsa (Ethel Haynes Francis), has written throughout her life, though her work remains unpublished. His family has remained deeply supportive of his creativity, providing insights and serving as mentors by listening, gently critiquing and supporting his ideas. As Francis states, "writing has always been part and parcel of what we did as a family (great uncle Vine Deloria, sisters, mother)—that and politics!"

Francis is currently the director-editor of the Native American Wordcraft Apprentices and Mentors Project and will be editing the Project's writings in preparation for their later publication. He is also a member of the Core Faculty of the Western Institute for Social Research in Berkeley.

Francis enjoys reading science fiction along with the works of his sisters, Leslie Silko, John M. Gunn and uncle Vine Deloria, Jr. He is an active participant in his Indian Community, attends pow-wows, councils and advises individuals, plays folk guitar, builds bookcases and especially enjoys working with his son, teaching and being taught by him.

NAME   P
Nia B. Francisco

OTHER NAMES USED
Bertha Francisco

TRIBAL AFFILIATION
Navajo

PERSONAL
Born: February 1952 in Ft. Defiance, Arizona

Education: A.A. from Navajo Community College, 1977

AWARDS, HONORS
National Endowment for the Arts, Writer in Residence, Washington, D.C., 1976; Poets on the Road Grant, Arizona Commission on the Arts, Phoenix, Arizona, 1974, 1975; Vincent Price Writing Contest, second place, Institute of American Indian Arts, Santa Fe, 1971

PUBLICATION HIGHLIGHTS
Blue Horses for Navajo Women (Greenfield Center, N.Y.: Greenfield Review Press, 1988); *The Sacred: Ways of Knowledge, Sources of Life,* ed. by Peggy Beck (Tsaile, Arizona: Navajo Community College, 1977)

Francisco's works have also appeared in several anthologies, including:

Harper's Anthology of 20th-Century Native American Poetry, first edition, ed. by Duane Niatum (San Francisco: Harper & Row, 1988)
Native American Renaissance, by Kenneth Lincoln (Berkeley: University of California Press, c1983)
The South Corner of Time: Hopi, Navajo, Papago, Yaqui Tribal Literature, ed. by Larry Evers et al. (Tucson: University of Arizona Press, 1980)
The Remembered Earth: An Anthology of Contemporary Native American Literature, ed. by Geary Hobson (Albuquerque: Red Earth Press, 1979)
American Indian Prose and Poetry: We Wait in the Darkness, ed. by Gloria Levitas et al. (New York: Putnam, 1974)
Arrow III, ed. by T. D. Allen ([Washington, D.C.?]: U.S. Bureau of Indian Affairs, Creative Writing Project, 1971)
Southwest: A Contemporary Anthology (Norman: Red Earth Press, [n.d.])

NARRATIVE

Francisco was raised by her grandparents in Crystal, New Mexico. Francisco learned Navajo as her first language. "I didn't know how to speak nor understand the English language until I was in the seventh grade. Didn't write until tenth grade. However, I was fluent in [the] Navajo language by the time I was three years old. My paternal grandfather had blessed me with a ritual that gave me the ability to learn languages without difficulty. He placed corn pollen, which was sprinkled on a mocking bird, on my head and into my mouth when I was a toddler. A Taos woman, Soge Track, spoke her native language well and I listened to rhythm and flow of the sounds, it fascinated me and it made me want to use language—Navajo and English, to express thoughts, dreams and stories."

"My experience at Navajo Community College and at the Institute of the American Indian Arts taught me that [the] American Indian has not vanished, as U.S. history books had begun to teach me in elementary and high school and had begun to instill in me the shame of being an American Indian. These two schools rescued me and gave me back my integrity."

Close to her traditions, Francisco relies on her people and their stories for much of her inspiration. "A lot of my writing has concepts that traditional Navajo people have—thinking, sayings that were repeated to us as we grew from children to young adults. Sometimes I like to use pure imagination." When Francisco was learning to write, she did not have a mentor to learn from, instead she has drawn strength from her responsive audiences. "There was no one person who taught me and showed me the value of my talent to write—there were many people, sometimes the audiences that validated my work and gave me the inspiration to keep working. I am very grateful for everyone who has come into my path."

The geographic surroundings of Francisco's home region play a significant role in her writing. "As a poet I'm isolated from other known writers, poets, and all around me is the vast land, massive mesas, mountain ridges and canyons—in varying hues, colors and shapes. All visible to everyone, so when I write, many readers relate well to the written material. The images give meaning to the context, I believe."

Currently Francisco is writing poetry in both Navajo and English. "I write both in Navajo [and] in English in hopes that I will have another book of poems. I would like to have a strong American Indian woman's voice as seen by a woman living in America. I believe it's important—through the world many societies have shut up their women and they have a lesser chance than I have to voice their view of their world. So I keep writing in Navajo and in English."

In finding her own voice, Francisco intently listens to the voices of others. "In my beginning years I liked Simon Ortiz, Greg Snyder. More recently is Sherman Alexie's writing. Many of the American Indian writers I read to become aware of the 'voices' of American Indians within myself; these voices are reunions of those who didn't speak this foreign language—English. I know that the thinking belongs to our people."

Currently Francisco is employed by the Navajo Tribal Government's Division of Social Services at the Ft. Defiance Agency. "I am a social service representative doing social working with families who have alleged to have abused their children. The job is demanding and intense."

During her leisure time Francisco enjoys painting and listening to others tell their stories. She is also an accomplished weaver, taking the first place award in tapestry and weaving at the 1988 Navajo Nations Fair Art Show in Window Rock, Arizona.

NAME   F, P

Della Frank

TRIBAL AFFILIATION

Navajo

PERSONAL

Born: May 6, 1959, in Aneth, Utah
Education: B.S., University of New Mexico; M.A., reading specialist from University of New Mexico; M.A., education specialist from University of New Mexico; M.A., guidance and counciling from Western New Mexico University; now working on a degree in Administration from Western New Mexico University

AWARDS, HONORS

Golden Poet Award from the World of Poetry Organization, 1990; Member of Honor Society in the New Mexico chapter of the National Education Organization, 1984

PUBLICATION HIGHLIGHTS

Storm Pattern: Poems from Two Navajo Women, by Della Frank and Roberta D. Joe (Tsaile, Ariz.: Navajo Community College Press, 1993)
"In grief ...," poem in *World of Poetry* (Sacramento: World of Poetry , Summer 1990)
"Shimasani/My Grandmother," poem in American Indian Literature ([S.l.: s.n.], vol. 2, no. 2, Summer 1990)

"Shima," poem in *Blue Mesa Review* (Albuquerque: University of New Mexico, 1989)

NARRATIVE

Della Frank grew up on the deserts of southeastern Utah near Aneth. At the age of 10 Frank was put in a Bureau of Indian Affairs dormitory at the Intermountain Indian School.

Frank writes about "traditional thoughts in Navajo life. Special moments in the life of a Navajo, and conflicts in cultural expressions." Poetry is her favorite expressive medium, as she explains, "I experience a 'release' of frustrations every time I write from a personal expression." She was close to her father: "... my dad [Frank Lansing] passed away in 1985, and since then I've been writing in his memory." And she corresponds with her friend writer Janice Gould: "I write personal letters to Janice Gould right now. She has had an influence in my life in her expressions of 'pains' in life." Some of her favorite writers also include Lynn V. Andrews, Mary Summer-Rain, Janice Gould and Luci Tapahonso, Blue Cloud and Linda Hogan.

Frank now works as a home living specialist in Aneth, Utah, where she overlooks a dormitory of one hundred Native American children, thirteen staff members and the building as well. She is enrolled in a graduate-level short story writing course with the Institute of Children's Literature. Her works have also appeared in the special Native American issue of the journal *Callaloo.*

G

NAME   E, F, P, VA

Jose L. Garza

OTHER NAMES USED

Blue Heron

TRIBAL AFFILIATION

Coahuilteco (Northern Mexico) and
Lipan Apache

PERSONAL

Born: November 24, 1942, in San Antonio,
Texas

Education: Two years of college coursework
at Wayne County Community College,
Detroit Michigan, and Wayne State University, Detroit, Michigan

AWARDS, HONORS

Michigan Council For the Arts, Individual
Artist Grant, 1988

PUBLICATION HIGHLIGHTS

"For Dr. Angela Debo," "Africa and Detroit"
in *Triage* ([S.l.: s.n.], vol. 1, no. 1, 1989)

Mascaras, tachuachitos, y un monton mas
(Roseville, Mich.: Ridgeway Press, 1989)

Masks, Folk Dances and a Whole Bunch More
(Detroit: Ridgeway Press, 1989)

"Where Are Our People," "Dad, The Dancing King" in *Wooster Review* (Wooster,
Ohio: College of Wooster, Winter 1989)

"Still Waiting," "My Strength" in the *Wayne
Review* ([S.l.: s.n.], Winter 1987)

"7th Cavalry Cultyre," "The Coyote and
The Buffalo," poems in *New Rain Anthology VI* ([S.l.: s.n.], 1986)

"Momentos," poems in *Casa De Unidad
Press* (Detroit Michigan: [s.n.], 1986)

"Cricket Neighbor," poem in *Akwekon Literary Journal* vol. 1, no. 1 (Ithaca:
Akwekon Press, 1985)

"My Strength," poem in the *Native Sun* vol.
5, no. 11 (Whitehorse, Yukon: Ye Ta So
Communications Society, 1985)

NARRATIVE

Jose L. Garza grew up in Detroit, Michigan, though he spent most of his summers with his grandparents back in San
Antonio. "I enjoyed summers with my
grandparents because they were able to
pass on much of their knowledge and experience before they passed into the Spirit
World. I remember how they used ceremony and herbal medicine for a variety
of illnesses. They owned a small chicken
farm and I have many good memories of
playing in the woods and doing some of
the farm chores. I remember riding in my
grandfather's 1928 Ford Model-T into
town." As a youth in school, Garza says
his favorite activity was probably recess.
As a college student Garza was a writer
for the school newspaper. Life as a college
student was full of high and low moments.
"They were the best of times. They were
the worst of times."

Garza's writings focus on Native
American and Latino culture, spirituality
and history. "[I came to] the realization
early on to write about what I know or
have experienced. And to write from the
'gut' intuition, with detail and description.
The subject matter generally has a universal appeal and often will record events
and characters that are viewed by some as
'commonplace.' I have always supported
multi-media work and like to include my
own drawings with the written text.
Sometimes within the written text itself I

will move works around to create a visual effect." The writings of Rod Serling, host of the popular television show "Twilight Zone" impressed Garza many years ago, because his stories often reflected life's unexpected experiences. "... life is often that way, with unexpected twists, and I often view the world not as something static, but wondrous and always changing.

"I had several mentors/tormentors early in my career who were already established writers. While living in near poverty they took the time to read my work, offer comments and encourage me to continue writing. Small press publications in Detroit played a key role by publishing my work, and Casa De Unidad Cultural Arts Center allowed us to form a community writers group that met to share work and ideas and to publish two anthologies of writings by the group." Garza enjoys the works of Wendy Rose, "[who is] is my favorite writer because she combines down-to-earth stories with her spiritual realities," Carlos Castaneda and Gabriel Garcia Marquez for the surreal images he creates in his writing. "They influence my writing in terms of content but not in writing style."

One of Garza's favorite works is also his most recent story *Apple Comes Home*, which, as he describes, "terminates the 'historical period' of writing about family and history which I felt obligated to record and pass on. As involvement with the spiritual aspects of my culture increased, so my writing has changed somewhat. *Apple Comes Home* ties up the move from an urban lifestyle in Detroit to a rural environment here in Pennsylvania."

He is currently finishing up work on the story *Apple Comes Home* and next plans to collect all of his drawings and graphics and turn them into an art book. He also wants to do a series of children's books "because I think it is important to address the facts and myths that surround

Native People. ..." Garza presents workshops on writing and native history, which, he adds, "... is a constantly changing project as new material presents itself." He is now working as a social worker on a part-time basis "because I want to devote as much time to my writing as possible." When he is not writing, Garza continues to work on graphic art, drawing and also enjoys gardening, camping, traveling and writing letters.

NAME PL
Hanay Geiogamah

TRIBAL AFFILIATION
Kiowa and Delaware

PERSONAL
Born: Lawton, Oklahoma, in 1945
Education: Coursework in journalism at the University of Oklahoma

PUBLICATION HIGHLIGHTS
The American Indian Resource Guide: Compiled for the Entertainment Industry (Los Angeles: American Indian Registry for the Performing Arts, 1987)
"Grandma: A Theatre Piece for One Indian Actress" ([S.l.: s.n.], 1985)
New Native American Drama: Three Plays, introduction by Jeffrey Huntsman (Norman: University of Oklahoma Press, 1980)

NARRATIVE
Geiogamah served as the artistic director of the Native American Theater Ensemble from 1972 to 1975 and currently writes and lectures in creative writing at universities throughout the world.

NAME P, PA, V

Phil George

OTHER NAMES USED

Phillip William George

TRIBAL AFFILIATION

Nez Perce and Alaskan Tsimshian

PERSONAL

Born: 1946 in Seattle, Washington
Education: Coursework at Gonzaga University, Spokane, Washington; coursework at the Institute of American Indian Arts, Santa Fe, New Mexico; coursework at the University of California at Santa Cruz

PUBLICATION HIGHLIGHTS

George's works have appeared in numerous anthologies, including:

Dancing on the Rim of the World: An Anthology of Contemporary Northwest Native American Writing, ed. by Andrea Lerner (Tucson: Sun Tracks, University of Arizona Press, c1990)

The Native American Reader: Stories, Speeches and Poems, ed. by Jerry D. Blanche (Juneau: Denali Press, c1990)

New and Old Voices of Wah'Kon-Tah, third edition, ed. by Robert K. Dodge and Joseph B. McCullough (New York: International Publishers, c1985)

The Remembered Earth: An Anthology of Contemporary Native American Literature, ed. by Geary Hobson (Albuquerque: Red Earth Press, 1979)

The Next World (Freedom, Calif.: Crossing Press, 1978)

Voices of the Rainbow, ed. by Kenneth Rosen (New York: Viking, 1975)

Voices from Wah'Kon-Tah: Contemporary Poetry of Native Americans, first edition, ed. by Robert K. Dodge and Joseph B.

McCullough (New York: International Publishers, 1974)

The Whispering Wind: Poetry by Young American Indians, ed. by T. D. Allen (New York: Doubleday, 1972)

The American Indian Speaks, ed. by John R. Milton (Vermillion: Dakota Press, University of South Dakota, 1969)

NARRATIVE

George grew up near his maternal great-grandmother, learning the traditional ways of his people. He served in the U.S. Army, spending two years in Vietnam and also worked as an army dental technician for a year in California. A member of the Nez Perce Nation, George is a traditional Plateau dancer. He has worked as a congressional intern in the U.S. House of Representatives, and he has toured with the Native American Theater Ensemble, which is based in New York City. His poems have appeared in many anthologies, have been translated into many languages and have been read on television and radio, including over the air on Radio Free Europe. George also wrote and narrated the film *A Season of Grandmothers* for the Public Broadcasting System.

NAME J

Tim Giago

TRIBAL AFFILIATION

Lakota

PERSONAL

Born: Mid-1930s on the Pine Ridge Reservation, South Dakota
Education: San Jose Junior College, California; University of Nevada at Reno; Harvard University

AWARDS, HONORS

H. L. Mencken Award

PUBLICATION HIGHLIGHTS

Notes from Indian Country, photographs by Tome Casey ([S.l.: K. Cochran, c1984])

"What's an Indian," [audiovisual] (Vermillion, S. Dak.: Telecommunications Center, 1992 [From the television program "On-line" by South Dakota Public Television])

The American Indian and the Media (Minneapolis: National Conference on Christians and Jews Minnesota-Dakotas Region, 1991)

The Aboriginal Sin: Reflections of the Holy Rosary Indian Mission School (Red Cloud Indian School) ([San Francisco: Indian Historian Press, 1978])

NARRATIVE

Giago is the editor of the newspaper *Indian Country Today,* which was formerly published as the *Lakota Times.* He recently started up a southwestern branch of *Indian Country Today.* His weekly column, *Notes from Indian Country,* is syndicated in 340 newspapers throughout the United States. His writings have also appeared in the journals *Newsweek, Nieman Reports, The New York Times* and *Editor and Publisher.*

Upon finding out that Mencken was a pro-Nazi racist after his diaries were revealed, Giago returned the H. L. Mencken Award for his work in the news media.

NAME   E, F, N

Robert Franklin Gish

TRIBAL AFFILIATION

Cherokee Nation of Oklahoma

PERSONAL

Born: April 1, 1940, in Albuquerque, New Mexico

Education: B.A., University of New Mexico, 1962; M.A., University of New Mexico, 1967; Ph.D., University of New Mexico, 1972

AWARDS, HONORS

Albuquerque High School, Distinguished Graduate Award; University of New Mexico Erna Fergusson Distinguished Alumni Award

PUBLICATION HIGHLIGHTS

First Horses: Stories of the New West (Reno: University of Nevada Press, 1993)

William Carlos Williams: The Short Fiction (Boston: McMillan, 1989)

Songs of My Hunter Heart: A Western Kinship (Ames: Iowa State University Press, 1992)

Frontier's End: The Life and Literature of Harvey Fergusson (Lincoln: University of Nebraska Press, 1988)

Paul Horgan (Boston: Twayne, 1983)

Hamlin Garland: The Far West, Boise Western writers series (Boise: Boise State University, 1976)

Gish's works have also appeared in: *Returning the Gift: Poetry and Prose from the First North American Naive Writers' Festival,* ed. by Joseph Bruchac with the support of the Association for the Study of American Indian Literatures (Tucson: University of Arizona Press, 1994).

NARRATIVE

Robert Franklin Gish is the son of Jesse and Lillian Gish, of Choctaw and Cherokee heritage. He grew up in Albuquerque's South Valley of the Rio Grande and on Albuquerque's West Mesa and attended Albuquerque High School, which he describes as being "a wonderful comprehensive school with a full mix of Anglos, Mexican-Americans, American Indians, African Americans, and Asian Americans. It was the future before the future was known. So was the University of New Mexico." Gish was raised surrounded by the support and encouragement of his friends in Albuquerque's South Valley and at Isleta Pueblo and his family, which included his parents, sisters, brothers-in-law, uncles, aunts, elders in northeast Oklahoma and relatives in Tulsa. "New Mexico was and is the single most influential force in my life. Next to that my wife and [two] children have most shaped my life, my perspective, and my values."

Gish remembers listening to his parents' stories about their days in Oklahoma. Their stories served "as a catalyst" for his own writings, which were "strongly influenced by my reading and my own critical studies of Hamlin Garland, Paul Horgan, Harvey Fergusson and William Carlos Williams. Among American Indian authors, I was most influenced by James Welch." Some of the many writers Gish enjoys reading include N. Scott Momaday, Leslie Silko, Louise Erdrich, Gerald Vizenor, James Welch, Paul Horgan, Harvey Fergusson, John Keeble, Russell Banks, R. G. Vliet, Wallace Stegner, Thoreau, Emerson, William Carlos Williams and Wallace Stevens.

Gish's works focus on the literature, history and ethnicity of the American West. Two of his favorite works are *Songs of My Hunter Heart: A Western Kinship,* because it is a lyrical memoir of growing up in a family of hunters, and *First Horses: Stories of the New West,* because they are stories that deal with cultural and physical stigmas in the multicultural West.

He has been a contributor of articles and reviews to several magazines and newspapers and has served as a contributing editor to the *Bloomsbury Review.* He has been a member of the editorial board of Western American Literature and of the *Journal of American Indian Culture and Research.* As he explains: "Yes, I must live in the West (and I count the West as beginning with the Mississippi). The Southwest and the Rocky Mountain West are tremendously inspiring to me. Same goes for the Central Coast of California."

Gish was a professor of English language and literature at the University of Northern Iowa in the 1960s and is now the director of ethnic studies and professor of English at California Poly State University at San Luis Obispo. He is working on a collection of short stories and a novella. His works have also appeared in the journal *American Indian Quarterly.*

NAME   E, F, N, P, PL
Diane Glancy

TRIBAL AFFILIATION
Cherokee

PERSONAL
Born: March 18, 1941, in Kansas City, Missouri
Education: B.A. in English literature, University of Missouri at Columbia, 1964; M.F.A., University of Iowa, 1988

AWARDS, HONORS
Blandin Private College Foundation Grants, 1990 and 1991
Mid-Ohio Chapbook Prize for *The West Pole,* 1991
Native American Prose Award for *Claiming Breath,* 1991
The Charles and Mildred Nilon Minority Award for *Trigger Dance,* 1990
Minnesota State Arts Board Grant, 1990
National Endowment for the Arts Grant, 1990
National Endowment for the Humanities, Summer Institute, Newberry Library, Chicago, 1990
Five Civilized Tribes Museum Play Writing Prize, 1984 and 1988

Five Civilized Tribes Laureate, 1984–1986

The Capricorn Prize for *Iron Woman*

Minnesota Book Award for Poetry for *Lone Dog's Winter Count*

Diverse Visions Grant, Intermedia Arts Minnesota, 1990

Borderlands Theater Festival Award, Tucson, Arizona, 1990

Frances C. Allen Fellowship, D'Arcy McNickle Center for the History of the American Indian, Newberry Library, Chicago, 1988

Edwin Piper Fellowship, University of Iowa, 1988

Pegasus Award from the Oklahoma Federation of Writers, 1985 for *Brown Wolf Leaves the Res*

Lakes and Prairies Prize from Milkweed Chronicle, Minneapolis, for *One Age in a Dream*

PUBLICATION HIGHLIGHTS

Monkey Secret (Evanston, Ill.: Triquarterly Books, 1995)

War Cries: A Collection of Plays (Duluth, Minn.: Holy Cow! Press, 1995)

The West Pole ([Minneapolis]: Minnesota Center for the Book Arts, 1994)

Claiming Breath (Lincoln: University of Nebraska Press, 1992)

Firesticks (Norman: University of Oklahoma Press, 1992)

The Heartlands Today, Lucien Stryk et al. (Huron, Ohio: Bottom Dog Press, 1991)

Lone Dog's Winter Count (Albuquerque, New Mexico: West End, 1991)

The West Pole ([Berkeley: The And/Or Press?], 1991)

Iron Woman (Minneapolis: New Rivers Press, 1990)

Trigger Dance (Boulder: Fiction Collective Two, 1990)

Offering (Duluth, Minn.: Holy Cow! Press, 1988)

One Age in a Dream (Minneapolis: Milkweed Editions, 1986)

Brown Wolf Leaves the Res (Marvin, S. Dak.: Blue Cloud Quarterly, 1984)

Ms. Glancy's works have also appeared in several anthologies:

Returning the Gift: Poetry and Prose from the First North American Native Writers' Festival, ed. by Joseph Bruchac with the support of the Association for the Study of American Indian Literatures (Tucson: University of Arizona, 1994)

Reinventing Ourselves in the Enemy's Language, ed. by Joy Harjo (Tucson: University of Arizona Press, 1992)

Braided Lives: An Anthology of Multicultural American Writing, by the Minnesota Humanities Commission and the Minnesota Council of Teachers of English (St. Paul: The Commission, 1991)

Stillers Pond (Minneapolis: New Rivers Press, 1991)

Talking Leaves, ed. by Craig Lesley (New York: Laurel, 1991)

House on Via Gombito (Minneapolis: New Rivers Press, 1990)

Looking for Home: Women Writing about Exile (Minneapolis: Milkweed Editions, 1990)

I Tell You Now, ed. by Brian Swann and Arnold Krupat (Lincoln: University of Nebraska Press, 1987)

Songs from this Earth on Turtle's Back, ed. by Joseph Bruchac (Greenfield Center, N.Y.: Greenfield Review Press, 1983)

NARRATIVE

Writer and educator Diane Glancy was born and raised in Kansas City, Missouri. Recalling her school years, Glancy says, "I think elementary and high school was mainly a matter of endurance. I don't remember being outstanding in anything."

Glancy was employed as an artist-in-residence for the State Arts Councils of Oklahoma and Arkansas, held the position of poet-in-the-schools for Tulsa, and was the writer-in-residence at Tulsa's Heller Theater. She is now an assistant professor at Macalester College, St. Paul, Minnesota, where she teaches Native American literature, creative writing and scriptwriting. She enjoys teaching, but admits that she's "mainly a writer."

In her work, Glancy writes primarily about her Native American heritage. "I also like historical voices [and] the impact of the ordinary on the imagination." Her grandmother's life and thoughts profoundly touched Glancy, moving her to write "because of the words she never got to say."

Glancy's poetry has appeared in dozens of periodicals and journals, among them the *Kansas Quarterly, Callaloo, New Letters, Wicazo Sa Review, Sulfur, the North Dakota Quarterly, Ironwood* and the *Mississippi Review.* Glancy is particularly pleased with three of her works: *Claiming Breath,* a collection of essays, which won the Native American Prose Award; *Lone Dog's Winter Count,* winner of the Minnesota book award for poetry, and *Trigger Dance,* a Charles Nilon Fiction Award recipient.

Glancy is now working on a long-term project titled *Pushing the Bear,* which is about the 1838–1839 Trail of Tears, and she has finished her second manuscript of nonfiction and is starting on her third. "I want to do more poetry also. I'm always at work writing."

NAME　　　F, P
Richard Glazer-Danay

OTHER NAMES USED
Brant Glazer-Danay

TRIBAL AFFILIATION
Mohawk of Kahnawake, Canada

PERSONAL
Born: April 21, 1973, in Chico, California
Education: Corona High School, Corona California, 1991; coursework at Riverside Community College, Riverside, California, 1991–1993

PUBLICATION HIGHLIGHTS
"A King of Wroldan," "Pool Fish" and "Ode to Matt Mack" in *Mosaic: A Journal for the Interdisciplinary Study of Literature,* twenty-eighth edition ([Winnipeg: University of Manitoba?]); "The Visitors" in *The Golden Treasury of Great Poets* (Sacramento: World of Poetry Press, 1989); "Pool Fish" in *Great American Poetry Anthology,* ed. by John Cambell. (Sacramento: World Poetry Press, 1988)

NARRATIVE
Richard Glazer-Danay spent the first seven years of his life in Chico, California and lived in Green Bay, Wisconsin from 1980 to 1985. He then moved back to Corona, California, where he now lives and works as a writer. Formerly writing under the name Brant Glazer-Danay, he writes poems and short stories about death and rebirth, the dark sides of love, suicide as salvation and good and evil. He enjoys reading the works of writers Michael Moorcock, Arthur Rimbaud, Edgar Allen Poe and Kahil Gibran.

NAME　　　P, SC
Mary Goose

TRIBAL AFFILIATION
Mesquakie and Chippewa

PERSONAL
Born: July 17, 1955, in Des Moines, Iowa
Education: B.A. in anthropology from Iowa

State University, Ames, Iowa, 1980; B.S. in speech communications, specializing in film and television, from Iowa State University, Ames Iowa, 1985

PUBLICATION HIGHLIGHTS

"Insight," "Cornfield Myth," "Last Night in Sisseton, S.D." and others, poems in *Songs from This Earth on Turtle's Back,* first edition, ed. by Joseph Bruchac (Greenfield Center, N.Y.: Greenfield Review Press, 1983); "Not About Snails," "Of Scavengers and Survivors in Like," "Interlude," poems in *The Clouds Threw This Light* (Santa Fe: Institute of American Indian Arts Press, 1983)

Goose's works have also appeared in *Returning the Gift: Poetry and Prose from the First North American Native Writers' Festival,* ed. by Joseph Bruchac with the support of the Association for the Study of American Indian Literatures (Tucson: University of Arizona, 1994).

NARRATIVE

Mary Goose spent her early years on the Mesquakie settlement in Tama Iowa. Her family moved back to Des Moines when she was in the third grade. Her early school experiences were marked by struggles with her teachers, who resisted her eagerness to learn about larger issues and more difficult, broader subjects. As a child in elementary school, Goose was discouraged from reading selected books in her school library because, according to her teachers, her test scores revealed that she was not capable of reading materials at such a level, and the books were not by authors that she was assigned to read. In response, her mother promptly went to the nearest public library and procured a library card for her daughter. Mary was soon reading the books that her teachers had discouraged her from exploring.

Goose is interested in filmmaking, science fiction and is an avid follower of the *Star Trek* film series. She finds a source of inspiration in the stories, adding that "... every time I feel like I can't do what I want, I watch an episode of *Star Trek,* especially the older episodes of the original shows."

In her college years, Goose found another source of inspiration and support in the form of two teachers: David Gradwohl, an anthropology professor, and Gretchen Bataille, and an English instructor who introduced Goose to other Native writers and pushed her in the direction of creative writing and native literature. Goose's writing career has also been assisted in part by her second cousin, writer Ray Youngbear, who has provided her with encouragement and practical working advice. Goose enjoys the work of authors Ray Bradbury, Frank Herbert, Ernest Hemingway and Arthur C. Clarke. She is writing poems and has one story that she has made into a screenplay. "This may sound funny or strange, but my long-term project is myself. If I can find out all that is in my mind and what I can do, I will have accomplished something." Her poems have also appeared in the *North Dakota Quarterly.*

NAME   F, M, N, P, VA

Roxy Gordon

TRIBAL AFFILIATION

Choctaw; adopted Assiniboine

PERSONAL

Born: March 7, Ballinger, Texas
Education: University of Texas at Austin

PUBLICATION HIGHLIGHTS

Gods and Indians (Dallas: Wowapi, 1989)

West Texas Mid-Century (Dallas: Wowapi, 1988)

At Play in the Lord's Fields, first edition ([Big Timber, Mont.: Seven Buffaloes Press], 1986)

Unfinished Business (Dallas: Wowapi Press, 1985)

Breeds (Austin: Place of Herons Press, 1984)

Some Things I Did (Austin: Encinco Press, 1971)

Gordon's works have also appeared in: *Returning the Gift: Poetry and Prose from the First North American Native Writers' Festival,* ed. by Joseph Bruchac with the support of the Association for the Study of American Indian Literatures (Tucson: University of Arizona, 1994).

NARRATIVE

Writer and performer Roxy Gordon cites the "rhythms of a Northern Plains Reservation" as a major influence on his life and writing. He spent several memorable years on the Fort Belknap Reservation in Montana, and in July of 1991 he was adopted by the John and Minerva Allen family (also of the Fort Belknap Reservation) at the Assiniboine Sundance. His new name after the adoption became Toe Ga Juke Juke Gan Hok Sheena, or First Coyote Boy. To this day, his association with the people of the reservation inspires him and gives direction to his creativity.

Gordon began writing seriously at the age of 17, because he felt that he had little choice in the matter; it was just "something he was compelled to do." Surprising his teacher and friends, Gordon won a state-sponsored writing contest while he was a senior in high school in West Texas, and through this early recognition gained confidence in his writing ability. In early 1969 Gordon met Richard Brautigan and from him learned about the life of a working writer and the balance that must exist between living and writing. This proved to be a valuable lesson, for Gordon has many interests. Outside of writing, he is an active musician who plays regularly at festivals and college events, as well as being a successful visual artist who illustrates books and has had a number of shows.

Raised in West Texas, Gordon spent much time as a young child listening to stories. Gordon's father (who is a storyteller) and his grandmother both helped to encourage his interest in books and reading. This interest developed as a young man, and some of his early favorite writers included William Faulkner for his choice of words, Jack Kerouac for his approach to writing, Jack Frost and the beatnik poets. His taste in music is revealed in his admiration for Hank Williams and Chuck Berry. R.A. Lafferty's "OKLA HANNALI" had also inspired his writing as have the works of Peter Matthiessen. When Gordon has time to read, his preferences include history and Indian and Western Americana. He now lives in the Dallas–Fort Worth area and finds that the close proximity of Indian people and events within the urban environment provides inspiration and reinforcement in his life and writing. He also spends as much time as possible at his rural home outside the metropolitan area.

Of writing Gordon says it's "something I've had to work out in my own mind and emotion with influences coming, naturally, from all direction." He has already published six books and has had approximately two hundred poems, short stories, articles and essays published. He has coauthored two plays with the Oklahoma Choctaw writer LeAnne Howe. He has also released three albums and has had several record pieces included in the National Public Radio series, "Running on the Edge of the Rainbow."

NAME E, F, L, M, N, P
Janice M. Gould

OTHER NAMES USED
Misha Gallagher

TRIBAL AFFILIATION
Maidu and Konkow

PERSONAL
Born: April 1, 1949, in San Diego, California

Education: Graduated from Berkeley High School, 1967; B.A. in linguistics from the University of California at Berkeley, 1983; M.A. in English, University of California at Berkeley, 1987; Ph.D. candidate in English, University of New Mexico at Albuquerque, 1996

PUBLICATION HIGHLIGHTS
Earthquake Weather (Tucson: University of Arizona Press, 1995)

"Companion," poem in *The Berkeley Poetry Review* (Berkeley: University of California at Berkeley, issue 25, 1991–1992)

"Foster Family," poem in *An Intimate Wilderness: Lesbian Writers on Sexuality,* ed. by Judith Barrington (Portland, Oreg.: Eighth Mountain Press, 1991)

Beneath My Heart, poems (Ithaca: Firebrand Books, 1990)

"We Exit," poem in *Making Face, Making Soul (Haciendo Caras: Creative and Critical Perspectives by Women of Color),* ed. by Gloria Anzaldua (San Francisco: Aunt Lute Foundation Books, 1990)

Gould's works have also appeared in the following anthologies: "Stories Don't Have Endings," short story in *Spider Woman's Granddaughters: Traditional Tales and Contemporary Writing by Native American Women,* ed. by Paula Gunn Allen (Boston: Beacon Press, 1989); *Living the Spirit: A Gay American Indian Anthology,* coordi-

nating editor Will Roscoe (New York: St. Martins Press, 1988) and *A Gathering of Spirit: A Collection by North American Indian Women,* ed. by Beth Brant (Ithaca: Firebrand Books, 1988, c1984).

NARRATIVE
Janice M. Gould spent her first nine years in San Diego, California. Between the ages of 10 and 18 she lived in Berkeley, California. "I grew up after I left home, living in Oregon, Washington and Colorado. I've lived most of my life, though, in Berkeley." Gould's high school years were difficult. "I hated junior high and high school. I almost flunked out, and I nearly dropped out in my senior year in high school. My home life was violent and disruptive. I was an angry and unhappy person. Because school was hard for me, I never thought I'd go to college; but as I grew up and grew older I began to heal from my abusive family. I realized I had the energy, interest and even the intelligence to make it through college. I graduated with high honors and distinction in scholarship from Berkeley (U.C.) in 1983. I went on to get a masters degree, and I'm currently completing my Ph.D."

"My family, because it's so apparently normal yet so inherently crazy, has had the most impact on my life and work as a writer." Of the death of her mother in 1986, Gould states that it "affected me profoundly, in the wake of her death I learned many secrets about my family. Much earlier, leaving home and living and working in other places (Oregon, Washington, Colorado, Alaska) was useful for me as a writer." Gould was fortunate to have an instructor who served as her mentor early in her writing career. "... [A] teacher named Edith Jenkins offered me much support when I first started writing. She encouraged me to publish, do public readings of my work and to read poetry that would get me writing."

Gould writes about "my past, people I've known, places I've lived, my family, Indianness (i.e., mixed blood) queerness, about what and whom I've loved, about what I've hated." She enjoys reading the works of many, many authors. "I like to read works by Joy Harjo, Lee Young Li, Gary Soto, Carolyn Forche, Robert Duncap, Robert Hass, Margaret Gibson and poets in translation: Milosz Zagajewski, Transtromer, Kaplirski, Akmatova, Neruda, Parra, Garcia-Lorea, Vallejos, Roque Dalton, Claribel Alegria. In terms of novelists: Kingsolver, Ishiguro, Margaret Drabble, Woold, Isabel Allende, Erdrich, James Joyce. I read widely and a lot."

She is currently working on an oral traditions and literacy project. " I am interested in oral traditions. I would like to understand more about the transition in cultures and in individuals from orality to literacy. I think this work has applications particularly for American Indian students who've struggled with writing, especially analytical writing. I see literacy as a tool of colonization but also a hope in resisting that colonization."

Gould is now a Ph.D. candidate in English at the University of New Mexico. Living in New Mexico, the Southwest has also been beneficial to her writing career. "I've been able to establish myself as a writer here in the Southwest. That might've happened in California too, but I think moving to New Mexico allowed me to open myself more."

When she is not writing, Gould practices her music, works on her studies ("I have to read and write a lot for academic publication"), works in her yard and takes care of her house and her eighteen cats. Her works have also appeared in the journals *Ariel, Callaloo* and *Frontiers.*

NAME   E, N, V
Rayna Green

TRIBAL AFFILIATION
Cherokee

PERSONAL
Born: July 18, 1942, in Dallas, Texas
Education: B.A. from Southern Methodist University, Dallas, Texas, 1963; M.A. from Southern Methodist University, Dallas, Texas, 1966; Ph.D. in folklore and American studies from Indiana University at Bloomington, 1973

AWARDS, HONORS
Fellows of the National Research Council, 1982; Smithsonian Fellow, 1970

PUBLICATION HIGHLIGHTS
American Indian Sacred Objects: Skeletal Remains, Repatriation and Reburial: A Resource Guide, 1992 updated edition (Washington, D.C.: Smithsonian Institution, 1992)

Women in American Indian Society (New York: Chelsea House, 1992)

Pissing in the Snow and Other Ozark Folktales, edited by Vance Randolph, Rayna Green and Frank A. Hoffmann (Urbana: University of Illinois Press, 1986)

That's What She Said: Contemporary Poetry and Fiction by Native American Women, ed. by Rayna Green (Bloomington: Indiana University Press, 1984)

An Annotated Bibliography on Native American Traditional Science, Medicine and Technology (Metuchen, N.J.: Scarecrow, 1983)

Native American Women: A Contextual Bibliography (Bloomington: Indiana University Press, 1983)

Indian SIA: The Social Impact Assessment of Rapid Resource Development on Native Peoples (Ann Arbor: School of Natural Resources, University of Michigan, 1982)

Energy Resource Development on Indian Lands: A Report on the Northern Plains (Washington, D.C.: American Association for the Advancement of Science, 1978)

American Indian Mathematics Education: A Report (Washington, D.C.: American Association for the Advancement of Science, 1977)

Talking Leaves: Contemporary Native American Short Stories, ed. by Craig Lesley (New York: Laurel; Dell, 1991)

Bridges of Power: Women's Multicultural Alliances, ed. by Albrecht and Brewer ([Philadelphia]: New Society Publishers, c1990)

Time and Temperature: A Centennial Retrospective, ed. by Charles Camp (Washington, D.C.: American Folklore Society, 1989)

Green's works have appeared in numerous anthologies, such as:

The Sacred Hoop: Recovering the Feminine in American Indian Traditions, by Paula Gunn Allen (Boston: Beacon, 1986)

Sisterhood Is Global, ed. by Robin Morgan (New York: Doubleday, 1984)

Handbook of American Folkore, ed. by Richard M. Dorson et al. (Bloomington: Indiana University Press, 1983)

Handicrafts of the Southern Highlands, ed. by Allan Eaton (New York: Dover, 1972)

NARRATIVE

A former resident of Texas and Oklahoma, Green now lives in the Washington, D.C., area where she is the director of the American Indian Program at the National Museum of American History at the Smithsonian Institution. Prior to her current position Green was an assistant professor of English and folklore, first at the University of Arkansas at Fayetteville, and later at the University of Massachusetts in Amherst. In 1975 she became the folklorist and program coordinator of Festival of American Folklore at the Smithsonian Institution. From 1976 to 1980

Green was the project director for the American Association for the Advancement of Science's project on Native American Science. From 1976 to 1980 she was an associate professor of Native American studies at Dartmouth College, in Hanover, New Hampshire, and while there she was the acting director of the American Indian Program.

A prolific writer of works on folklore, anthropology, Native American traditional science, women and ethics, Green's writings have appeared in numerous anthologies and popular and academic journals such as *Science, Ms., Folklore Forum, American Indian Quarterly, Southern Folklore Quarterly, Corona, the Massachusetts Review, American Art Magazine* and the *Northeast Indian Quarterly.* Green is also a contributing editor to the journals *Corona* and *Sweetgrass.*

Green has also worked in the fields of television and film as a consultant and advisor in numerous projects since 1974. Her most recent projects include work in script development and as an advisor for a thirteen-part radio series on the 1992 observance of Columbus's voyage to America produced by Radio Smithsonian/Native American Public Broadcasting Corporation, and she was also a member of the advisory board for script development for the Children's Television Workshop titled "Sesame Street Discovers America" in 1991.

Green has been a member of the board of directors of Ms. Foundation for Women and of the Indian Law Resource Center. Since 1985 she has been the president of the American Folklore Society.

NAME   F, J, SC
Richard Green

OTHER NAMES USED
Richard G. Green

TRIBAL AFFILIATION

Osweken Kaniengeheiga (Mohawk)

PERSONAL

Born: March 21, 1940, at the Six Nations Indian Reserve, Ontario, Canada
Education: High school graduate, 1958

AWARDS, HONORS

Journeyman Award for High School Journalism, Diablo High School, Concord, California, 1958
Awarded by the *New York Times* for high school journalism, presented by St. Bonaventure University, 1954

PUBLICATION HIGHLIGHTS

The Raspberry Chronicle," short story in *Nativebeat* ([S.l.: s.n.], vol. 1, no. 11, 1991)
"Everett's Visit," "Reunion," short stories in *Turtle Quarterly* (Niagara Falls, N.Y.: Native American Center for the Living Arts, vol. 3, no. 3, 1990)
"Jewel's Choice," short story in *Turtle Quarterly* (Niagara Falls, N.Y.: Native American Center for the Living Arts, vol. 3, no. 2, 1989)
"Revelation," short story in *Turtle Quarterly* (Niagara Falls, N.Y.: Native American Center for the Living Arts, vol. 3, no. 1, 1989)
"The Last Raven," short story in *Canadian Fiction Magazine* (Vancouver, B.C.: s.n., no. 60, 1987)

Green's works have also appeared in: *Returning the Gift: Poetry and Prose from the First North American Native Writers' Festival,* ed. by Joseph Bruchac with the support of the Association for the Study of American Indian Literatures (Tucson: University of Arizona, 1994).

NARRATIVE

Richard Green was raised on the Six Nations Indian Reserve and in Niagara Falls, New York. He now lives back on Six Nations, which Green describes as a "sacred area and a very special place." Deeply moved by the political turmoil that has occurred during his lifetime, Green enumerates several influential events in his life: the Alcatraz Island occupation, the Wounded Knee occupation and the Bureau of Indian Affairs takeover in Washington, D.C.

Now busy teaching, speaking and writing in a variety of formats, from short stories to scripts, Green believes that "as a Native people we have to know how to write correctly before we can tell our true histories and stories." He is currently a freelance writer and a writer-in-residence at the Missassaugas of New Credit First Nation Library, and he is also a columnist and feature writer for the newspaper the *Branford Expositor,* which has a daily circulation of thirty-six thousand.

In his written and graphic work as a cartoonist, Green addresses many issues that appear in contemporary Native life in North America, the Mohawk people and urban Indians. "My short stories reflect contemporary Indian life in a literary fashion which I think is important." Green has also been the editor of the journal *Indian Voice Magazine,* and his short stories have appeared in several periodicals and journals such as *Turtle Quarterly* and *Indian Voice Magazine.*

He is now finishing a collection of short stories that have been individually published in American and Canadian anthologies and in the Indian media. He is also working on a feature film, one television series pilot movie, a television documentary and a thirty-minute video. Green enjoys reading the works of authors John Updike, George Plimpton and Joyce Carol Oates, and when he is not writing, he spends his spare time working on graphics, cartooning and listening to jazz.

NAME   E, N
Don Grinde

OTHER NAMES USED
Donald Andrew Grinde Jr.

TRIBAL AFFILIATION
Yamasee

PERSONAL
Born: 1946 in Savannah, Georgia
Education: B.A. in history from Georgia Southern College; M.S. in history from the University of Delaware; Ph.D. in history, *magna cum laude,* from the University of Delaware in 1973

PUBLICATION HIGHLIGHTS
Ecocide of Native America: Environmental Destruction of Indian Lands and Peoples (Santa Fe: Clear Light, 1994); *Exemplar of Liberty: Native America and the Evolution of Democracy,* by Donald Grinde, Bruce E. Johansen (Los Angeles: American Indian Studies Center, University of California at Los Angeles, 1991); *The Iroquois and the Founding of the American Nation* ([San Francisco]: Indian Historian Press, 1977)

NARRATIVE
Grinde is on the faculty at the University of California at San Luis Obispo. His areas of specialization include American history, American Indians, economics and archives. He was an assistant professor of history and museology at State University of New York at Buffalo from 1973 to 1977. His works have also appeared in the journals the *Indian Historian, Journal of Erie Studies, Western Pennsylvania Historical Magazine* and *Pennsylvania History.*

H

NAME   E, P, S
Regina Hadley-Lynch

TRIBAL AFFILIATION
Navajo

PERSONAL
Born: September 17, 1946, in Chinle, Arizona,

Education: St. Michael's High School, St. Michael's, Arizona; Arizona State University, Tempe; University of New Mexico, Albuquerque; Navajo Community College, Tsaile, Arizona; Prescott College, Prescott, Arizona

PUBLICATION HIGHLIGHTS
To Be a Navajo, poems, (Chinle, Ariz.: Navajo Curriculum Center, Rough Rock A Demonstration School, 1987)

Native Foods and Edible Wild Plants (Cortez, Colo.: Mesa Verde Press, 1986)

Saad Ahaah Sinil: Dual Language, a Navajo-English Dictionary (Albuquerque: Mirage Printing, 1986)

History of Navajo Clans (Chinle, Ariz.: Navajo Curriculum Center, Rough Rock Demonstration School, 1986)

NARRATIVE
Regina Hadley-Lynch was raised in Kitsillie, Arizona, on Black Mesa, in the center of the Navajo Reservation. She was born of the Kin yaa'aanii (Towering House People) clan, and her upbringing instilled in her the traditional Navajo values of hard work and harmonious relationships with others and with the land. Hadley-Lynch was employed as a social worker.

A mother and grandmother, Hadley-Lynch imparts her values to others as a writer and editor of Navajo books. She has authored, coauthored and edited many bilingual texts on subjects such as Navajo history, Navajo mythology and short stories for kindergarten through high school students. "There is a need for bi-lingual/bi-cultural Navajo material. [There is a] need in our school and [I] find that so much can be done, but hardly anyone is doing any writing."

She has also written a Navajo dictionary, has recorded a version of the Navajo Blessingway, Hozhooji Hane, and has written a history of the Navajo clans. She was initially encouraged to write by author Luci Tapahonso and Teresa McCarty, and later by the enthusiastic reception her early writing efforts elicited from her audience.

Currently working as a curriculum writer, Hadley-Lynch is developing curriculum materials for her school. "It is an on-going project year-round (long term), the grades are from K through 12." She also travels widely, helping teachers to incorporate Native American literature into their curriculum and sharing her ideas on bilingual and bicultural education. She has also coauthored several other publications for the Rough Rock Demonstration School (formerly Navajo Curriculum Center) in Rough Rock from 1980 to 1987.

❖❖❖

NAME   F, L, N, M, P, PA, PL, S, VA
Raven Hail

TRIBAL AFFILIATION
Cherokee

PERSONAL

Born: January 27, 1921, in Dewey, Oklahoma
Education: Oklahoma State University,
Stillwater; Southern Methodist University,
Dallas, Texas

PUBLICATION HIGHLIGHTS

"Cherokee Wisdom: Balance the Earth,"
article in *Arizona Women's Voice* (Phoenix:
[s.n.], November 1988)

*The Pleiades Stones: A Journey into the Un-
known by Way of a Magic Crystal and the
Mysterious Circle of Stones* (Scottsdale,
Ariz.: Raven Hail Books, 1988)

*The Raven Speaks: Cherokee Indian Lore in
Cherokee and English* (Scottsdale, Ariz.: R.
Hail Books, 1987)

*Windsong, Texas Cherokee Princess: The Ad-
ventures of Rebecca Bowles on the Texas
Frontier* (Scottsdale, Ariz.: R. Hail Books,
1986)

"Where the Dog Ran," story in *Odyssey*
([Brattleboro, Vt.?: Experiment Press],
vol. 6, no. 8 August 1984)

"Danaga Echodiyi," "Legend of the Chero-
kee Rose," "Ritual to Insure Long Life,"
"Cherokee Invocation," "The Tiger" in *The
Remembered Earth,* ed. by Geary Hobson
(Albuquerque: Red Earth Press, 1979)

"Pick a Pawpaw," article the *Cherokee Advocate* (Tahlequah, Okla.: Cherokee Nation
Oklahoma, Nov. 1977)

The Magic Word (Marvin, S. Dak.: Blue
Cloud Abbey, 1971?)

*The Raven and the Redbird: Sam Houston and
His Cherokee Wife* (Dallas: R. Hail, 1965)

Hail's works have also appeared in: *Re-
turning the Gift: Poetry and Prose from the
First North American Native Writers' Festi-
val,* ed. by Joseph Bruchac with the sup-
port of the Association for the Study of
American Indian Literatures (Tucson:
University of Arizona, 1994) and *Neon
Pow-Wow: New Native American Voices of
the Southwest,* first edition, ed. by Anna Lee
Walters (Flagstaff: Northland, [1993]).

NARRATIVE

Poet, storyteller, musician and herbalist,
Raven Hail was born on an oil lease north
of Dewey, Oklahoma, and lived on her
mother's Cherokee land allotment near
Welch, Oklahoma, as a child, where, while
still a preschooler, she was taught to read
by her mother. She later attended Okla-
homa State University and Southern
Methodist University and lived in Dallas
until her marriage. Her articles and po-
ems have appeared numerous publica-
tions, including *Callaloo, the Cherokee
Advocate,* the *Cherokee Nation News,
Nimrod, Cimarron Review, Translation,
The State, Quetzal, Indian Voice,* the *Blue
Cloud Quarterly, Daybreak,* the *Wayside
Quarterly,* the *Herb Quarterly* and *Bestways
Magazine.* From 1968 to 1972 she edited
a monthly newsletter *The Raven Speaks,
A Journal of Cherokee Culture.*

Hail writes about Native American
issues and subjects, particularly Cherokee
Indian. "When I was in Texas I was interested in Texas subjects. When I retired, I
moved to Arizona, and now I like to write
about this area. I feel that writers should
write about what they know about." Writers she enjoys include Edgar Allen Poe,
Vine Deloria Jr., Mary Austin's translation of *Neither Spirit or Bird* and the works
of Cherokee writers.

Hail is working on a forthcoming
book titled *The Raven's Tales* to be published by Snowbird Publishing. She will
have a prose piece titled "The Sun Goddess" and a legend titled "Double Trouble"
in a Cherokee anthology. She is also writing short articles on the Cherokee religion
and the Goddess, and is contemplating a
book on the Cherokee religion. Hail is
actively studying herbs and wild plants,
and does basketry and beadwork, plays the
guitar and "studies the magic crystal." She
is now retired.

NAME   E, N
Duane K. Hale

TRIBAL AFFILIATION
Mixed-Blood Creek

PUBLICATION HIGHLIGHTS
Researching and Writing Tribal Histories (Grand Rapids: Michigan Indian Press, 1991)
The Chickasaw (New York: Chelsea House, 1990)
Peace Makers on the Frontier: A History of the Western Oklahoma Delaware (Anadarko, Okla.: Delaware Tribal Press, 1987)
Turtle Tales: Oral Traditions of the Delaware Tribe of Western Oklahoma (Anadarko, Okla.: Delaware Tribe of Western Oklahoma Press, 1984)

NAME   F, N
Janet Campbell Hale

TRIBAL AFFILIATION
Coeur d'Alene

PERSONAL
Born: January 11, 1946, in Riverside, California
Education: B.A. from the University of California at Berkeley, 1974; M.A. from the University of California at Davis, 1984

AWARDS, HONORS
First Prize in the Vincent Price Poetry Competition, 1963; New York Poetry Day Awards, 1964

PUBLICATION HIGHLIGHTS
The Owl's Song (New York: Doubleday; Bantam, 1976, 1995)

Bloodlines: Odyssey of a Native Daughter (New York: Random House, 1993, 1994)
The Jailing of Cecelia Capture (New York: Random House; Albuquerque: University of New Mexico Press, 1985, 1988)
Custer Lives in Humboldt County (Greenfield Center, N.Y.: Greenfield Review Press, 1977)

Hale's works have also appeared in several anthologies, including:

American Indian Literatures: An Introduction, Bibliographic Review and Selected Bibliography, by A. LaVonne Brown Ruoff (New York: Modern Language Association, 1990)
Dancing on the Rim of the World: An Anthology of Contemporary Northwest Native American Writing, ed. by Andrea Lerner (Tucson: Sun Tracks; University of Arizona Press, 1990)
American Indian Novelists: An Annotated Critical Bibliography, by Tom Colonnese and Louis Owens (New York: Garland, 1985)
Native American Literature, by Andrew Wiget (Boston: Twayne, 1985)
New and Old Voices of Wah'Kon-Tah, ed. by Robert K. Dodge and Joseph B. McCulugh (New York: International Publishers, 1985)
Voices of the Rainbow, ed. by Kenneth Rosen (New York: Viking, 1975)

NARRATIVE
Janet Campbell Hale was raised in the Pacific Northwest. Her tribal affiliation is Coeur d'Alene, though she is also part Kootenai (on her mother's side). "I was born on the Coeur d'Alene Reservation in northern Idaho. When I was ten my family moved to Wapato Washington on the Yakima Reservation. I disliked school and did poorly in it. I didn't attend school at all the year I was supposed to have been in the ninth grade, just began the next year in the tenth grade. I worked as a waitress, I

picked cherries, apricots, peaches, stripped hops. I painted, wrote poetry, read serious books. In 1963, with a tenth-grade education, twenty dollars in my pocket, and a youthful optimism I now find amazing, I went to San Francisco to seek my fortune. Times were hard for a long, long time. In 1968 without ever going any further in high school, I took a City College of San Francisco's entrance exam, passed and began my college career. I had a three-year-old son by this time and worked at a variety of odd jobs. The following year I transferred to the Berkeley campus. I earned my undergraduate degree in rhetoric, did graduate work in journalism" (*Voices of the Rainbow,* 1975).

Hale worked as an editor trainee for Harcourt Brace Jovanovich in 1972 and then worked as an instructor of reading and composition for one year in the Department of Native American Studies at the University of California at Berkeley. In the course of her subsequent academic career, Hale has taught language and literature courses at the University of California's Berkeley and Davis campuses, the University of Oregon, the Centrum Foundation in Port Townsend, Washington, and at Lummi Community College and Western Washington University, both in Bellingham, Washington. She has lived in New York City and is now a visiting distinguished writer at Eastern Washington University, Cheney, Washington.

An early mentor in her career was writer Toni Morrison, who was supportive of her early work. She enjoys reading the works of writers Toni Morrison, Joyce Carol Oates, James Welch, Louise Erdrich, Wallace Stegner, James Baldwin, D. H. Lawrence and Gustav Flaubert. *The Jailing of Cecilia Capture* was nominated for six literary awards, including the Pulitzer Prize. She is married and has two children.

NAME   N, M, P
Joy Harjo

TRIBAL AFFILIATION
Muscogee (Creek)

PERSONAL
Born: May 9, 1951, in Tulsa, Oklahoma
Education: High school diploma from the Institute of American Indian Arts, Santa Fe, New Mexico, 1968; B.A. from the University of New Mexico, 1976; M.F.A. from the University of Iowa, Writers Workshop, 1978; completed program of study at the Anthropology Film Center, Santa Fe, New Mexico

AWARDS, HONORS
William Carlos Williams Award, 1991; Poetry Society of America for Best Book of Poetry, 1990

PUBLICATION HIGHLIGHTS
Reinventing the Enemy's Language: Contemporary Native Women Writing of North America (New York: W. W. Norton and Company, 1997)
"My Sister, Myself: Two Paths to Survival" in *Ms.* vol. 6 (2) September–October 1995, p. 70 (4)
The Spiral of Memory: Interviews, by Joy Harjo, ed. by Laura Coltelli (Ann Arbor: University of Michigan Press, c1996)
The Woman Who Fell from the Sky (New York: W. W. Norton, 1994)
A Circle of Nations: Voices and Visions of American Indians, ed. by John Gattuso (Hillsboro, Oreg.: Beyond Words Publishing, 1993)
The Submuloc Show—Columbus Wohs: A Visual Commentary on the Columbus Quincentennial from the Persepective of America's First People, ed. by Carla Roberts (Phoenix: s.n., 1992)
In Mad Love and War (Middletown, Conn.: Wesleyan University Press, 1990)

Secrets from the Center of the World (Tucson: Sun Tracks; University of Arizona Press, 1989)

She Had Some Horses (New York: Thunder Mouth Press, 1983)

What Moon Drove Me to This? (New York: I. Reed Books, 1979)

The Last Song ([Las Cruces, N.M.?]: Puerto del Sol, 1975)

Ms. Harjo's poems have also been published in numerous anthologies:

Returning the Gift: Poetry and Prose from the First North American Native Writers' Festival, ed. by Joseph Bruchac with the support of the Association for the Study of American Indian Literatures (Tucson: University of Arizona, 1994)

Talking Leaves: Contemporary Native American Short Stories, An Anthology, ed. by Craig Lesley (New York: Laurel, Dell, 1991)

American Indian Literatures: An Introduction, Bibliographic Review and Selected Bibliography (New York: Modern Language Association, 1990)

Winged Words: American Indian Writers Speak, ed. by Laura Coltelli (Lincoln: University of Nebraska Press, 1990)

A Gathering of Spirit: A Collection by North American Indian Women, ed. by Beth Brant (Ithaca: Firebrand Books, 1988, c1984)

I Tell You Now: Autobiographical Essays by Native American Writers, ed. by Brian Swann and Arnold Krupat (Lincoln: University of Nebraska Press, c1987)

Survival This Way: Interviews with Native American Poets, ed. by Joseph Bruchac (Tucson: Sun Tracks; University of Arizona Press, 1987)

The Sacred Hoop: Recovering the Feminine in American Indian Traditions, by Paula Gunn Allen (Boston: Beacon Press, 1986)

New and Old Voices of Wah'Kon-Tah, ed. by Robert K. Dodge and Joseph B. McCollugh (New York: International Publishers, c1985)

Native American Literature, ed. by Andrew Wiget (Boston: Twayne, 1985)

The Remembered Earth: An Anthology of Contemporary Native American Literature, ed. by Geary Hobson (Albuquerque: Red Earth Press, 1979) *Circle of Motion: Arizona Anthology of Contemporary American Indian Literature,* ed. by Kathleen Mullen Sands (Tempe, Ariz.: Historical Foundation, c1990)

Native American Renaissance, ed. by Kenneth Lincoln (Berkeley: University of California Press, c1983)

NARRATIVE

Joy Harjo is one of the most gifted and respected poets of her generation. Her mother is Cherokee and French and her Creek father is descended from a long line of tribal speakers and leaders. The oldest of four siblings who were raised in a non-traditional Cree household, Harjo lived on the north side of Tulsa in a neighborhood among many other mixed-blood Indian and white families. At the age of 16 she moved to Santa Fe, New Mexico, to finish high school at the Institute of American Indian Arts. "The IAIA [Institute of American Indian Arts] literally saved my life. I'd felt invisible in Tulsa and was dealing with some heavy-duty emotional chaos. Suddenly I was affirmed as a young Native woman who was gifted, had something to say. I was among kindred souls, other artists of my age. If it hadn't been for the affirmation of my experience at IAIA, I probably wouldn't have made it past eighteen years old."

After graduating from the University of New Mexico, Harjo's career path took a turn. As a young woman Harjo had intended to pursue a career in art, but at the age of twenty-two she made a different choice. "I was going to be a painter.

My grandmother Naomi Harjo was a painter as well as my Aunt Lois Harjo. [In her] I found a kindred soul. She gave me the stories of the people, our family herself. I was born painting, drawing images. It was my way of speaking. It was when I was in my early twenties that I turned to writing. It was a painful turn because I knew the challenge for me in writing was even greater than in painting. Painting was a familiar language. Writing seemed more foreign." In another interview, Harjo adds, "I found that poetry was taking on more magical qualities than my painting. I could say more when I write. Soon it wasn't a choice. Poetry speaking 'called me' in a sense and I couldn't say no" (*Winged Words: American Indian Writers Speak,* 1990).

One of the first Native writers whose works Harjo read was Simon Ortiz, to whom she was briefly married. "He was the first Native writer I ever heard. What clicked was the notion that I too could write of my experience, with my own sense of the world as a Native writer." While she was beginning to write as an undergraduate at the University of New Mexico, Harjo was fortunate to have three instructors who helped her to find her artistic voice: David Johnson, Gene Frumkin and Leslie Marmon Silko. "By their acknowledgment I was given confidence."

She has taught Native American literature and creative writing at the Institute of American Indian Arts in Santa Fe, New Mexico; at Arizona State University and at the University of Colorado at Boulder, where she was an assistant professor of English.

She is now an associate professor of English at the University of Arizona at Tucson. Harjo is a contributing editor of *Contact II,* the poetry editor of High *Plains Literary Review* and contributing editor for *Tyuonyi.* She is also active as a member of the Steering Committee of the En'owkin Centre International School of Writing (for Native American writers) and was on the board of directors for the National Association for Third World Writers. Harjo is on the policy panel of the National Endowment for the Arts and is a member of the board of directors for the Native American Public Broadcasting Consortium.

Harjo's written works have been published together as monographs and individually in numerous anthologies, journals and magazines, among them *Dacotah Territory, New America,* the *Kenyon Review, Ploughshares,* the *Progressive* and *Southwest Women's Poetry Exchange.*

Reflecting on her responsibility as a writer, she says, "I feel strongly that I have a responsibility to all the sources that I am: to all past and future ancestors, to my home country, to all places that I touch down on and that are myself, to all voices, all women, all of my tribe, all people, all Earth and beyond that to all beginnings and endings. In a strange kind of sense it frees me to believe in myself, to be able to speak, to have a voice, because I have to; it is my survival" (*Winged Words: American Indian Writers Speak,* 1990). "[My] struggle to stand tall as a whole person is at the root."

About her choice of subjects Harjo writes, "I don't think I particularly preselect subjects, they come to me. I notice I tend to write about the mysteries of life ... with a kind of bittersweetness." Some of her favorite works are *The Palm Wine Drinkard,* by Amos Tutuola; *Beloved,* by Toni Morrison; *Ceremony,* by Leslie Silko and *The Book of Nightmares,* by Galway Kinnell. "These books all change and disturb me ... there are more, of course," says Harjo. Aside from her academic duties and writing, she also works as a musician. "I'm now a saxophonist and have a Native band, Poetic

Justice. We play a kind of reggae-jazz-tribal music. I'm working on a CD for the band. We just finished our demo tape." Harjo has worked as a dramatic screenwriter and has produced works for Silvercloud Video Productions. She has also conducted workshops and given readings of her poetry throughout the United States. She is now working on an anthology of Native women's writing as well as three other books. She has two children and a granddaughter, Krista, who she spends as much time with as she can.

NAME   E, N
Lisa Davis Harjo

TRIBAL AFFILIATION
Choctaw Nation of Oklahoma

PERSONAL
Born: August 23, 1952, Rifle, Colorado
Education: B.A. from the University of California at Davis, 1974; M.A. in education from the University of California at Davis, 1991

AWARDS, HONORS
National Indian Education Association for Curriculum Development; Bank of American Award for Business

PUBLICATION HIGHLIGHTS
Indian Country: A History of Native People in America, with Karen Harvey (Golden, Colo.: North American Press, 1994)
Indian Country Teacher's Guide, with Karen Harvey (Golden, Colo.: North American Press, 1994)
The Circle Never Ends (Denver, Colo.: Denver Indian Center, 1990)
Teaching About Native Americans (Washington, D.C.: National Council for the Social Studies, 1990)

NARRATIVE
Lisa Harjo grew up in California, Colorado and Wyoming, spending her summers in Oklahoma. She attended grade school in Colorado Springs, Colorado, and Laramie, Wyoming. As a young woman Harjo describes herself as a "normal kid, nothing outstanding," though she was raised in a cross-cultural setting, the culture of her non-Indian mother and that of her Choctaw father. As a student active in politics and government at the University of California at Davis, Harjo helped start the Tecumsah Center, the Native American Center on campus, with the help of her friends David Risling, Jack Forbes and Carl Borman Sr.

Several people have served as her mentors, including Karen Harvey, her husband, Mody B. Harjo, and her father-in-law George B. Harjo, an oral historian with whom she confers and discusses issues and ideas. Another individual who has helped Harjo with her personal life and identity is Semn Hua Ute, a medicine man and an elder in the Chumash community in California.

Harjo has always written, and she considers her work *Teaching About Native Americans* to be her most rewarding creative endeavor to date. Writers who have influenced her work include Tony Hillerman, Louise Erdrich and Karen Harvey. She is a mother, gardener and is currently working on a textbook.

Harjo is the executive director of the Early Childhood Program at the Denver Indian Center and is also the director of the Circle of Learning, an elementary education program at the Center.

NAME   P
Patty Leah Harjo

TRIBAL AFFILIATION
Seneca and Seminole

PERSONAL
Born: December 29, 1947, in Miami, Oklahoma

Education: Institute of American Indian Art, Santa Fe, New Mexico, 1965–1969; University of Colorado at Boulder, 1969–1971

AWARDS, HONORS
Vincent Price Writing Awards, 1968

PUBLICATION HIGHLIGHTS
Harjo's works have also appeared in numerous anthologies:

Voices of the Rainbow: Contemporary Poetry by American Indians, ed. by Kenneth Rosen (New York: Viking, 1975)

Voices from Wah'Kon-Tah: Contemporary Poetry of Native Americans, first edition, ed. by Robert K. Dodge and Joseph B. McCullough (New York: International Publishers, 1974)

Literature of the American Indian, compiled by Thomas Sanders and William Peek (Beverly Hills: Glencoe Press, 1973)

The Way: An Anthology of American Indian Literature, ed. by Shirley H. Witt (New York: Knopf, 1972)

The American Indian Reader, ed. by Jeanette Henry (San Francisco: Indian Historian Press, 1972, 1977)

The American Indian Speaks, ed. by John R. Milton (Vermillion: Dakota Press; University of South Dakota, 1969)

NARRATIVE
Harjo has had her works published in numerous journals and periodicals, such as *Sun Tracks, Blue Cloud Quarterly, South Dacotah Review, Indian Historian, Amon Carter* and *The Way.* She was formerly the conservator of anthropology and liaison and community coordinator of Native American Affairs for the Center Museum of Natural History in Denver, Colorado.

NAME   J, L, P, PA
Suzan Shown Harjo

TRIBAL AFFILIATION
Cheyenne, Hodulgee Muscogee and Arapaho

PERSONAL
Born: June 2, 1945, in El Reno, Oklahoma

PUBLICATION HIGHLIGHTS
Harjo's works have appeared in: *The Remembered Earth: An Anthology of Contemporary Native American Literature,* ed. by Geary Hobson (Albuquerque: Red Earth Press, 1979) and *Come to Power: Eleven Contemporary American Indian Poets* (Trumansburg, N.Y.: Crossing Press, [1974]).

NARRATIVE
Harjo grew up on her Muscogee grandparents' farm outside of Beggs, Oklahoma. During the Second World War Harjo's family moved to Naples, Italy, where her father was stationed while he was in the service with the Allied forces. After the war her family returned to live in Oklahoma City, where she graduated from high school.

Harjo recalls three very memorable teachers she had as a young woman. "[a] second grade teacher in Oklahoma … pushed me out a second story window because he didn't like Indian kids or my attitude or version of the Battle of Little Big Horn (which I knew about from my family history on the winning side and which he knew next to nothing about)." Another instructor, Mrs. diGiovanni, wrote the music for the school song for which Harjo wrote lyrics (and won a school contest). Of Mrs. Bell, her seventh grade English teacher from Texas, Harjo says, "[She] taught me in an American military school in Naples, Italy, and used the plays and poetry of Shakespeare to instruct in use of words, style of language and ideas. English, Texas, Italy and Shakespeare were all so foreign, especially in that combination, that I paid attention and learned a lot about what to do and not to do in word games."

Of the significant events in Harjo's life, she says, "Loving and mourning two husbands, my grandparents and my youngest brother. The births of my children. Incidents of emotional and physical violence at several points in my life. Meeting nearly all my heroes." She adds that she benefits from the support of her family, her mother, father, brothers, daughter and son, "who always listen and offer the best comments."

Encouraged by her mother to pursue writing, Harjo's works speak about Native peoples traditional and cultural rights, negative and positive images of Indian people in film, theatre, sports, advertising and the arts and letters. She strives to provide a historical context for modern problems and a vision of the future of Native peoples and all people of color. Her writings have appeared in anthologies and journals, such as *Quest,* the *New York Quarterly* and *Nimrod.* Harjo enjoys reading works by authors Vine Deloria Jr., N. Scott Momaday, Michael Dorris, Louise Erdrich, Joy Harjo, Lillian Hellman, John Lennon, Bob Dylan, Dylan Thomas, Pablo Neruda, Robert Bolt, Tennessee Williams and Thomas Shappard. She is currently writing poetry, editing a book titled *Our Visions: The Next Five Hundred Years,* and is writing a book of interviews and profiles on personal courage.

Now living in Washington, D.C., Harjo frequently travels to South Dakota for ceremonies. She also travels to "Santa Fe and Taos, New Mexico, where I go for business and pleasure, and New York City, where I go for stimulation. Every setting influences what I think and write, although they are not always apparent or explicit." Harjo is active in politics, policy development that affects Indian affairs and human rights, and performing. "Helping make people the best they can be."

Harjo was formerly the executive director of the National Congress of American Indians and worked as a special assistant in the Office of the Assistant Secretary of Indian Affairs in the Department of the Interior. "I also write a lot of the stuff that becomes federal Indian law." She is currently the president and executive director of the Morning Star Foundation and national coordinator of the 1992 Alliance. She is also the personal manager of an Indian rock and roll singer/songwriter who leads the Native rock band Red Thunder.

NAME F, M, N, P, PL
Gordon Henry

TRIBAL AFFILIATION
White Earth Chippewa (Anishinabe)

PERSONAL
Born: October 19, 1955, in Philadelphia
Education: M.S. in journalism and public relations from the University of Iowa, 1960

PUBLICATION HIGHLIGHTS

Outside White Earth (Marvin, S. Dak.: Blue Cloud Quarterly Press, 1986); *Sleeping in Rain* (Tsailie, Ariz.: Navajo Community College, 1983)

Henry's works have also appeared in: *Returning the Gift: Poetry and Prose from the First North American Native Writers' Festival*, ed. by Joseph Bruchac with the support of the Association for the Study of American Indian Literatures (Tucson: University of Arizona, 1994).

NARRATIVE

Gordon Henry spent his early years on the White Earth Reservation in Minnesota, and later traveled extensively with his family as his father pursued a twenty-year career in the navy. Gordon was close to his great-grandparents, grandparents and extended family despite the many moves he had made as a child. His family's caring and encouragement are reflected in his works. An important event in his life was his opportunity to meet with Turtle Mountain elder Francis Cree, an individual whose influence also shaped his life.

Henry has been interested in the works of several musicians and writers, including Caroll Arnett, Lance Henson, Gerald Vizenor, Garcia Marquez and Neruda, Rumi, Carlos Fuentes, Momaday and Leslie Marmon Silko, as well as the music of Bob Dylan and John Prine. Currently Henry is working on a collection of poems, a collection of stories, several plays and some "folk-rock-country-western-pre-Columbian protest songs."

NAME   N

Jeannette Henry

TRIBAL AFFILIATION

Eastern Cherokee of North Carolina

PUBLICATION HIGHLIGHTS

The American Indian Reader, ed. by Jeannette Henry (San Francisco: Indian Historian Press, 1973); *Index to Literature on the American Indian,* ed. by Jeannette Henry et al (San Francisco: Indian Historian Press, 1970)

NAME   E, L, M, P, PL

Lance Henson

OTHER NAMES USED

Lance D. Henson

TRIBAL AFFILIATION

Southern Cheyenne

PERSONAL

Born: September 20, 1944, in Washington, D.C.

Education: B.A. in English and minor in film as literature, Oklahoma College of Liberal Arts, Chickasha, Oklahoma, 1972; M.A. in creative writing, Tulsa University, Tulsa Oklahoma, 1975

AWARDS, HONORS

Winner of the National Poetry Film Festival in San Francisco, California, 1990; Ford Foundation Scholarship, Tulsa University, Tulsa, Oklahoma, 1976; Funding from the National Endowment for the Arts through the New York Foundation for the Arts for the musical theatre piece *Winter Man*

PUBLICATION HIGHLIGHTS

Strong Heart Song: Lines from a Revolutionary Text (Albuquerque: West End Press, 1997)

Le Orme del Tasso (The Badger Tracks) (Torinno, Italy: Soconos Incomindios, 1989)

Another Song for America (Norman, Okla.: Point Rider's Press, 1987)

Selected Poems, 1970–1983 (Greenfield Center, N.Y.: Greenfield Review Press, 1985)

A Circling Remembrance (Marvid, S. Dak.: Blue Cloud Quarterly, 1982)

In a Dark Mist (Long Island, N.Y.: Cross Cultural Communications Press, 1982)

Buffalo Marrow on Black (Edmond, Okla.: Full Count Press, 1979)

Mistah (New York: Strawberry Press, [1977?], 1978)

Naming the Dark (Norman, Okla.: Point Rider's Press, 1976)

Keeper of Arrows: Poems for the Cheyenne (Chickasha, Okla.: Renaissance Press, 1971)

Henson's works have also appeared in numerous anthologies:

Circle of Motion: Arizona Anthology of Contemporary American Indian Literature, ed. by Kathleen Mullen Sands (Tempe: Arizona Historical Foundation, c1990)

Harper's Anthology of 20th-Century Native American Poetry, first edition (San Francisco: Harper & Row, 1988)

The Sacred Hoop: Recovering the Feminine in American Indian Traditions, by Paula Gunn Allen (Boston: Beacon Press, 1986)

Songs from This Earth on Turtle's Back, ed. by Joseph Bruchac, first edition (Greenfield Center, N.Y.: Greenfield Review Press, 1983)

The Remembered Earth: An Anthology of Contemporary Native American Literature, ed. by Geary Hobson (Albuquerque: Red Earth Press, 1979)

Carriers of the Dream Wheel: Contemporary Native American Poetry, ed. by Duane Niatum (New York: Harper & Row, 1975)

Voices of the Rainbow: Contemporary Poetry by American Indians, ed. by Kenneth Rosen (New York: Viking, 1975)

NARRATIVE

Henson was raised by his grandparents in Texas and near Calumet, Oklahoma, where he now resides. An ex-marine, he is a member of the Cheyenne Dog Warrior Society and the Native American Church.

Henson has held the post of master poet for the Oklahoma State Arts Council's writer-in-residence program from 1975 to 1985, in 1988 he was the writer-in-residence at the Olean Public Library in Olean, New York, and since 1989 Henson has held the position of writer-in-residence for the Alternative Literature Programs in the Schools for the city of Albany, New York. Throughout his career, Henson has traveled the length of the United States and Europe to lecture, give readings of his works and conduct independent workshops in over five hundred schools and universities.

Of his writing Henson says, "I am most interested in capturing as loosely as I can the imagery of immediate experience. Within the images there are finite clues that mirror what is real within the contextual surfaces of the portray. I write about nature, native rights and issues, and my relationships with family and the larger world (extended) family." He continues, "My early influences were the artists of the Beat Generation. My Cheyenne training has availed me of a great many mentors within the spiritual life of the tribe. My life as a poet has introduced me to an enormous array of literary heroes. My influences have taught me to respect the earth and it's mystery. The Earth's consciousness is my teacher."

He enjoys reading the works of W. S. Merwin, Thomas Transtromer, Georg Trakl, James Wright, Charles Simic, Neruda, Lorca and other Spanish poets "... and all of my brothers and sisters who are writing from their own tribal experiences." Henson is currently in the midst of several projects. "I am always writing poetry. I also periodically write a song or collaborate on a play. There are several long-term projects on my agenda, including a play, poetry recorded with voice and electronic music in collaboration with a composer, and the compilation of a large book of poems suitable for a major or university press publication."

Henson's works have appeared in numerous journals and periodicals, such as *Konza, Mid-America Review, Harvard Magazine, Coyote's Journal, Nimrod, Scarab, Tamaqua, World Literature Today, Calapooya Collage, Studies in American Indian Literature,* and he has had work published in the European journals *Fire, Teepee, Sur le dos de la Tortue, De Kiva* and *Sovremennik.*

Henson has also been active in music and film. His poem "Another Wind Is Moving" was made into a film of the same title in 1986 at the University of Kansas. Another of his poems, "Ghost Dance," was also made into a film in 1990 by Unity Productions of Aberdeen, South Dakota, and won the 1990 National Poetry Film Festival in San Francisco, California. He recorded an album of music in Pisa, Italy, in 1989 titled *Song of Myself,* and he wrote the lyrics and was a technical advisor for the musical theatre work *Winter Man.* The play has received funding and the endorsement of the National Endowment for the Arts through the New York Foundation for the Arts. "My work as a poet has given me the opportunity to engage, through my poetry in several other areas in the arts. I have co-written with my wife (Jeanetta Calhoun) lyrics for a rock-and-roll album composed and recorded with the rock group Not Moving who are based in Pisa, Italy. In 1991, I co-wrote a light opera entitled *Winter Man.* This play had an off-Broadway run and a good review in *The New York Times.* In 1992 I co-wrote a play with Jeff Hooper of Mad River Theatre Works in Ohio. The play *Coyote Road* was presented in the summer of 1992. ... I am always looking

for new ways to present poetry. My poetry has also led me to the opportunity to speak on behalf of the Southern Cheyenne and in solidarity with other indigenous people in forums such as the United Nations in Geneva and New York, the Bertrand Russell Forum in Amsterdam ... and in public forums all over the U.S. and Europe. ... I always use whatever opportunities I have to speak about issues like Leonard Peltier, treaty rights, the struggle of the Dann sisters and the possible destruction of the Serpent Mound in Ohio. I believe it is our duty as Native American writers to discuss these issues."

NAME   M, PL
Tomson Highway

TRIBAL AFFILIATION
Cree

PERSONAL
Born: December 6, 1951, in northwest Manitoba
Education:
Guy Hill Indian Residential School, The Pas, Manitoba, 1957–1966
Churchill High School, Winnipeg, Manitoba, 1970
University of Manitoba, Faculty of Music
B.A. in music, with honors, from the University of Western Ontario, 1975
B.A. in English, University of Western Ontario, 1977

AWARDS, HONORS
One Dora Mavor Moore Award for *The Rez Sisters* and four for *Dry Lips Oughta Move to Kapuskasing,* 1987–1988; *The Rez Sisters* was chosen to represent Canada at the Endinburgh Festival, Edinburgh Scotland, 1988.

PUBLICATION HIGHLIGHTS

Dry Lips Oughta Move to Kapuskasing in Modern Canadian Plays, vol. 2 (Vancouver, B.C.: Talon Books, 1994); *Dry Lips Oughta Move to Kapuskasing: A Play* (Saskatoon, Sask.: Fifth House, 1989); *The Rez Sisters: A Play in Two Acts* (Saskatoon, Sask.: Fifth House, 1988)

NARRATIVE

Tomson Highway spoke the Cree language until he began attending Catholic school at the age of 6. He displayed a gift for music and later studied music and English at the University of Western Ontario. Highway began writing plays after he had worked for many years with Native assistance programs. He has worked with several people on many theater productions: with James Reancy on the plays *Wacousta* and *The Canadian Brothers,* with Rene Highway on the dance production *New Song ... New Dance* in 1987–1988, he was the artistic director of Native Earth performing Arts, Inc., of Toronto, Ontario, and worked with the De-ba-jeh-mu-jig Theatre Group from West Bay, Ontario. His play *Aria* (Monologues) was produced at the Makka Kleist Annex Theatre, Toronto, Ontario, in 1987.

NAME   P
Roberta Hill

OTHER NAMES USED
Roberta Hill Whiteman

TRIBAL AFFILIATION
Oneida

PERSONAL
Born: February 17, 1947, in Baraboo, Wisconsin

Education: B.A. in psychology from the University of Wisconsin; M.F.A. in writing from the University of Montana, Missoula

PUBLICATION HIGHLIGHTS

Hill's works have appeared in numerous anthologies:

Returning the Gift: Poetry and Prose from the First North American Native Writers' Festival, ed. by Joseph Bruchac with the support of the Association for the Study of American Indian Literatures (Tucson: University of Arizona, 1994)
Braided Lives: An Anthology of Multicultural American Writing, ed. by the Minnesota Humanities Commission and the Minnesota Council of Teachers of English (St. Paul: The Commission, 1991)
Native American Renaissance, ed. by Kenneth Lincoln (Berkeley: University of California Press, c1983)
Carriers of the Dream Wheel: Contemporary Native American Poetry, ed. by Duane Niatum (New York: Harper & Row, 1975)
Voices of the Rainbow: Contemporary Poetry by American Indians, ed. by Kenneth Rosen (New York: Viking, 1975)

NARRATIVE

Hill's work has appeared in the journals *Southern Review, Poetry Northwest* and *American Poetry Review.* She was a poet-in-residence in the Schools Program in St. Paul, Minnesota, and is currently teaching at Sinte Gleska College in Rosebud, South Dakota. Hill is married and has a son.

NAME   E, F, L, N
Geary Hobson

TRIBAL AFFILIATION
Cherokee, Quapaw and Chickasaw

PERSONAL

Born: June 12, 1941, in Chicot County, Arkansas

Education:

A.A. in liberal arts from Phoenix Junior College, 1963–1964

B.A. in English from Arizona State University, 1968

M.A. in English from Arizona State University, 1969

Ph.D. in American studies from the University of New Mexico, 1970–1976, 1985–1986

PUBLICATION HIGHLIGHTS

Deer Hunting and Other Poems (New York: Strawberry Press; Norman, Okla.: Renegade/Point Riders Press, 1990); *The Remembered Earth: An Anthology of Contemporary Native American Literature,* ed. by Geary Hobson (Albuquerque: Red Earth Press, 1979)

Hobson's works have appeared in numerous anthologies:

Returning the Gift: Poetry and Prose from the First North American Native Writers' Festival, ed. by Joseph Bruchac with the support of the Association for the Study of American Indian Literatures (Tucson: University of Arizona, 1994)

American Indian Literature: An Anthology, revised edition, ed. by Alan R. Velie (Norman, Okla.: University of Oklahoma Press, 1991)

The Sacred Hoop: Recovering the Feminine in American Indian Traditions, by Paula Gunn Allen (Boston: Beacon Press, 1986)

The Clouds Threw This Light: Contemporary Native American Poetry, ed. by Phillip Foss (Santa Fe: Institute of American Indian Arts Press, 1983)

Earth Power Coming: Short Fiction in Native American Literature, ed. by Simon J. Ortiz (Tsaile, Ariz.: Navajo Community College Press, c1983)

Songs from This Earth on Turtle's Back: Contemporary American Indian Poetry, ed. by Joseph Bruchac (Greenfield Center, N.Y.: Greenfield Review Press, 1983)

Structure and Meaning: An Introduction to Literature, second edition, ed. by Anthony Dube et al. (Boston: Houghton Mifflin, 1983)

From the Center: A Folio, ed. by Maurice Kenny (New York: Strawberry Press, 1980)

Southwest: A Contemporary Anthology (Albuquerque: Red Earth Press, 1977)

NARRATIVE

Hobson graduated from Desha Central High School in Rohwer, Arkansas, in 1959. He worked in many different jobs after high school: a farm laborer and a trapper and a U.S. marine from 1959 to 1965 as a sergeant. Hobson also worked as a salesman, a bridge construction worker, a surveyor's assistant. He was a semi-professional baseball player, a lumber yard employee and a bookstore clerk before he later became an educator.

Hobson began his teaching career as a special tutor at Arizona State University and has since worked in several teaching positions. He was a teacher at the Dumas Arkansas Public Schools, a teaching assistant in English and a special assistant in the Native American studies/English American studies programs at the University of New Mexico, and he was also the university's Native American Studies program coordinator. Hobson was an English instructor at the University of Arkansas at Little Rock. He later returned to the University of New Mexico as a lecturer and faculty associate in Native American studies. He also was a visiting assistant professor in the American studies program at the University of New Mexico. Hobson is currently an assistant professor in the English department of the University of Oklahoma.

An active member of the academic community, Hobson has participated in many university councils and committees, and through the years, he has had his short stories, poems and reviews published in numerous journals, such as *La Confluencia, Sun Tracks, New America: A Review, Southwest Women's Poetry Exchange, A Journal Of Contemporary Literature, Arizona Quarterly,* the *Blue Cloud Quarterly, World of Literature Today* and the *Greenfield Review.*

Hobson has been married twice and has a daughter from each marriage.

NAME E, N, P, PLP

Linda Hogan

TRIBAL AFFILIATION

Chickasaw

PERSONAL

Born: 1947 in Denver, Colorado
Education: Masters degree in English from the University of Colorado

AWARDS, HONORS

American Book Award from the Before Columbus Foundation for *Seeing Through the Sun*
Five Civilized Tribes Playwriting Award for *A Piece of Noon*
National Endowment for the Arts Fellowship in Fiction, 1986
Yaddo Colony Fellowship, 1982
Newberry Library Fellowship, 1980
Colorado Writers Fellowship in Fiction
Minnesota Arts Board Grant in Poetry

PUBLICATION HIGHLIGHTS

Dwellings: Reflections on the Natural World (New York: W. W. Norton and Company, 1995)

Solar Storms: A Novel (New York: Scribner, c1995)
Book of Medicines: Poems (Minneapolis: Coffee House Press, 1993)
Red Clay: Poems and Stories (Greenfield Center, N.Y.: Greenfield Review Press, 1991)
Mean Spirit: A Novel (New York: Anetheum, 1990)
Savings: Poems (Minneapolis: Coffee House Press, 1986)
Seeing Through the Sun (Amherst: University of Massachusetts Press, 1985)
Eclipse (Los Angeles: University of California at Los Angeles American Indian Studies Center, [1984?])
Daughters, I Love You (Denver: Loretto Heights College, [1981])
Calling Myself Home (Greenfield Center, N.Y.: Greenfield Review Press, [1978?])
That Horse (Acoma, N. Mex.: Pueblo of Acoma Press, [n.d.])

Hogan's works have also appeared in many anthologies:

Returning the Gift: Poetry and Prose from the First North American Native Writers' Festival, ed. by Joseph Bruchac with the support of the Association for the Study of American Indian Literatures (Tucson: University of Arizona, 1994)
Braided Lives: An Anthology of Multicultural American Writing, ed. by the Minnesota Humanities Commission and the Minnesota Council of Teachers of English (St. Paul: The Commission, 1991)
Winged Words: American Indian Writers Speak, ed. by Laura Coltelli (Lincoln: University of Nebraska Press, 1990)
Spider Woman's Granddaughters: Traditional Tales and Contemporary Writing by Native American Women, ed. by Paula Gunn Allen (Boston: Beacon Press, 1989)
Harper's Anthology of 20th-Century Native American Poetry, first edition (San Francisco: Harper & Row, 1988)
I Tell You Now: Autobiographical Essays by Native American Writers, ed. by Brian

Swann and Arnold Krupat (Lincoln: University of Nebraska Press, c1987)

Survival This Way: Interviews with Native American Poets, ed. by Joseph Bruchac (Tucson: Sun Tracks; University of Arizona Press, 1987)

The Sacred Hoop: Recovering the Feminine in American Indian Traditions, ed. by Paula Gunn Allen (Boston: Beacon Press, 1986)

That's What She Said: Contemporary Poetry and Fiction by Native American Women, ed. by Rayna Green (Bloomington: Indiana University Press, 1984)

Earth Power Coming: Short Fiction in Native American Literature, ed. by Simon J. Ortiz (Tsaile, Ariz.: Navajo Community College Press, c1983)

The Remembered Earth: An Anthology of Contemporary Native American Literature, ed. by Geary Hobson (Albuquerque: Red Earth Press, 1979)

NARRATIVE

Hogan spent most of her childhood in Oklahoma. Her mother was the daughter of white immigrants living in Nebraska, and her father was Chickasaw. Hogan has held the position of associate professor of American Indian and American studies at the University of Minnesota and is now an associate professor of Native American and American studies at the University of Colorado at Boulder, where she teaches literature and creative writing. Educator, poet and playwright, Hogan has been a poet-in-residence for the Oklahoma and Colorado arts councils, has won numerous grants and writing awards and is the editor of the Indian women's issue of the journal Frontiers. She is also the coeditor of *The Stories We Hold Sacred* for the *Greenfield Review Press.* Her works have been published in many journals, such as the *Beloit Poetry Journal, The Little Magazine, Greenfield Review, Prairie Schooner, Ms., Callaloo,* the *American Poetry Review, Parabola* and *Hiram Review.*

Hogan lives in Colorado with her two daughters.

NAME   N, P
Andrew Hope III

TRIBAL AFFILIATION
Tlingit

PERSONAL
Born: December 23, 1949, in Sitka, Alaska

PUBLICATION HIGHLIGHTS
"Raven's Bones Journal" in *Alaska Native* magazine (Anchorage: Alaska Native News, June 1986); *Raven's Bones,* ed. by Andrew Hope III (Sitka, Alaska: Sitka Community, 1982); "Rootless Primitives Need Land Masters" in *Quilt* magazine ([Wheatridge, Colo.: Leman Publications], Summer, 1981)

Hope's works have appeared in: *Returning the Gift: Poetry and Prose from the First North American Native Writers' Festival,* ed. by Joseph Bruchac with the support of the Association for the Study of American Indian Literatures (Tucson: University of Arizona, 1994) and *Raven Tells Stories: An Anthology of Alaskan Native Writing,* first edition, ed. by Joseph Bruchac (Greenfield Center, N.Y.: Greenfield Review Press, 1991)

NARRATIVE
Hope was born in Sitka, Alaska, the home of his father's family. He is a member of the board of directors of the Before Columbus Foundation and is the founder of Raven's Bone Press, in 1985. He now lives in Juneau with his wife and two sons. Hope's works have also appeared in the journal *Chicago Review.*

NAME E, F, J, N, P, PA, PL
LeAnne Howe

TRIBAL AFFILIATION
Choctaw

PERSONAL
Born: April 29, 1951, in Edmond, Oklahoma
Education: B.A. in English

AWARDS, HONORS
National Endowment for the Humanities, 1991

PUBLICATION HIGHLIGHTS
"The Bone Picker" and "Dance of the Dead" (chap. 1) in *The Looking Glass,* ed. by Clifford Trafzer (San Diego, Calif.: San Diego State University Press, 1991)
"The Red Wars" and "Moccasins Don't Have High Heels," short stories in *American Indian Literature: An Anthology,* revised edition, ed. by Alan Velie (Norman: University of Oklahoma Press, 1991)
"An American in New York," short story in *Spider Woman's Granddaughters,* ed. by Paula Gunn Allen (Boston: Beacon Press, 1989)
A Stand Up Reader (Dallas: Into View Press, 1987)
Coyote Papers (Dallas: Wowapi Press, 1984)

Howe's works have also appeared in: *Returning the Gift: Poetry and Prose from the First North American Native Writers' Festival,* ed. by Joseph Bruchac with the support of the Association for the Study of American Indian Literatures, (Tucson: University of Arizona, 1994).

NARRATIVE
Howe's family name is Anolitubbee, which means "one who tells and kills." Her writings have appeared in journals, such as the *Callaloo, The Dallas Morning News, USA Today, Johnson County News, Azle News* and other regional Texas magazines and publications.

Howe's written works focus on the areas of Choctaw culture, history and cross-cultural experiences. She frequently gives lectures and presents papers on the subjects of reburial and repatriation of American Indian remains, Native American literature, hazardous waste sites that are planned to be located on Indian reservations and the waste companies that contract with foreign governments to dump on reservation lands, a topic which Howe covered in a paper with coauthor Scott Morrison titled "Sewage of Foreigners."

A paper that Howe coauthored with Scott Kela Morrison, Jim Wilson and Joel Martin, titled "Love and Money: A Critical Evaluation of *Fisher versus Allen,*" received support from a grant from the National Endowment for the Humanities in June 1991. The paper is about a landmark 1838–legal case that established women's property rights in Mississippi. The defendant in the case was a Chickasaw woman, and the Mississippi State Supreme Court affirmed Chickasaw tribal customary law, which held that the "property" in southeastern tribal society was owned by the women. This case was instrumental in helping to define women's property laws in the United States.

Howe wrote a paper titled "Choctaw Mortuary Practices and the Nanih Waiya," a play in collaboration with Roxie Gordon titled *Big Pow Wow,* a collection of short fiction titled *Please Don't Shoot Me I'm Only a Choctaw Indian Disguised As a Palestinian … OK I Chose the Wrong Disguise* and is finishing a historical novel, *The Bone Picker.* She is also working on a novel on the Choctaws' contact with Europeans.

Howe is currently a producer and educational/editorial associate in the Office of International Education and Services,

University of Iowa. When she is not writing, Howe enjoys cooking, photography, political activism and reading the works of writers Leslie Silko, Roxy Gordon, Anna Lee Walters, Vine Deloria, Ward Churchill, Beth Brant and Margurite Duras.

NAME   A, E, F, P

Ruth A. Hunsinger

OTHER NAMES USED

Hunt Singer

TRIBAL AFFILIATION

Rosebud Lakota

PERSONAL

Born: April 15, 1927, at Rosebud, South Dakota
Education: B.S., Black Hills State College; M.A., University of Northern Colorado; completed coursework for Ed.D. Arizona State University

AWARDS, HONORS

Kappa Delta Pi, honorary sorority; Lambda Theta Pi, honorary sorority

PUBLICATION HIGHLIGHTS

"Drum Song" in *The Desert Candle* (Alpine, Tex.: Dr. J. Brueske, 1990)
"A Dakota Story" in *American Indian Historian,* ed. by J. Henry (San Francisco: American Indian Historian, 1973)

"Stochunger" in *American Indian Horizon* (New York: Henri Ben Ami, 1963)
"Dreams," "As I Do" in Pasque Pedals (Sioux Falls: *South Dakota Poetry Magazine,* [n.d.])

NARRATIVE

Ruth Hunsinger was raised in Rapid City, South Dakota. She was initially inspired to try writing after reading the works of Vine and Ella Deloria. While honing her skills as a writer, she worked with colleagues in an organization called the Black Hills Writers Group in Rapid City, where she enjoyed the camaraderie and exchange of ideas with other writers. Rapid City librarian and friend Mrs. Mary Maragret Morrett provided Hunsinger with invaluable help in editing and critiquing her early efforts at writing. Hunsinger now finds herself reading mostly nonfiction and enjoys the works of author Carl Sagan. She recalls many events in her past that have shaped her philosophy and writings about social concerns and historical accounts: the Great Depression in the 1930s, the South Dakota Blizzard in 1948, the floods that racked Rapid City in 1962 and 1972, the Deadwood South Dakota forest fire and each of the wars that the United States has been involved in since the Second World War.

Currently retired and living in Alpine, Texas, Hunsinger says she is "… trying to survive, but I do volunteer work at museums and national parks and schools." She also conducts research and works on handicrafts.

I

NAME   P

Bruce Ignacio

TRIBAL AFFILIATION

Ute

PERSONAL

Born: Utah and Duray Reservation in Ft. Duchesne, Utah

Education: Coursework at the Institute of American Indian Arts, Santa Fe, New Mexico

PUBLICATION HIGHLIGHTS

Ignacio's works have appeared in the anthologies:

New and Old Voices of Wah'Kon-Tah, third edition, ed. by Robert K. Dodge and Joseph B. McCullough (New York: International Publishers, c1985)

Voices from Wah'Kon-Tah: Contemporary Poetry of Native Americans, first edition, ed. by Robert K. Dodge and Joseph B. McCullough (New York: International Publishers, 1974)

Literature of the American Indian, by Thomas Sanders and William Peek (Beverly Hills: Glencoe Press, 1973)

The American Indian Speaks, ed. by John R. Milton (Vermillion: Dakota Press; University of South Dakota, 1969)

NARRATIVE

Ignacio studied creative writing and jewelry-making for three years at the Institute of American Indian Arts in Santa Fe, New Mexico. His written works have appeared in the journal the *South Dakota Review.*

NAME   F, J, L, N, P, VA

Alootook Ipellie

TRIBAL AFFILIATION

Inuit

PERSONAL

Born: August 11, 1951, in a camp on Baffin Island, north shore at Frobisher Bay, Northwest Territories, Canada

PUBLICATION HIGHLIGHTS

Arctic Dreams and Nightmares (Penticton, B.C.: Theytus, 1993)

Paper Stamp Pot—A Collection of Inuit Writing (Edmunton: Hurtig Publishers, [1980?], 1981)

The Dancing Sun (S.l.: Press Porcepic, 1981)

"Signing the Sun," short story in *Canadian Fiction Magazine* (Vancouver: s.n., 1980)

NARRATIVE

Alootook Ipellie was raised in Iqaluit, on Baffin Island. Close to his family, Ipellie recalls the important lessons they taught him. "My grandfather was a carver, taught me patience and sense of belonging to our culture and traditions. An uncle ... taught me the secrets of living on the land." Ipellie excelled as a student. He received two awards, "... for having the highest academic marks in class and then the entire school."

Considering himself a self-taught writer, he explains that he has been motivated by the plight of his people, their social strife and cultural upheaval, which has been caused "mostly by alcohol abuse and [the] difficulty adjusting to a new lifestyle in a community, as opposed [to] camp life on the land." He also writes about the Arctic region, where he has lived for over twenty-five years. Though his writing focuses on the Far North, Ipellie says he also needs " to do comparison[s] and to write about differences in cultures and traditions and lifestyles, which also encompasses differences in views and opinions as well as outlook on life and the world."

Among the body of work he has created, he considers his fiction, prose, essays and poetry to be some of his best work. In his leisure time he enjoys reading "A lot of nonfiction, human interest, autobiographies, poetry (many by Native writers)." He is now working on three book projects: a novel, some nonfiction works and several illustrated stories. His long-term projects include a book of poetry, a cartoon book, a short story collection and another volume of illustrated stories. When he is not writing Ipellie works as a freelance writer and editor of the Inuit fiction magazine *Kivioq*. He is also a freelance artist, creating pen-and-ink drawings, cartoons and illustrations, also designing posters, logos and letterheads.

NAME   F, P, PL, VA
Morris Isaac

OTHER NAMES USED
Nujaweekuget ("one who writes" [Micmac])

TRIBAL AFFILIATION
Micmac

PERSONAL
Born: October 20, 1943, in Restigouche Reserve, Quebec, Canada
Education: B.A. in business administration, 1973; B.A. in Native American law, 1987

AWARDS, HONORS
Scholarship to attend the Vermont School of Arts, 1989

PUBLICATION HIGHLIGHTS
"The Diary of a Mad Ironworker" in *Towaw* magazine (Ottawa, Ont.: Department of Indian Affairs, vol. 3, no. 4, 1979); "Trapped in the 'Express' at Indian Affairs" in *The Native Perspective* (Ottawa, Ont.: [s.n.], vol. 2, no. 6, 1978); "Funny—I'm Still Looking for That Place" in *Anthropology* (Ottawa, Ont.: St. Paul's University, vol. 13, 1971)

NARRATIVE
Born and raised on the Restigouche Reserve, Quebec, Morris Isaac attended the only English school in Quebec as a boy. During his twenty years as a writer, Isaac's works have been published in several magazines, newspapers and books. His favorite and most frequent subjects have been satirical pieces about the government, works on societal issues and stories for children. "I seemed to find [it] easy to be funny when I attacked stupid [government] programs." Though he now lives in an urban area, he prefers being in the country or back on the reserve where he grew up as a youth.

He was encouraged to pursue a writing career by his friends editor Diane Armstrong, and writer, social scientist, researcher and consultant Jim Lotz, of whom Isaac says, "gave me the feeling that I can write," and was further motivated to continue writing when he had one of his early articles published in two books and four newsletters. Writer Diane Armstrong also assisted him when he was starting out as a writer, by editing his first book and guiding him in his creative endeavors. "She influenced me a lot." Isaac enjoys reading the works of Margaret Atwood, Robert Frost, W. C. Mitchell and Jim Lotz.

In 1980 Isaac was informed that he had Parkinson's disease, a condition that eventually forced him to retire from his position at Indian Affairs and assume a long-term disability pension. Though he had always been a writer, submitting pieces to Native publications, Isaac decided to start writing seriously: "I figured that I might not be able very soon." He also works with video and radio productions and creates watercolor paintings. Now retired, Isaac "works at home to stay sane and keep the wolf out of the door!"

In 1993 Isaac had his play *Thanks to Peter, I Know Where the North Is* produced at the University of Ottawa. He is currently active in radio, with his own show, "Thirty Minutes with Morris Isaac," and is completing a video for the Assembly of First Nations on the loss of Native languages. He is also active in various audio/visual productions and works as a counselor, career planner and cross-cultural and Native awareness workshop facilitator.

J

NAME E, F, J, P

Roger Jack

TRIBAL AFFILIATION

Member of the Colville Confederated
Tribes

PERSONAL

Born: October 7 in Nespelem, Washington
Education:
B.A. in English and journalism, Eastern
Washington University, Cheney, Wash-
ington, 1977
Associate of fine arts degree, Institute of
American Indian Arts, Santa Fe, New
Mexico, 1982
B.A. in education, Eastern Washington
University, Cheney, Washington, 1984
M.F.A. in creative writing, Eastern Wash-
ington University, Cheney, Washington,
1987

PUBLICATION HIGHLIGHTS

"The Pebble People" in *Talking Leaves: Con-
temporary Native American Short Stories,
An Anthology,* ed. by Craig Lesley and
Katheryn Stavrakis (New York: Laurel,
1991); "An Indian Story" in *Dancing on
the Rim of the World,* ed. by Andrea Lerner
(Tucson: Sun Tracks and the University
of Arizona Press, 1990); "The Pebble
People" in *Earth Power Coming,* ed. by
Simon J. Ortiz (Tsaile, Ariz.: Navajo
Community College Press, 1983)

NARRATIVE

Roger Jack was born and raised in
Nespelem, Washington. As a young man
he attended a parochial school. "As the
saying goes, my early years were spent in
Catholic boarding school ... Jesuit priests
and Dominican nuns straight out of the
old country .. what some kids believe
untrue may very well be true. Also did
time in BIA boarding schools where they
punished you for speaking your tribal languages, and all that. Things we tend to
laugh about now, now that it's over, but
suffered/survived when it was all too real
and happening."

Jack's ninety-one-year-old maternal
grandmother related many legends, family history and tribal history to him as he
was growing up. "She's held fast to her
tribal identity for so many years it's a wonder I ended up a mixed (full) blood Indian! I mean, I'm a descendant of
hard-core Colvilles, who were pretty paci-
fistic, and warrior societies from 'off-res-
ervation' tribes."

His works are about the basis of Indian culture and day-to-day survival, his
perspective shaped by the death of his
mother. "The death of my mother held a
major impact in my life story so much so
perhaps I write some out of bitterness and
some out of concern for what's left of my
people and their culture. Symbolically, is
one not representative of the other?"
While a student, Jack met and befriended
writer Elizabeth Cook-Lynn, who influenced his academic and writing career.
Jack says, "If you've got it, you've got it!
No one actually made me become a writer,
or anything."

His writings have been published in
many journals and anthologies, such as
*Earth Power Coming, Spawning the Medi-
cine River, The Clouds Threw This Light*
and the *New York Quarterly.* A play titled
Buckskin Curtains is one of his favorite
works: "I wrote a play called *Buckskin*

Curtains that's never been acted out on stage—it's kind of my favorite because it deals with what is old and new in the Indian world. Tidbits of seriousness, humor and tragedy." He is working on a chapbook of short stories, written in the style of *Buckskin Curtains*. As he adds, "Gotta keep writing, my fan insists upon it!"

When asked about the writers he enjoys reading, he responded: "I tend to relish the old Indian classical writing that created and/or embellished the newfound genre of Indian literature, but I try to keep up on the latest writings as well. My oldest inspiration came out of IAIA's [Institute of American Indian Arts] poetry and verse publication, and then N. Scott Momaday and James Welch, the likes of them."

Jack now works at his former childhood school. "Believe it or not! I'm back at the school I attended in my days of youth, except it's run by the tribe now. I'm a part-time aide in the gifted and talented program, and a part-time instructor. The former St. Mary Mission is now Paschal Sherman Indian School, Omak, Washington." When he is not working in the school, or writing, he enjoys going to pow-wows and beading.

NAME   P

Alex Jacobs

NARRATIVE

Karoniaktatie

TRIBAL AFFILIATION

Cayuga

PUBLICATION HIGHLIGHTS

Jacob's works have appeared in the anthologies:

Returning the Gift: Poetry and Prose from the First North American Native Writers' Festival, ed. by Joseph Bruchac with the support of the Association for the Study of American Indian Literatures (Tucson: University of Arizona, 1994)

New Voices from the Longhouse: An Anthology of Contemporary Iroquois Writing, first edition, ed. by Joseph Bruchac (Greenfield Center, N.Y.: Greenfield Review Press, c1989)

The Native American in American Literature: A Selectively Annotated Bibliography, compiled by Roger O. Rock (Westport, Conn.: Greenwood Press, 1985)

NARRATIVE

Jacobs is now employed at the Institute of American Indian Arts in Santa Fe, New Mexico. He was the editor of *Akwesasne Notes* in the early 1970s.

NAME   E, L, N

M. Annette Jaimes

NARRATIVE

Marie Annette Jaimes

TRIBAL AFFILIATION

Juaneno (California Mission Band) and Yaqui

PERSONAL

Born: September 10, 1946, in Mesa, Arizona

Education: B.A. in American history with minor in psychology, Western civilization, Arizona State University, Tempe; M.A. in secondary education, emphasis on "ethnic/minority" history and education, Arizona State University, Tempe; Ed.D. in higher education and policy studies with emphasizes in federal Indian policy and socio-cultural issues, Arizona State University, 1990

AWARDS, HONORS

Award from the Society for the Humanities at Cornell University, Ithaca, New York, for postdoctoral fellowship work in "Politics of Identity," award also included a visiting professorship on the subject of "American Indians, identity, race and nationalism," 1991–1992

Congressional internship at George Washington University, Washington, D.C.

Scholarships and fellowships in Federal Indian Education, Inter-American Schooling and Research (in Guatemala and Mexico), which includes certificates from the United Nations in the area of rights for indigenous people

PUBLICATION HIGHLIGHTS

Fantasies of the Master Race: Literature, Cinema and the Colonization of American Indians, by Ward Churchill, ed. by M. Jaimes (Monroe, Maine: Common Courage Press, 1992)

The State of Native America: Genocide, Colonization and Resistance, ed. by M. Jaimes (Boston: South End Press, 1992)

"The Pit River Indian Land Claim Dispute in Northern California," ed. by Ward Churchill, in *Critical Issues in Native North America,* Vol. II (Copenhagen: IWGIA, 1991)

"Federal Indian Identification Policy: A Usurpation of Indigenous Sovereignty in North America," ed. by Ward Churchill, in *Critical Issues in Native North America* (Copenhagen: IWGIA, 1989)

NARRATIVE

Marie Annette Jaimes was born in Mesa, Arizona, and now lives in Boulder, Colorado, where she is the assistant director of social projects for the University Learning Center at the University of Colorado at Boulder. She teaches American Indian studies courses for the Universities Center for Studies of Ethnicity and Race in America. She has published extensively in the fields of American Indian policy issues, spirituality and environmental ethics, American Indians and colonization, media images of Native American women and Native women's issues and pre-contact Native America and other related subjects.

NAME L, N
Alex Jamieson

NARRATIVE
Gawitrha'

TRIBAL AFFILIATION
Bear Clan of the Cayuga Nation

PERSONAL
Born: June 19, 1933, in the Six Nations Territory, near Brantford, Ontario
Education: Five years of post-secondary coursework

PUBLICATION HIGHLIGHTS

Dwanoha: One Earth, One Mind, One Path (Hagersville, Ont.: Pine Tree Publishing Group, 1991)

"I Do Not Want to Be a Canadian" in *The Branford Expositor* (Brantford, Ont.: *The Branford Expositor,* July 13, 1991)

"Man Caught in Monkey Trap" in *The Branford Expositor* (Brantford, Ont.: *The Branford Expositor,* November 4, 1989)

NARRATIVE

Jamieson was born and raised on the Six Nations Territory near Brantford, Ontario. As a young man he was familiar with the ugliness of racism present throughout his years as a student in city schools. Jamieson's writings are a response to the myriad of people and mindsets he has encountered in his life: "Arrogant bureaucrats, racist bigots, unscrupulous politicians, greed-driven businessmen and destroyers of nature, smug educators, self-righteous missionaries and all other ethnocentric enemies of tribalism." He continues, "I am not a professional writer. My book *Dwanoha'* was meant to be a one-shot gift to all my relations. My essay reflects my life-long observations and is an attempt to reveal the One Cause of the problems in the world." When asked about his favorite writers, he responds, "I rarely read fiction and never read poetry. Writers speak to me through the facts and figures they present. However, I am capable of emotions other than anger. In fact I believe *Dwanoha'* was a labor of love, and in spite of my disinterest in fiction, I have written a novel. It is called *The Pipe Carrier* [unpublished]." Jamieson is currently working on several broad, long range projects "Many, mostly to preserve our language and revitalize tribalism. Language instruction, awakening our community to the need of maintaining our tribal traditions, trying to revive our agricultural practices. I am currently occupied in trying to discredit and destroy "Western civilization" and most of its supporting institutions. ... [I am] attempting to discredit and destroy civilization and replace it with a more female-oriented global tribalism."

NAME P
Rex Lee Jim

TRIBAL AFFILIATION
Navajo

PUBLICATION HIGHLIGHTS
Dancing Voices: Wisdom of the American Indian (White Plains, N.Y.: Peter Pauper Press, 1994)
Ahi Ni' Nikisheegiizh, poems (Princeton, N.J.: Lenape Yaa Deez'a, 1989)

Living from Livestock (Rock Point, Ariz.: Rock Point Community School, 1984)
Naakaiitahgoo Yazhdiiya (Rock Point, Ariz.: Rock Point Community School, 1981)

NAME N
Donna John

TRIBAL AFFILIATION
Athabascan

PUBLICATION HIGHLIGHTS
"Donna John Shares Her Life Story" in *Tundra Times* (Fairbanks, Alaska: *Tundra Times,* December 16, 1992); "Parents Need Self-Esteem to Raise Healthy Kids" in *Fairbanks Daily News Miner* (Fairbanks, Alaska: The News, 1992); "Tribute to Horace Smoke, Sr.," poem in *FNA 1992: 19th Annual Festival of Native Arts* (Fairbanks, Alaska: [University of Alaska Fairbanks?], 1992)

NAME E, J, L, N
Basil H. Johnston

TRIBAL AFFILIATION
Anishinaubae (Ojibway/Pottawatomi)

PERSONAL
Born: July 13, 1929, on the Parry Island Indian Reserve, Canada
Education:
Cape Croker Indian Reserve Public School, Canada
Spanish Indian Residential School, Canada, graduated in 1950
Loyola College, *cum laude,* Montreal, Canada, 1954
Secondary school teaching certificate from the Ontario College of Education, 1962

AWARDS, HONORS

Order of Ontario for Service of the Greatest Distinction and of Singular Excellence Benefiting Society in Ontario and Elsewhere, 1989

Samuel S. Fells Literary Award for the first publication "Zhowmin and Mandamin" by the Coordinating Council of Literary Magazines, New York, 1976

Centennial Medal in Recognition of Work on Behalf of the Native Community, 1967

PUBLICATION HIGHLIGHTS

Indian School Days (Norman: University of Oklahoma Press, 1989)

By Canoe and Moccasin (Lakefield, Ont.: Waapoone Publishing and Promotion, 1986)

Ojibway Ceremonies (Toronto: McClelland and Stewart, 1983)

Tales Our Elders Told (Ontario: Royal Ontario Museum, 1981)

Moose Meat and Wild Rice (Toronto: McClelland and Stewart, 1978)

How the Birds Got Their Colours (Toronto: Kids Can Press, 1978)

Ojibway Heritage (Toronto: McClelland and Stewart, 1976)

Johnston's works have also appeared in numerous anthologies:

Boreal (Hearst, Canada: University College of Hearst, 1975)

Starting Points in Reading (Toronto: Ginn and Company, 1974)

Read Canadian (Toronto: James Lewis and Samuel, 1972)

Teachers Manual for History Series (Toronto: Ginn and Company, 1972)

The Only Good Indian: Essays by Canadian Indians (Toronto: New Press, 1970)

Travel Ontario (Toronto: New Press, 1971)

Dictionary of Canadian Biography, vol. 3 1741–1770 (Toronto: University of Toronto Press, [n.d.])

NARRATIVE

Basil Johnston was raised by his grandmother and mother until he reached the age of 10, when he and his four-year-old sister were taken by an Indian agent to St. Peter Claver's School, also known as "Spanish" to the local population. A Catholic school run by priests, Spanish was located in Sudbury, Ontario, and is the subject of Johnston's book *Indian School Days,* which recalls his life and experiences at the notorious school. Graduating from Spanish in 1950, Johnston spent the following years before and during college working a variety of jobs that kept him close to the land, first as a hunter and trapper, farmer and angler, and later as a lumber and timber worker. He also worked in the mining industry in Wawa, Ontario.

Since 1962 Johnston has worked as an educator in a variety of capacities. He has taught history to students in secondary school as well as in colleges and adult groups, and at the Royal Ontario Museum he has taught English as a second language. Multilingual, Johnston speaks Ojibway, French, English and Spanish. He has taught Ojibway language and culture for many years in the classroom and privately to individuals, and over the years has translated numerous documents from English to Ojibway. He currently works as a lecturer in the subject of ethnology at the Royal Ontario Museum, Toronto, Ontario. As a well-known and sought-after speaker and lecturer Johnston has traveled extensively throughout the United States and Canada to speak at private, state and provincial universities and colleges on the subjects of Native studies, modern languages, Native communications, anthropology, education, English literature, humanities and theological studies.

Johnston has also had extensive experience in the field of broadcasting and media since the early 1970s. In 1972 he was a consultant to the production "Native to the Land," which was produced by the Canadian Broadcasting Corporation (CBC); in 1973 he was a consultant to "Canadian Indians," again by the CBC; he was the scriptwriter and narrator for the program "The Man, the Snake and the Fox," which was produced by Directions Films in Toronto in 1977. Johnston was a consultant to "Serie televisee legendes Indiennes," which was produced by Vie le monde Canada in 1980, and he was the narrator for several programs: "Ojibway Traditions," produced by Radio Station WJOB in Hayward, Wisconsin, in 1982; "Wild in the City," by Rogers Cable 10 Production in 1989 and "Micmac: Seasonal Life," produced by the National Film Board of Canada in 1983. Johnston again worked as a scriptwriter and narrator for the film *Hunting Traditions and Customs* by the National Film Board of Canada, 1982; was a consultant in the making of the film *The Spirit of Maize*, TV Ontario, Toronto, 1986, and he was a script reviewer for the program "Where the Spirit Lives," produced by Amazing Spirit Productions in Toronto, Ontario, in 1988.

Active in his community, Johnston has been an office holder in several organizations. He was the president of the Toronto Indian Club in 1957, he served as the executive and vice president of the Canadian Indian Centre of Toronto from 1963 to 1969, and he was the executive and a member of the Legal Committee and Speakers Committee of the Indian Eskimo Association from 1965 through 1968, among other memberships.

A prolific writer, Johnston has had numerous stories, essays articles and poems published over the years in journals and periodicals, such as *Tawow*, the *Educational Courier, Toronto Native Times, Canadian Fiction Magazine, Many Smokes*, the *Ontario Indian, Whetstone, T.V. Guide, Wildflower Magazine, Sweetgrass Magazine* and *Canadian Children's Literature*, among many others.

Of his life's work Johnston says that it is his wish to take his people's heritage and "improve upon [it] and give [it] to future generations"—that it is a "part of [my] commitment to heritage and to the future." He enjoys the works of N. Scott Momaday and William Shakespeare, and added that the novel *The Cain Mutiny* was one of his recent favorites. As a resident of Toronto, Johnston says that he "doesn't like the city" and that he "writes better outside than inside." He is currently working on five books, which are scheduled to be coming out over the next three years. When he is not writing Johnston enjoys taking walks and visiting many of the lakes in his region. He is married and has three children.

K

NAME   P, VA
Michael Kabotie

OTHER NAMES USED
Lomawywesa

TRIBAL AFFILIATION
Hopi

PERSONAL
Born: 1942 in Shungopavi, Arizona
Education: Graduated from the Haskall Institute, Lawrence, Kansas, 1961; coursework in engineering at the University of Arizona, Tucson

PUBLICATION HIGHLIGHTS
Migration Tears: Poems about Transitions (Los Angeles: University of California at Los Angeles, 1987)

Kabotie's works have appeared in: *Circle of Motion: Arizona Anthology of Contemporary American Indian Literature,* ed. by Kathleen Mullen Sands (Tempe: Arizona Historical Foundation, c1990) and *The South Corner of Time: Hopi, Navajo, Papago, Yaqui Tribal Literature,* ed. by Larry Evers et al. (Tucson: University of Arizona Press, 1980)

NARRATIVE
A visual artist as well as a poet, Kabotie has had a one-man show at the Heard Museum in Phoenix, Arizona, and has exhibited throughout the United States.

NAME   P, PL, S, SC
Geri Keams

OTHER NAMES USED
Geraldine Keams

TRIBAL AFFILIATION
Navajo, Streak-of-Black-Forest Clan

PERSONAL
Born: August 19, 1951, in Winslow, Arizona
Education: Boarding school; graduated from Coconino High School, Flagstaff; B.F.A. in drama education from the University of Arizona, Tucson, 1978

PUBLICATION HIGHLIGHTS
Broken Peacepipe, poems (Tempe, Ariz.: Arizona Historical Foundation, 1990); *Canyon Day Woman Blues,* poems (Ithaca, N.Y.: Firebrand Books, 1984); *Flight of the Army Worm,* play (Albuquerque: Red Earth Press, 1979)

NARRATIVE
Writer and actor Geri Keams was born in Winslow, Arizona, and raised in the town of Castle Buttes, Arizona. She also spent time as a child both on and off the Reservation, in the Painted Desert Region of Northern Arizona, as the oldest child in a family of nine brothers and sisters. Keams was raised by her grandmother, a traditional Navajo rugweaver who still lives at Navajo. "Her life is an example of truth. The integrity and the pain of living gives you your truths when others don't."

She attended thirteen schools before she graduated from high school, which provided her with a large number of acquaintances and gave her a great deal of experience with various kinds of people, both Native and non-Native. Keams always enjoyed performing before an audience. "I was performing at age 6 in boarding school; I was always willing to talk, to be in front of an audience. Since many people thought Indians were shy, I was always changing that, not consciously. I was just being myself." In 1978 Keams toured with the Native American Theatre Ensemble, which is based in New York City. While touring and working with the Ensemble, she helped create a theater production based on the Navajo creation myth. Keams is still an actor, in TV and motion pictures, with one of her more memorable roles in the movie *The Outlaw Josie Wales*, with Clint Eastwood.

The political mood of the country, the Reagan presidency, the Wounded Knee Massacre in 1973 and the tumultuous events of the times all prompted her to seek writing as a form of expression by which to cleanse, heal and communicate "my truth." Keams enrolled in Larry Evers's writing class at the University of Arizona and was able to meet many prominent Native writers in person. "They were an inspiration." Such meetings affected Keams profoundly. "My life needed its own voice. [I had the] need to communicate in a world that wanted me to live by its rules." Consequently, Keams now writes about traditional and modern Native Americans, women and her own past, reflecting upon her own traditional Navajo upbringing. She also writes about her present life in Los Angeles and her move off the Reservation and into an urban setting. As she describes her perspective: "I see things in this world which clash with my world on my grandmother's land. Many times I write after a trip to my home in Arizona."

Keams is currently working on several projects: a series of children's books,

a series of screenplays, and she is continuing her work on her one-woman show, *Legends and Creation Stories,* which she takes to schools. She also works occasionally as an actor in films and in the television commercials industry. Keams sums up her life and work saying, "I basically make my living by living the life I love! It's great!"

NAME   L, P, S
Lenore Keeshig-Tobias

TRIBAL AFFILIATION
Saugeen Ojibway

PUBLICATION HIGHLIGHTS
Bird Talk (Bineshiinh Dibaajmowin), trans. by Shirley Pheasant Williams (Toronto, Ont.: Sister Vision, 1991); "The Porcupine" in *Tales for an Unknown City,* collected by Dan Yashinsky (Montreal: McGill-Queen's University Press, 1990); *The Short Cut* (Don Mills, Ont.: Fitzhenry & Whiteside, 1985)

Keeshig-Toias' works have also appeared in: *Returning the Gift: Poetry and Prose from the First North American Native Writers' Festival,* ed. by Joseph Bruchac with the support of the Association for the Study of American Indian Literatures (Tucson: University of Arizona, 1994) and *Indigena: Contemporary Native Perspectives in Canadian Art* (Tortola, BVI; New York: Craftsman House, 1992).

NARRATIVE
Storyteller, writer and lecturer Keeshig-Tobias has spoken to a number of groups in the United States and Canada, such as the PEI Women's Festival, the National Museum of Civilization, Pennsylvania State University and Carleton University.

She is a workshop leader and an editor and consultant who has worked on the journals *Sweetgrass* from 1982 to 1985 and *Ontario Indian* from 1981 to 1982. Her children's stories, plays, poems, short stories articles and reviews have appeared in journals such as *Saturday Night, Fuse,* the *Globe and Mail, Books in Canada, Ontario Indian, Utne Reader* and *Sweetgrass.* Her plays *Quest for Fire or How the Trickster Brought Fire to the People* and *Word Magic* were produced by De-Ba-Jeh-Mu-Jig Theatre Group in 1990.

Keeshig-Tobias is a founding member of the Committee to Reestablish the Trickster (CRET), a Native writers' group formed to promote Native contributions to literature.

NAME   E, N
Maude Kegg

TRIBAL AFFILIATION
Mille Lacs Band Chippewa

PERSONAL
Born: August 1904 in Crow Wing County, Minnesota
Education: Completed eighth grade

AWARDS, HONORS
National Endowment for the Arts National Heritage Award

PUBLICATION HIGHLIGHTS
Portage Lake: Memories of an Ojibwe Childhood, ed. by Maude Kegg, transcribed by John D. Nichols (Minneapolis: University of Minnesota Press, 1991; Edmonton: University of Alberta Press, 1993)
"The Little Turtle" in *Signs of Spring* (Toronto: Fitzhenry and Whitside, 1988)
Nookomis Gaa-inaajimotawid: What My

Grandmother Told Me: With Texts in Ojibwe (Chippewa) and English, told by Maude Kegg, ed. and transcribed by John D. Nichols (St. Paul: Minnesota Archaeological Society, 1983)
Gabekanaansing: At the End of the Trail: Memories of a Chippewa Childhood with Texts in Ojibwe and English, by Maude Kegg, ed. by John D. Nichols (Greeley, Colo.: University of Northern Colorado, 1978)
Gii-ikwezen Siwiyaan: When I Was a Little Girl, by Maude Kegg, ed. by John D. Nichols (Onamia, Minn.: [s.n.], 1976)

Kegg was a primary contributor to *Ojibwewi-ikidowinan: An Ojibwe Word Resource Book,* ed. by Earl Nyholm and J. D. Nichols (St. Paul: Minnesota Archaeological Society, 1979).

NARRATIVE
Kegg was born in 1904 in her family's wigwam while they were at rice camp in Crow Wing County, Minnesota. Her family was one of the few of the Mille Lacs band that stayed in the Mille Lacs area instead of being forcibly moved to the White Earth Reservation in Minnesota. Because of this resistance her band is also known as the "Non-removable Band." Kegg was bilingual from an early age. Her family followed the traditional seasonal cycles of the Minnesota Anishinaabeg. They would pick berries, fish, garden and make maple sugar in the spring, and in late summer they would move to the many lakes near their homes to set up wild rice camp. In 1920 she married Martin Kegg, who later died in 1968. In that same year, Kegg began working as an interpretive guide at the Mille Lacs Indian Museum, which is part of the Minnesota Historical Society. She now lives at Vineland, Minnesota, on the Mille Lacs Reservation.

Kegg's stories recall the experiences of her youth and the tales she heard from her elders. She is a vital and active member of the Minnesota Archaeological Society and other organizations, working to record her native language and preserve the stories and traditions of her people.

NAME E, F, N, P
Maurice Kenny

TRIBAL AFFILIATION
Mohawk

PERSONAL
Born: August 16, 1929, in Watertown, New York

Education: Butler University, Indianapolis, Indiana; St. Lawrence University; M.A. from New York University, New York 1959

AWARDS, HONORS
New York State Fellowship, 1992

The Signal Award, 1990

American Book Award for *The Mama Poems,* 1984

Citation from St. Lawrence University: Distinguished Service to Literature

Corporation for Public Broadcasting Award for *Black Robe*

PUBLICATION HIGHLIGHTS
Independence (Buffalo, N.Y.: Just Buffalo Literary Center, 1995)

On Second Thought: A Compilation (Norman: University of Oklahoma Press, 1995)

"Bear" in *Callaloo,* January 1994

Tekonwatonti: Molly Brant: Poems of War (Fredonia, N.Y.: White Pine Press, 1992)

Last Mornings in Brooklyn: Poems (Norman: Point Riders Press, 1991)

Rain and Other Fictions (Fredonia, N.Y.: White Pine Press, 1990)

The Short and Long of It: New Poems (Little Rock: University of Arkansas, 1990)

Hand Into Stone, Elizabeth Woody, ed. by Maurice Kenny and J. G. Gosciak (Contact Two Publications, 1988)

These Waves of Dying Friends, Michael Lynch, ed. by Maurice Kenny and J. G. Gosciak (Contact Two Publications, 1988)

Between Two Rivers: Selected Poems (Fredonia, N.Y.: White Pine Press, 1987)

Greyhounding This America: Poems and Dialog, first edition (Chico, Calif.: Heidelberg Graphics, 1987)

The Man with the White Liver, Angela Jackson, ed. by Maurice Kenny and Josh Gosciak (New York: Contact II Publications, 1987)

Vigil of the Wounded, Philip Minthorn, ed. by Maurice Kenny and Josh Gosciak (New York: Contact II Publications, 1987)

Wounds Beneath the Flesh: Anthology of Native American Poetry, ed. by Maurice Kenny (New York: White Pine Press, 1987)

Brooklyn Branding Parlors, James Purdy, ed. by Josh Gosciak and Maurice Kenny (New York: Contact II Publications, 1986)

W. C. Fields in French Light, Rochelle Owens, ed. by Josh Gosciak and Maurice Kenny (New York: Contact II Publications, 1986)

Is Summer This Bear ([S.l.]: Chauncy Press, 1985)

The Mama Poems (West Linn, Oreg.: White Pine Press, 1984)

Black Robe (Saranac Lake, N.Y.: North Country Community College Press, 1982)

Dancing Back Strong the Nation, second edition (Buffalo, N.Y.: White Pine Press, 1981)

Kneading the Blood (New York: Strawberry Press, 1981)

From the Center: A Folio, ed. by Maurice Kenny (New York: Strawberry Press, 1980)

Only as Far as Brooklyn (Boston: Good Gay Poets, 1979)

North: Poems (Marvin South Dakota: Blue Cloud Quarterly, 1977)

Kenny's works have also appeared in the following anthologies:

Returning the Gift: Poetry and Prose from the First North American Native Writers' Festival, ed. by Joseph Bruchac with the support of the Association for the Study of American Indian Literatures (Tucson: University of Arizona, 1994)

Braided Lives: An Anthology of Multicultural American Writing, by the Minnesota Humanities Commission and the Minnesota Council of Teachers of English (St. Paul: The Commission, 1991)

Wounds Beneath the Flesh: Anthology of Native American Poetry (Fredonia, N.Y.: White Pine Press, 1987)

Earth Power Coming: Short Fiction in Native American Literature, ed. by Simon Ortiz (Tsaile, Ariz.: Navajo Community College Press, 1983)

Songs from This Earth on Turtle's Back, ed. by Joseph Bruchac (Greenfield, N.Y.: Greenfield Review Press, 1983)

The Remembered Earth: An Anthology of Contemporary Native American Literature, ed. by Geary Hobson (Norman, Okla.: Red Earth Press, 1978)

From the Belly of the Shark, ed. by Walter Lowenfels (New York: Random House, 1973)

NARRATIVE

Renowned poet and educator Maurice Kenny was born and raised in Watertown, New York, near the St. Lawrence and Black Rivers. He was the youngest of three children and the only boy. While growing up he suffered from various allergies and so struggled with feelings of being "different." He spent his youth in three places: on his aunt's farm in the town of Cape Vincent, at his father's cabin on Chaumont Bay and on the farm of his prankster uncle, near the towns of Verona and Enterprise. It was in Watertown when he was between six and nine years old that he had three great childhood friends: a young Italian "ruffian," an African American and a Native American. Kenny was close to all three, and together they found mutual pride and faith in their individual abilities. His father, Andrew, was also a great supporter of his son's creativity, but it was a childhood neighbor named Aunt Flo, who introduced him to the world of books. Later, as a college student at Butler, St. Lawrence and New York Universities Kenny had three memorable instructors who were to have a dominant influence on his writing: Werner Beyer, Louise Bogan and Douglas Angus. Kenny's choice to pursue a writing career was not sudden but instead assumed throughout his life. "I fear it was wished on me. I had no choice in the matter. [It is] pretty much all I have ever been capable of doing well. In college I prepared myself to write, [with] no other career even though I have been teaching the last seven years." In 1974 Kenny's life took an abrupt turn when he suffered a heart attack and was later told by his cardiologist that he "saved his life so that he could continue writing."

Kenny now lives in the high peak regions of the Adirondack Mountains in upper New York state, which "constantly work their way into both my spiritual life and in my writing." He is the founding editor and owner of the Strawberry Press, which publishes works of art and literature by Native people. He is also the owner and editor of the press Contact II, which is dedicated to poetry and book reviews. Kenny is also working on a brief memoir about his early years growing up.

Kenny enjoys reading works by William Faulkner, W. Somerset Maugham,

Thomas Hardy, Gerard Manley Hopkins, Robinson Jeffers, E. Arlington Robinson, Leslie Silko, Simon Ortiz and Maria Campbell. "They have all influenced me to some degree, but the writer who has held the strongest influence would be William Carlos Williams. I also pay much attention to traditional story song and poetry, as well as William Shakespeare."

Throughout the years Kenny has also lived in the Virgin Islands, Mexico, California and Oklahoma. He enjoys gardening, picking berries, reading, "gossiping, cooking, hiking, traveling and football in the fall."

NAME   P, M

Wayne Keon

TRIBAL AFFILIATION

Ojibway

PERSONAL

Born: December 12, 1946, in Pembroke, Ontario, Canada
Education: Degree in business administration, 1969

PUBLICATION HIGHLIGHTS

Storm Dancer: Poems (Stratford, Ont.: Mercury Press, 1993)
"Down to Ogawa," poem in *Carousel* (Bethesda, Md.: Writers Center, no. 7, 1991)
Sweetgrass II: Poems (Stratford, Ont.: Mercury Press, 1991)
Sweetgrass: An Anthology of Indian Poetry (Elliot Lake, Ont.: W.O.K. Books, 1972)

NARRATIVE

Wayne Keon was born and raised in Pembroke, Ontario, the Ottawa Valley region and the Elliot Lake Ontario, Lake Huron–

Algoma Highlands areas. Keon's youth was spent among his relatives, namely his aunts, uncles, many of whom were storytellers who inspired Keon and supported his creative endeavors. His father, who is also a writer, encouraged him to write and was a strong influence on his life and works. Keon's work appeared in college publications while still in school, which encouraged him to pursue writing as a career. He enjoys the works of Mark Twain, Bill Bissett, Leonard Cohen, B. P. Nichol and e.e. cummings. Keon also plays and writes music and has had his poetry put to music and performed by the Ontario Youth Choral Group. Keon's works have also appeared in the journals *Dalhousie Review, Ariel* and *Canadian Literature.*

NAME   N

Anna Grits Kilpatrick

TRIBAL AFFILIATION

Cherokee

PUBLICATION HIGHLIGHTS

New Echota Letters, with Jack Frederick Kilpatrick (Dallas: Southern Methodist University, 1968)
Run Toward the Nightland: Magic of the Oklahoma Cherokees, ed. by A. G Kilpatrick and J. F. Kilpatrick (Dallas: Southern Methodist University, 1967)
The Shadow of Sequoyah: Social Documents of the Cherokees, 1962–1964, trans. and ed. by A. G. Kilpatrick and J. F. Kilpatrick (Norman: University of Oklahoma Press, 1965)
Walk in Your Soul: Love Incantations of the Oklahoma Cherokees, ed. by A. G. Kilpatrick and J. F. Kilpatrick (Dallas: Southern Methodist University, 1965)
Friends of Thunder: Folktales of the Oklahoma Cherokees, trans. by Anna G. Kilpatrick

and Jack F. Kilpatrick (Dallas: Southern Methodist University, 1964)

NARRATIVE

Kilpatrick is now deceased.

NAME N

Jack Frederick Kilpatrick

TRIBAL AFFILIATION

Cherokee

PUBLICATION HIGHLIGHTS

New Echota Letters, with A. G. Kilpatrick (Dallas: Southern Methodist University, 1968)

Run Toward the Nightland: Magic of the Oklahoma Cherokees, ed. by A. G Kilpatrick and J. F. Kilpatrick (Dallas: Southern Methodist University, 1967)

The Shadow of Sequoyah: Social Documents of the Cherokees, 1962–1964, trans. and ed. by A. G. Kilpatrick and J. F. Kilpatrick (Norman: University of Oklahoma Press, 1965)

Walk in Your Soul: Love Incantations of the Oklahoma Cherokees, ed. by A. G. Kilpatrick and J. F. Kilpatrick (Dallas: Southern Methodist University, 1965)

Friends of Thunder: Folktales of the Oklahoma Cherokees, trans. by A. G. Kilpatrick and Jack F. Kilpatrick (Dallas: Southern Methodist University, 1964)

NARRATIVE

Kilpatrick has also had his work published in the journals *Southern Folklore Quarterly, Southern Indian Studies* and *American Anthropologist.* He is now deceased.

NAME F, N

Bruce King

TRIBAL AFFILIATION

Mohawk

PUBLICATION HIGHLIGHTS

Dustoff (Santa Fe: Institute of American Indian Art, 1982)

King's works have also appeared in: *New Voices from the Longhouse: An Anthology of Contemporary Iroquois Writing,* first edition, ed. by Joseph Bruchac (Greenfield Center, N.Y.: Greenfield Review Press, c1989) and *Native American Literature,* by Andrew Wiget (Boston: Twayne, 1985).

NARRATIVE

King's works have also been published in the journal *Akwesasne Notes.*

NAME E, F, N

Thomas King

TRIBAL AFFILIATION

Cherokee

PERSONAL

Born: 1943
Education: Bachelors degree in agricultural economics, University of Tennessee, Knoxville, 1986; M.S. from South Dakota State University, Brookings, 1990; Ph.D. from University of Oklahoma, 1994

PUBLICATION HIGHLIGHTS

Neo-Classical Furniture Designs: A Reprint of Thomas King's "Modern Style of Cabinet Work Exemplified," 1829 (Mineola, N.Y.: Dover Publications, 1994)

Green Grass, Running Water (Boston: Houghton Mifflin, 1993)

All My Relations: An Anthology of Contemporary Canadian Native Fiction (Norman: University of Oklahoma Press, 1992)

Medicine River (Markham, Ont.: Viking, 1989)

Allegories of Genesis (West Chester, Pa.: Swedenborg Foundation, 1982)

"The One About Coyote Going West," short story in *Journal of Wild Culture* ([Toronto]: Society for the Preservation of Wild Culture, Fall, vol. 11, nos. 2, 3)

King's works have also appeared in: *Talking Leaves: Contemporary Native American Short Stories, An Anthology,* ed. by Craig Lesley (New York: Laurel, Dell, 1991) and *The Last Map Is the Heart* (Saskatoon, Sask.: Thistledown Press, 1989).

NARRATIVE

King is of Greek, German and Cherokee descent. He is presently teaching creative writing, Native literature and American studies at the University of Minnesota, and he is also a member of the Native studies department at the University of Lethbridge. His works have also appeared in the journals *Canadian Literature* and *Film Quarterly.*

NAME   P, VA
King D. Kuka

TRIBAL AFFILIATION
Blackfeet

PUBLICATION HIGHLIGHTS

Kuka's works have appeared in numerous anthologies:

Dancing on the Rim of the World: An Anthology of Contemporary Northwest Native American Writing, ed. by Andrea Lerner (Tucson: Sun Tracks; University of Arizona Press, c1990)

New and Old Voices of Wah'Kon-Tah, third edition, ed. by Robert K. Dodge and Joseph B. McCullough (New York: International Publishers, c1985)

The Remembered Earth: An Anthology of Contemporary Native American Literature, ed. by Geary Hobson (Albuquerque, N.M.: Red Earth Press, 1979)

Voices of the Rainbow: Contemporary Poetry by American Indians, ed. by Kenneth Rosen (New York: Viking, 1975)

Voices from Wah'Kon-Tah: Contemporary Poetry of Native Americans, first edition, ed. by Robert K. Dodge and Joseph B. McCullough (New York: International Publishers, 1974)

The Whispering Wind: Poetry by Young American Indians, ed. by Terry Allen (New York: Doubleday, 1972)

NARRATIVE

Kuka, a writer and well-known visual artist, has works in the permanent collections of many prominent museums, such as the Gilcrease Institute of American History and Art in Tulsa, Oklahoma, the Heye Foundation in New York City, the Heard Museum in Phoenix, Arizona, the Museum of the Plains Indian in Browning, Montana, and the National Museum of Man in Ottawa, Canada, among many others.

L

NAME
Vincent LaDuke

OTHER NAMES USED
Sun Bear

TRIBAL AFFILIATION
Chippewa

PUBLICATION HIGHLIGHTS
Buffalo Hearts (Heraldsburg, Calif.: Naturegraph Publishers, 1970); *At Home in the Wilderness* (Heraldsburg, Calif.: Naturegraph Publishers, 1969)

NARRATIVE
LaDuke is now deceased.

NAME
Winona LaDuke

OTHER NAMES USED
Winona LaDuke Kapashesit

TRIBAL AFFILIATION
Ojibwa

PERSONAL
Education: M.A. from Antioch University, 1988

PUBLICATION HIGHLIGHTS
"Chippewas Take on Congress: Constitutional Challenge to Take Back Their Land," article in *Wildfire* (Spokane, Wash.: Wildfire, vol. 3, no. 1/2, 1987)

A Heritage at Risk: Native Americans and Poverty, audio recording (Iowa State University Lecture Series, 1988)

Environmental and Social Justice, audio recording (Iowa State University Lecture Series, 1993)

Indigenous Women and Feminism, audiovisual (Madison, Wisc.: University of Wisconsin, 1992)

Indigenous People and Environmental Concerns, audiovisual (Madison, Wisc.: University of Wisconsin, 1992)

LaDuke's works have appeared in: *A Gathering of Spirit: A Collection by North American Indian Women,* ed. by Beth Brant (Degonwadonti)(Ithaca, N.Y.: Firebrand, 1988, c1984).

NARRATIVE
LaDuke now lives in Massachusetts.

NAME
Lame Deer

OTHER NAMES USED
Tahca Ushte
John Fire
John Fire Lame Deer

TRIBAL AFFILIATION
Sicangu Lakota

PERSONAL
Born: Various sources give his birth date as: 1876, 1900 or 1903. Born on the Rosebud Reservation, South Dakota.

PUBLICATION HIGHLIGHTS
Lame Deer, Seeker of Visions: The Life of a Sioux Medicine Man, with Richard Erdoes (New York: Simon & Schuster, 1972)

Lame Deer's work has also appeared in these anthologies:

The Sacred Hoop: Recovering the Feminine in American Indian Traditions, by Paula Gunn Allen (Boston: Beacon Press, 1986)

Native American Renaissance, by Kenneth Lincoln (Berkeley: University of California Press, c1983)

Literature of the American Indians: Views and Interpretations: A Gathering of Indian Memories, Symbolic Contexts and Literary Criticism, ed. by Abraham Chapman (New York: New American Library, 1975)

NARRATIVE

Lakota holy man Lame Deer attended reservation schools until he reached the third grade. He died in 1976.

NAME   E, L,N,P,VA

Frank LaPena

OTHER NAMES USED

Tauhindauli

TRIBAL AFFILIATION

Wintu-Nomtipom

PERSONAL

Born: October 5, 1937, San Francisco, California

Education: Coursework in liberal arts, California State University–Chico, 1965; teaching credential, San Francisco State University, 1968; M.A. in ethnography, California State University, Sacramento

PUBLICATION HIGHLIGHTS

The World Is a Gift (San Francisco: Limestone Press, 1987)

The Extension of Tradition: Contemporary Northern California Native American Art in Cultural Perspective, ed. by Frank R. LaPena and Janice T. Driesbach (Sacramento: Crocker Art Museum, 1985)

Legends of the Yosemite Miwok, comp. by Frank LaPena and Craig D. Bates (Yosemite National Park: Yosemite Natural History Association, 1981)

Wintu Ethnography Revised (Sacramento: California State University, 1978)

CALAFIA: California Poetry (Berkeley: A Y'Bird Book, 1979)

LaPena's works also appear in the anthology: *Songs from This Earth on Turtle's Back,* first edition, ed. by Joseph Bruchac (Greenfield Center, N.Y.: Greenfield Review Press, 1983).

NARRATIVE

Frank LaPena was raised by his grandmother. His father died when he was five years old, and he soon lost his mother, who he never knew. As a child he was sent to Indian boarding schools in Stewart, Nevada, and Chemawa, Oregon, and he later lived in a foster home in Northern California during his high school years. Active in sports a youth, LaPena also had several good instructors in English and mathematics, although (he says) "I was more interested in getting out." His most meaningful education has been from the medicine people, elders and singers in his tribe, and of the tribes of Northern California among other tribes. He was close to his elders, his uncles and aunts, a medicine woman and dance captain and singers he has known. He was also close to Wallace Burrows, who was over 101 when he passed on. LaPena currently works as a painter, photographer, sculptor and poet, and is presently the director of Native American studies and associate professor of art at California State University, Sacramento, and is also active as a singer and dancer in traditional activities.

LaPena's short stories, prose and poetry are about art, traditions and culture.

His artwork has appeared in numerous galleries and shows throughout the United States, Europe, Cuba and South America. LaPena also gives readings of his works and was involved in the PBS Television production "California Indian Performing Arts." He writes an art column for the journal *News from Native California,* which he considers to hold some of his best written work. He enjoys reading the works of authors John Hersey, John Steinbeck, N. Scott Momaday, Leslie Silko, Galeano, Jorge Luis Borges and Ernest Hemingway. "Lots of different people and poets."

He is now working on a book about the history of the Wintun Tribe and an art book, and he is in the continuous process of writing poems and prose. When he in not writing, he works as a visual artist first, but he adds: "I write to gain some sanity on some other level of clarity for myself. Both art and writing are different aspects of the same thing."

NAME E, J
Frank LaPointe

TRIBAL AFFILIATION
Sicangu Lakota

PERSONAL
Born: November 1, 1936, in Rosebud, South Dakota
Education: B.A. from Rockhurst College, Kansas City, Missouri, 1958; coursework at Black Hills State College, Spearfish South Dakota

AWARDS, HONORS
South Dakota Indian Educator of the Year from the South Dakota Indian Education Association, 1979; John Hay Whitney Fellowship, 1967

PUBLICATION HIGHLIGHTS
The Sioux Today (New York: Macmillan, 1972); "Millie's Gift" in *An American Indian Anthology,* comp. by Benet Tvedten (Marvin, S. Dak.: Blue Cloud Abbey, 1971)

NARRATIVE
Born in Rosebud, South Dakota, LaPointe worked as a ranch hand until he attended Rockhurst College. LaPointe served in the U.S. Navy as a journalist from 1959 to 1963. He worked as a newspaper reporter and editor for the *Rosebud Sioux Herald: Eyapaha* and also the *Littleton Independent and Arapahoe Herald* from Littleton, Colorado. LaPointe became the executive director of the Sicangu Oyate Ho, Inc. school in St. Francis, South Dakota, in 1971 and in 1977 was the institution's fiscal officer. He has also worked as an instructor at Sinte Gleske College, where he was a charter member of the American Indian Leadership Council. LaPointe is a member of the Rosebud Sioux Council.

NAME E, F, L, N, P
Emma LaRocque

TRIBAL AFFILIATION
First Nations affiliation Plains Cree Metis

PERSONAL
Born: January 2, 1949, in Big Boy, Alberta
Education:
Completed two years in the faculty of education, majoring in English and sociology, Camrose Junior College, Camrose, Alberta, 1969–1971
B.A. in English and communications, Goshen College, Goshen Indiana, 1973
M.A. in religion (peace studies), AMBS, Elkhart, Indiana, 1976

M.A. in history, University of Manitoba, Winnipeg, Manitoba, 1980

Currently working on Ph.D. in Interdisciplinary Program, University of Manitoba

AWARDS, HONORS

Interim Fellowship for Doctoral Studies, Graduate Studies, University of Manitoba, 1992

Faculty of Arts (Dean's Office) Grant (Native Women Speaker Series, 1987/1989) University of Manitoba, 1986

Staff Research Support Grant, Academic Development Fund, for Manitoba Native History Research Project, University of Manitoba, 1982

Manitoba Graduate Fellowship, University of Manitoba, 1977

Rockefeller Fellowship from Princeton University, 1974

PUBLICATION HIGHLIGHTS

Among many academic publications and works appearing in newspapers over the years, Laroque's creative works include the following:

Violence in Aboriginal Communities ([Ottawa]: National Clearinghouse on Family Violence, 1994)

"My Hometown Northern Canada South Africa" in *Border Crossings* (Winnipeg, Manitoba: Arts Manitoba Publications, November 1992)

"Tides, Towns and Trains" in *Living the Changes,* ed. by Joan Turner (Winnipeg, Manitoba: University of Manitoba Press, 1990)

"On the Ethics of Publishing Historical Documents" in *The Orders of the Dreamed: George Nelson on Cree and Northern Ojibwa Religion and Myth, 1823,* ed. by Jennifer S. H. Brown and Robert Brightman (Winnipeg, Manitoba: University of Manitoba Press, 1988)

"An Evening Walk," poem in *Prairie Fire* (Winnipeg, Manitoba: MWN Publica-

tions, vol. III, no. 1, Spring 1986)

Three Conventional Approaches to Native People in Society and Literature ([Regina]: Saskatchewan Library Association, 1984)

LaRocque, E., and Beaucage, M., "Two Faces of the New Jerusalem: Indian/Metis Reaction to the Missionaries," in *Visions of the New Jerusalem: Religious Settlement of the Prairies,* ed. by B. Smillie (Edmonton, Alberta: NeWest Pub., l983)

"Brown Sister," and "The Geese Over the City," poems in the *Mennonite Reporter* (Waterloo, Ont.: Mennonite Public Service, April 19, 1982)

Defeathering the Indian (Agincourt, Ont.: Book Society of Canada, 1975)

LaRocque's poems have also been included in the following monographs:

Four Feathers: Poems and Stories by Canadian Native Authors, ed. by Harmut Lutz (SLOBEMA Co-operative, 1991)

Writing the Circle: Native Women of Western Canada: An Anthology, ed. by Jean Perreault and Sylvia Vance, (Edmonton, Alberta: NeWest Pub., 1990)

Canadian Literature Quarterly, Special Issue on Native writers and Canadian writing, ([Vancouver: University of British Columbia?], Spring 1990)

Our Bit of Truth, ed. by Agnes Grant (Winnipeg, Manitoba: Pemmican Publications, 1990)

NARRATIVE

Emma LaRocque was raised in northeastern Alberta in a small Metis community, "a very racist town" that made its livelihood on trapping (as did her own family) and railroad work, and supplied her with "many poignant experiences" throughout her early years. She grew up in a very close and loving family. She vividly remembers the racism and cruelty of grade school, but loved learning and had a wonderful and skilled teacher who contributed to her "quality of life" and helped her succeed in school.

Until 1971, LaRocque worked as an intern-teacher for the Northland School Division on the Janvier Reservation, Alberta. From 1971 until 1972 she was a reporter, then assistant editor for the Alberta Native Communications Society's *Native People* newspaper. LaRocque set up the Alberta Native Communications Society (ANCS) education programming and was coordinator of the programming until she returned to the University of Manitoba. The program was in conjunction with the Alberta School broadcasts, which produced dramatic radio programs on Native people. In 1972 she produced six original dramatic radio scripts on Metis history and Riel, for the Alberta School Broadcasts in Edmonton, and worked as a freelance journalist for various magazines in the United States and Canada. She worked as a scriptwriter in 1974 for the Alberta Native Communications Society (ANCA) in Edmonton, and also produced radio and television scripts for ANCA. From 1976 until the present time, LaRocque has worked as a teaching assistant for the Department of History at the University of Manitoba, steadily working up in academic rank to her present position as a full-time professor in the Department of Native Studies. In 1989 she was invited to teach a semester at the University of Osnabruck, West Germany, and in the same year she taught Native identity and history of colonization in Canada for the Native Communications Program, Grant McEwan Community College, Edmonton.

In addition to her teaching workload at the University of Manitoba, LaRocque is working on her doctoral degree at the same university. Her doctoral studies area is focused on the colonizer and the colonized in Canadian historiography and literature regarding Native peoples. She is also working on a continued research project for the Manitoba Native History Project, which is now tentatively titled "The Dichotomy of Civilization/Savagery," or as listed in the project outline "Canadian Perspectives on Native Peoples: An Historiographical Study." Areas in which Larocque lectures include Native Peoples of Canada, the Metis of Canada, American Native literature, Canadian Native literature, Images of Indian People in North American society and seminars on Native women.

LaRocque has been published in numerous scholarly and academic works, has participated in conferences, often as a presenter, and has written many government, industrial and technical reports, as well as poems and fictional works on subjects such as colonization, racism, sexism and education. She has also been interviewed on radio programs and in newspapers in the United States and Canada. She enjoys the works of Pablo Neruda and considers some of her strongest written works to be her essays in *Writing the Circle and Living the Changes,* her recent poetry, her 1978 masters thesis in *Native Education* and her work *Defeathering the Indian.*

❖❖❖

NAME   P
Patrick Russell LeBeau

TRIBAL AFFILIATION
Mniconju Lakota

PUBLICATION HIGHLIGHTS
"The Dawes General Allotment Act" in *Book of Days* (Ann Arbor, Mich.: Pierian Press, 1986)

Profiles of Natural Resources on the Reservations of North Dakota and South Dakota, report published for the Native American Task Force (New York: The Ford Foundation, September, 1986)

"Energy Interests Endanger Indian Lands"

in *The People's Voice* ([Jamesburg, N.J.: Wictor Wilusz?], March 1982)

NAME   P
Lanniko Louelle Lee

TRIBAL AFFILIATION
Mniconju Lakota

PERSONAL
Born: On the Cheyenne River Reservation, Eagle Butte, South Dakota
Education: Coursework for an M.A., Bread Loaf School of English, Middlebury College, Middlebury, Vermont

PUBLICATION HIGHLIGHTS
"Invitation to Lakota Territory" in *Writers' Forum* (Colorado Springs, Colo.: University of Colorado at Colorado Springs, vol. 17, Fall 1991)
"Awash in Wool" in *Yeast* (Middlebury, Vt.: Bread Loaf School of English, Middlebury College, no. 6, Summer 1990)
"Bird Song Woman" in *Yeast* (Middlebury, Vt.: Bread Loaf School of English, Middlebury College, no. 3 Summer 1990)
"School Words" in *Bread Loaf News* (Middlebury, Vt.: Bread Loaf School of English, Middlebury College, vol. 5, no. 1, [n.d.])

NAME   P
June Leivas

TRIBAL AFFILIATION
Chemehuevi

PERSONAL
Born: 1950 in Parker, Arizona

PUBLICATION HIGHLIGHTS
Leivas' works have appeared in *From the Belly of the Shark: A New Anthology of Native Americans,* ed. by Walter Lowenfels (New York: Vantage, 1974); "America," "Don't Let Time's Conquest Be Final" in *American Indian Culture Center Journal* ([S.l.: s.n.], vol. 2 Winter 1971) and "The Battle's Not Over Yet," "No Indians Here," "Shadow People," "Yesterday" in *Akwesasne Notes* (Rooseveltown, N.Y.: Mohawk Nation, vol. 3, 1971).

NAME   L, N, P, PA, S, VA
Mary Jane Litchard

OTHER NAMES USED
Anuqsraaq

TRIBAL AFFILIATION
Inuit and Commanche

PERSONAL
Born: January 3, 1951, in Eotzebue, Alaska
Education: Mt. Edgecumbe, Alaska High School; A.A. in education; two courses short of B.A. in ethnic arts and culture/ education

AWARDS, HONORS
Golden Poet Award, 1986

PUBLICATION HIGHLIGHTS
"Fanny," story in *Brilliant Star* (Hixson, Tenn.: National Spiritual Assembly of the Baha'is of the United States, vol. 21, no. 5, Nov./Dec. 1989)
"The Aleuts: Eskimos Distant Relatives," poem in *Alaska Native News* ([S.l.: s.n.]: vol. 2, no. 8, August 1984)
"A Reminiscence," poem in *Alaska Native News* ([S.l.: s.n.]: vol. 2, no. 5 April 1984)

"Female Beings," "Eskimo Blood," poems in *Canadian Encounter* ([S.l.: s.n.], vol. 1, no. 1, 1981)

NARRATIVE

Mary Jane Litchard was raised in the areas of Lost River, Teller, Anchorage, Fairbanks and Barrow, Alaska. One vivid memory from her childhood is of the time she and her brother were selected to greet the president of the United States. "When we lived in Anchorage, Alaska, I was chosen by [the] Mother's Club to greet John F. Kennedy at the airport. He was campaigning for presidency. My little brother Steven [Brown] and I wore our hot parkas and greeted him."

In her youth Litchard turned to writing as an outlet, a means of expressing her emotions. "I couldn't trust talking or sharing with anyone so I turned to pen and paper as a teenager to write about my life problems." She is now a self-employed artist, Eskimo dancer and writer. Her literary subjects include Inuit, or Eskimo, culture and life experiences, women's issues and recovery issues. She feels her strongest works have been her children's stories and poems. The Russian poet Pushkin is one of Litchard's favorite writers. She also enjoys early Native American writings, particularly poems written by "Young Doctor," a Makah Indian of the early 1900s.

Litchfield now lives in the state of Washington. "Up north I had difficult time writing because I did crafts in order to survive the high cost of living. Down south I can concentrate more time on writing because cost of living is lowered." She is also a craftsperson. "I make finger puppets that are little Eskimos, Eskimo yo-yos I also paint, stencil and draw variety of pictures. I also like to visit and share at recovery meetings. I also hold Bahai' children classes once a week." She is now working on five writing projects, four of which are long term, and all will include her illustrations.

NAME   P, PA, VA

Harold Littlebird

TRIBAL AFFILIATION

Laguna Pueblo, Santo Domingo Pueblo

PERSONAL

Born: 1951 in Albuquerque, New Mexico
Education: Graduated from the Institute of American Indian Art, Santa Fe, New Mexico, 1969

AWARDS, HONORS

First Place from the Vincent Price Awards in Poetry, 1969; Special Award from the Scottsdale National Poetry Contest, 1968

PUBLICATION HIGHLIGHTS

"A Circle Begins" in *National Geographic* magazine (Washington, D.C.: National Geographic Society, vol. 180, no. 4, October 1991); *Beyond Tradition* (Flagstaff: Northland Press, 1990); *On Mountains' Breath* (Santa Fe: Tooth of Time Books, 1982)

Littlebird's works have also appeared in several anthologies:

Returning the Gift: Poetry and Prose from the First North American Native Writers' Festival, ed. by Joseph Bruchac with the support of the Association for the Study of American Indian Literatures (Tucson: University of Arizona, 1994)

Survival This Way: Interviews with Native American Poets, by Joseph Bruchac (Tucson: Sun Tracks; University of Arizona Press, 1987)

New and Old Voices of Wah'Kon-Ta, third edition, ed. by Robert K. Dodge and Joseph B. McCullough (New York: International Publishers, c1985)

Words in the Blood: Contemporary Indian Writers of North and South America, ed. by Jamaike Highwater (New York: New American Library, 1984)

The Remembered Earth: An Anthology of Contemporary Native American Literature, ed. by Geary Hobson (Albuquerque: Red Earth Press, 1979)

Voices of the Rainbow: Contemporary Poetry by American Indians, ed. by Kenneth Rosen (New York: Viking, 1975)

NARRATIVE

Littlebird lived in California and Utah as a young man. His works have appeared in the journals the *New York Quarterly, Alcheringa* and the *New Mexico Review.* Littlebird is also known for his pottery and performance art.

NAME   P, N

Mary Lockwood

TRIBAL AFFILIATION

Inupiaq Malemute

PERSONAL

Born: April 12, 1952, in Unalakleet, Alaska
Education: B.A. in community studies, University of California at Santa Cruz

AWARDS, HONORS

University of California Regents Scholarship 1970

PUBLICATION HIGHLIGHTS

"Caribou" in the *Greenfield Review Press* (Greenfield, N.Y.: Greenfield Review Press, 1991); "Cold Wars" in *Matrix* ([S.l.:

s.n.], vol. 15, no. 2 May 1991); "Mother Earth Meets the Holy Trinity" in *Twanas* (vol. 5, issue 4, June 1985)

Lockwood's works have also appeared in: *Returning the Gift: Poetry and Prose from the First North American Native Writers' Festival,* ed. by Joseph Bruchac with the support of the Association for the Study of American Indian Literatures (Tucson: University of Arizona, 1994).

NARRATIVE

Raised in Unalakleet, Alaska, Mary Lockwood attended the upward bound programs at the University of Alaska during her high school summers. An early mentor was T. D. Allen, who came to Unalakleet to offer her a regents scholarship in 1970. Writer Sally Carrighan, who wrote two books about Unalakleet in the mid-1950s, inspired Lockwood in her decision to become a writer as did several others writers, including two filmmakers and her aunt, who wrote two books when Lockwood was a young girl. Two monumental events in her life that appear in her writings are the establishment of Alaska statehood in 1958 when she was six years old, and the consequent fall in social position of the Native population.

Now living in Santa Cruz, California, Lockwood considers her quiet, reminiscent stories of her Alaskan girlhood experiences her strongest works because "they convey the beauty, security, adventure and wildness of my ancient race." Deeply moved by her geographical surroundings, Lockwood writes about her northern upbringing in a Southern California environment "span[ning] thirty years of rigorous living and move[ing] them aside to come to images of my faraway childhood." Favorite writers include Barry Lopez, early Leslie Marmon Silko, Sally Cunningham and Simon Schwartz-Bart. She is working on an autobiographical novel from her Alaska childhood through her California years. The remaining portion of her novel recounts her affiliation with the Native American Church. Lockwood is also working on articles and essays that "respond to current situations in the world." In her spare time, Lockwood enjoys sewing, beading and cooking.

NAME   E, P, VA

Ramson Lomatewama

TRIBAL AFFILIATION

Hopi

PERSONAL

Born: October 20, 1953, in Victorville, California
Education: B.A. liberal studies, Goddard College, Vermont

AWARDS, HONORS

American Indian Arts Foundation Award for Poetry; Arizona Senator's Art Award for Contribution to Community; Awards in juried art shows

PUBLICATION HIGHLIGHTS

Drifting Through Ancestor Dreams: New and Selected Poems, first edition (Flagstaff Ariz.: Entrada Books, 1993); *Ascending the Reed, Poems* (Flagstaff, Ariz.: Badger Claw Press, 1987); *Silent Winds: Poetry of One Hopi,* fourth edition (Flagstaff, Ariz.: Badger Claw Press, 1987)

NARRATIVE

Ramson Lomatewama grew up in Flagstaff, Arizona, and attended a Mennonite school in Hoteville, on the Hopi Reservation. Several years later, he began pre-medical studies at Northern Arizona

University, which he relinquished, admitting he was "fulfilling someone else's dream." Instead, he earned a bachelors degree in Liberal Studies from Goddard College, Vermont, and returned to the Hopi Reservation. Such dramatic relocations and changes had a cataclysmic effect on his life and his writings. Lomatwewama credits his uncle with helping him define his role in the world by educating him in clan history and tradition. His friend artist Charles Loloma was also an early influence.

He worked as an educator in Flagstaff for a number of years but found that his art and writing were his true calling. His works help in the process of "healing," and by "watering his own seeds" he is now able to go out and give to the world. Part of his evolution as a writer is due to the force of the Hopi oral tradition that permits him to "step over the edge" creatively.

He was a resident of Flagstaff for many years, and he now lives outside the city, where he gardens and lives a "natural course of life." Writers he enjoys include Jung, Campbell, as well as various Japanese poets.

NAME   P

Charles C. Long

TRIBAL AFFILIATION

Navajo

PUBLICATION HIGHLIGHTS

"Yei-ie's Child," poem in *Blue Cloud Quarterly* (Marvin, S. Dak.: Blue Cloud Quarterly, vol. 15, no. 3, [n.d.])

Long's works also appear in *New and Old Voices of Wah'Kon-Tah,* third edition, ed. by Robert K. Dodge and Joseph B.

McCullough (New York: International Publishers, c1985) and *Voices from Wah'Kon-Tah: Contemporary Poetry of Native Americans,* first edition, ed. by Robert K. Dodge and Joseph B. McCullough (New York: International Publishers, c1974).

NAME P
Alonzo Lopez

TRIBAL AFFILIATION
Tohono O'dham

PERSONAL
Born: Pima County, Arizona
Education: Coursework at the Institute of American Indian Arts, Santa Fe, New Mexico; coursework at Yale University, New Haven, Connecticut; coursework at Wesleyan University, Middletown, Connecticut

PUBLICATION HIGHLIGHTS
Celebration (Littleton, Mass.: Sundance Publishing, 1991, 1972)

Lopez's works have appeared in numerous anthologies:

The American Indian Speaks, ed. by John R. Milton (Vermillion: Dakota Press; University of South Dakota, 1969)
New and Old Voices of Wah'Kon-Tah, third edition, ed. by Robert K. Dodge and Joseph B. McCullough (New York: International Publishers, c1985)
Native American Reader: Stories, Speeches and Poems, ed. by Jerry D. Blanche (Juneau: Denali Press, c 1990)
Literature of the American Indian, by Thomas Sanders and William Peek (Beverly Hills: Glencoe Press, 1973)

NARRATIVE
While a student in his sophomore year at the Institute of American Indian Arts, Lopez was accepted for an interim year of studies at Yale University. Lopez's works have also appeared in the journal the *South Dakota Review.*

NAME F, N, VA
Oren Lyons

TRIBAL AFFILIATION
Onondaga

PUBLICATION HIGHLIGHTS
Exiled in the Land of the Free: Democracy, Indian Nations, and the U.S. Constitution, by Oren Lyons et al. (Santa Fe: Clear Light, 1992); *Wilderness in Native American Culture* (Moscow, Idaho: University of Idaho Wilderness Research Center, 1989)

Lyon's works have appeared in: *New Voices from the Longhouse: An Anthology of Contemporary Iroquois Writing,* first edition, ed. by Joseph Bruchac (Greenfield Center, N.Y.: Greenfield Review Press, c1989) and *American Indian Authors for Young Readers: A Selected Bibliography,* comp. by Mary Gloyne Byler (New York: Association on American Indian Affairs, [1973]).

NARRATIVE
Lyons has also illustrated two publications by Virginia Driving Hawk Sneve: *High Elk's Treasure* (New York: Holiday House, 1992) and *When Thunder Spoke* (Lincoln: University of Nebraska, 1993)

NAME F, N
Sarah D. Lyons

TRIBAL AFFILIATION
Isleta Pueblo

PUBLICATION HIGHLIGHTS
"Poem to the National Alliance in Memorium of David Sohappy" in the newspaper the *National Alliance* (New York: National Alliance Foundation, vol. 12, no. 23, June 13 1991)

"Sister You Are Mixed Like Me," "Walk On," poems in *Gatherings: The En'owkin Journal of First North American Peoples* (Penticton, B.C.: Theytus Books, 1991)

"Proudly of Mixed Heritage in a White Racist Society" in *Present Time* (Seattle, Wash.: Rational Island Publishers, 1989)

NARRATIVE
Lyons works as a paste-up artist for a publishing company and does volunteer work on the newsletter of the Native American Program of the Oregon Legal Services (NAPOLS).

M

NAME N

George Manuel

TRIBAL AFFILIATION

Shuswap

PERSONAL

Born: February 17, 1921, in Chase, British Columbia

Education: Coursework at Laval University, Quebec

PUBLICATION HIGHLIGHTS

The Fourth World: An Indian Reality and Social Change (Don Mills, Ontario: Collier-MacMillan of Canada, 1973)

White Man's Whitewash, with Michael Poslums ([S.l.]: National Indian Brotherhood, 1972)

District Six, with Denis Hatfield (White Plains, N.Y.; Toronto: Longman's Green, 1967)

Manuel's works have appeared in: *The Only Good Indian: Essays by Canadian Indians* (Toronto: New Press, 1970).

NARRATIVE

Manuel served as the president of the National Indian Brotherhood in Ottawa, Ontario, from 1970 to 1976. He was the president of the Union of British Columbian Indian Chiefs in Vancouver from 1977 to 1981. In 1975 and 1981 Manuel served as the president of the World Council of Indigenous Peoples. Manuel also worked as the community development officer for the town of Duncan, British Columbia.

NAME N

Brian Maracle

OTHER NAMES USED

Owenadeka

TRIBAL AFFILIATION

Mohawk

PERSONAL

Born: March 18, 1947, in Detroit, Michigan

Education: Bachelor of arts, Dartmouth, Hanover, New Hampshire, 1969; Bachelor of journalism, Carleton University, Ottawa, Ontario, Canada, 1982

AWARDS, HONORS

Ottawa Association of Canadian Television and Radio Artists Award for Best Commentary, 1991

Canadian National Radio Award for Best Commentary, 1989

Ottawa Association of Canadian Television and Radio Artists Award for Best Documentary, 1987

PUBLICATION HIGHLIGHTS

Crazywater: Native Voices on Addiction and Recovery (Toronto; New York: Penguin, 1994)

"Our Native Land" in the *Saskatchewan Indian Magazine* (Saskatoon, Sask.: *Saskatchewan Indian Magazine,* April 1988)

"Trading Secrets" in the *Saskatchewan Indian Magazine* (Saskatoon: *Saskatchewan Indian Magazine,* May 1988)

"The Stockholm Syndrome" in *Ontario Indian Magazine* (Toronto, Ont.: [s.n.], July/August 1984)

"Strings Attached" in *Ontario Indian Magazine* (Toronto, Ont.: *Ontario Indian Magazine,* May 1982)

"Limitations Statute Invoked: Time Could Be Running Out" in *Perception* (Ottawa, Ont.: Canadian Council on Social Development, November/December 1981)

NARRATIVE

Brian Maracle was raised on the Six Nations Reserve, Ontario, in Buffalo and Rochester, New York, and in Niagara-on-the-lake in southern Ontario. Son of writer Lee Maracle, he is the author of numerous magazine articles and commentaries in various Canadian journals, on the subjects of Native people, politics and current affairs.

Maracle expresses the belief that he and probably many other writers of his generation were not encouraged by anyone to be a writer. "I did not write when I was young so I did not have a mentor. I didn't get any special help or inspiration to become a writer—it just happened, believe it or not." He currently resides in Ottawa, Ontario, where he works as a writer.

NAME   E, F, N, P

Lee Maracle

OTHER NAMES USED

Bobbi Lee Maracle

TRIBAL AFFILIATION

Cree/Metis and Salish

PERSONAL

Education: Vancouver Community College; Simon Fraser University, British Columbia

PUBLICATION HIGHLIGHTS

Raven Songs: A Novel (Vancouver, B.C.: Press Gang, 1993)

Sundogs: A Novel (Penticton, B.C.: Theytus Books, 1992)

Seeds (Vancouver: Write-On, 1991)

Bobbi Lee: Indian Rebel (Toronto: Women's Press, 1990)

Linked Lives (Montreal: Trois Editions, 1990)

Oratory: Coming to Theory (North Vancouver, B.C.: Gallerie Publications, 1990)

Sojourner's Truth and Other Stories (Vancouver: Press Gang, 1990)

Telling It: Women and Language Across Culture, ed. by Telling It Book Collective (Vancouver: Press Gang, 1990)

I Am Woman: A Native Perspective on Sociology and Feminism (North Vancouver, B.C.: Write-On, 1988)

Maracles's works have also appeared in: *Gatherings* (S.l: Theytus Books, 1990); *Native Writers and Canadian Writing* (Vancouver: University of British Columbia Press, 1990); *Rediscovery* (Vancouver: Western Canada Wilderness Communications, 1989).

NARRATIVE

Lee Maracle is a writer of poetry, fiction and nonfiction and has had numerous articles published in literary and historical journals, such as *Trivia, Canadian Literature* and *Fireweed.* She has taught courses in indigenous history and awareness, cross-cultural writing, cultural appropriation, contemporary Native women's issues, women and violence, empowerment, healing through writing, Native literature and contemporary social issues. She has also been involved in curriculum development and course delivery. She has taught at the En'owkin International School of Writing, the University of Saskatchewan, the British Columbia Federation of Writers, Saskatchewan Indian Federated College and the British Columbia Native Youth Association.

NAME   N

Peter Markoosie

OTHER NAMES USED

Markoosie
Markoosie Patsang

TRIBAL AFFILIATION

Inuit

PERSONAL

Born: June 19, 1942

PUBLICATION HIGHLIGHTS

Harpoon of the Hunter (Montreal: McGill-Queen's University Press, 1970)

NARRATIVE

Markoosie attended the Port Harrison Elementary School as a young man. He later earned his commercial pilot's license and a carpentry diploma. One of the first Canadian Inuit to hold a commercial flying license, Markoosie worked as a pilot from 1969 to 1975, flying charter trips, and as a translator from 1975 to 1976. His novel *Harpoon of the Hunter* was the first long work by an Inuit to be published into English.

NAME   F, N, M, PL, PA, V

Rudy Martin

TRIBAL AFFILIATION

Tewa, Navajo and Apache

PERSONAL

Education: M.F.A. in playwriting, Tisch School of the Arts, New York University, New York

PUBLICATION HIGHLIGHTS

"Medicine War," *Kainai News* (Stand Off, Alberta: Indian News Media, vol. XXIV, no. 6, Feb. 21, 1991)

"A View from New York," *Turtle Quarterly* (Niagra Falls, New York: Native American Center for the Living Arts, Spring-Summer, 1991, vol. 4, no. 1)

"Urban Indian Artists," *Northeast Indian Quarterly,* Cultural Encounter Edition *Unbroken Circles: Traditional Arts of Contemporary Woodland Peoples* (Ithaca, New York: Cornell University, American Indian Program, Winter 1990, vol. VII, no. 4)

"Building Bridges," *A World of Difference: Supplement to The New York Times* (New York: *The New York Times,* April 18, 1980)

NARRATIVE

Playwright, composer and entertainer Rudy Martin spent his youth in New Mexico, Los Angeles and New York City. His mother's family is from Isleta Pueblo and his father's family is from Santa Clara Pueblo. While a student at the Tesch School of the Arts, he produced a play he co-wrote with Claudia Howard Queen, titled *The Gleaners,* a one-act opera based on the biblical Book of Ruth. Martin also co-wrote with Claudia Howard Queen *The Coyote Brothers,* a two-act American Indian musical, which he produced and developed. Their most recent collaboration is *500 Years of Prophecy,* a fifteen-minute chorus for sixteen voices, commissioned for the Columbus Quincentenary by the DaCamera Singers. Martin also writes for the Off the Beaten Path Theatre Company, a Native American theater company of which he is also a member.

Martin is writing a children's play for the Pittsburgh Playhouse Jr. Children's Theater. He also worked on a symphony commissioned by Absolut Vodka for the 1993–1994 season of their Concert Concerto Series. His articles and essays have been published in several journals, including *The New York Times,* the *Village Voice,* the *Lakota Times,* the *Northeast Indian Quarterly* and the *Turtle Quarterly.* Martin has produced works through commissions from the Smithsonian National Museum of the American Indian, and The American Indian Film Festival, and he has been featured in articles in *National Geographic* and *Taxi* magazine. To Martin his piece *Medicine War* is significant because "the prevention of the exploitation of our spirituality is so important."

Martin has worked as a consultant to Scholastic Productions, WNET Television, ABC's *Good Morning America, 20/20,* NBC's *Today Show* and the CBS television corporation, as well as various film and radio productions. He has also worked as a character consultant for the PBS children television show "Shining Time Station." Martin has also served as a consultant on contemporary Native American issues and has given presentations and lectures at numerous educational institutions, such as Princeton University, West Point, Columbia University and Cornell University.

Rudy Martin is a member of the Native Writers Circle of the Americas, and Wind and Glacier Voices: The Native American Film and Media Celebration. He is the managing editor of the *American Indian Community House Community Bulletin,* a bi-monthly information newsletter concerning Indian issues, and is also a member of the Ethnic Equal Opportunities Committee of the Screen Actors Guild of America, the New York Native American Heritage Committee, the New York Native American Advisory Committee, the Native American Council of New York City for 1992, and was the Public Relations Director for the American Indian Community House for eleven years.

Martin is currently retired and living in New Mexico. His current projects include writing his column "Reviews" for the *American Indian Community House Community Bulletin* in which he reviews books, film, theater and other media events with Native American themes.

NAME P

David Martinez

OTHER NAMES USED

Dave Martin Nez

TRIBAL AFFILIATION

Navajo

PUBLICATION HIGHLIGHTS

"New Way, Old Way," "This Is Today" in *Blue Cloud Quarterly* (Marvin, S. Dak.: Blue Cloud Quarterly, vol. 15, no. 3)

"New Way, Old Way" in *Future Directions in Native American Art* (Santa Fe: Institute of American Indian Arts, [1973])

"New Way, Old Way" in *The Way: An Anthology of American Indian Literature* (New York: Knopf, 1972)

Martinez' works have appeared in: *New and Old Voices of Wah'Kon-Tah,* third edition, ed. by Robert K. Dodge and Joseph B. McCullough (New York: International Publishers, c1985) and *Voices from Wah'Kon-Tah: Contemporary Poetry of Native Americans,* first edition, ed. by Robert K. Dodge and Joseph B. McCullough (New York: International Publishers, 1974).

NAME N
John Joseph Mathews

TRIBAL AFFILIATION
Osage

PERSONAL
Born: November 16, 1895, in Pawhuska, Oklahoma

Education:

B.A. from the University of Oklahoma, 1920

B.A. from Oxford University, Oxford England, 1923

Coursework at the University of Sewanee, 1915

Certificate from the School of International Relations, University of Geneva, Switzerland, 1923

AWARDS, HONORS
Guggenheim Fellowship, 1939–1940

Distinguished Service Citation, University of Oklahoma, 1962

Award Merit from the American Association for State and Local History for *The Osages: Children of the Middle Waters,* 1962

PUBLICATION HIGHLIGHTS
The Osages: Children of the Middle Waters (Norman: University of Oklahoma Press, 1961)

Life and Death of an Oilman (Norman: University of Oklahoma Press, 1951)

Talking to the Moon (Chicago: University of Chicago Press, 1945)

Sundown (New York: Longman's Green, 1934)

Wah'Kon-Tah: The Osage and the White Man's Road (Norman: University of Oklahoma Press, 1932)

NARRATIVE
Mathews is the great-grandson of William Shirley Williams, also known as "Old Bill Williams" to western history readers. Though one-eighth Osage, Mathews received Osage allocated land in 1906 and was financially independent because of his Osage oil rights. He began studying geology at the University of Oklahoma, but his studies were delayed by his service in France as a U.S. air service pilot in 1918, during World War I. After completing his studies, Mathews returned to the United States where he worked as a realtor in Los Angeles from 1926 to 1928 and in 1928 began his long career as a writer, returning to his native Oklahoma, where he also worked as a rancher.

Mathews has served as a member of the Osage Tribal Council from 1934 to 1942 and in 1935 was a member of the Oklahoma State Board of Education.

NAME E, F, L, P, S, V
Art James McConville Jr.

TRIBAL AFFILIATION
Nez Perce (Nii-Mii-Pu) and Cayuse

PERSONAL
Born: June 16, 1944, in Pendleton, Oregon

Education: Community college coursework in criminal justice, management and alcohol and drug therapy

PUBLICATION HIGHLIGHTS
"Clothing Reflects Attitude" in: *Madras Pioneer* (Madras, Oreg.: Michael L. Williams, January 28, 1990)

In Search of Interpretive Illustration and Authentication: Curriculum Development Instruction, Handbook for Cultural Curriculum Development for American Indian Tribes and First Nations (Norman: University of Oklahoma, American Indian Institute, 1990)

"Columnist Hopes to Remove Stereotypes" in *Madras Pioneer* (Madras, Oreg.: Michael L. Williams, January, 21, 1988)
"Return to Childhood Considered an Honor" in *Madras Pioneer* (Madras, Oreg.: Michael L. Williams, February 4, 1988)

NARRATIVE

Of his upbringing, Art James McConville Jr. says he was raised "deep in the mountains, then on a reservation in a house with no running water or electricity which was just old planks ready to fall at any time. During grade school years, we lived in the car or in a tent along rivers which fed us. At age 13 I was placed in foster homes (three different homes I didn't like) until I escaped into the marines."

"School was easy but was full of prejudice and racism. I was never satisfied with school and studied encyclopedias to learn what I wanted to know about. I'm still the same way, I always want to know more than what someone is offering." His mother instilled in him the love of stories and the need to create. "My mother was a storyteller who told us a different story every evening for years. I know that many times she made up stories to teach us about specific situations. We were very poor, so it was like being mandated to be creative if you wanted anything out of life exciting, so I learned to write also." McConville served as a marine in Vietnam as a young man, and the experience and its aftermath dramatically changed his life. "My life changed from being a U.S. Marine, who after Vietnam was self-destructive, full of anger, hurt and hate, who sought of who he was as a Human Being. In discovering the 'Indian Spirit' gifted to me at birth, I started rediscovering who I should be, and turned my life around 180 degrees in to a person searching for spirituality which I found."

Since that time he has taken this understanding and used it, along with his storytelling abilities, to help others in need. "Many friends ask me to write stories for them to help them understand how they got where they are, good or bad, which 'awaken' the Spirit within themselves. I write for individuals who everyone has given up on, and help them re-discover their true potential and beauty as Human Beings. I use ancient thought and understanding to guide them through a series of changes they must make to accomplish specific goals."

McConville currently enjoys reading works by Victor Frankel. "I like Victor Frankel. He writes about things most people have no understanding of, but should. I usually just read educational books, manuals or books on weightlifting science. I also read comic books at night (*Archie* series), which are more real to me than the world I see people trying to hide or deny." McConville's own writings focus on the subjects of self-awareness, rebuilding lifestyles and realities and American Indian Spirituality. "Stories which help you understand where you are as a person, and how to become your best self through harmony and balance. Why? Because I've seen many people ready to give up on life, or who don't even HAVE a life, become everything they can be, using a Spiritual approach."

He is now working on several chapters that he plans to gather together into a book. "It's chapters about the Indian spirit, and is designed specifically to help Indian youth or Indian people who are having serious problems in their lives and want out. I've been writing it for a few years now." McConville currently works for the Confederated Tribes of Warm Springs, Oregon, as a curriculum developer, Interpretive graphic illustrator, video technician, researcher and writer for the Culture and Heritage Department. In his leisure time he works as an artist and graphic designer, beadworker and researcher in the areas of American Indian traditions and spirituality.

NAME   E, N
Ed McGaa

OTHER NAMES USED
Eagleman

TRIBAL AFFILIATION
Oglala Lakota

PERSONAL
Born: April 16, 1936, on the Pine Ridge Reservation, South Dakota
Education: B.S. from St. Johns University, Collegeville, Minnesota, 1960; J.D. from the University of South Dakota Law School, Vermillion, 1970

AWARDS, HONORS
Bush Fellowship, 1974–1975; Donner Scholarship; Joel McCrea Indian Scholarship

PUBLICATION HIGHLIGHTS
Rainbow Tribe: Ordinary People Journeying on the Red Road (San Francisco: HarperSanFrancisco, 1992)
Mother Earth Spirituality: Native American Paths to Healing Ourselves and Our World (San Francisco: Harper & Row, 1990)
The Last Buffalo, by W. R. Rosenfelt, introduction by Ed McGaa (Minneapolis: Denison, 1973)
Red Cloud: The Story of an American Indian (Minneapolis: Dillon Press, 1971)

NARRATIVE
McGaa served in Korea as a U.S. Marine from 1953 to 1955, and five years later he went to Vietnam, where he flew Phantom fighter jets from 1960 to 1967. McGaa was promoted to the rank of major and because of his distinguished service, was decorated with eight Air Medals, a Vietnam Cross of Gallantry and the Presidential Unit Citation. McGaa decided to pursue a legal career upon his return to the United States and enrolled at the University of South Dakota Law School, where he later graduated. Since that time McGaa has worked as an attorney. He has also worked as the assistant director for the Minnesota Department of Indian Education in St. Paul. He was the deputy director of human rights for the City of St. Paul, Minnesota, and since 1975 has been the manager of the Metropolitan Airports Commission. He has also written television scripts and has been a contributor to the journal *Northern States Power Quarterly.*

NAME   J, N, P
June McGlashan

TRIBAL AFFILIATION
Aleut

PERSONAL
Born: June 23, 1963, in Akutan, Alaska
Education: Unalaska High School; A.A., Sheldon Jackson College

AWARDS, HONORS
Deans List, Sheldon Jackson College, 1993

PUBLICATION HIGHLIGHTS

McGlashan's works have appeared in the following anthologies:

Raven Tells Stories: An Anthology of Alaskan Native Writing, first edition, ed. by Joseph Bruchac (Greenfield Center, N.Y.: Greenfield Review Press, 1991)

Village Voices: Rural Cap Newsletter, ed. by Jan Kennedy (Anchorage: [s.n.], 1991)

Dancing on the Rim of the World: An Anthology of Contemporary Northwest Native American Writing, ed. by Andrea Lerner (Tucson: Sun Tracks: University of Arizona Press, 1990)

Moonlark, ed. by Cheryl Morse (Sitka, Alaska: Orca Press, 1983)

NARRATIVE

June McGlashan was born and raised "in Akutan, Alaska, like wild natives. Running up and down hills. By the ocean. In the summers fog. Lory grasses, berries, fish and sea mammals with dogs and cats and at least fifty more wild barefooted children to play with." McGlashan was close to her family, particularly her mother and her father's second wife, and her friend Jerah Chadwick "—fellow poet of Unalaska was always there for me."

McGlashan's natural writing abilities and interests were apparent at a young age. "My mother ... couldn't figure out how I inherited the writing skills. ... As a young girl I was very quiet, shy but observed everything with an unusual perspective. As I began to write as a teenager (age 15) it opened a new life for me. I had found my reason for living almost. It was very natural and I didn't need many inspirational teachers to talk me into writing poetry. It became almost a need. I cannot explain how I felt then except I was very excited and very proud of myself. Secretly I hoped to become a published poet before I started writing poetry seriously. I never gave up. I accepted criticism and used it in my rewriting. As others began finding an interest in my writings, I became more interested in writing. I knew as soon as I began reading and analyzing poetry that was what I'd be doing—writing." McGlashan recalls that it was not through school, but in the many writing workshops that she was introduced to well-known writers and their works. Some memorable meetings include "one with John Haines where I met soon-to-be-famous writers and clicked on to their thoughts. A poetry reading by Mary TallMountain. In college taking a course with Fred Big Jim. Writers I loved to read and eventually met were the biggest moments in my life."

McGlashan writes about the Aleut Native culture, nature, persons close to her, prejudice and stories told by her elders. She considers some of her best works to be *About Old Ladies* and *Ache, Ache.* *About Old Ladies* is "about old ladies taking a steam bath. *Ache, Ache* is about a relationship between a younger Native and older Native that lasts a lifetime." She enjoys reading the works of Luci Tapahonso. "If she ever has a poetry reading up here or I can attend her readings I will give my eye teeth. Strong, realistic, spiritual and almost psychic writers attract me." McGlashan is currently working on a short-term project. "I am to transcribe the last Aleut Chief's dairies. [I'm] excited [for] Akutan/Aleutians' world [to] have a document from one of their own." She is working on a book of her poetry and is attending college for a teacher's degree so she can come home and teach. Role model for younger Natives needed!"

Sobriety, the birth of her two children ("not at the same time, thank goodness") and divorce are events in her life that she has endured and grown strong from, as she says, "You know the saying: 'Bad events are a good learning experience.'" She is currently employed in a commercial fishery plant. "Because poets aren't rich I work at a local fishery plant, at quality central as a secretary/clerk. The fisheries has been a major interest of mine because the Natives depend on commercial fishing for the income. Off season— [they] work at odd jobs." When not writing, McGlashan spends time with two children ages 6 and 7. She beachcombs, does research on native plants and how they were used to heal and keeps reading. "Reading, reading and reading. Classic novels, Indian nonfiction and the newspapers. T.V. is not a good idea—reading is more profitable, memorable."

NAME   E, L, P
Glen M. McGuire

TRIBAL AFFILIATION
Pawnee

PERSONAL
Born: 1920
Education: Haskell Indian Institute, Lawrence, Kansas; English coursework, Tulsa University, Tulsa, Oklahoma; B.A. in music, Phillips University, Enid, Oklahoma

AWARDS, HONORS
First Prize from the Sixth Annual California State Poetry Contest, 1991
Franklin G. Dill, Scholarship, Tulsa University
Second Prize from the Bicentennial Division Poetry Contest, St. Louis Poetry Center

PUBLICATION HIGHLIGHTS
Spider Spins Between Two Worlds (Little Rock: American Native Press Archives; University of Arkansas, 1992)
"Note to a Mexican Lady," poem in *Wicazo Sa Review* (Rapid City, S. Dak.: *Wicazo Sa Review*, vol. 3, no. 2, 1987)
"Vacancy," poem in *California State Poetry Quarterly* (Long Beach, Calif.: The Quarterly, vol. 14, no. 1, 1987)

NARRATIVE
Glen McGuire was separated from his Pawnee mother at the age of 4 by his white relatives. When he reached the age of 14 McGuire was sent to the Haskell Indian School in Lawrence, Kansas, where he struggled to adjust to his new life. "I learned to cope with it, but all these different copings ... I just couldn't see any end to it."

McGuire graduated from Haskell after five years and entered the U.S. Army and served with the 5th cavalry in the Southwest Pacific during World War II. Before he enlisted, McGuire recalled that he felt that the service would be a good place to be because he would get treated fairly. He also recalled that once in the service he was expected to be a great fighter, but he later admitted that fighting really "wasn't in my nature." As a result of his combat in the Pacific, McGuire suffered from battle fatigue, also known as post-traumatic stress syndrome, and was given thirteen shock treatments and additional therapy, which he described as being "... really inhuman. My memory has great weaknesses. I can remember seeking help. I can remember being belligerent." After the war, McGuire left the army and took advantage of the GI bill, enrolling at Tulsa University as an English major. He was later awarded an English scholarship in his sophomore year.

After two years in Tulsa, McGuire hitchhiked to Kansas City to look for a job writing for the *Kansas City Star*. With no luck in Kansas City, McGuire went back to Oklahoma and spent time hitchhiking, picking fruit and doing odd jobs. Again looking for a change, McGuire went back to school and earned his bachelors degree in music. Since his graduation from Phillips, McGuire has worked as an educator in a variety of places. He has taught music and English in St. Louis, Missouri, inner-city schools, worked as an educator at a government boarding school for the Bureau of Indian Affairs in Kansas and taught in many Midwest farming communities. He later taught special education at the Sherman Indian School in Riverside, California, until his retirement.

A writer of poetry, McGuire's works have been published in numerous journals and publications, such as the *California State Poetry Society Quarterly, Mosaic, Poetry Center Speaking, Seven Buffaloes Press* and the *Wicazo Sa Review*. He has given poetry readings for many groups, organizations, conferences and special events, such as the Ibero-American Writers Society in Santa Ana, California, the Laguna Poets Performance and Reading in Laguna Beach, California, and the telecast event, *The Riverside County Almanac,* a drama and poetry performance in Riverside, California. When he is not writing, McGuire avidly plays tennis.

(Quotes taken from an article by Pat O'Brien, which appeared in the Sunday, October 18, 1992, issue of the *Press-Enterprise* [Riverside, Calif.: Press-Enterprise]).

❖❖❖

NAME   N

Gary McLain

OTHER NAMES USED

Eagle Walking Turtle

TRIBAL AFFILIATION

Choctaw

PERSONAL

Born: January 11, 1941, in Vermillion, South Dakota
Education: Kansas State University; University of Wyoming

AWARDS, HONORS

Ben Franklin Award at Publishers Convention, 1991 for *The Indian Way;* American Library Association Denali Press Award, 1990 for *Indian America*

PUBLICATION HIGHLIGHTS

The Indian Way: Learning to Communicate with Mother Earth, first edition (New York; Santa Fe: John Muir Publications, 1990); *Indian American* (Santa Fe: John Muir Publications, 1990); *Keepers of the Fire* (Santa Fe: Bear & Company, 1987)

NARRATIVE

Gary Mclain grew up in the small Kansas town of Blue Rapids. He attended country schools, where he was taught by his mother until he reached the sixth grade. McLain worked as a miner until 1975, when ill health forced him to retire. With more free time he was able to devote himself to art and writing. Individuals who have had a great influence on McLain include his son, Jesse; his wife Ruby; his friends Kaare Evensen and Black Elk, a holy man of the Oglala Sioux who inspired him to become a writer. McLain enjoys reading works by Tony Shearer, who has influenced his thought on writing about the spirit of all living things, and Kaare Evensen, who "opened my mind to new horizons."

Mclain now lives in New Mexico, where "the spirit of the land ... influences artists of all kinds." He considers his best work to be *Keepers of the Fire,* where the vision of Black Elk is "portrayed in fiction and the reality is still to be." He is currently writing a novel and more full moon stories in the tradition of *The Indian Way.*

❖❖❖

NAME   E, F, S

D. Joseph McLellan

OTHER NAMES USED

Daniel Joseph (Joe) McLellan

TRIBAL AFFILIATION

Metis

PERSONAL

Born: September 27, 1945, in Monterey, California

Education: B.A. plus additional coursework

PUBLICATION HIGHLIGHTS

Nanabosho Dances (Winnipeg, Manitoba: Pemmican Publications, 1991); *Nanabosho Steals Fire* (Winnipeg, Manitoba: Pemmican Publications, 1990); *The Birth of Nanabosho* (Winnipeg, Manitoba: Pemmican Publications, 1989)

NARRATIVE

McLellan was raised in North Dakota. Brought up in a close and secure family, it was difficult for McLellan to leave home to attend boarding school. He missed his family terribly. "I stayed awake late into the night worrying about them." Two individuals who have influenced his life are his wife, Matrine, and his great-grandmother Bragg. McLellan writes primarily about legends and feels that his work *Nanabosho Dances* is one of his strongest, adding that "It was a great collaboration with a wonderful artist; it was the easiest to write."

McLellan regards his friend and poet Tom McGrath as his mentor. Of McGrath, who passed away in 1990, McLellan says, "He taught me the values of honesty and showed me how words hide in and out of the clouds and under beds and in old closets." He was also challenged to continue writing by an old man he had met, who told him to "... write these stories, so they will light the fires in childrens eyes again."

McLellan enjoys authors Basil Johnson, Terry Tafoya ("his storytelling was a great influence on my life"), Geary Hobson's poem about the buffalo at the airport, the works of Louise Erdich and any good mystery writer. He is now working on a novel about a Cree man who becomes a cardinal, and at least eight more Nanabosho books. He is now a teacher in Beedabun, a special school for non-attending junior high students in Manitoba.

❖❖❖

NAME

Gerald R. McMaster

TRIBAL AFFILIATION

Plains Cree (Nehiyawuk)

PERSONAL

Born: March 9, 1953, in Red Pheasant Reserve, Saskatchewan, Canada

Education: B.F.A. from the Minneapolis College of Art and Design, Minneapolis, 1977; M.A. candidate in anthropology, Carleton University, Ottawa, Ontario

PUBLICATION HIGHLIGHTS

Edward Poitras: Canada XLVI Biennale di Venezia (Hull, Quebec: Canadian Museum of Civilization ([Musee Canadien des Civilizations], 1995)

"Colonial Alchemy: Reading the Boarding School Experience" in *Partial Recall: Photographs of Native North Americans,* ed. by Lucy Lippard (New York: The New Press, 1992)

Indigena: Contemporary Native Perspectives, ed. by Gerald McMaster and Lee-Ann Martin (Vancouver: Douglas & McIntyre, 1992)

"The Persistence of Land Claims" in *Robert Houle: Indians from A to Z* (Winnipeg: Winnipeg Art Gallery, 1990)

"Tenuous Lines of Descent: Indian Arts and Crafts of the Reservation Period" in the *Canadian Journal of Native Studies* ([Winnipeg, Manitoba]: Brandon University, vol. 9, no. 2, 1989)

"How the West Was Lost: An Artist's Perspective" in *Gatherings: The En'owkin Journal of First North American Peoples,* vol. 2 (Pentecton, B.C.: En'owken Center, [n.d.])

NARRATIVE

Gerald McMaster was born and raised on the Red Pheasant Reserve near north Battleford, Saskatchewan. He is currently conservator of contemporary Indian art at the Canadian Museum of Civilization in Hull, Quebec. Artist and museum curator, McMaster writes about museums, art, art history and issues, Native peoples and artist's biographies. He was motivated to pursue writing because of the "the lack of Native writers in the area of museums and the visual arts." He enjoys reading the works of Trinh Minha-ha, Bell Hooks, Lucy Lippard and Gerald Vizenor, and remains an active painter, exhibiting in solo and group shows and participating in juried competitions as either an exhibitor or invited juror. His works have also appeared in *Art Journal.*

NAME   E, J, N
D'Arcy McNickle

OTHER NAMES USED
William D'Arcy McNickle

TRIBAL AFFILIATION
Salish and Kootenai

PERSONAL
Born: January 18, 1904, in St. Ignatius, Montana, died December 1977
Education: Coursework at the University of Montana, Missoula, 1925; coursework at Oxford University, Oxford, England, 1925–1926; coursework at the University of Grenoble, Switzerland, 1931

AWARDS, HONORS
Guggenheim Fellowship, 1963–1964; Sc.D. degree from the University of Colorado, 1966

PUBLICATION HIGHLIGHTS
The Hawk Is Hungry and Other Stories (Tucson: University of Arizona, 1993)
Native American Tribalism: Indian Survivals and Renewals (New York: Oxford University Press, 1993, 1971)
The Surrounded, seventh paperbrand printing edition (Albuquerque: University of New Mexico, 1992, 1978)
Wind from an Enemy Sky (New York: Harper & Row, 1978)
Captives Within a Free Society: Federal Policy and the American Indian (S.l.: s.n., 1977)
Indian Man: A Life of Oliver La Farge (Bloomington: Indiana University Press, 1962)
The Indian Tribes of the United States: Ethnic and Cultural Survival (New York: Oxford University Press, 1962)
Indians and the Other Americans: Two Ways of Life Meet, with Harold E. Fey (New York: Harper & Row, 1959)
Runner in the Sun: A Story of Indian Maize (New York: Holt, Rinehart and Winston, 1954)
They Came Here First: The Epic of the American Indian (Philadelphia: J. B. Lippincott, 1949)

McNickle's works have appeared in numerous anthologies, including: *Forever There: Race and Gender in Contemporary Native American Fiction,* by Elizabeth I. Hanson (New York: P. Lang, c1989) and *American Indian Fiction,* first edition, by Charles R. Larson (Albuquerque: University of New Mexico Press, c1978).

NARRATIVE
McNickle was Creek by blood but adopted into the Confederated Salish and

Kootenai Tribes. He was a student at local mission schools as a young man. After college, McNickle worked as an editor in New York from 1926 to 1935, and for a year afterward worked as a staff writer for the Federal Writers Project in Washington, D.C. In 1936 he began a long tenure at the Bureau of Indian Affairs in Washington, D.C., first as an assistant to the commissioner, then as a field representative and later as the director of the Branch of Tribal Relations for the Bureau until 1952.

From Washington McNickle moved to Boulder, Colorado, where he worked as the Director of the American Indian Development, Inc., and in 1966 he joined the faculty of the University of Saskatchewan as a professor of anthropology until 1971. In 1972 McNickle became the program director of the Newberry Library's Center for American Indian History, Chicago. Active in Indian affairs throughout his life he was also a cofounder of the National Congress of American Indians.

He was married with two children. He is now deceased.

NAME   N, P
Beatrice Medicine

TRIBAL AFFILIATION
Blackfoot (Sihasapa Lakota)

PERSONAL
Born: August 1, 1923, in Wakpala, South Dakota
Education: B.S., South Dakota State University; M.A., Michigan State University; Ph.D., University of Wisconsin, Madison

AWARDS, HONORS
Among her many awards and honors, the most recent include:

Martin Luther King & Rosa Park Professorship, Wayne State University, 1989
Outstanding Minority Professor (First) University of Michigan, 1987
Faculty Award for Meritorious Service, California State University at Northridge, 1984
Outstanding Minority Researcher, American Educational Research Association, 1983

PUBLICATION HIGHLIGHTS
The Hidden Half: Studies of Plains Indian Women, with Patricia Albers (Washington, D.C.: University Press of America, 1983)
The Native American Woman: A Perspective (Las Cruces, N. Mex.: ERIC/CRESS: Austin: National Educational Laboratory Publishers, 1978)
Speaking Indian: Parameters of Language Use among American Indians (Rosslyn, Va.: National Clearinghouse for Bilingual Education, 1981)

NARRATIVE
Anthropologist Beatrice Medicine grew up in Wakpala, South Dakota, on the Standing Rock Reservation, and throughout her life she has lived all over North American in context with Native groups.

She is now writing poetry and is working on a book on contemporary Native women. She has recently retired and is living in Mobridge, South Dakota, near Standing Rock. Medicine is still conducting ethnographic and anthropological research and presenting papers at conferences.

NAME   N, S
Howard Meredith

TRIBAL AFFILIATION
Cherokee/Akokisa

PERSONAL

Born: May 25, 1992, in Galveston, Texas

Education: B.S., University of Texas at Austin, 1961; M.A., Stephen F. Austin State University, Nacogdoches, Texas, 1963; Ph.D., University of Oklahoma, Norman, Oklahoma, 1970

AWARDS, HONORS

Murial Wright Endowment Award, 1980; Westerners' International Best Book Award, 1989

PUBLICATION HIGHLIGHTS

"N. Scott Momaday: A Man of Words" in *World Literature Today* (Norman, Okla.: *World Literature Today;* University of Oklahoma Press, vol. 64 Summer 1990)

"Nuh-Ka-Oashun: Hasinai Turkey Dance Tradition" in *Songs of Indian Territory: Native American Music Traditions of Oklahoma,* with Irving Whitebead (Oklahoma City: Center of the American Indian, 1989)

Hasinai: A Traditional History of the Caddo Confederacy (College Station: Texas A&M University Press, 1988)

NARRATIVE

Howard Meredith grew up on the southern plains of Texas and Oklahoma, where he now lives and works as an associate professor of American Indian studies at the University of Science and Arts of Oklahoma. His life in the southern plains is critically important to his writing, which is about "specific tribal traditions, governance, [and] spirituality on the Southern Plains."

Several people in life guided Meredith and his writing: Gerald One Feather (Lakota) and Margaret Hawk (Lakota) (during the Wounded Knee conflict in 1973), Tom Jackson (Navajo), Stephen Plummer (Navajo), Lennie Nez (Navajo) (on the creation of the Navajo jurisdiction), Archis Sam (Cherokee/Natchez) (on Cherokee community organization), Mary Ellen Milam Meredity (Cherokee), Gayle Nunez Godard (Shawnee), teachers James Nichols (from Stephen F. Austin State University) and Arrell Gibson (from the University of Oklahoma). Meredith reads William Faulkner, Vine Deloria Jr., Simon Ortiz, and Anna L. Walters for pleasure because "they each offer content and style that are extraordinarily important."

He is working on a "free-verse expression of Akokisa tradition and a work of synthesis of Native American thought and images" and enjoys working in the mediums of photography and painting when not writing. His writings have also appeared in the journals the *Western Historical Quarterly, American Indian Quarterly* and *World Literature Today.*

NAME   F, P, VA

Barry G. Milliken

TRIBAL AFFILIATION

Chippewa/Pottawattami

PERSONAL

Born: February 10, 1944, in Windsor, Ontario, Canada

Education: Completed grade 10 in high school; completed three-year art course at the Central Technical School, Toronto, Ontario Canada

PUBLICATION HIGHLIGHTS

"Run" in *Destinations 12, In Flight* (Toronto, Ont.: Prentice-Hall Canada, 1991)

"Run" in *All My Relations, an Anthology of Contemporary Canadian Native Fiction* (Toronto, Ont.: McClelland & Stewart, 1988)

"Run" in *Canadian Fiction Magazine* (Toronto, Ont.: *Canadian Fiction Magazine,* 1987)

"In Memory of Nelson" in *Ontario Indian Magazine* ([S.l.: s.n.], vol. 4, no. 9, 1981) Milliken's work has also appeared in *Braided Lives: An Anthology of Multicultural American Writing,* by the Minnesota Humanities Commission and the Minnesota Council of Teachers of English (St. Paul: The Commission, 1991)

NARRATIVE

Barry Milliken was born in Windsor, Ontario, was adopted as a child and grew up on the Kettle Point Reservation on the shore of Lake Huron, which had a population of about seven hundred, with "one Anglican church, and one United." The main industry of the town was fishing. As a child, Milliken's school years were not happy ones. "Though in some ways I would like most to forget those years, I suppose that in another sense they are most responsible for who I am today. At times I was made to feel burning shame at being a Native person, but perhaps if not for those times I would not feel the pride I do today for being that same Native person." He adds that "Being adopted and consequently growing up on a reserve has been the one event which has influenced the way I think, feel, respond."

His older brother encouraged him to write ("I have also used him as a basis for several characters"). And he recalls that his earliest and probably most profound influence was the works of writer John Steinbeck, whose style and diversity of characters "made me want to write. ... I have always loved to read, and the knowledge that one could create whole other worlds through writing, the process of which, though agonizing, seemed to fill a need."

Milliken writes about circumstances as related to the human condition. "Because my formative years were spent on the reservation, much of my work has been subjective, through (young) Native eyes. As with most writers, I rely mainly on recollection conjured from my youth which colors landscape, etc., with many strange and wonderful hues."

When not writing he works in the visual arts: "I have always found satisfaction in art and have tried over the years to develop this to its fullest degree, through in some ways it does not compare, in terms of depth, to writing." Milliken enjoys the works of English writers Charles Dickens, Somerset Maugham and D. H. Lawrence; Canadian writers Margaret Laurence and Alice Munro and American writers Truman Capote, John Steinbeck and Ernest Hemingway. He is now rewriting four stories that were first written about twenty-five years ago, which all have a common theme and may eventually be published in a single volume. His current occupation is artist and writer.

NAME E, L, M, VA
Emerson Blackhorse Mitchell

OTHER NAMES USED
Emerson Blackhorse Barney Mitchell

TRIBAL AFFILIATION
Navajo

PERSONAL
Born: March 3, 1945, in Shiprock, New Mexico
Education:
A.A. in 1977
B.S. in 1978
M.A. in secondary education in 1993
Coursework at the Institute of American Indian Arts, Santa Fe, New Mexico

Coursework at Fort Lewis College, Durango, Colorado

AWARDS, HONORS

Vincent Price Creative Writing Award for "Talking to His Drum," 1965; National Poetry Day Award for *Miracle Hill: The Story of a Navajo Boy,* 1964; Scottsdale Award for Short Story

PUBLICATION HIGHLIGHTS

The Whispering Wind (New York: Doubleday, 1972); *Miracle Hill: The Story of a Navajo Boy,* with T. D. Allen (Norman: University of Oklahoma Press, 1967)

Mitchell's works have also appeared in numerous anthologies, among them: *Voices from Wah'Kon-Tah: Contemporary Poetry of Native Americans,* first edition, ed. by Robert K. Dodge and Joseph B. McCullough (New York: International Publishers, 1974) and *Literature of the American Indian,* by Thomas Sanders and William Peek (Beverly Hills: Glencoe Press, 1973).

NARRATIVE

Son of a professor of history and culture, Mitchell was born in a hogan and raised in northern New Mexico in "a place called Popping Rock Ranch ... next to the Northern Ute Reservation on a remote area of the mesa." He spent a great deal of time with his maternal grandparents, learning the traditional ways of his Navajo people. As a young man he attended school in Ignacio, Colorado, and later transferred to the Institute of the American Indian Arts in Santa Fe, New Mexico while a junior in high school.

Mitchell has worked as an educator throughout his life. He taught Navajo social studies at the Rock Point Community School in Chinle, Arizona, and was a teacher of Navajo music at the Rough Rock Demonstration School. He also worked as the community development supervisor at the Office of Navajo Economic Opportunity in Chinle, Arizona. He is currently teaching multicultural education in secondary school in the areas of curriculum development and instruction, and he is also teaching multicultural education at the Aneth Community School in Aneth, Utah, "a BIA school setting working with professional teaching staff from kindergarten through sixth grade, implementing cultural values into the classroom."

Mitchell presently lives in northern New Mexico. "I am surrounded with mesas, mountains, desert, rolling hills, plateaus, the San Juan River, snowy mountain tops and creatures, species that live within the terrain. And of course the famous rock, Shiprock, and the Four Corners area." Books he enjoys reading include the Don Coldshith's reading series, Joseph M. Lander's reading series, Madelene Baker's Indian novels, Jean Auel's books and books by Linda L. Shuler, Constance Bennett, Tony Hillerman and Katherine and Michael O'Neal Gear. "I feel that these people are great writers, and it helps me a great deal in my determination to write."

He also recalls the influence that dancers, comedians, actors, entertainers and rock and roll have had on his career as a writer, especially stars Fats Domino, Little Richard, Wanda Jackson and Chubby Checker. Movies like *Dances with Wolves, Wind Walker* and *A Man Called Horse* have also influenced his artistic expression, as did his friendship with the late actor Vincent Price. "He was a dear friend that I could talk with during his visit to the Institute of American Indian Arts in 1964, 1966 and 1967."

When out of the classroom and not working on his writing project, Blackhorse

Mitchell makes Navajo moccasins, pottery and basketry and studies Navajo medicine. He also takes his sheep out into the range, hikes, rides horseback and studies American history.

❖❖❖

NAME   N
Rosalio Moises

TRIBAL AFFILIATION
Yaqui

PERSONAL
Born: c1896 in Sonora, Mexico

PUBLICATION HIGHLIGHTS
A Yaqui Life: The Personal Chronicle of a Yaqui Indian (Lincoln: University of Nebraska Press, 1977, 1971); *The Tall Candle: The Personal Chronicle of a Yaqui Indian,* with Jane Holden and William Curry Holden (Lincoln: University of Nebraska Press, 1971)

NAME   F, L, N, P, S, VA
N. Scott Momaday

OTHER NAMES USED
Navarre Scott Momaday

TRIBAL AFFILIATION
Kiowa and Cherokee

PERSONAL
Born: February 27, 1934, in Lawton, Oklahoma
Education:
Augusta Military Academy
A.B. from the University of New Mexico, Albuquerque, 1958

M.A. from Stanford University, Stanford, California, 1960
Ph.D. from Stanford University, Stanford, California, 1963

AWARDS, HONORS
Premio Letterario Internazionale Mondelo, Italy, 1979
Western Heritage Award shared with David Muench for *Colorado, Summer/Fall/Winter/Spring,* 1974
National Institute of Arts and Letters Grant, 1970
Pulitzer Prize for Fiction for *The House Made of Dawn,* 1969
Guggenheim Fellowship, 1966–1967
Academy of American Poets Prize for "The Bear," 1963

PUBLICATION HIGHLIGHTS
Conversations with N. Scott Momaday (Jackson: University Press of Mississippi, 1997)
The Man Made of Words: Essays, Stories, Passages (New York: St. Martin's Press, 1997)
The Names: A Memoir (Tucson: University of Arizona Press, 1996)
Circle of Wonder: A Native American Christmas Story (Santa Fe: Clear Light, 1994)
The Native Americans: Indian Country, N. Scott Momaday and Linda Hogan (Atlanta: Turner Publishing, 1993)
In the Presence of the Sun: Stories and Poems 1961–1991 (New York: St. Martin's, 1991, 1992)
The Ancient Child (New York: Doubleday, 1989)
House Made of Dawn (New York: HarperCollins, 1989)
The Journey of Tai-me (Santa Barbara: University of California Press, 1987)
The Names: A Memoir (New York: Harper, 1976)
"Angle of Geese" and Other Poems (Boston: David Godine, 1974)
Colorado, Summer/Fall/Winter/Spring, ill. with photographs by David Muench (Chicago: Rand McNally, 1974)

The Gourd Dancer (New York: Harper, 1974)
The Way to Rainy Mountain (Albuquerque: University of New Mexico Press, 1969)
The Complete Poems of Frederick Goddard Tuckerman, ed. by N. Scott Momaday (New York; Oxford: Oxford University Press, 1965)

NARRATIVE

Momaday is the son of painter and art instructor Alfred Morris Momaday (shortened by his father from Mammedaty) and writer and teacher Mayme Natachee Scott. Part Cherokee, Momaday's mother descended from early pioneers, and his father is Kiowa. His parents were both attending the Haskall Institute in Kansas, where they met and were later married. They moved to New Mexico to work among the Jemez people and then moved to Oklahoma, where Momaday was raised on the family farm.

Momaday began his career as an educator as an assistant professor at the University of California at Santa Barbara and was promoted to associate professor of English from 1968 to 1969. Then he was an associate professor of English and comparative literature at the University of California at Berkeley from 1969 to 1973. Momaday became professor of English at Stanford University from 1973 to 1982. And since 1982 Momaday has worked at the University of Arizona at Tucson as a professor of English.

A visual artist as well as an educator, Momaday has had his prints and drawings exhibited at numerous galleries. He has been a consultant for the National Endowment for the Humanities and National Endowment for the Arts since 1970. Momaday is married and has three daughters. The recipient of many awards and honors, his works have appeared in numerous anthologies and he has been the subject of many stories and articles.

NAME   F, N, P
Victor D. Montejo

TRIBAL AFFILIATION
Maya

PERSONAL
Born: October 9, 1951, in Guatemala
Education:
Primary Schoolteacher Certification, 1972
B.A., State University of New York, Albany
M.A., State University of New York, Albany, 1989
Ph.D., University of Connecticut, 1993

AWARDS, HONORS
Plumsock Mesoamerican Fellowship, 1990–1992; Fellowship of Onaway Fund, 1992; Cornell University Research Fellowship

PUBLICATION HIGHLIGHTS
Sculpted Stones: Piedras labradas, first edition (Willimantic, Conn.: Curbstone Press, 1995)
Brevisima relacion testimonial de la continua destruccion del Mayab' (Guatemala) (Providence, R.I.: Guatemala Scholars Network, 1992)
The Bird Who Cleans the World and Other Mayan Fables, first edition (Willimantic, Conn.: Curbstone Press, 1991)
Testimony: Death of a Guatemalan Village (Willimantic, Conn.: Curbstone Press, 1987)
El Kanil: Man of Lightning (Carrboro, N.C.: Signal Books, 1984)
El Kanil, Man of Lightning: A Legend of Jacaltenango, Department of Huehuetenango, Guatemala, Spanish-English edition (Carrboro, N.C.: Signal Services, 1984)
El Kanil, Man of Lightning: A Legend of Jacaltenango, Department of Huehuetenango, Guatemala, first and limited edition (Pittsboro, N.C.: Signal Services, 1982)

NARRATIVE

Victor Montejo was born in the highlands of Guatemala and raised by his parents Eusebio Montejo, a farmer, and weaver Juana Mendez. He was educated by the Maryknoll Benedictines and the Brothers of La Salle. Montejo has worked as a schoolteacher and has served as the president of the Maya Education Foundation. Active in volunteer work providing aid to refugees in Chiapas, Mexico, he is interested in Mayan literature, politics, religion and history. He was married in November 1977 and has three children. He lives in Willimantic, Connecticut.

NAME E, F, L, N, VA

Joel Monture

TRIBAL AFFILIATION

Mohawk

PERSONAL

Born: July 4, 1953, in Lewistown, Pennsylvania

Education: B.A. in literature and creative writing, Bennington College, 1987; M.A. in literature and creative writing, Dartmouth, 1991

AWARDS, HONORS

Honor Citation in Fiction, Dartmouth, 1990

PUBLICATION HIGHLIGHTS

Cloudwalker: Contemporary Native American Stories (Golden, Colo.: Fulcrum Publishing, 1996)

The Complete Guide to Traditional Native American Headwork: A Definite Study of Authentic Tools, Materials, Techniques and Styles, first Collier Books edition (New York; Toronto: Collier; Maxwell Macmillan Canada, 1993)

Turtle Belly (Flagstaff, Ariz.: Northland Press, 1992)

"The Animal Gift" in *Northeast Indian Quarterly* (S.l.: s.n., Winter 1991)

"Over One Hundred Miles an Hour," fiction in *The Oracle* (St. Paul: Hamline University, Spring 1991)

NARRATIVE

Joel Monture was raised in Canada until the age of 12, then moved to Connecticut, where he graduated in 1971 from Greenwich High School. He later wrote, "I hated high school and didn't much care for college—writing was a way to assert my individuality and buck the system." His mother was his creative supporter and sustainer, and it was her death and the birth of his son Rowe':ren (Joseph Brandt) that precipitated changes in his life and his writings. Monture was raised in a family that emphasized the importance of reading. He grew up among a number of oral historians within his family, all of whom inspired him in his decision to pursue writing as a profession.

Early mentors of Monture include Bernard Malamud and Joe McGinnis at Bennington College, and Nick Delbanco and Arturo Vivante, who read and critiqued his early writings and provided guidance in his works. Writers who Monture reads include Momaday, Bruchac and Salinger. Monture regards his novel *Turtle Belly* to be his strongest work to date, as it is a "truthful portrayal of contemporary res [reservation] life." He has worked as an artist and writer, curator and lecturer in a multitude of areas, including Native American and eighteenth-century colonial arts and handicrafts. He is currently an instructor of beadwork at the Santa Fe Institute of American Indian Art. Monture is also a painter and sculptor. Monture's works have also appeared in the journals *Parabola* and *Ariel.*

NAME   P

Irvin Morris

TRIBAL AFFILIATION

Navajo

PUBLICATION HIGHLIGHTS

"The Snake of Light," short story in *Circle of Motion: Arizona Anthology of Contemporary American Indian Literature,* ed. by Kathleen Mullen Sands (Tempe, Ariz.: Arizona Historical Foundation, c1990)

"Squatters," short story; "August," poem and "Eagle and Rabbit," play in *Desire and Time* (Santa Fe: Institute of American Indian Arts, 1990)

"Monday," "Birdman," "Crazy River," "Christmas Eve," short stories in *New Work* (Santa Fe: Institute of American Indian Arts, 1989)

"The Skinwalker," short story in *Maazo Magazine: Navaho Life Styles* (Window Rock, Ariz.: Maazo Publishing, vol. 1, no. 9, 1987)

"The Homecoming," short story in *Maazo Magazine: Navaho Life Styles* (Window Rock, Ariz.: Maazo Publishing, vol. 1, no. 7, 1986)

"The Blood Stone" in *Northeast Indian Quarterly* (Ithaca, N.Y.: American Indian Program, Cornell University, [n.d.])

Morris's works have also appeared in: *Neon Pow-wow: New Native American Voices of the Southwest,* first edition, ed. by Anna Lee Walters (Flagstaff: Northland, [1993]).

NAME   P, PL

Daniel David Moses

TRIBAL AFFILIATION

Delaware

PERSONAL

Born: 1952, Ohsweken Six Nations Reservation, Ontario

Education: Honours B.A. in general fine arts, York University, 1971–1975; M.F.A. in creative writing, University of British Columbia, 1975–1977

AWARDS, HONORS

Nominated for the Governor General's Award for Drama, 1990

PUBLICATION HIGHLIGHTS

Almighty Voice and His Wife: A Play in Two Acts (Stratford, Canada: William-Wallace, 1992)

Delicate Bodies (Sechelt, B.C.: Nightwood Editions, 1992)

Feast for the Dead, radio play produced by Clarke Rogers for Vanishing Point, CBC Radio, November 15, 1991

Coyote City, play (Stratford, Ont.: Williams-Wallace, 1990)

The White Line, poems (Saskatoon, Saskatchewan: Fifth House, 1990)

Moses's works have also appeared in *Returning the Gift: Poetry and Prose from the First North American Native Writers' Festival,* ed. by Joseph Bruchac with the support of the Association for the Study of American Indian Literatures (Tucson: University of Arizona, 1994).

NARRATIVE

Daniel David Moses grew up on a farm on the Six Nations lands near Brantford, Ontario. His first six years of schooling were spent in a one-room schoolhouse, in an "enriched environment." Moses's early years were spent with two grandmothers, both of whom were quite different from one another; one was unconsciously traditional and the other was "mainstream," yet they each fostered and encouraged his creative growth.

Moses is working on the third of four plays, which have the same characters and are interrelated. Among the writers he reads, science fiction writer Ursula LeGuinn has been especially important to him, because her family came before her career.

NAME P

Julie Moss

TRIBAL AFFILIATION

Cherokee

PUBLICATION HIGHLIGHTS

"The Indigenous Women's Role in Experimentation to Create Alternative Economies" in *Indigenous Woman: A Publication of the Indigenous Women's Network* (Lake Elmo, Minn.: Indigenous Women's Network, vol. 1, no. 1, Spring 1991)

"Beginning to End," "For Your Presence," "Today, I Saw Yesterday and Tomorrow," "Rattles, Gourds and Drums," "Native Voices," "Spring Comes Dancing," "Another Chance" in *Echoes of Our Being*, by the Tahlequah Indian Writer's Group, ed. by Robert J. Conley (Muskogee, Okla.: Indian University Press, Barcone College, 1982)

Moss's works have also appeared in: *Returning the Gift: Poetry and Prose from the First North American Native Writers' Festival*, ed. by Joseph Bruchac, with the support of the Association for the Study of American Indian Literatures (Tucson: University of Arizona, 1994).

N

NAME   F, N, VA
Joe Dale Tate Nevaquaya

TRIBAL AFFILIATION
Comanche and Yuchi

PERSONAL
Education: Coursework at the Institute of American Indian Arts, Santa Fe, New Mexico

PUBLICATION HIGHLIGHTS

Nevaquaya's works have appeared in the following anthologies:

Returning the Gift: Poetry and Prose from the First North American Native Writers' Festival, ed. by Joseph Bruchac with the support of the Association for the Study of American Indian Literatures (Tucson: University of Arizona, 1994)

SAIL: Studies in American Indian Literatures, New Native American Writing (New York: Association for the Study of American Indian Literatures, Series 2, vol. 2, no. 2, Summer 1990)

Living the Spirit: A Gay American Indian Anthology, by Will Roscoe (New York: St. Martin's Press, c1988)

The Clouds Threw This Light (Santa Fe: Institute of American Indian Arts, 1983)

NARRATIVE
Nevaquaya spent his early years in Oklahoma and was raised by his Yuchi grandmother in a household that spoke Yuchi as a primary language.

NAME   F, N, P
Duane Niatum

OTHER NAMES USED
Duane McGinnis

TRIBAL AFFILIATION
Klallam (Jamestown Band)

PERSONAL
Born: February 13, 1938, in Seattle, Washington

Education: B.A. in English, University of Washington, 1970; M.A., Johns Hopkins University, 1972; Ph.D. candidate in American culture, University of Michigan

AWARDS, HONORS
Community Scholar Grant, Smithsonian Institution, Washington, D.C., 1990

The American Book Award from the Before Columbus Foundation for *Songs for the Harvester of Dreams,* 1982

Poetry in Motion Award, Allied Arts Foundation, Seattle, Washington, 1981

Poetry in Public Places Award, American International Sculptor's Symposiums, New York, 1979

Writers Grant Award, International PEN Fund, 1976

Authors Grant Award, Carnegie Fund, 1975

Governor's Award, Office of the Governor, State of Washington, 1971

Pacific Northwest Writers Conference: First Prize 1966, 1970; Third Prize, 1968.

PUBLICATION HIGHLIGHTS
The Submuloc Show/Columbus Wohs: A Visual Commentary on the Columbus Quincentennial from the Perspective of

America's First People, (Phoenix: Atlatl, 1992)

Drawing of the Song Animals: New and Selected Poems (Duluth, Minn.: Holy Cow! Press, 1991)

Stories of the Moons (Marvin, S. Dak.: Blue Cloud Quarterly, 1989)

Stories of the Moons (Marvin, S. Dak.: Blue Cloud Quarterly, 1987)

Pieces (New York: Strawberry Press, 1981)

Songs for the Harvester of Dreams (Seattle: University of Washington Press, 1981)

To Bridge the Dream (Laguna, New Mex.: A. Press, 1978)

The Canoe (New York: Strawberry Press, 1977)

Digging Out the Roots (New York: Harper & Row, 1977)

Turning to the Rhythms of Her Song (Seattle: Jawbone Press, 1977)

Carriers of the Dream Wheel, ed. by Duane Niatum (San Francisco: Harper & Row, c1975)

Ascending the Red Cedar Moon (New York: Harper & Row, 1974)

A Cycle for the Woman in the Field (Baltimore: Laughing Man Press, 1973)

Taos Pueblo (Greenfield Center, N.Y.: Greenfield Review Press, 1973)

After the Death of an Elder Klallam (Phoenix: Baleen Press, 1970)

Niatum's works have also appeared in numerous anthologies:

Durable Breath: Contemporary Native America Poetry, ed. by D. L. Birchfield and John E. Smelcer (Anchorage: Salmon Run Press, 1994).

Returning the Gift: Poetry and Prose from the First North American Native Writers' Festival, ed. by Joseph Bruchac with the support of the Association for the Study of American Indian Literatures (Tucson: University of Arizona, 1994)

The Before Columbus Foundation Poetry Anthology, ed. by Shawn Wong, et al. (New York: W. W. Norton, 1992)

Parole Nel Sangue: Poesia Indiana Americana Contemporanea, ed. by Franco Meli (Milan, Italy: Arnoldo Mondadori, 1991)

Talking Leaves: Contemporary Native American Short Stories, ed. by Lesley Craig (New York: Laurel Paperbacks Dell, 1991)

Harper's Anthology of Twentieth-Century Native American Poetry, ed. by Duane Niatum (San Francisco: Harper & Row, 1988)

Recovering the Word: Essays on Native American Literature, ed. by Brian Swann and Arnold Krupat (Berkeley: University of California Press, 1987)

Earth Power Coming: Short Fiction in Native American Literature, ed. by Simon Ortiz (Tsaile, Ariz.: Navajo Community College Press, 1983)

This Song Remembers: Self Portraits of Native Americans in the Arts (Boston: Houghton Mifflin, 1980)

The Remembered Earth: An Anthology of Contemporary Native American Literature, ed. by Geary Hobson (Albuquerque: University of New Mexico Press, 1978)

From the Belly of the Shark, ed. by Walter Lowenfels (New York: Vintage Books, 1973)

NARRATIVE

Educator and writer Duane Niatum was born Duane McGinnis in Seattle, Washington, on the Olympic Peninsula near Hadlock Bay, an area where his family had lived for generations. He is a member of the Klallam Tribe and is of Klallam, French and Irish descent. Niatum is Klallam on his mother's side and was raised among her family until he left home at the age of 17. As a youth, Niatum lived in Seattle, Hadlock California and Alaska, where his family had been salmon anglers for generations. His father and mother were divorced when he was between five and six years old, and he never saw his father until he was 21 and out of the service. Niatum admits that while growing up he was the "black sheep of the family" until he was in his teenage years. He was able to survive such a stigma through the tremendous love, understanding and guidance of his grandfather. It was to his grandfather that Niatum made a solemn promise to uphold his Coast Salish traditions, not abandon his own roots and to honor the Earth and its creatures.

At the age of 17, Niatum left home and enlisted in the navy, where he spent two years in Japan. He reveled in the cultural differences and similarities in areas such as art, philosophy and traditions between the Japanese people and his own people. "It was one of the best influences I ever had." While in Japan, he came to understand the idea of restraint: how to understand and appreciate objects, how to use restraint, or hold back, by understating the feeling for the object and the object itself as well. In time, his poetry came to reflect this powerful influence.

As a young man, he played the alto saxophone and dreamed of becoming a great musician, though he quit while he was stationed in Japan. He never played again, discouraged because he could not "purify the tone of my sax." The night he decided to quit playing the saxophone, he started his first poem while getting quite drunk in a Yokosura bar. "I've never stopped writing since. And I never played music again."

Not long after he began his first poem, he decided to dedicate himself to the work of becoming a writer and storyteller. Having always been interested in visual art, Niatum was inspired by the lives and works of the impressionist and post-impressionist artists, whose brilliant paintings and drawings still provide a source of illumination in his life. As he started to study poetry, Niatum began with the works of the beat poets, and then moved to the writings of Theodore Roethke and Nelson Bentley. Next he read the works

of poets Thomas Hardy, T. S. Eliot, Dylan Thomas, W. H. Auden, Louise Bogan, Octavio Paz, W. B. Yeats, Pablo Neruda and Wallace Stevens, all of whose works fired his love of poetry. Of all the modes of expression he had tried up to this point, poetry and fiction became the two most enduring and driving forces in his life.

From 1964 to 1965, he lived in New York City. In the spring of 1971, his great-aunt gave him her father's Indian name "Niatum," and in 1973 he legally changed his name from McGinnis to Niatum. In that same year he returned to New York City to work for the publishers Harper & Row. Since then, Niatum has taught at a number of institutions: Johns Hopkins University, Evergreen State College, Seattle Central Community College and the University of Washington. Now living in Seattle, he taught for a semester at Seattle High School and for over a year at Seattle Elementary School. He has also taught poetry and short fiction writing to senior citizens in Seattle senior centers for nearly a year. In June 1983 he was invited to participate in Rotterdam's International Poetry Festival. Niatum currently teaches college courses on a part-time basis and is a Ph.D. candidate in American culture at the University of Michigan.

A widely published writer of poems, fiction and nonfiction, Niatum has had his works translated into ten languages, published in innumerable journals, such as the *Chicago Review, Prairie Schooner, Callaloo, Ariel,* the *Michigan Quarterly Review* and the *Northwest Review,* and has had several monographs of his work published.

Of all Niatum's works, his favorite is his last book *Drawings of the Song Animals.* "I spent six years working on it and it is the best of the first four books, plus new poems that cover over twenty-five years of writing." He is currently about to submit a short-story collection to a publisher, has a new poetry collection at a publisher now and is compiling a collection of essays for another. "I am also writing a dissertation on the Aleut artist, John Hoover."

NAME   P
Linda Noel

TRIBAL AFFILIATION
Concow Maidu

PUBLICATION HIGHLIGHTS
"Understanding Each Other," "A Little Light from Somewhere," poems in *Newsletter Interview* (Fort Bragg, Calif.: [s.n.], issue 7, 1985); "Knowing of the Time: A Time for Gathering," poem in *The Clouds Threw This Light* (Santa Fe: Institute of American Indian Art, 1983); *Where You First Saw the Eyes of Coyote* (Brooklyn, N.Y.: Strawberry Press, 1982)

NAME   N
Adam Nordwall

OTHER NAMES USED
Adam Fortunate Eagle

TRIBAL AFFILIATION
Red Lake Band Chippewa

PERSONAL
Born: July 18, 1929, in Red Lake, Minnesota, Red Lake Indian Reservation
Education: Federal boarding schools for Indians; (Pipestone Indian Boarding School, Pipestone, Minnesota; Haskall Institute, Lawrence, Kansas)

AWARDS, HONORS
Lifetime Teaching Credential, University Level, State of California

PUBLICATION HIGHLIGHTS
Alcatraz! Alcatraz!: The Indian Occupation of 1969–1971 (Berkeley: Heyday Books, 1992)

NARRATIVE
Adam Fortunate Eagle was born Adam Nordwall July 18, 1929, on the Red Lake Indian Reservation, in northern Minnesota. He was taken from his parents as a child and sent to a Bureau of Indian Affairs boarding school in Pipestone, Minnesota, which "historically suppress[ed] the cultural identity of children." After ten years at Pipestone, he moved to Lawrence, Kansas, to attend the Haskall Indian Institute and studied commercial art. While he was attending the Haskall School, he met his future wife, Bobbie. After they were married, they moved to San Francisco, where Fortunate Eagle worked as an exterminator and later began his own extermination business in Oakland. During this time he also taught classes in Native American cultures at California State University at Hayward for four and one-half years.

While living in California, Fortunate Eagle became acquainted with various American Indians around the Bay Area who were native Californians, former Haskall colleagues and individuals who were brought to the Bay Area under the federal program of relocation. Through these acquaintances he became involved in meetings with local Indian groups and urban pow-wows, and later became politically active within the Indian community, serving as chair of the United Bay Area Council of American Indian Affairs during the years 1962–1976. As the chair of the council in 1969, Fortunate Eagle oversaw the organization's plans to overtake Alcatraz Island and became one of the leading organizers of the occupation, which lasted for nineteen months. The occupation was intended to accomplish many goals, to provide an Indian center to replace the one that burned down earlier, to create a cultural center, spiritual center, vocational training facility and museum for all of the Indian nations, to be bought from the U.S. government for $24 in beads, "the exact same amount the Dutch paid the Indians for the island of Manhattan. This was clearly a bargain. ..."

Fortunate Eagle, who was closely associated with the events surrounding the historic Alcatraz occupation, writes to present a recording of history from an Indian point of view. On the process of writing, he says that "writing is a pain in the ass as well as a strain on the brain. I'd rather sculpt and carve pipes, my main source of income." Fortunate Eagle is an award-winning pipe maker and sculptor. He also attends pow-wows and ceremonies, where he serves as a pipe carrier and ceremonial leader.

The name Fortunate Eagle was given to him when he was adopted into the Whistling Water Clan of the Crow Nation, though he is careful to point out that he is also a member of the Teasing Clan. He is known in some circles for his ongoing exchange of good-humored gibes with author Vine Deloria Jr.

Fortunate Eagle currently operates an art gallery on the Shoshone-Paiute Reservation near Fallon, Nevada, his Shoshone wife's reservation, where he also makes pipes, sculpts, writes short stories and is working on three or four books.

NAME J, P
Jim Northrup

TRIBAL AFFILIATION
Anishinabe, Fond du Lac Band of Lake Superior Chippewa

PERSONAL
Born: April 28, 1942, at the Fond du Lac Reservation, Minnesota

AWARDS, HONORS
Best Feature Story—Native Journalists Association; 1987 Lake Superior regional Writers, 1986

PUBLICATION HIGHLIGHTS
Days of Obsidian, Days of Grace: Selected Poetry and Prose by Four Native American Writers, Adrian C. Louis, et al. (Poetry Harbor, 1994)

Walking the Rez Road (Stillwater, Minn.: Voyageur Press, 1993)

Three More (Minneapolis: Minnesota Center for Book Arts and the Loft, 1992)

Native American Minnesotans, videorecording, (St. Paul: KTCA, 1991)

Celebration of Indian Culture, videorecording, (Duluth, Minn.: College of St. Scholastica, 1989)

Northrups's works also appear in *Returning the Gift: Poetry and Prose from the First North American Native Writers' Festival,* ed. by Joseph Bruchac with the support of the Association for the Study of American Indian Literatures (Tucson: University of Arizona, 1994).

NARRATIVE
Seeing the works of his grandfathers in the public library and listening to the many storytellers present in his young life led Jim Northrup to pursue a life of literature and writing. Throughout his work, the members of the reservation community and the reservation lifestyle have provided Northrup with a source of ideas, inspiration and strength. Northrup attended a federal boarding school, where his years were spent in "isolation and cultural emptiness." His later experience as an infantry soldier in the Vietnam War

changed his life and, consequently, his writings. Currently living and writing on the reservation, Northrup is involved in seasonal activities such as spear fishing and basket making, participating in pow-wows in the summer, gathering wild rice and moose hunting in the fall, teaching, writing and storytelling in the winter. He is now working on several short stories, a historical novel, a screenplay, poetry and is writing a syndicated column called "Fond du Lac Follies." Writers whose works Northrup enjoys include Joe Northrup, Simon Ortiz, Carroll Arnett and Marcie Rendon.

NAME P

Nila Northsun

TRIBAL AFFILIATION

Shoshone/Chippewa

PERSONAL

Born: February 1, 1951, in Schurz, Nevada
Education: B.A. in art, University of Montana, Missoula

AWARDS, HONORS

Commisioner, Nevada State Commission on Women, 1992

PUBLICATION HIGHLIGHTS

"Peeping Toms" in *Callaloo* vol. 17 (1), Winter p. 301 (2), 1994
Small Bones, Little Eyes, poems, with Jim Sagel (Fallon, Nev.: Duck Down Press, 1982)
Coffee, Dust Devils and Old Rodeo Bulls, poems, with Kirk Robertson ([S.l.]: Canada: OPAC Nations, 1978)
After the Drying Up of the Water (Fallon, Nev.: Fallon Paiute-Shoshone Tribe, 1977)
Diet Pepsi and Nacho Cheese, poems (Fallon, Nev.: Duck Down Press, 1977)

Northsun works also appear in the following anthologies:

American Visions: Multicultural Literature for Writers, by Delores La Guardia and Hans P. Guth (Mountain View, Calif.: Mayfield, 1995)
Returning the Gift: Poetry and Prose from the First North American Native Writers' Festival, ed. by Joseph Bruchac with the support of the Association for the Study of American Indian Literatures (Tucson: University of Arizona, 1994)
American Indian Literature: An Anthology of Contemporary American Indian Fiction, ed. by Alan Velie (Norman: University of Oklahoma Press, 1991)
Desert Wood: An Anthology of Nevada Poets, ed. by Shawn Griffin (Reno: University of Nevada Press, 1991)
Dancing on the Rim of the World: An Anthology of Contemporary Northwest Native American Writing, ed. by Andrea Lerner (Tucson: Sun Tracks and University of Arizona Press, 1990)
The Sacred Hoop: Recovering the Feminine in American Indian Traditions, Paula Gunn Allen (Boston: Beacon Press, 1986)
The Remembered Earth: An Anthology of Contemporary Native American Literature, ed. by Geary Hobson (Albuquerque: Red Earth Press, 1979)

NARRATIVE

Northsun grew up in the San Francisco Bay Area. She now lives on her reservation in Fallon, Nevada, and is a single parent of three children. In 1989 Northsun became the social services director for her tribe. She has work published in the *Wormwood Review, Callaloo, Vagabond, Sun Tracks, Dacotah Territory, Nitty Gritty,* the *Greenfield Review, Poetry East* and *In Focus,* among many other journals.

Northsun writes about "abnormally normal people, commonly referred to as dysfunctionals." She regards her strongest work to be the *Gramma* series "because they were the earliest and most effortless, and become history for my extended family." Her first husband, Kirk Robertson, exposed her to great reading and writing and encouraged and edited her efforts. Many authors Northsun reads are Sherman Alexie, Adrian Louis, Raymond Carver and Richard Ford. Charles Bukowski is one of her favorite authors: "He didn't write 'pretty stuff.'" He seemed to enjoy regaling the exploits of the down and dirty. I like that, I could relate to that." Northsun is now the director of Stepping Stones Tribal Youth Shelter and is beginning to write again after a long hiatus.

NAME   N
Jack Norton

TRIBAL AFFILIATION
Hupa and Cherokee

PUBLICATION HIGHLIGHTS
"Traversing the Bridge of Our Lives," essay in *American Indian Quarterly* (Horst, Tex.: Southwestern American Indian Society, 1989)

"The Path of Genocide: From El Camino Real to the Gold Mines of the North," essay in *The Missions of California: A Legacy of Genocide* (San Francisco: Indian Historian Press, 1988)

Genocide in Northwestern California (San Francisco: Indian Historian Press, 1979)

Q

NAME   J, P
William Oandasan

TRIBAL AFFILIATION
Yuki

PERSONAL
Born: 1947 at the Round Valley Reservation in Northern California

PUBLICATION HIGHLIGHTS
Moving Inland: A Cycle of Lyrics (York Stn., Calif.: A. Publications, 1993)

A Yukian Bibliography ([Los Angeles]: A. Publications, 1991)

"Los Angeles, Southern California for Lorca's 'Paisaje,'" poem in the *Colorado Review* (Fort Collins, Colo.: Colorado State University, 1989)

"Grandmother's Land," poem in *Harper's Anthology of Twentieth-Century Native American Poetry* (San Francisco: Harper & Row, 1988)

Round Valley Verses (Marvin, S. Dak.: Blue Cloud Quarterly, 1987)

Round Valley Songs (Minneapolis: West End Press, 1984)

"Starlight," poem in *Moving Inland* (Los Angeles: Writer's Circle, 1983)

A Branch of California Redwood (Los Angeles: University of California at Los Angeles Indian Study Center, 1980)

A Branch of California Redwood, poems (Los Angeles: American Indian Studies Center at the University of California, 1980)

Taking Off a Turning Point ([Laguna, N. Mex.]: A. Press, 1976)

Earth and Sky: A Series of Contraries in Haiku ([Laguna, N. Mex.]: A. Press, 1976)

Oandasan's works have also appeared in the anthologies: *A Nation Within: Contemporary Native American Writing,* selected by Ralph Salisbury (Hamilton, New Zealand: Outrigger Publishers, 1983) and *The Remembered Earth: An Anthology of Contemporary Native American Literature,* ed. by Geary Hobson (Albuquerque: Red Earth Press, 1979)

NARRATIVE
Oandasan was the founder and publisher of A. Press, through which he published three poetry chapbooks: *Earth and Sky, Taking Off* and *Sermon and Three Waves.*

Oandasan was a member of the Multicultural Arts Panel of the California Arts Council, he was a member of the Board of Directors of the Santa Monica (California) Cultural Center and he held the position of executive director of A Writers' Circle of Los Angeles. He also taught contemporary Native American poetry at the University of California at Los Angeles and was a community scholar fellow in the department of English and comparative literary studies at Occidental College in Los Angeles. Oandasan's works have appeared in the journals *Akwesasne Notes, Mississippi Valley Review* and *New America.* He has also worked as the senior editor of the *American Indian Culture and Research* journal and has produced his own periodical titled *A Journal of Contemporary Literature.* Oandasan is now deceased.

NAME   P
Calvin O'John

TRIBAL AFFILIATION
Ute and Navajo

PERSONAL

Born: Denver, Colorado

Education: Graduate of the Institute of American Indian Arts, Santa Fe, New Mexico, 1967

PUBLICATION HIGHLIGHTS

O'John's works have appeared in the following anthologies:

New and Old Voices of Wah'Kon-Tah, third edition, ed. by Robert K. Dodge and Joseph B. McCullough (New York: International Publishers, c1985)

Voices from Wah'Kon-Tah: Contemporary Poetry of Native Americans, first edition, ed. by Robert K. Dodge and Joseph B. McCullough (New York: International Publishers, [1974])

Future Directions in Native American Art (Santa Fe: Institute of American Indian Arts, [1973])

The Whispering Wind: Poetry by Young American Indians, ed. by Terry Allen (New York: Doubleday, 1972)

The Way: An Anthology of American Indian Literature, by Shirley H. Witt (New York: Knopf, 1972)

The American Indian Speaks, ed. by John R. Milton (Vermillion, S. Dak.: University of South Dakota, 1969)

NARRATIVE

In addition to writing poetry, O'John works as a painter and exhibits regularly.

NAME   P

Louis Oliver

OTHER NAMES USED

Littlecoon

TRIBAL AFFILIATION

Creek

PERSONAL

Born: 1904 in Cowera, formerly Koweta Town, Oklahoma

PUBLICATION HIGHLIGHTS

Chasers of the Sun: Creek Indian Thoughts (Greenfield Center, N.Y.: Greenfield Review Press, 1990)

NARRATIVE

Oliver was raised by his grandmother and aunts after being orphaned as a youth. He attended high school at Bacone College where he graduated in 1926. In high school he enjoyed studying the poetry and prose of American and British writers. He did not pursue writing through his middle years, and for his first fifty years he lived, worked, hunted, fished and gardened in the vicinity of his home in eastern Oklahoma. In his later years, Oliver came to feel that he needed to leave a record of his Native peoples' knowledge, their understanding of the world, past history and traditions to the younger generations, so he took up the pen and began to write. Other works by Oliver have been published in the journals *Northeast Indian Quarterly, Mildred* and the *Wooster Review.*

NAME   F, L, S

Lela K. Oman

OTHER NAMES USED

Lela Kiana Oman

TRIBAL AFFILIATION

Inupiaq (Eskimo)

PERSONAL

Born: December 15, 1915, in Noornik, Alaska

Education: 10th grade of high school

AWARDS, HONORS

Certificate of Appreciation, Youth Leadership Organization, 1991

Woman of the Year, 1980

Citation from the Alaska Legislature (two times), 1980

Arctic Native Brotherhood Queen, 1979

Certificate of Merit by the publishers of *Writers Digest,* 1967

Centennial Year Story Teller, Anchorage, 1967

Mrs. Nome, 1966

PUBLICATION HIGHLIGHTS

Eskimo Legends, second edition (Anchorage: Methodist University Press, 1975)

The Ghost of Kingikty (ee-ahk-meute) and Other Eskimo Legends (Anchorage: Printed by K. Wray's Print Shop, 1967)

Eskimo Legends: Authentic Eskimo Tales of Suspense and Excitement (Nome, Alaska: Nome Publishing, 1956)

NARRATIVE

Lela Oman spent her early years in Noornik, Selawik and the region around the White Mountains. She attended school at the Eklutna Vocational School, Alaska, where she played basketball, was a member of the school choir and enjoyed dancing. She later completed a nursing course through the American Red Cross in 1934. As a young woman Oman was deeply influenced by her father, Jim Kiana, and her aunt, Susie Larkhart, and she takes pride in her exceptional heritage. "I am a descendent of the great Umialiks [chiefs] of the Kobib Valley."

When she was a young woman attending school, Oman remembers a school teacher she had, Miss Brooke, who encouraged her to write. She has been translating and recording Eskimo legends since 1947 and works with children in schools as a storyteller. Oman has also given lectures on Alaska and is a bilingual teacher to adults.

As she describes her work with legends and storytelling, Oman says "People, non-Natives, think Eskimos are lacking, to me this was a challenge; I always represent my people in many ways." Oman enjoys the works of authors James Michener, Edna Ferber, Louis Thomas Jones, Edward William Nelson and articles published in the periodical *Reader's Digest.* She is still actively translating Eskimo legends and has completed a book titled *Epic of Kayak* (qayaq).

Oman is now a retired social worker, though she is an active lecturer. Her activities outside writing and lecturing include fishing, berry-picking and attending her church.

NAME E, N

Alfonso A. Ortiz

OTHER NAMES USED

Alfonso Alex Ortiz

TRIBAL AFFILIATION

San Juan Pueblo

PERSONAL

Born: April 30, 1939, in San Juan Pueblo, New Mexico

Education: A.B. from the University of New Mexico, 1961; M.A. from the University of Chicago, 1963; Ph.D. from the University of Chicago, 1967

PUBLICATION HIGHLIGHTS

The Pueblo: Southwest (New York: Chelsea House, 1994)

North American Indian Anthropology: Essays on Society and Culture, by A. Ortiz, Raymond DeMallie, F. Eggan (Norman: University of Oklahoma, 1994)

"Origins: Through Tewa Eyes" in *National Geographic,* vol. 180 (4), October, p. 4 (10), 1991

American Indian Myths and Legends, by A. Ortiz and R. Erdoes (New York: Pantheon, 1984)

Handbook of North American Indians, Volume 10: Southwest, by William C. Sturtevant and Alfonso Ortiz (United States Government Printing Office, 1983)

Southwest, ed. by Alfonso Ortiz (Washington, D.C.: Smithsonian Institution Press, 1980)

To Carry Forth the Vine: An Anthology of Native North American Poetry, with Margaret D. Ortiz (New York: Columbia University Press, 1974)

The Tewa World: Space, Time, Being and Becoming in a Pueblo Society (Chicago: University of Chicago Press, 1969)

Project Head Start in an Indian Community (Bethesda, Md.: ERIC Document Reproduction Service, n.d.)

"Ritual Drama and the Pueblo World View" in *New Perspectives on the Pueblos,* first edition, ed. by Alfonso Ortiz (Albuquerque: University of New Mexico Press, 1972)

NARRATIVE

Ortiz began his academic career as an assistant professor of anthropology at Pitzer College in Claremont California. He was an assistant professor of anthropology at Princeton University in Princeton, New Jersey, from 1967 to 1970 and later taught as an associate professor at Princeton. Ortiz worked as a consultant for the John Hay Whitney Foundation in 1971, for the Ford Foundation from 1969 to 1970 and for the Xerox Corporation in 1968. He is currently a professor of anthropology at the University of New Mexico.

Ortiz was as a member of the Native American Rights Fund Advisory Council and served as the vice president of the Association on American Indian Affairs. He is married to Margaret Ortiz, and they have three children.

NAME F, J, N, P, S, E

Simon J. Ortiz

TRIBAL AFFILIATION

Acoma Pueblo

PERSONAL

Born: May 27, 1941, in Albuquerque, New Mexico

Education: Ft. Lewis College, Durango, Colorado, 1961–1962; University of New Mexico, 1966–1968; M.F.A. from the University of Iowa, 1968–1969

AWARDS, HONORS

Returning the Gift Lifetime Achievement Award, University of Oklahoma, Norman, 1993

New Mexico Humanities Council Humanitarian Award for Literary Achievement, 1989

National Endowment for the Arts Fellowship, 1981

Honored Poet at a White House Salute to Poetry and American Poets, Washington D.C., 1980

National Endowment for the Arts Discovery Award, 1970

PUBLICATION HIGHLIGHTS

The People Shall Continue (Emeryville, Calif.: Children's Book Press, 1988, 1995)

After and Before the Lightning (Tucson: University of Arizona, 1994)

Fight Back: For the Sake of the People, for the Sake of the Land (Albuquerque: After and Before the Lightning) (Tucson: University of Arizona, 1994)

Chaco Canyon: A Center and Its World (Santa Fe: Museum of New Mexico Press, 1994)

"Seed" in *Ploughshares,* vol. 20 (1), Spring, p. 34, 1994

Columbus and Beyond: Views from Native Americans, ed. by Randolph Jorgen (Tucson, Ariz.: Southwest Parks and Monuments Association, 1992)

Woven Stone (Tucson: University of Arizona Press, 1992)

A Good Journey (Tucson, Ariz.: Sun Tracks; University of Arizona Press, 1984, c1977)

Fightin': New and Collected Stories (New York: Thunder's Mouth Press, 1983)

The Importance of Childhood (Acoma Pueblo, N. Mex.: Pueblo of Acoma Press, 1982)

From Sand Creek: Rising in This Heart Which Is Our America (New York: Thunder's Mouth Press, 1981)

Howbah Indians: Stories (Tucson, Ariz.: Blue Moon, 1978)

Going for the Rain (New York: Harper & Row, 1976)

Naked in the Wind ([S.l.]: Quetzal-Vihio Press, 1971)

Ortiz has been coeditor of the books *A Ceremony of Brotherhood: 1680–1980,* with Rudolfo A. Anaya and Simon Ortiz (Albuquerque: La Academia Publications, 1980) and *Califia: The California Poetry* (S.l.: Yardbird Wing, 1978)

Mr. Ortiz is the editor of: *Earth Power Coming: Anthology of Native American Short Fiction* (Tsaile, Ariz.: Navajo Community College Press, 1983).

Ortiz' works have also appeared in numerous anthologies:

Returning the Gift: Poetry and Prose from the First North American Native Writers' Festival, ed. by Joseph Bruchac with the support of the Association for the Study of American Indian Literature (Tucson: University of Arizona, 1994)

The Lightning Within: An Anthology of Contemporary American Indian Fiction, ed. by Alan Velie (Lincoln: University of Nebraska Press, 1991)

Winged Words: American Indian Writers Speak, ed. by Laura Coltelli (Lincoln: University of Nebraska Press, 1990)

I Tell You Now: Autobiographical Essays by Native American Writers, ed. by Brian Swann and Arnold Krupat (Lincoln: University of Nebraska Press, 1987)

Survival This Way: Interviews with Native American Poets, ed. by Joseph Bruchac (Tucson: Sun Tracks; University of Arizona Press, 1987)

Native American Renaissance, ed. by Kenneth Lincoln (Berkeley: University of California Press, 1983)

Four American Indian Literary Masters, by A. R. Velie (Norman: University of Oklahoma Press, 1982)

The Remembered Earth: An Anthology of Contemporary Native American Literature, ed. by Geary Hobson (Albuquerque: Red Earth Press, 1979)

The American Indian Reader, ed. by Jeanette Henry (San Francisco: Indian Historian Press, 1972–1977)

Carriers of the Dream Wheel: Contemporary Native American Poetry, ed. by Duane Niatum (New York: Harper & Row, 1975)

From the Belly of the Shark, ed. by Walter Lowenfels (New York: Vantage, 1974)

The Man to Send Rain Clouds: Contemporary Stories by American Indians, ed. by Kenneth Rosen (New York: Viking, 1974)

NARRATIVE

Ortiz was raised "at Deetsegaimah—or McCartys—at Acoma Pueblo in New Mexico." He spent his first twenty years at the Acoma Pueblo, in a close and supportive environment with "my parents, relatives, people in my Acoma community." He remembers that as a youth all of his years as a student were memorable. "There were many moments I remember as being significant, although they're not remembered fondly in some instances." After he graduated from high school, Ortiz worked in the uranium mines and processing plants of the Grants Ambrosia Lake area for one year. He enrolled at Ft. Lewis College in Durango, Colorado, from 1961 to 1962 with the intention of becoming a chemist. Before completing his studies, Ortiz enlisted in the U.S. Army and served from 1963 to 1966. After his service he enrolled as a student at the University of New Mexico from 1966 to 1968, and he later earned his masters of fine arts degree from the University of Iowa, where he was also a Fellow in the University's International Writing Program. During his student years Ortiz began to publish his poems in small magazines and presses.

Ortiz has worked as an educator and journalist for many years, beginning as a public relations worker at the Rough Rock Demonstration School in Rough Rock, Arizona, then becoming a newspaper editor for the National Indian Youth Council in Albuquerque, New Mexico, from 1970 to 1973. He then moved into academia, first working as an instructor at San Diego State University and as an instructor at the Institute of American Indian Arts in Santa Fe, New Mexico, both in 1974. He worked as an instructor at the Navajo Community College in Tsaile, Arizona, from 1975 to 1977, an instructor at the College of Marin in Kentfield, California, an instructor at the University of New Mexico, Albuquerque, an instructor and co-director of the creative writing program at Sinte Gleska College in Mission, South Dakota, and instructor at Lewis and Clark College, Portland, Oregon.

He has served as consulting editor at the Navajo Community College Press, Tsaile, Arizona, and consulting editor of the Pueblo of Acoma Press, Acoma, New Mexico. He was also the editor of the *Navajo Rough Rock News* and now edits the literary journal *Wanbli Ho*. Ortiz served as the arts coordinator of the Metropolitan Arts Commission for Portland, Oregon, in 1990. He has had his works published in numerous journals and publications, such as *Alcheringa, New Mexico Quarterly, South Dakota Review* and *Pembroke* magazine.

Ortiz writes about the Native American life and people in contemporary contexts. His works are based on his Native American heritage and oral traditions and are influenced by the social and political changes that took place in the 1950s–1980s, such as the civil rights struggles, the Third World Liberation Movement and the Indian human rights actions. "I like the works (and things I heard or read they did) of the 1950s' and 1960s' 'beats.'" When asked about his choice to pursue a writing career, Ortiz responded, "I think realizing that Indian people worked so hard to be who they were—at times against insurmountable odds, made me decide [to be a writer]."

He considers one of his favorite works to be *From Sand Creek* "because it was written during a period of real serenity. And I also really like *Woven Stone* because it's my latest book and is very inclusive of a large amount of my work." Writers he enjoys include Raymond Carver, Richard Nelson, Leslie Marmon Silko and Eduardo Galcono.

Ortiz was briefly married to writer Joy Harjo. He now lives at Acoma, New Mexico, with his three children, Raho, Rainy Dawn and Sara Ortiz. In 1990 Ortiz was appointed lieutenant governor of the Acoma Pueblo, where he is currently serving in that capacity. He is also writing, beginning work in film and storytelling.

NAME E, F, N, J
Louis Owens

TRIBAL AFFILIATION
Cherokee/Choctaw

PERSONAL
Born: July 18, 1948, in Lompoc, California
Education: B.A. from the University of California, Santa Barbara; M.A. from the Uni-

versity of California, Santa Barbara; Ph.D. from the University of California, Davis

AWARDS, HONORS

National Endowment for the Arts Creative Writing Fellowship, 1990; National Endowment for the Humanities Fellowship, 1988; Fulbright Fellowship, 1980

PUBLICATION HIGHLIGHTS

Wolfsong (Norman: University of Oklahoma, 1994)

Bone Game: A Novel (Norman: University of Oklahoma, 1994)

Other Destinies: Understanding the American Indian Novel (Norman: University of Oklahoma Press, 1992, 1994)

American Literary Scholarship: An Annual, 1990, ed. by Louis Owens (Durham, N.C.: Duke University Press, 1992)

The Sharpest Sight (Norman: University of Oklahoma Press, 1992)

The Grapes of Wrath: Trouble in the Promised Land (Boston: Twayne, 1989)

John Steinbeck Re-vision of America (Athens: University of Georgia Press, 1985)

NARRATIVE

Owens moved back and forth between Mississippi and California until he was about seven years old. "In Mississippi we lived north of Vicksburg, along the Yazoo River—way out in the sticks." After the age of 7 he lived in California and occasionally lived in Nevada. His school experience was marked by his decision to drop out—at an early age. "I ran away from kindergarten after two weeks and never had to go back; I was a kindergarten drop out. A formative experience." Owens was raised in a close and supportive family, as he explains, "My mother, who was part Cherokee, had a powerful impact on my life and especially my patterns of thought. She emphasized our

Cherokee identity as I was growing up. My father, who is part Choctaw, taught me about the outdoors in great depth, and taught me how to work. My eight brothers and sisters had a great impact [on my life]."

Owens spent seven years working for the U.S. Forest Service as a wilderness ranger and a fire fighter on a Hot Shot crew.

Owens writes about the environment, Native American mixed-blood identity, and Native American literature. "I believe ecology to be the most important subject in my writing. I always liked to write and wanted to write. Perhaps it came from my mother's stories, who knows?" He considers his best work to be *The Sharpest Sight,* but *Wolfsong* is his favorite "because it represents a personal and rather intense attempt to get at Native American ecological concerns. Geography is absolutely central to everything I write. I've set work in Mississippi, California and Washington [state] because each of those places were very important to me at some point in my life. The natural environment is a crucial subject for me." He enjoys reading the works of most Native American novelists, such as Gerald Vizenor, James Welch, N. Scott Momaday, Leslie Marmon Silko, Thomas King, Louise Erdrich, Michael Dorris, Linda Hogan, the Navajo poet Luci Tapahonso, novelist Cormac McCarthy ("I want to write like him when I grow up"), John Steinbeck, William Butler Yeats and Wallace Stevens. He adds that, "Everyone is an influence; no one is a major influence."

He is working on two projects: a novel and a long, reflective nonfiction piece about wilderness and wilderness rangering. He is currently professor of literature at the University of California at Santa Cruz. In addition to writing and teaching, Owens is a builder: "I like to build additions to my house, chicken coops, anything."

P

NAME E, L, P, S, VA

Juanita Pahdopony

OTHER NAMES USED

Pahdopony

TRIBAL AFFILIATION

Comanche

PERSONAL

Born: January 18, 1947, in Portland, Oregon

Education: M.Ed. from Oklahoma City University, 1990; graduated from the American Indian Teacher Training Program, 1990

AWARDS, HONORS

Outstanding Teacher of the Gifted, Oklahoma City University, 1989

PUBLICATION HIGHLIGHTS

"Creative Perspectives," paper presented at Encircling Our Forgotten: conference proceedings (Norman, Okla.: American Indian Institute, University of Oklahoma, 1989)

"Tattered, Torn and Dusty Lace," poem in *Up Against the Wall Mother* ([S.l.]: Poetry Periodical Publishers, 1985)

"Art Therapy to Strengthen Tribal Identity," conference paper presented at the Seventh Annual National American Indian Conference on Child Abuse and Neglect, 1985

Pahdopony's works also appear in the following anthology. *Returning the Gift: Poetry and Prose from the First North American Native Writers' Festival*, ed. by Joseph Bruchac with the support of the Association for the Study of American Indian Literatures (Tucson: University of Arizona, 1994)

NARRATIVE

Educator, lecturer, poet, storyteller and visual artist, Juanita Pahdopony writes about southern Plains culture, the Comanche people, landscape of the Plains, relationships and the whimsy of everyday life. She spent her early years at the Comanche Indian Mission in Lawton, Oklahoma, where she also attended high school. Pahdopony recalls an incident in high school that became a pivotal point in her path to becoming an educator and writer " ... I think when an aptitude test in high school said I had the aptitude to be a paper bag inspector, ... my father blew his proverbial stoic stack and advocated for me. He stated to me that he knew I was bright; he knew from the questions I asked ... that those educators were stupid! I think that's why I'm an educator—to advocate for paper bag inspectors who are really artists, educators and writers." She describes her parents, who were her mentors, "My parents ... are unlike me ... they are patient. I always admired the way my father responded to a question. He thought for a time and responded only when he was ready. My mother never reacted to me with shock (and I tried often to get this response in my early years). She was patient."

She was encouraged to become fluent in the English language by her family, all of whom speak fluent Commanche. "[They] wanted me to be English-speaking and modern and progressive."

Pahdopony now lives in Oklahoma. "I live on the southern plains in the shadow of a mesa, the locals call it 'Red

Hill,' equidistant between Watonga (Cheyenne country) and Geary Oklahoma (Arapaho country). Sometimes I drive to work and look at the flat, flat land and see a brilliant Oklahoma sunrise, and at times I drive home and see an incredible sunset. The land is flat as far as I can see east or west." Pahdopony paints when she is not writing, giving presentations and teaching, and her subject matter encompasses the landscape of Oklahoma's Cheyenne and Arapaho country, and the people of the Plains.

Throughout her writing career, Pahdopony has been inspired by the works of writers Charlotte De Clue, Lance Henson and Louis Little Coon Oliver. "Being a friend of Charlotte has encouraged me a lot to develop confidence and share her passion for writing." She also enjoys the works of James Welch and Barbara Warner Ross, a Ponca poet and friend.

Pahdopony is currently working in Geary, Oklahoma, Elementary School as a title VC coordinator for half-days working with Cheyenne and Arapaho Tribes, and she is an art instructor for half-days at Geary High School. She also attends and gives presentations at numerous workshops and conventions.

NAME　　　P, VA
Ted Palmanteer

TRIBAL AFFILIATION
Colville

PERSONAL
Born: 1943 near Omak, Washington
Education: Coursework at the Institute of American Indian Arts, Santa Fe, New Mexico

PUBLICATION HIGHLIGHTS
"Pass It on Grandson" in *The Remembered Earth: An Anthology of Contemporary Native American Literature,* ed. by Geary Hobson (Albuquerque: University of New Mexico Press, 1979)

"Chinook Dance" in *Sun Tracks* (Tucson, Ariz.: Sun Tracks Literary Quarterly, vol. 1, Winter 1971/1972)

"The Strings of Time," "Hit," "Judgement," "Spring Dew," "This Is Real," "We Saw Days" in *The Whispering Wind: Poetry by Young American Indians,* ed. by Terry Allen (New York: Doubleday, 1972)

NARRATIVE
Palmanteer worked as an instructor at the Institute of American Indian Arts in Santa Fe, New Mexico. He was a painter and sculptor as well as a poet. He is now deceased.

NAME　　　N
Ron Paquin

TRIBAL AFFILIATION
Chippewa

PUBLICATION HIGHLIGHTS
Not First in Nobody's Heart: The Life Story of a Contemporary Chippewa, first edition, by Ron Paquin and Robert Doherty (Ames: Iowa State University Press, 1992)

NAME　　　E, P
Wilfred Pelletier

TRIBAL AFFILIATION
Odawa

PERSONAL
Born: 1927

PUBLICATION HIGHLIGHTS

Le silence d'un cri (Sainte-Foy, Quebec: A. Sigier, 1985)

Frei wie ein Baum: ein Indianer erzahlt sein Leben (Koln: E. Diederichs, 1983, 1973)

No Foreign Land: The Biography of a North American Indian (New York: Pantheon, 1973)

"Childhood in an Indian Village" in *The American Indian, The First Victim*, ed. by Jay David (New York: Morrow, 1972)

"For Every North American Indian Who Begins to Disappear, I Also Begin to Disappear," "Traditional Concepts of Organization" in *For Every North American Indian Who Begins to Disappear, I Also Begin to Disappear* (Toronto: Neewin Publishing, 1971)

Childhood in an Indian Village (Toronto: Neewin Publishing, 1969)

Some Thoughts About Organization and Leadership (Toronto: Neewin Publishing, 1967)

NAME   F, N
Jerry Pelley

TRIBAL AFFILIATION
Comanche

PUBLICATION HIGHLIGHTS

"War" in *Concepts: A Prison News Publication* (Lexington, Okla.: Joseph Harp Correctional Center, vol. 7, no. 3, 1991)

"Revised Grooming Code Shaves Religious Exemptions" in *Concepts: A Prison News Publication* (Lexington, Okla.: Joseph Harp Correctional Center, vol. 7, no. 4, 1991)

"Native Americans Hold Council Fire," "Prisoners Run for Common Goal," "Red Rum and Broken Treaties" in *Concepts: A Prison News Publication* (Lexington,

Okla.: Joseph Harp Correctional Center, vol. 6, no. 6, 1990)

NAME   F, N, P
Bill Penn

OTHER NAMES USED
W. S. Penn

TRIBAL AFFILIATION
Nez Perce and Osage

PERSONAL

Born: March 21, 1949, in Los Angeles, California

Education: B.A. in English, University of California at Davis, 1970; M.A. in creative writing and nineteenth- and twentieth-century American literature, Syracuse University, Syracuse, New York, 1977; Doctor of Arts in creative writing, Syracuse University, Syracuse New York, 1979

AWARDS, HONORS

Finalist, the *Missouri Review* National Essay Contest, University of Missouri Press, 1993

All University Research Completion Grant from Michigan State University for *All My Sins Are Relatives* (narrative essays on urban mixed-blood life and literature), 1993

Nominated for Elmer Holmes Bobst Awards, New York University Press, for story collection *This Is the World,* 1991

Michigan Council on the Arts Grant for *The Absence of Angels,* 1990

New York Foundation for the Arts Prize for *The Absence of Angels,* 1988

All University Research Initiation Grant for *Killing Time with Strangers,* Michigan State University, 1988

Finalist, P.E.N. Nelson Algran Awards, New York, 1987

Ludwig Vogelstein Foundation Supporting Grant for *The Absence of Angels,* 1985

Yaddo Fellowship, Yaddo Writer's Colony, Saratoga Springs, New York, State University of New York Grant, 1983

Honorable Mention, James B. Phelan Awards, San Francisco Foundation, for a collection of stories and *Dreaming in Place,* 1982

Stephen Crane Prize in Fiction for "Tarantulas," 1979

Michael Alssid Prize for "A Structural Accommodation of Beatrice" in *La Vita Nuova,* 1979

Stephen Crane Prize in Fiction for "Old Bird Young Bird," 1977

PUBLICATION HIGHLIGHTS

The Absence of Angels (New York: Permanent Press, [1994?])

"My Baby Sings Beethoven's Ninth," essay in *Wayzgoose Anthology of New Canadian-American Writing,* no. II ([S.l.: s.n.], Spring 1991)

"Quotients" in *Wayzgoose Anthology of New Canadian-American Writing,* no. I ([S.l.: s.n.], Spring 1990)

"Special Report: Preserving the English Language" in the *Encyclopedia Americana Annual: 1988, An Encyclopedia of the Events of 1987* (Danbury, Conn.: Grolier, [1988])

"This Is the World" in *Anataeus: Special Fiction Issue* ([S.l.: s.n.], Fall 1983)

NARRATIVE

Penn was raised in the suburbs of Los Angeles and Palo Alto, California. Penn's grandfather was an immense influence on his life, as was his sister Patricia Penn Hilden, both of whom "encouraged me to keep writing and telling stories in spite of rejections." He had numerous memorable instructors in school: Mrs. Robinson, Miss Marion McNamara, Art Amos and Jack Hicks. He says that another teacher,

George P. Elliott, served not only as an instructor but his mentor. There were many significant events in Penn's life. "The circumstances of my own birth, time spent at Second Mesa, Arizona, and the people I met there, years spent bouncing around from place to place and job to job, and the births of my two children."

Penn taught English, creative writing, and literature at Syracuse University from 1976 until 1981, first as a teaching assistant and later as a postdoctoral teaching fellow. He was an assistant professor at the State University of New York at Oswego from 1981 to 1984, an adjunct assistant professor at Pace University and the Fashion Institute of Technology from 1985 to 1986 and he taught as an assistant professor of English at the City University of New York in 1986 to 1987. Penn is currently the resident fiction writer and teacher of Native literature and comparative literature at Michigan State University in East Lansing, Michigan, and he is the regional coordinator for the Wordcraft Circle of Native American Writers.

Penn writes about "urban mixblood life and experiences, perceptions of death, time, humor (no, all that isn't incompatible). My current geographical surroundings play little or no part in my writing, which seems to be set where there are mountains, rivers or desert (California, Arizona, Oklahoma, upstate New York)."

He regards his work *The Absence of Angels* to be one of his strongest because "... it's funny but also records the life and perceptions of the (fictional) Albert Hummingbird. *All My Sins Are Relatives* (narrative essays) because it's true and represents some of the most difficult writing I've done."

Penn has had many of his articles, stories, essays and poems published in numerous journals, such as *L.A. Parent* magazine, *San Diego Parent* magazine, *Parenting, Southern Humanities Review,*

Portland Review, California Quarterly, Quarry, Passages, the *Northern Review,* the *William and Mary Review, Black Ice, Vanderbilt Street Press* and the *Vanderbilt Review,* among many others. He has also held reading of his works throughout the United States and Canada. Penn has held numerous program director positions within the academic community, he has served as a guest editor for the journal *Callalloo* and he has served as coordinator and workshop director for various writing programs throughout his academic career.

He enjoys reading works by writers "Tom King, Faulkner, Paul Auster, Jane Austen, Homer, Boccaccio, Vizenor, Louis Owens, Silko, McNickle, Mourning Dove, Conrad, Melville, Garcia Marquez, Ernest Gaines, J. J. Mathews, James A. McPherson, Linda Hogan, Wendy Rose, Carter Revard, Vine Deloria Jr. All these 'speak' truly to me as storytellers or poets who are tied into their oral traditions. I read any and all books which have a sense of storytelling and/or truthfulness."

Penn is now working on a manuscript titled *Killing Time with Strangers,* which is "a novel about Nez Perce religion, invention, sense of 'time.'" In his spare time, Penn stays in tough with the written word, as he explains, "I don't enjoy not writing. Essentially, I write, read, spend time with family and friends. Beyond that, I enjoy mentoring in the Wordcraft Circle of Native American Mentors and Apprentice writers, giving back a bit of the lot that has been given to me."

NAME   F, N
Clarence Pickernall

TRIBAL AFFILIATION
Inuit

PUBLICATION HIGHLIGHTS
"This Is My Land" in *From the Belly of the Shark: A New Anthology of Native Americans,* ed. by Walter Lowenfels (New York: Vantage, 1974)

Pickernall's works have also appeared in: *Native American Reader: Stories, Speeches and Poems,* ed. by Jerry D. Blanche (Juneau: Denali Press, c1990).

NAME   F, N
Chief George Pierre

TRIBAL AFFILIATION
Colville

PERSONAL
Born: 1926

PUBLICATION HIGHLIGHTS
Autumn's Bounty (San Antonio: Naylor, 1972)
American Indian Crisis (San Antonio: Naylor, 1971)

Pierre's works are also mentioned in: *Native American Literature,* by Andrew Wiget (Boston: Twayne, 1985); *American Indian Novelists: An Annotated Critical Bibliography,* by Tom Colonnese and Louis Owens (New York: Garland, 1985) and *American Indian Fiction,* first edition, by Charles R. Larson (Albuquerque: University of New Mexico Press, c1978).

NAME   F, S
Opal Popkes

OTHER NAMES USED
Lee Rogers

TRIBAL AFFILIATION

Choctaw

PERSONAL

Born: February 14, 1920, in Roswell, New Mexico

Education: B.A. from Eastern New Mexico University, Portales, 1948; graduate coursework at the University of New Mexico, Albuquerque, 1950; writing courses at Stephens College, 1975, 1977, 1979, 1981, 1985

PUBLICATION HIGHLIGHTS

Popkes's works have appeared in several anthologies, among them are: *The Remembered Earth: An Anthology of Contemporary Native American Literature,* ed. by Geary Hobson (Albuquerque: Red Earth Press, 1979) and *The Man to Send Rain Clouds: Contemporary Short Stories by American Indians,* ed. by Kenneth Rosen (New York: Viking, 1974).

NARRATIVE

Opal Popkes, born Lee Rogers, was raised in Portales, New Mexico, and is of Choctaw and Irish descent. Her father was illiterate, but her mother could read and stressed the importance of an education to her daughter, encouraging her to excel in her studies. While in college, Popkes remembers that she "... was voted Fall Festival Queen in 1947." During World War II, Popkes worked as General Marshall's cryptographer. She wrote an unpublished manuscript about these experiences titled *The Pigeons of the Pentagon.*

In her writing, Popkes tries to put herself in her subject's place: "I write to learn to visualize and understand any subject; I try to get behind the popular concept and understand the anonymous actors." Popkes has taught at Stephens College in Clearview, Missouri, and is currently retired. In her spare time she enjoys traveling, "going to auctions, babysitting my grandchildren, researching, reading and learning how to sew well."

NAME   F

Susan Power

TRIBAL AFFILIATION

Yanktonnai Sioux

PERSONAL

Born: October 12, 1961, in Chicago, Illinois

Education: A.B. in psychology from Harvard/Radcliffe, 1983; Juris Doctorate from Harvard Law School, 1986; M.F.A. from the University of Iowa Writer's Workshop, 1992

AWARDS, HONORS

James Michener Fellowship, University of Iowa, 1992–1993; Iowa Arts Fellowship, 1990–1992

PUBLICATION HIGHLIGHTS

The Grass Dancer (New York: Putnam, 1994, 1995)

"Morse Code" in *The Atlantic Monthly,* vol. 273 (6) June 1994, p. 88 (11)

"Snakes" in *The Paris Review,* vol. 35 (130) Spring 1994, 20 (38)

NARRATIVE

Power's mother is a Yanktonnai Dakota who was raised on the Standing Rock Reservation in North Dakota, and her father is a white Anglo-Saxon Protestant from New England who died when she was 11. As a youth, Power's school years were stressful: "I was always doing battle given that I was the only Native American in my school from kindergarten through twelfth grade."

With her mother teaching her tribal heritage, stories and legends, and her father reading aloud to her practically every night, Power was brought up with a love of works and language. She was encouraged to write by her mother. "My mother always encouraged my writing, and certainly gave me a wealth of materials to draw from, given the stories she told me, and her own eventful (and political) life."

"Attending the writer's workshop was a tremendous experience." Of the many inspirational teachers Power's had at Iowa, one worked closely with her and served as her mentor. "Margot Livesey taught a workshop and went over my manuscripts with thoughtful care and insight. She helped me develop into a better, more disciplined writer."

She enjoys the works of writers Linda Hogan, Joy Harjo, Amy Tan, Toni Morrison and Alan Gurganus, and says, "I am endlessly inspired by the writers Louise Erdrich and Michael Dorris."

Power's short stories have been published in several journals. "Beaded Soles" appeared in the Summer/Fall 1991 issue of *Other Voices,* "Red Moccasins" was published in the Fall issue of *Story,* the short story "Wild Turnips" appeared in the 1992 *High Plains Literary Review* and "Stone Woman" can be found in the vol. II, no. 3 1991 issue of *Iowa Woman.*

NAME E, F, N, P

Agnes Pratt

TRIBAL AFFILIATION

Suquamish

PERSONAL

Born: December 23, 1945, in Bremerton, Washington, on the Port Madison Indian Reservation

Education: Coursework at the Institute of American Indian Art, Santa Fe, New Mexico; graduate of the Northwest College of Art

PUBLICATION HIGHLIGHTS

Pratt's works have appeared in the following anthologies:

Dancing on the Rim of the World: An Anthology of Contemporary Northwest Native American Writing, ed. by Andrea Lerner (Tucson: Sun Tracks; University of Arizona Press, c1990)

New and Old Voices from Wah'Kon-Tah, third edition, ed. by Robert K. Dodge and Joseph B. McCullough (New York: International Publishers, c 1985)

Voices from Wah'Kon-Tah: Contemporary Poetry of Native Americans, first edition, ed. by Robert K. Dodge and Joseph B. McCullough (New York: International Publishers, 1974)

Future Directions in Native American Art (Santa Fe, N.Mex.: Institute of American Indian Art, [1973])

The Whispering Wind: Poetry by Young American Indians, ed. by Terry Allen (Garden City, N.J.: Doubleday, 1972)

The American Indian Speaks, comp. by John R. Milton (Vermillion, S. Dak.: University of South Dakota, 1969)

NARRATIVE

Pratt was raised on the Port Madison Indian Reservation. She is a descendent of Salmon Bay Curley, who was one of Chief Seattle's sub chiefs. Her work has also appeared in the journal *Literary Cavalcade.*

Q

NAME N
Polingaysi Qoyawayna

OTHER NAMES USED
Elizabeth Q. White

TRIBAL AFFILIATION
Hopi

PERSONAL
Born: 1892 in Oraibi, Arizona, on the Hopi Reservation
Education: Coursework at Bethel Academy and the Los Angeles Bible Institute

PUBLICATION HIGHLIGHTS
No Turning Back: A True Account of a Hopi Indian Girl's Struggle to Bridge the Gap Between the World of Her People and the World of the White Man, as Told to Vada F. Carlson (Albuquerque: University of New Mexico Press, 1964)

NARRATIVE
Qoyawayna was a member of her mother's Coyote Clan, and her father was a member of the Kachina Clan. As a child she was sent to the government boarding school at Keams Canyon, and in 1906 she was sent with many other Hopi children to the Sherman Institute in Los Angeles. Qoyawayna stayed at the Institute for four years, then returned home to Oraibi. Unhappy and ready for more challenges, Qoyawayna went to live with Mennonite pastor Jacob Frey's family near Oraibi. She traveled to Newton, Kansas, with Frey to learn typesetting and was later enrolled at the Bethel Academy with the intent of becoming a missionary. She returned to the Hopi Reservation in 1914 and worked in a nearby Mennonite mission until about 1919, when she became a teaching assistant at the Kayenta Indian Boarding School, thus ending her missionary work. Qoyawayna worked as a substitute teacher at the Tuba City Boarding School but traveled to Los Angeles for a semester at the Los Angeles Bible Institute. After her class ended, she returned to Oraibi and became the housekeeper and later a full-time instructor at the government school in Hotevilla, where she taught Hopi children, using a mix of Hopi language and legends instead of a diet of strictly English and European stories. Qoyawayna moved to Toadlena, New Mexico, where she was employed as an instructor. She married Lloyd White in 1931, though they were shortly separated. Qoyawayna later taught at Polacca and Oraibi. She is now deceased.

NAME E, F, N
Ronald Burns Querry

TRIBAL AFFILIATION
Choctaw

PERSONAL
Born: March 22, 1943, in Washington, D.C.
Education: B.A. in English, Central State University, Edmond, Oklahoma, 1969; M.A. in English, New Mexico Highlands University, 1970; Ph.D. in American studies, University of New Mexico, 1975

AWARDS, HONORS
Visiting Lecturer, Oklahoma University English Department, Spring 1993
Invited Writer, Returning the Gift Project: A North American Native Writers Festival, Norman, Oklahoma, July 1992

Recipient of a Professional Development Grant from the Arizona Commission on the Arts, July 1992

PUBLICATION HIGHLIGHTS

Death of Bernadette Lefthand (New York: Bantam, 1995, 1993)

I See By My Get-up (Norman: University of Oklahoma, 1994, 1987)

Review/essays in *Masterplots II* (Pasadena, Calif.: Salem Press, 1994)

Native American Struggle for Equality (Vero Beach, Fla.: Rourke Corp, 1992)

Growing Old at Willie Nelson's Picnic: And Other Sketches of Life in the Southwest, ed. R. Querry, (College Station, Tex.: Texas A&M University Press, 1983)

NARRATIVE

Ronald Burns Querry grew up in Oklahoma City. He is the son of Woodrow Borns and Beverly Burns Querry Corbett, and is married to Elaine Breece Stribling, with one child, Isabel Kathleen. Querry is a descendent of the Sixtown Clan of the Choctaw Nation (Oklahoneli) and is a member of the Choctaw Tribe. During graduate school he supported himself by working on ranches. After graduation, he served in the U.S. Marine Corps from 1960 to 1963. Querry worked as a instructor of English and American studies at Eastern New Mexico University's Project NewGate, at the New Mexico State Penitentiary, 1971–1972. "Service in the U.S. Marine Corps and teaching in the New Mexico State Penitentiary persuaded me that I simply had to find another way to live—thus, I write." He worked in various jobs as a ranch hand and wrangler, horse trainer, horse-shoer and served as a racing official for the American Quarter Horse Association. From 1977 to 1978 Querry was associate professor of American studies and director of Equestrian Center, Erie Lake College for Women, Painesville, Ohio, and from 1979 to 1983 was instructor of English at the University of Oklahoma. Querry was the assistant dean of education at the New Mexico State Penitentiary in 1988. From 1983 he has been a writer and rancher, and was visiting professor/fiction writer at the University of Oklahoma for the 1993 spring semester. Querry is working on a book to be published by the University of Oklahoma Press, retracing the long walk of the Choctaw along the Trail of Tears during the forced removal by the U.S. government in the 1830s of the tribe from their ancestral homeland in Mississippi to the wilderness of what is today the state of Oklahoma.

Querry enjoys working on cross-cultural subjects—Native American/non-Native American and the clash of the two. He considers his best work to be *Death of Bernadette Lefthand* "because it is my most recent work and my first novel." Of the many people in his life who contributed to his work as a writer, Querry credits his wife, who "... has been and continues to be supportive of my work. Without her support and encouragement this writing life would be much more difficult." As a young writer, Querry met author/playwright Larry L. King. "I was influenced heavily by King's humor and conversational tone." Other writers whose works Querry enjoys are Louis Owens, Linda Hogan, Gerald Vizenor, Leslie Silko and N. Scott Momaday. "I suspect every writer I've read has, in some way, influenced my world, and so my work." He adds that his chosen form of expression is literature because of "My love of the 'word'—first the spoken work, and then the word on a page. I do not 'enjoy' writing, I enjoy having written."

Querry's works have also appeared in the journals the *Chicago Tribune,* the *Dallas Times Herald, New Mexico Magazine, Albuquerque Journal, Albuquerque Living, Sunday Oklahoman, Speedhorse Magazine, Bishinik, Santa Fe New Mexican, Livestock Digest, New Mexico Stockman, World Literature Today, New Mexico Horse Breeder* and the *Taos News.*

R

NAME   P
Suzanne S. Rancourt

TRIBAL AFFILIATION
Abenaki

PUBLICATION HIGHLIGHTS
"Child Woman Kachina," "Earth Woman Kachina," "Dance Kachina Man," poems in *Tamaqua* (Champaign, Ill.: Humanities Dept., Parkland College, vol. 2, issue 2, 1991)

"Harvesting the Spring," poem in *Rooster Bay* ([S.l.: s.n.], Spring 1990)

"Mining the Hardshell," poem in *Mildred* ([Schenectady, N.Y.]: Mildred Publishing, vol. 2, no. 2, 1988)

"Embryonic Weave," "Silver Side," poems in the *Albany Review* (Albany, N.Y.: Albany Review Association, 1988)

Rancourt's works have also appeared in: *Returning the Gift: Poetry and Prose from the First North American Native Writers' Festival,* ed. by Joseph Bruchac with the support of the Association for the Study of American Indian Literatures (Tucson: University of Arizona, 1994).

NAME   P
William Michael Ransom

OTHER NAMES USED
W. M. Ransom

TRIBAL AFFILIATION
Cheyenne and Arapaho

PERSONAL
Born: June 6, 1945, in Puyallup, Washington

AWARDS, HONORS
Nominated for Pulitzer Prize for *Finding True North and Critter,* 1974; Nominated for National Book Award for *Finding True North and Critter,* 1974

PUBLICATION HIGHLIGHTS
Waving Arms at the Blind: Poems (Denver: Copper Canyon Press, 1975); *Finding True North and Critter* (Denver: Copper Canyon Press, 1973); *Soul Siftings* (Cottage Printers, 1968)

Ransom's works have also appeared in *Carriers of the Dream Wheel: Contemporary Native American Poetry,* ed. by Duane Niatum (New York: Harper & Row, 1975) and *From the Belly of the Shark: A New Anthology of Native Americans,* ed. by Walter Lowenfels (New York: Vantage, 1974).

NARRATIVE
Ransom also wrote the screenplay for the film *Look and Listen* in 1975.

NAME   L, P, PL, SC, V, VA
Duke Redbird

TRIBAL AFFILIATION
Chippewa

PERSONAL
Born: March 18, 1939, on the Saugeen Indian Reserve, Ontario, Canada

Education: M.A. in interdisciplinary studies, York University, Toronto, Canada, 1978; Ph.D. candidate in sociology, York University, Toronto, Canada, 1985–present

PUBLICATION HIGHLIGHTS

Loveshine and Red Wine, poems (Toronto: Woodlands Publishing, 1981)

We Are Metis: A Metis View of the Development of a Native Canadian People (Willowdale, Ont.: Ontario Metis & Non-Status Indian Association 1980)

I Am a Canadian (Toronto: Wacacro Productions, 1978)

"I Am a Canadian" in *Canada Century* (Scarsborough, Ont.: McGraw Hill Ryerson, 1977)

"My Lodge" in *Language Patterns Impressions* (Toronto: Holt, Rinehart & Winston, 1977)

"I Am the Redman" in *English Quarterly* (Toronto: Canadian Council of Teachers of English, 1977)

"The Beaver" in *High School Anthology* (Toronto: MacMillan, 1973)

"My Moccasins" in *The Melting Snowman* (Ottawa: Department of Indian Affairs, 1971)

Redbird's works have also appeared in these publications:

Canada Picture Book (West Germany: Jurgen F. Boden, 1976)

Effective Reading I (Toronto: Gage Educational Publishing, 1975)

Kites and Cartwheels and Toboggans and Turtlenecks (Toronto: Thomas Nelson & Sons, 1973)

Red on White (Toronto: New Press, 1971)

NARRATIVE

Duke Redbird has given numerous poetry readings, performances and television interviews throughout Canada and is a member of the Indian, Metis and Inuit Resource and Research Council at Harvard University, Cambridge, Massachusetts. Redbird is the president of Native Development Network Associates, where he is involved in the sale of Indian handicrafts, food and food service and computer telecommunications. He has recently retired from the position of grand chief of the Ontario Native Alliance.

Redbird was a former president of the Ontario Metis and Non-Status Indian Association from 1980 to 1983, and was the former director of Land Claims Research during the years 1978–1980. He was also the former vice president of the Native Council of Canada for the years 1974 to 1976. Redbird delivered a lecture at the Upper Canada College on Native people and the Constitution in 1982 and addressed the same issues on television. A multi-media musical based on his poetry was presented in 1978 in a command performance in honor of the Queen and Duke of Edinburgh. In 1985 he was invited by the president of India to open the Valmiki World Poetry Festival in New Delhi, India.

Redbird has directed a ninety-minute color documentary titled *National Assembly of the Fifth Annual Convention of the Native Council of Canada,* and he was co-director and writer of the National Film Board documentary *The Paradox of Norval Morriseau.* He also wrote and co-directed a thirty-minute drama documentary for TV Ontario in 1993, and he wrote and worked as the associate director for the CBS Four Directions drama series titled *A Canoe for the Making.*

Redbird now owns and operates the Wilderness Discovery Centre in Madawaska, Ontario, and he divides his time between his studio in Bark Lake, Ontario, and Toronto, where he paints and makes films.

NAME   P

Fred Red Cloud

TRIBAL AFFILIATION

Seneca

PUBLICATION HIGHLIGHTS

Red Cloud's works have appeared in the following anthologies:

New and Old Voices of Wah'Kon-Tah, third edition, ed. by Robert K. Dodge and Joseph B. McCullough (New York: International Publishers, c1985)

Native American Renaissance, by Kenneth Lincoln (Berkeley: University of California Press, c1983)

American Indian Prose and Poetry: We Wait in the Darkness, by Gloria Levitas et al. (New York: Putnam, 1974)

Voices of Wah'Kon-Tah: Contemporary Poetry of Native Americans, first edition, ed. by Robert K. Dodge and Joseph B. McCullough (New York: International Publishers, [1974])

From the Belly of the Shark: A New Anthology of Native Americans, ed. by Walter Lowenfels (New York: Vantage, 1974)

NARRATIVE

Red Cloud's works have also appeared in the journals *Akwesasne Notes, Prairie Schooner, Wisconsin Review* and *Voices International.* He also served as an editor for the poetry journal the *Mustang Review.*

NAME   N, F, VA

Philip H. Red Eagle

TRIBAL AFFILIATION

Sisseton Wapeton and Clallam

PERSONAL

Born: February 16, 1945, in Tacoma, Washington

Education: B.F.A. in art from the University of Washington, 1983; B.A. in communications from the University of Washington, 1987

AWARDS, HONORS

Louis Littlecoon Oliver Memorial Prose Award for "Red Earth," 1993

PUBLICATION HIGHLIGHTS

"Crown of Columbus" in *Raven Chronicles* (Seattle, Wash.: Raven Chronicles, vol. 1, no. 1, 1991)

"Red Earth" in *Seattle Arts Commission Newsletter* ([Seattle, Wash.: The Commission, July 1990])

"Native American Sport" in *Humanities Today* ([S.l.: s.n.] , vol. 4, no. 1, [n.d.])

NARRATIVE

Red Eagle is the founder, coeditor and co-publisher of the journal *Raven Chronicles.* He is also on the editorial board of the journal *Northwest Ethnic News* and is the co-chair of the Northwest Multi Cultural Arts Task Force. Red Eagle is a partner in the graphic design studio of Red-Foot Productions and works as a photographer and silversmith. He has taught art at the Seattle Community College and was a co-producer of the film titled *Voices and Visions* in 1990. Red Eagle is also the founder and co-director of the Windhorse Gallery and through the years has served as the organizer and project coordinator of numerous art exhibits and events.

NAME   P

Lois Red Elk

TRIBAL AFFILIATION

Yankton Sioux from Ft. Peck

PUBLICATION HIGHLIGHTS

"Tonight the Fists Will Start," poem in

Wambli Ho/Eagle's Voice (Mission, S. Dak.: Sinte Gleska College, 1992)

"The Give-away," poem in *Tamaqua,* Native American issue (Champaign, Ill.: Humanities Department of Parkland College, vol. 2, issue 2, 1991)

"Winter Solstice," poem in *Wotanin Wowapi* (Poplar, Mont.: Fort Peck Tribal Executive Board, vol. 20, no. 50, 1989)

NAME E, P
Carter Revard

TRIBAL AFFILIATION
Osage

PERSONAL
Born: March 25, 1931, in Pawhuska, Oklahoma
Education:
Buck Creek Rural Schol (District 66) Osage County, Oklahoma
Bartlesville, Oklahoma secondary schools
B.A. from University of Tulsa, 1952
B.A. from Oxford University, 1954
Ph.D. from Yale University, 1959

AWARDS, HONORS
Rhodes Scholarship, 1952

PUBLICATION HIGHLIGHTS
An Eagle Nation (Tucson: University of Arizona, 1993)

Cowboys and Indians (Norman, Okla.: Point Riders Press, 1992)

Ponca War Dancers (Norman, Okla.: Point Riders Press, 1980)

Nonymosity (Richford, Vt.: Samisdat, 1980)

My Right Hand Don't Leave Me No More (S.l.: Eedin Press, 1970)

Revard's works have also appeared in numerous anthologies:

Returning the Gift: Poetry and Prose from the First North American Native Writers' Festival, ed. by Joseph Bruchac with the support of the Association for the Study of American Indian Literatures (Tucson: University of Arizona, 1994)

Talking Leaves: Contemporary Native American Short Stories, An Anthology, ed. by Craig Lesley (New York: Laurel; Dell, 1991)

American Indian Literature: An Anthology of Contemporary American Indian Fiction, ed. by Alan Velie (Lincoln: University of Nebraska Press, 1979, 1991)

Native American Reader: Stories, Speeches and Poems, ed. by Jerry D. Blanche (Juneau: Denali Press, 1990)

I Tell You Now: Autobiographical Essays by Native American Writers, ed. by Brian Swann and Arnold Krupat (Lincoln: University of Nebraska Press, 1987)

Survival This Way: Interviews with Native American Poets, by Joseph Bruchac (Tucson: Sun Tracks; University of Arizona Press, 1987)

New and Old Voices of Wah'Kon-Tah, ed. by Robert K. Dodge and Joseph B. McCullough (New York: International Publishers, 1985)

Native American Literature, by Andrew Wiget (Boston: Twayne, 1985)

Earth Power Coming: Short Fiction in Native American Literature, ed. by Simon J. Ortiz (Tsaile, Ariz.: Navajo Community College Press, 1983)

Native American Renaissance, by Kenneth Lincoln (Berkeley: University of California Press, 1983)

The Remembered Earth: An Anthology of Contemporary Native American Literature, ed. by Geary Hobson (Albuquerque: Red Earth Press, 1979)

Voices of the Rainbow, ed. by Kenneth Rosen (New York: Viking, 1975)

NARRATIVE
Carter Revard grew up in the Bird Creek Valley of Osage County, Oklahoma, five

miles west of Bartlesville. Part Osage on his father's side, Revard grew up with his sister and four more half brothers and sisters and his Ponca cousins in the freedom of a rural environment and the security of a close-knit family.

Revard's grandfather Alex Camp, his Osage grandmother Josephine Jump and his dignified Ponca aunt Jewell McDonald Camp were especially close to him during his formative years. "My grandfather Alex Camp, just before he died in 1942, told me to go to college. None of our family had ever gone to college. They would have had to kill me to keep me from going, after I told him I would." A famous relative of Revard's is Carter Camp, the American Indian Movement leader who was sentenced to three years in prison for his part in Wounded Knee. Earlier in Oklahoma history his great-great-grandfather Joseph Revard ran the first trading post in the territory.

As a teenager Revard attended high school during the day and worked as a greyhound trainer and caretaker after school in the evenings. He remembers with fondness his English teacher Mary Paxton, one of the most influential teachers he ever had. Revard graduated as co-valedictorian of the Osage County school in 1944. In 1948 he won a Quiz Kids Radio Quiz Show Scholarship to the University of Tulsa.

"I was writing what teachers called for and [in] about 1943 began trying to write stories; in high school it was essays. At the University of Tulsa I started writing poems to say things to and for friends. People encouraged this." He had two notable teachers at the University of Tulsa, professors Franklin Eikenberry and Donald Hayden. "In college, professor Eikenberry gave invaluable help and support from 1948 through 1956. ... [Eikenberry] supported my intellectual growth, helped financially and was a wise,

gentle, generous guide and companion in literary explorations." In 1972 *Nimrod* magazine published some of his poems, which led to getting his works published in numerous other anthologies. Revard received a Rhodes Scholarship to study in Oxford, England, where he rowed on the Merton crew.

His work has since appeared in anthologies and journals, such as *Callaloo, Massachusetts Review, Epoch, Denver Quarterly, River Styx, Sun Tracks* and *Nimrod*. He considers some of his strongest works to be two collections of poems, *Ponca War Dancers* (1980), *Cowboys and Indians* (1992) and *An Eagle Nation,* his forthcoming book.

He enjoys reading the works of "Wendy Rose, Simon Ortiz, Linda Hogan ... Robert Frost ... Elizabeth Woody ... Chaucer, Shakespeare, Milton, Old English poets. There is no influence from the American Indian poets or novelists that I know of, because I am walking alongside, not following. I have learned metaphor and compression and closure form Frost and Shakespeare, and rhythm and sense of unapologetic self from Milton, narrative from Chaucer."

When he is not writing, Revard enjoys working with medieval documents, "solving their old mysteries and clarifying and revising history and literature by these solutions. I like to read every sort of thing—science, history, politics, some literature. I like walking and sunrise and birds, trees, meadows, streams, valleys and hills. I like pow-wows if I'm not overwhelmed by the work of putting them on. I teach and like to talk with students. My wife and I go to Shakespeare plays when we're in England. ... It is all work and play, learning and responding."

Revard has taught at Amherst, but since 1961 he has been at Washington University in St. Louis, Missouri, where he is currently a professor of English, specializing in medieval literature, Chaucer and historical linguistics.

In 1952 Revard was given his Osage name Nom-Pe-Wa-The or "Fear Inspiring" in a naming ceremony given by his Grandma Josephine Jump and his Oasge elders. "The name giving ceremony which Grandma Josephine sponsored in 1952 committed me for life to try and live up to and honor Osage ways."

NAME
Ron Rogers

OTHER NAMES USED
Ronald Rogers

TRIBAL AFFILIATION
Cherokee

PERSONAL
Born: 1948 in Claremore, Oklahoma
Education:
Graduated from the Institute of American Indian Arts, Santa Fe, New Mexico
Coursework at San Francisco State College
Coursework at the University of California at Los Angeles
Coursework at the University of California at Santa Cruz

PUBLICATION HIGHLIGHTS
New and Old Voices from Wah'Kon-Tah, third edition, ed. by Robert K. Dodge and Joseph B. McCullough (New York: International Publishers, c1985); The Remembered Earth: An Anthology of Contemporary Native American Literature, ed. by Geary Hobson (Albuquerque: Red Earth Press, 1979)

Rogers's works have appeared in numerous anthologies, among them:

Voices from Wah'Kon-Tah: Contemporary Poetry of Native Americans, first edition, ed. by Robert K. Dodge and Joseph B. McCullough (New York: International Publishers, 1974)
The American Indian Reader: Literature, ed. by Jeannete Henry (San Francisco: Indian Historian Press, 1973)
The Whispering Wind: Poetry by Young American Indians, ed. by Terry Allen (Garden City, N.J.: Doubleday, 1972)
The American Indian Speaks, comp. by John R. Milton (Vermillion: University of S. Dak., 1969)

NARRATIVE
Rogers's works have also appeared in the journals: Akwesasne Notes, the Indian Historian, A: A Journal of Contemporary Literature, the South Dakota Review, Cavalcade and New America.

NAME   E, L, N, P, VA
Wendy Rose

OTHER NAMES USED
Chiron Khanshendel

TRIBAL AFFILIATION
Hopi and Miwok

PERSONAL
Born: May 7, 1948, in Oakland, California
Education:
Coursework at Cabrillo College, Aptos, California and Conta Costa College, San Pablo, California
B.A. in cultural anthropology and Native American studies, University of California, Berkeley, 1976
M.A. in cultural anthropology and Native American studies, University of California, Berkeley, 1978

AWARDS, HONORS

National Endowment for the Arts Fellowship, 1981–1982

PUBLICATION HIGHLIGHTS

Now Poof She Is Gone: Poetry (Ithaca, N.Y.: Firebrand, 1994)

Bone Dance: New and Selected Poems 1965–1993 (Tucson: University of Arizona, 1994)

Going to War with All My Relations: New and Selected Poems (Flagstaff, Ariz.: Entrada, 1993)

"December 1890–1990" in *Boundary 2,* January 1992

The Halfbreed Chronicles and Other Poems (Los Angeles, Calif.: West End Press, 1985)

Nuke Chronicles: Writers and Artists on the Future, Ed Sanders, A. Ginsberg and Wendy Rose, ed. by Josh Gosciak (Contact II Publications, 1985)

What Happened When the Hopi Hit New York (New York: Contact II Publications, 1982)

Long Division: A Tribal History, second edition ([S.l.]: Strawberry Press, 1980)

Lost Copper: Poems (Banning, Calif.: Malki Museum Press, 1980)

Builder Kachina: A Home-Going Cycle (Marvin, S. Dak.: Blue Cloud Press, 1979)

Aboriginal Tattooing of California ([S.l.]: Archaeological Research Facility, University of California, 1979)

Poetry of the American Indian Series ([S.l.]: American Visual Communications Bank, 1978)

Academic Squaw: Reports to the World from the Ivory Tower (Marvin, S. Dak.: Blue Cloud Quarterly Press, 1977)

Hopi Roadrunner Dancing (Greenfield Center, N.Y.: Greenfield Review Press, [1974], c1973)

Rose's works have also appeared in numerous anthologies:

Returning the Gift: Poetry and Prose from the First North American Native Writers' Festival, ed. by Joseph Bruchac with the support of the Association for the Study of American Indian Literatures (Tucson: University of Arizona, 1994)

Winged Words: American Indian Writers Speak, by Laura Coltelli (Lincoln: University of Nebraska Press, 1990)

I Tell You Now: Autobiographical Essays by Native American Writers, ed. by Brian Swann and Arnold Krupat (Lincoln: University of Nebraska Press, 1987)

Survival This Way: Interviews with Native American Poets, by Joseph Bruchac (Tucson: Sun Tracks; University of Arizona Press, 1987)

The Sacred Hoop: Recovering the Feminine in American Indian Traditions, by Paula Gunn Allen (Boston: Beacon Press, 1986)

New and Old Voices of Wah'Kon-Tah, ed. by Robert K. Dodge and Joseph B. McCollugh (New York: International Publishers, 1985)

That's What She Said: Contemporary Poetry and Fiction by Native American Women, ed. by Rayna Green (Bloomington: Indiana University Press, 1984)

A Gathering of Spirit: A Collection by North American Indian Women, ed. by Beth Brant (Ithaca, N.Y.: Firebrand Books, 1988, c1984)

A Nation Within: Contemporary Native American Writing, selected by Ralph Salisbury (Hamilton, New Zealand: Outrigger Publishers, 1983)

Native American Renaissance, by Kenneth Lincoln (Berkeley: University of California Press, 1983)

The South Corner of Time: Hopi, Navajo, Papago, Yaqui Tribal Literature, ed. by Larry Evers et al. (Tucson: University of Arizona Press, 1980)

The Remembered Earth: An Anthology of Contemporary Native American Literature, ed. by Geary Hobson (Albuquerque: Red Earth Press, 1979)

Carriers of the Dream Wheel: Contemporary Native American Poetry, ed. by Duane Niatum (New York: Harper & Row, 1975)

NARRATIVE

Wendy Rose grew up in Oakland, Richmond and on a ranch in Chico, California. Her father is Hopi and her mother is Miwok. She founded the Native American Student Union of Contra Costa College while a student there. She has worked as the manager of the museum bookstore at the Lowie Museum of Anthropology on the campus of the University of California, Berkeley, and was a lecturer of Native studies at the same university. She is currently a full-time instructor and co-ordinator of American Indian studies at Fresno City College, Fresno, California, where she teaches five or six classes per semester and advises a Native student club. Living in California, Rose explains her ties to the land. "I live near the ancestral land of the Miwots side of my family."

Writer, educator and anthropologist, Rose has lectured and given readings of her works to numerous groups. She has had articles and poems published in several periodicals such as *Many Smokes, Early American, Contra Costa Advocate, Journal of California Anthropology, San Francisco Bay Guardian* and *Janus.* She has also served as the editor for the journal *American Indian Quarterly* for one year. Rose has recently completed three manuscripts. Her book *Lost Copper* was nominated for the American Book Award in 1981. An illustrator of numerous books and periodicals, Rose has also had exhibits and shows throughout the United States and has also worked as a writer and cover artist for the journal *Many Smokes.* She is one of the cofounders of the Light of Dawn Temple, a metaphysical research center, and has served as a member of the

Board of Directors of the Coordinating Council of Literary Magazines.

Rose's works deal with political and social issues and autobiographical symbolism. As a young woman Rose was fortunate to have an instructor that encouraged her to write. "When I was about 18, a teacher said I had 'a flair' for it. Otherwise most people consistently discouraged me—said I couldn't do it." If there were others who helped her develop as a writer it was "Definitely not family. Early college English instructor [named] Levy, Maurice Kenny, Scott Momaday, [and] Duane Niatum."

She enjoys reading the works of Robinson Jeffers, N. Scott Momaday, Simon Ortiz, Leslie Marmon Silko, Maurice Kenny, Gladys Cardiff, Judy Grahn and Linda Hogan's poetry. In her spare time she works with her collection of cacti and succulents and plays Baroque music on the piano.

NAME   E, N
A. C. Ross

OTHER NAMES USED
Allen Ross

TRIBAL AFFILIATION
Santee Dakota/Sicanqu Lakota

PERSONAL
Born: October 25, 1940, in Pipestone, Minnesota
Education:
B.S. in education, Black Hills State College, Spearfish, South Dakota, 1967
M.A. in education, Arizona State University, Tempe, Arizona, 1971
A.B.D. doctoral studies in education administration, University of Minnesota, Minneapolis, 1973

Ed.D. in education administration, Western Colorado University, Grand Junction, Colorado, 1980

AWARDS, HONORS

Special Recognition Award for Contribution to Indian Education, National Indian Education Association, 1992

Honoree "Top 50" selection at the International Book Fair, Frankfurt, Germany, and Recognition for *Mitakuye Oyasin: We Are All Related,* 1992

Participant, Hubert Humphrey Institute, Evaluation of NATO, Brussels, Belgium, 1987

Who's Who Among the Sioux, sponsored by the University of South Dakota, 1986

Gubernatorial Appointment, North Dakota Teacher's Professional Practices Commission, 1985

PUBLICATION HIGHLIGHTS

Ehanamani "Walks Among": An Autobiography (Kyle, S. Dak.: Bear Publishing, 1992)

Mitakuye Oyasin: We Are All Related (Ft. Yates, N. Dak.: Bear Publishing, 1989)

"Should Educators Pay Closer Attention to Hemispheric and Other Brain Characteristics of Students?" in *ASCD Update* (Alexandria, Va.: Association for Supervision and Curriculum Development, May 1987)

"Walk the Red Road for Sobriety" in *Linkages/IAADA* ([S.l.: s.n.], April 1987)

"Brain Hemispheric Functions and the Native American" in *Journal of American Indian Education* (Tempe, Ariz.: College of Education, Arizona State University, May 1982)

NARRATIVE

A. C. Ross was raised on three different reservations throughout South Dakota. Influential people in his life include his parents and friends Dawson No Horse and Dorothy Brave Eagle. Of his school years, Ross remembers that for him it was a "terrible struggle to complete a left-brain school system." Upon graduation from high school, he became a member of the U.S. Army Airborne 505 Paratroopers, and in 1965 ended his military service with an honorable discharge.

Author and international consultant, Ross previously worked as the superintendent of the Little Wound School in Kyle, South Dakota, from 1990 to 1991. He was the agency superintendent for education for the Bureau of Indian Affairs in Ft. Yates, North Dakota, from 1983 to 1990, and throughout the years 1983 to 1990 was actively teaching: as an instructor of doctorate-level graduate classes in education administration for the International College, Los Angeles and as an Instructor of Native American Studies at the Oglala Lakota College in Kyle, South Dakota. He was an instructor at the Fort Peck Community College in Popular, Montana, and was also an Instructor at Standing Rock College in Ft. Yates, North Dakota. Prior to these positions, Ross worked as a business manager, health and education consultant, housing rehabilitation specialist and principal educational coordinator in the fields of education and human services in North and South Dakota, Colorado and Arizona.

Ross has given talks and presentations throughout Europe and the United States on the subjects of spirituality and Native American history and culture. Ross is also active in various aspects of filmmaking and production. He was the technical advisor for the film *Sacred Buffalo People* in which he also made an appearance. The film was produced by Deb Wallwork and the Prairie Public Television in 1992. He was the technical advisor for *Keep Your Heart Strong* in 1989, which was distributed by the North Dakota Humanities Project. Ross was the producer and technical advisor for the film by the same title as his book *Mitakuye Oyasin: We Are All Related,* distributed by KXJB-TV, in 1987 and was the technical advisor for the 1986 film *Brain Hemispheric Functions,* the Circle television program produced by South Dakota Public Television, KUSD-TV. Ross had been the technical advisor for two prior films: *Running Brave* (the Billy Mills story), distributed by Buena Vista Distribution in 1985 and for *Native American Art* produced by the North Dakota Humanities Project in 1984.

Ross is also a member of the National Advisory Caucus of the Wordcraft Circle, a Native American mentor and apprentice writers program. In his own writings, Ross addresses the topics of Native American history, culture and spiritualism, and he considers his strongest work to be *Mitakuye Oyasin: We Are All Related.* Ross regards sacred sites to be significant elements in his works, and he is an active participant in spiritual ceremonies. For enjoyment, he relaxes with the works of Edgar Cayce and Black Elk. He is currently working on a movie script.

NAME F, S
Gayle Ross

TRIBAL AFFILIATION
Cherokee

PUBLICATION HIGHLIGHTS
Dat-so-la-lee, Artisan (Morristown, N.J.: Modern Curriculum Press, 1995)

The Legend of Windigo: A Tale from Native North America, first edition (New York: Dial, 1996)

The Story of the Milky Way: A Cherokee Tale, first edition, by Joseph Bruchac and Gayle Ross (New York: Dial, 1995)

The Girl Who Married the Moon: Tales from Native North America, by Joseph Bruchac

and Gayle Ross (Mahwah, N.J.: Bridgewater Books, 1994)

How Rabbit Tricked Otter and Other Cherokee Trickster Stories, first edition (New York: HarperCollins, 1994)

The Girl Who Married the Moon: Tales from Native North America, poster (Mahwah, N.J.: Bridgewater Books, 1994)

How the Whale Got His Throat, by Gayle Ross et al., videocassette and viewer's guide (New York: H. W. Wilson, 1986)

To This Day Native American Stories, audio recording (Fredricksburg, Tex.: Gayle Ross, 1986)

NAME F, P
Armand Garnet Ruffo

TRIBAL AFFILIATION
Ojibway

PERSONAL
Born: January 22, 1955 in Chapleau, Ontario
Education: Bachelors and masters degrees

PUBLICATION HIGHLIGHTS
Opening in the Sky (Penticton, B.C.: Theytus, 1994)

"Grey Owl: The Mystery of Archie Belaney," poem in *Canadian Native Literature in English* (Don Mills, Ont.: Oxford University Press Canada, 1992)

"Angele, Bell of Temagemi," "Bill Draper," poems in *Orbis—An International Quarterly,* Canadian issue ([United Kingdom]: s.n., 1991)

"Creating a Country," "Bear Death," poems in *Gatherings* (Penticton, B.C.: Theytus Press, 1990)

"Selected Poems" in *Contemporary Native Writing—Seventh Generation* (Penticton, B.C.: Theytus Press, 1989)

Ruffo's works also appear in anthologies *Returning the Gift: Poetry and Prose from the First North American Native Writers' Festival*, ed. by Joseph Bruchac with the support of the Association for the Study of American Indian Literatures (Tucson: University of Arizona, 1994) and *Looking at the Words of Our People: First Nations Analysis of Literature*, ed. by Jeannette Armstrong (Penticton, B.C.: Tyeytus, 1993).

NARRATIVE

Ruffo grew up in northern Ontario. He is working on a book-length poetic fictional biography of the life of writer Archie Belaney. Ruffo reads a wide variety of books, but admits that he is drawn to Native American and post-colonial writing, adding that he recently enjoyed Keri Hulme's *The Bone People*. He is currently a graduate assistant at the University of Windsor in Windsor, Ontario.

NAME   E, L, N, P
Norman H. Russell

TRIBAL AFFILIATION
Cherokee

PERSONAL
Born: November, 28, 1921, in Big Stone Gap, Virginia
Education: B.S. from Slippery Rock State Teachers College, 1946; graduate study, University of Tennessee, 1946–1947; Ph.D. University of Minnesota, 1951

AWARDS, HONORS
National Science Foundation Grants, 1954–1970

PUBLICATION HIGHLIGHTS

Mr. Russell's scientific publications include:

The Plant Kingdom: A Laboratory Manual (St. Louis, Missouri: Mosby, 1959) third edition published as *General Botany Manual: Exercises on the Life Histories, Structures, Physiology and Ecology of the Plant Kingdom,* 1970
Violets (Viola) of Central and Eastern United States: An Introductory Survey (Dallas: Lloyd H. Shinners, 1965)
An Introduction to the Plant Kingdom, with Paul C. Lemon (St. Louis, Missouri: Mosby, 1958)

Mr. Russell's poetic works include:

Indian Thoughts: The Children of God (Los Angeles: University of California Indian Studies Center, 1985, 1975)
Indian Thoughts: My Journey (Marvin, S. Dak.: Blue Cloud Quarterly, 1980)
The Longest March (Fairbury, Nebr.: Southeast Community College, 1980)
Indian Thoughts: The Ways of the World (La Jolla, Calif.: Inca Press, 1974)
Open the Flower (Mt. Horeb, Wisc.: Perishable Press, 1974)
Collected Poems (Menomonee Falls, Wisc.: Northwoods Press, 1974)
The Ways of the World ([S.l.]: Inca Press, 1974)
I Am Old (Albuquerque, N.M.: San Marcos Press, 1974)
Indian Thoughts: The Small Songs of God (La Crosse, Wisc.: Northeast/Juniper Books, 1972)
At the Zoo ([S.l.]: JRD Publishing, 1969)

Mr. Russell's works have also appeared in numerous anthologies:

New and Old Voices of Wah'Kon-Tah, ed. by Robert K. Dodge and Joseph B. McCullough (New York: International Publishers, 1985)
The Remembered Earth, ed. by Geary Hobson (Albuquerque: University of New Mexico Press, 1979)

From the Belly of the Shark, ed. by Walter Lowenfels (New York: Vintage, 1973)

Literature of the American Indian, ed. by Thomas E. Sanders and Walter W. Peek (Westerville, Ohio: Glencoe Press, 1973)

Messages, ed. by X. J. Kennedy (New York: Little, Brown, 1973)

The Turquoise Horse, ed. by Flora Hood (New York: Putnam, 1972)

Poems and Perspectives, ed. by Robert H. Ross and William E. Stafford (Glenview, Ill.: Scott Foresman, 1971)

American Literary Anthology 3, ed. by George Plimpton and Peter Ardery (New York: Viking Press, 1970)

The Blue Guitar, ed. by Bethel Bodine (Redding, Mass.: Addison-Wesley, 1970)

Like It Is, ed. by Bethel Bodine (Redding, Mass.: Addison-Wesley, 1970)

NARRATIVE

Poet, botanist and university administrator, Russell has had his poetic and scientific writings published in more than 220 magazines, journals and monographic publications. He has been a contributor to reference works such as the *Encyclopaedia Britannica,* and the *Reinhold Scientific Encyclopedia,* and his poems have been published in the journals *Virginia Quarterly Review, Educational Forum, Poetry Northwest* and *South Dakota Review,* among many others. He is the author of eleven books of poetry, and he has written several scientific books on botany.

Russell served in the U.S. Air Force for four years from 1942 to 1946. He was stationed in India for two years and rose to the rank of staff sergeant. He began his academic career as an instructor at Grinnell College in Grinnell, Iowa, from 1951 to 1954, and moved up through the academic ranks to become assistant professor from 1954 to 1955, associate professor from 1955 to 1956 and professor of biology from 1957 to 1959.

Russell moved to Tempe, Arizona, to assume the position of professor of biology and department chair at Arizona State University from 1959 to 1963, he then accepted the position of visiting professor of botany from 1963 to 1965 at Rutgers University in Newark, New Jersey. In 1966 he moved to Central State University in Edmond, Oklahoma, to work as an associate professor until 1968 and was visiting professor at Buena Vista College from 1968 to 1970. In 1970 Russell became professor of biology, where he remained until 1973 when he accepted the position of dean of the School of Science at Central State University.

Mr. Russell is currently a "partly retired professor of biology," a position that finds him teaching on a part-time basis in Oklahoma, a state which he says "inspires poetry."

S

NAME   E, F, N, P

Ralph Salisbury

TRIBAL AFFILIATION

Cherokee (Eastern)

PERSONAL

Born: January 24, 1926, in northeastern Iowa
Education: B.A. from the University of Iowa;
M.F.A. from the University of Iowa

PUBLICATION HIGHLIGHTS

One Indian and Two Chiefs: Short Fiction
(Tsaile, Ariz.,: Navajo Community Col-
lege Press, 1991)
*A White Rainbow: Poems of a Cherokee Heri-
tage* (Marvin, S. Dak.: Blue Cloud Quar-
terly Press, 1985)
*Going to the Water: Poems of a Cherokee Heri-
tage* (Eugene, Oreg.: Pacific House Books,
1983)
*A Nation Within: Contemporary Native
American Writing*, selected by Ralph
Salisbury (Hamilton, New Zealand:
Outrigger Publishers, 1983)
Spirit Beast Chant (Marvin, S. Dak.: Blue
Cloud Quarterly, 1982)
*Pointing at the Rainbow: Poems from a Chero-
kee Heritage* (Marvin, S. Dak.: Blue Cloud
Quarterly, 1980)
"Ghost Grapefruit" and Other Poems (Ithaca,
N.Y.: Ithaca House, 1972)
*Three Northwest Poets: Albert Drake, Lawson
Inada, Douglas Lawder* (Madison, Wisc.:
Quixote Press, 1970)

Salisbury's works have also appeared in
numerous anthologies:

*Returning the Gift: Poetry and Prose from the
First North American Native Writers' Festi-*
val, ed. by Joseph Bruchac with the sup-
port of the Association for the Study of
American Indian Literatures, (Tucson:
University of Arizona, 1994)
*American Indian Literatures: An Introduction,
Bibliographic Review and Selected Bibliog-
raphy,* by A. LaVonne Brown Ruoff (New
York: Modern Language Association,
1990)
*Circle of Motion: Arizona Anthology of Con-
temporary American Indian Literature,* ed.
by Kathleen Mullen Sands (Tempe, Ariz.:
Arizona Historical Foundation, 1990
*Dancing on the Rim of the World: An Anthol-
ogy of Contemporary Northwest Native
American Writing,* ed. by Andrea Lerner
(Tucson, Ariz.: Sun Tracks; University of
Arizona Press, 1990)
*I Tell You Now: Autobiographical Essays by
Native American Writers,* ed. by Brian
Swann and Arnold Krupat (Lincoln: Uni-
versity of Nebraska Press, 1987)
Native American Literature, by Andrew
Wiget (Boston: Twayne, 1985)
*Earth Power Coming: Short Fiction in Native
American Literature,* ed. by Simon J. Ortiz
(Tsaile, Ariz.: Navajo Community Col-
lege Press, 1983)

NARRATIVE

Salisbury was born on a farm in northeast Iowa and lived a life of hunting and
farming. He spent his first seventeen years
with his three brothers and a sister, his
father, a traditional Cherokee storyteller
and singer, and his mother, an Irish storyteller. At the age of 17 he had enlisted
in the Air Force, learned electronic weap-
onry and was trained to take part in the
bombing raids over Tokyo. Afer the war he
was a member of the Air Force Reserves,

but was not called into active duty for the Korean War. As he recalls his youth, Salisbury touches upon bittersweet memories: "Struck by lightning at age 15, visions, dreams, World War II, deaths of some friends, a few narrow escapes myself, books loaned by college trained buddies, six plus years of university education as reward for service."

Salisbury is professor of English at the University of Oregon, Eugene. "The wilderness here keeps me in touch with the wilderness of my childhood." Throughout his life he has worked a wide variety of occupations, from farm worker to poet, photographer and journalist to construction worker, and janitor and literary editor to fiction writer. While in school he studied with writers Robert Lowell and R. V. Cassill, both of whom he considered to be his mentors along with James Hearst. "All valued my working-class, mixed-race, dream-cursed-and-blessed roughness and encouraged me."

Salisbury's poems and stories have appeared in the journals *Callaloo, Chariton Review, New Letters, New Yorker, Poetry Northwest* and *Transatlantic Review,* among many others. Current projects include a series of four connected novels, a book of short stories and a book of poems. Salisbury enjoys William Faulkner, who he describes as "my father's southern voice at literary edge" and with "his mind-opening style, his feeling for Native Americans' reality." He also likes reading William Butler Yeats: "like the best Irish poets a natural 'tribal visionary.'"

NAME   E, L, N, P, PL, VA

Carol Lee Sanchez

TRIBAL AFFILIATION

Laguna Pueblo

PERSONAL

Born: January 13, 1934, in Albuquerque, New Mexico

Education:

Loretto Heights College, Denver, Colorado, 1950–1951

University of New Mexico, Albuquerque, Fall 1951

San Francisco State University, 1977–1978

B.A. in arts administration-multicultural arts focus, San Francisco State University, 1978

AWARDS, HONORS

Nominated for Pulitzer Prize for *Message Bringer Woman,* 1977

Nominated for the Edgar Allen Poe Award by the American Academy of Poets for *Conversations from the Nightmare,* 1975

Master Poet Teacher with the California Poets in the Schools Program, 1974

PUBLICATION HIGHLIGHTS

She) Poems (Goshen, Conn.: Chicory Blue Press, 1995)

"Corn Children," poem in *She Rises Like the Sun: Invocations of the Goddess* (Freedom, Calif., Crossing Press, 1989)

Excerpts from a Mountain Climber's Handbook: Selected Poems, 1971–1984 (Santa Margarita, Calif.: Taurean Horn Press/ Out West Limited, 1985)

Message Bringer Woman, poems (San Francisco: Taurean Horn Press, 1977)

Conversations from the Nightmare, poems (San Francisco: Casa Editorial, 1975)

Sanchez has also had poems published in the following anthologies: *Returning the Gift: Poetry and Prose from the First North American Native Writers' Festival,* ed. by Joseph Bruchac with the support of the Association for the Study of American Indian Literatures (Tucson: University of Arizona, 1994); *That's What She Said: Contemporary Poetry and Fiction by Native*

American Women, ed. Rayna Green. (Bloomington, Ind.: Indiana University Press, 1984) and *The Remembered Earth,* ed. by Geary Hobson (Albuquerque: Red Earth Press, 1980).

NARRATIVE

Writer, painter and educator Carol Lee Sanchez is the daughter of parents of Laguna Pueblo and Lebanese descent. Her sister is writer and educator Paula Gunn Allen, and her brother is writer and educator Lee Francis. She spent her first four years in Paguate Village, New Mexico, which is located on the Laguna Reservation. Her parents moved to Cubero Village, New Mexico, a town located on the old Cubero Land Grant (originally a Spanish Land Grant), and then moved again to Seboyeta, on the old Cebolleta Land Grant, near Paguate, New Mexico, where they lived for six months. When Sanchez was six years old, her family moved back to Cubero just before her sister Paula Gunn Allen was born. Later, Sanchez attended St. Vincent Academy in Albuquerque and the Radford School for Girls in El Paso, Texas, graduating in 1950 from St. Vincent's. As a young woman in school, Sanchez's mixed ethnic background made it difficult to interact with some of her peers: "Realizing in high school that I was somehow 'different' because of the strangeness of my heritage and bloodlines. As a mixed blood who 'was' Indian and Lebanese mostly—I wasn't exactly shunned but was never accepted as 'part of the group' either." She continued her studies at Loretto Heights College in Denver, Colorado, the University of New Mexico in Albuquerque, and San Francisco State University.

When Sanchez moved to San Francisco in 1964, she was brought in contact with the Coffee House Poetry scene, and she began writing poetry at that time because, as she says, "I had something to

say as a bi-racial multicultural simple mother of three. Ultimately I was a member of the Bay Area Third World Writers Group in the seventies." At this time Sanchez had also met and befriended essayist and editor Carol Christ, who encouraged her to write an article for her anthology on spirituality titled *Weaving the Vision.* Following such experiences, Sanchez has gone on to have her essays, stories and poems published in numerous journals and publications, such as the *Beloit Poetry Journal, Callaloo, Emotions, Shaman's Drum, Venus Rising, National Women's Studies Association Newsletter* and in anthologies and individually as monographs. She became statewide director of the California Poets in the Schools in 1974 and wrote and read her poetry in various reading forums throughout Northern and Southern California. She also taught American Indian studies in the School of Ethnic Studies at San Francisco State University.

Sanchez has since worked as an educator in several states, and she is an active participant in academic organizations on the state and national level. She is a conference presenter, and she is still active in reading her poetry in public and participates in many arts organizations. She is also involved in community arts activities, art administration, and was involved in the coordination of the first Western States Biennial Exhibition. She is also involved in the Women's Movement, teaching feminist literature.

In her poems and essays, Sanchez focuses on the human condition and human interaction with the natural world. In nonfiction essays, she writes about the contributions of North and South American tribal peoples to global cultures, and the life-preserving ways of Native peoples. Now living and teaching in Missouri, she is currently studying Osage history and traditions, "as where I live was once their home lands. My recent works (poetry) reflect this environment to some extent. My twenty years in California and my native New Mexico [are] more prominent in [the] poetic imagery of [my] published works." She is also now working on a collection of essays, a play and short stories. Sanchez is now adjunct creative writing instructor for State Fair Community College in Sedalia, Missouri, for the Community College Branch at Whiteman Air Force Base in Knob Noster, Missouri, is the women's studies instructor for University of Missouri and is the master poet teacher for the Honstonia Elementary School, R-V District in Pettis County, Missouri.

NAME   F, N, P
Georgiana Valoyce Sanchez

TRIBAL AFFILIATION
Papage, Pima and Chumash

PERSONAL
Education: B.A. in English and creative writing, California State University at Long Beach, 1984; M.A. Califonia State University at Long Beach, 1992

PUBLICATION HIGHLIGHTS
"Chumash Man," "Fat of the Land" in *Invocation L.A.* (Albuquerque: West End Press, 1990)

"The Heart of the Flower," short story in *The Stories We Hold Secret* (Greenfield Center, N.Y.: Greenfield Review Press, 1986)

"Cahuilla Bird Song" in *Riprap* (Long Beach, Calif.: CSULB Publications, vol. 3, 1981)

Sanchez' works have also appeared in: *Returning the Gift: Poetry and Prose from the First North American Native Writers' Festival,* ed. by Joseph Bruchac with the support of the Association for the Study of American Indian Literatures (Tucson: University of Arizona, 1994).

NARRATIVE
Sanchez is Pima and Papago on her mother's side and Chumash on her father's side. She is married and has five children.

NAME   E, N
Joe S. Sando

TRIBAL AFFILIATION
Jemez Pueblo

PERSONAL
Born: August 1, 1923, in Jemez Pueblo, New Mexico
Education: B.A. from Eastern New Mexico University, 1949; M.S. in Audiology from Vanderbilt University, 1960

PUBLICATION HIGHLIGHTS
Nee Hemish: The History of Jemez Pueblo (Albuquerque: University of New Mexico Press, 1982); *The Pueblo Indians* (San Francisco: Indian Historian Press, 1976) revised edition 1982; *Pueblo Indian Biographies* ([S.l.]: Southwestern Indian Polytechnic Institute, 1976)

NARRATIVE
Born and raised at the Jemez Pueblo in New Mexico, Sando began writing at an early age and later learned to speak English as his second language while he was in the ninth grade at the Santa Fe Indian School. In World War II, he served in the U.S. Navy as petty officer second class from 1943 to 1946 and was part of the invasion of the Marianna and Gilbert Islands. As a result of his service during the

war, Sando was decorated with four battle stars.

Sando began his career in education in 1949 working as a school teacher in Sedona, Arizona, and became a school guidance counselor for the Bureau of Indian Affairs in Dulce, New Mexico, from 1954 to 1959. In 1962 he worked again as a guidance counselor in Dulce. Sando served as an assistant to the chair in the Extension Division at New Mexico State University and later developed and evaluated curriculum materials for the Southwestern Cooperative Educational Laboratory in Albuquerque. He also worked as an education specialist and instructor at the University of New Mexico from 1970 until 1978. At this time Sando worked as a writer and lecturer until 1982, when he joined the faculty of the Institute of American Indian Art in Santa Fe, New Mexico. Sando's works have also appeared in the journal the *Indian Historian.*

Active in his community and state, Sando has served as the chair of the New Mexico Judicial Council and was the chair of the All Indian Pueblo Housing Authority and its educational committee. He is married and has three children.

NAME   F, N
Greg Sarris

TRIBAL AFFILIATION
Pomo, Miwok

PERSONAL
Born: 1952
Education: Undergraduate degree, University of California at Los Angeles; Ph.D. from Stanford University

PUBLICATION HIGHLIGHTS
Grand Avenue (New York: Hyperion, 1994)

The Sound of Rattles and Clappers: A Collection of New California Indian Writing (Tucson: University of Arizona Press, 1994)
Mabel McKay: Weaving the Dream (New York: Hyperion, 1994)
Keeping Slug Woman Alive: A Holistic Approach to American Indian Texts (Berkeley: University of California Press, 1993)

NARRATIVE
Greg Sarris's family was a mixture of many cultures: his mother was of Jewish, German and Irish heritage and his father's family was Filipino, Miwok and Pomo. As a youth Sarris belonged to a gang that was in and out of trouble until his aunt, Pomo basket weaver Mabel McKay caught his attention with traditional stories and legends. He excelled in sports and academics and later attended the University of California at Los Angeles. Sarris has recently been working on getting the Bureau of Indian Affairs to acknowlegdge the existance of the Miwok Tribe, which in 1923 had forty acres of land set aside for its use, but through a federal clerical error the tribe never formally received recognition from the government and never received the land.

Sarris currently is a professor of American Indian literature at the University of California at Los Angeles and is the chair of the California Coastal Miwok Tribe. His work has also appeared in the journal *Callaloo.*

NAME   E, F, L, P, S
Cheryl Savageau

TRIBAL AFFILIATION
Abenaki

PERSONAL
Born: April 14, 1950, in Worcester, Massachusetts

Education: B.S. in general studies, Clark University, Worcester, Massachusetts

AWARDS, HONORS

Fellowship in Poetry from the Massachusetts Foundation for the Arts

PUBLICATION HIGHLIGHTS

Dirt Road Home (Willimantic, Conn.: Curbstone Press, 1995)

Home Country (Cambridge, Mass.: Alice James Books, 1992)

"In Franconia," poem in *The Eagle* ([S.l.: s.n.], vol. 9, no.2, March–April 1991)

"Trees," "At the Pow Wow," poems in *SAIL* (Studies in American Indian literature) (New York: Columbia University, vol. 2, no. 2, Summer 1990)

"Barbie—The Discovery," "Barbie Worries about Her Hips," poems in *Sojourner* (Cambridge Mass.: Massachusetts Institute of Technology, vol. 15, no. 10, 1990)

"Bones—A City Poem," "Henri Toussaints," poems, in *An Ear to the Ground* (Athens, Ga.: University of Georgia Press, 1989)

"Bones—A City Poem" originally published as "Bones" in the *Worcester Review*, vol. 7, 1984

NARRATIVE

Cheryl Savageau is of mixed Abenaki and French-Canadian heritage and was raised on a small lake in central Massachusetts. "Our neighborhood was actually on an island that had been connected by a road to both shores of the lake—the lake was a living presence that affected our lives in every season and it has been a presence in my writing as well." As a young woman in school, studying and learning came easily to Savageau, and she was encouraged to love reading. "Also, I think, because I was successful at school, I developed confidence that I could be successful at other things and not have to work in the factory as most in my family had at that time."

Savageau's family, particularly her father and grandmother, provided her with a strong sense of identity and were instrumental in helping Savageau and her family maintain their Native identity despite great pressures to "assimilate and forget." Her grandmother passed on many family stories and carried forward to the next generation her family's history and sense of solidarity. "My grandmother was a wonderful storyteller. My first story was about her telling stories while she ironed clothes. I think I wanted to continue in writing what she was doing, orally—telling the family stories, preserving our history."

Savageau now lives in Massachusetts and works as a writer-in-the-schools and as a storyteller, and also teaches courses at a local university. Very much tied to her northeastern roots, Savageau lives in the city but contemplates an eventual return to the rural environment of her youth. "I still live in central Massachusetts, but in the city. Cities never seem completely real to me—not in the way the land, water and forest do. I am very much a Northeastern writer, have felt since childhood that in spite of technological society's encroachment, all [of this forested land] will return."

Savageau's writings address family issues, cultural identity, racism, working-class issues, and "the Earth and all our relatives." Savageau vividly remembers an occasion when writer Ethride Knight taught a course on writing that changed her perspective on poetry and how she could use it as a vehicle for her own self expression. Ethride Knight started a "Free Peoples Poetry Workshop" in Worcester, Massachusetts, which lasted for four years after his brief stay. "He encouraged us to write out of our own communities, the voices of our communities and connected to the body. He let me see that the Anglo-academic male poetry was not the only kind."

Savageau enjoys the works of many authors. "I enjoy Joy Harjo, Linda Hogan, Mary Tallmountain, Chrystos, Joe Bruchac, Simon Ortiz and other Native writers. Also Toni Morrison, Gwendolyn Brooks, Louise Erdrich, Alice Walker, Sandra Cizneros, Martin Espada. ... I am nourished by the great outpouring of Native and multicultural literature. At last, our stories are being told. I am hoping to write about the history of Native people in New England in my poetry. I'm also working on a couple of ideas for children's books and some short stories.

When she is not writing or working in the schools, Savageau enjoys physical activities, beadwork, gardening, knitting, cooking and playing the piano.

NAME E, F, L, M, N, P, PL, S, VA

Diane L. Schenandoah

TRIBAL AFFILIATION

Oneida and Iroquois

PERSONAL

Born: October 21, 1958, in Syracuse, New York

Education: associate fine arts degree in creative writing; associate fine arts degree in three dimensional arts, Institute of American Indian Arts, Santa Fe, New Mexico

AWARDS, HONORS

Silver Poets Award; numerous awards for sculpture

PUBLICATION HIGHLIGHTS

"Empty Minds" in *The Clouds Threw This Light* (Santa Fe: Institute of American Indian Arts Press, 1983)

"On Eagles Wings," poem in *Spawning the Medicine River* (Santa Fe: Institute of American Indian Arts Press, Spring issue, vol. 9, 1982)

"Heh Heh Heh" in *Spawning the Medicine River* (Santa Fe: Institute of American Indian Arts Press, Spring issue, 1981)

NARRATIVE

Diane L. Schenandoah was raised in upstate New York, at the foothills of the Adirondacks. She now resides in Oneida, New York, the heart of Iroquois country. Her mother, a Clan Mother of the Oneida Nation, has been a strong and positive influence in Schenandoah's life by virtue of her great inner strength and spirituality.

As a young woman Schenandoah was compelled to become a writer when she realized that she had a unique ability to communicate a whole new dimension of her person to others. She writes works of fiction, pieces that reveal a "slice of life," works about children and family and stories that are about her visual art. She particularly enjoys reading the works of writers Roberta Hill Whitman, N. Scott Momaday, V. C. Andrews and Alfred Hitchcock. Now working as a writer, artist and sculptor, Shenandoah has received numerous awards for sculpture. She is currently working on a nonfiction television script.

NAME F, N, P

Doris Seale

TRIBAL AFFILIATION

Santee/Cree

PERSONAL

Born: July 7, 1936 in Vermont

Education: Undergraduate degree; degree in library science

PUBLICATION HIGHLIGHTS

Thanksgiving: A Native Perspective (Berkeley: Oyate, 1990)

Blood Salt, Poems (Little Rock: American Native Press Archives, University of Arkansas at Little Rock, 1989)

How to Tell the Difference: A Checklist for Evaluating Native American Children's Books, by Beverly Slapin, Doris Seale and Rosemary Gonzales (Berkeley: Oyate, 1989)

Books Without Bias: Through Indian Eyes, ed. by Doris Seale and Beverly Slapin (Berkeley: Oyate, 1988)

"Indians Without Hope, Indians Without Options—The Problematic Theme of Hatter Fox," in *Interracial Books for Children Bulletin* (New York: Council on Interracial Books for Children, vol. 15, no. 3, 1984)

NARRATIVE

Doris Seale was born and raised in Vermont, and is of Dakota, Cree and white background. As a child she suffered the pain of being separated from her family. "I'm still trying to write myself home." Her father was a source of strength and support to her, as were other individuals, a Bear Clan woman who has been a sister to her, her sisters, "because of what we went through together, and apart" and "a brother/friend who set my feet on the road and is walking with me on the long journey back to myself." In school she had two memorable teachers "... one in high school, one in college. The first taught me that the English language was beautiful, and how to use it; the second, that human creativity has at least a thousand faces, and that none of them is the 'right one.'" Seale had always been writing. "Writing was just something I did. ... In college, there was a creative writing class, the professor told me to forget it. ...

"Beth Brant was the first person to publish a poem of mine, the first to say to me 'Of course you are a writer.' She has given me support and encouragement all the way." Another individual who got Seale started in publishing her works was Beverly Slapin, "... who, unbeknownst to me, sent my poems to the Native writers project at the University of Arkansas at Little Rock, because she knew I would never do it myself."

Seale was deeply affected by the events at Wounded Knee in 1973. "Wounded Knee II was a huge awakening to the need for all of us to speak out; living in this white world, no more closet Indian." She writes about many of the aspects of "our lives as Native people and the land that is ours and to which we belong forever. Thats what it's about." She also writes about children's literature, multicultural literature analysis and poetry. "I feel most connected to the poems, because they have allowed me to speak in my own true voice, and to say things that I could not, in any other way. And some of them have been a lot of fun to write."

When asked about the works of other writers and the influence they've had on her works, she responds, "Even if I do not feel particularly drawn to a given individual, I am always interested to see what they are doing. There are writers who have had a profound effect on how and what I think, how I feel about myself, and our lives and history. Among them are Beth Brant, Awiakta, Jimmie Durham, Linda Hogan, N. Scott Momaday, Mary Tallmountain. Louis Oliver's (Little Coon) poem, 'The Stout of Heart' burned its way into my mind and will never leave."

She is now working on starting a newsletter, a supplement to *Books Without Bias: Through Indian Eyes* and is catching up on reviews of children's books. She is also working a piece titled *The People with Six Fingers* that will either become a novel or a collection of connected stories.

She also works on silversmithing in her spare time. Doris Seale is now the supervisor of children's services at the Brookline Massachusetts Public Library.

NAME
Vickie L. Sears

E, F, N, P, SC, VA

TRIBAL AFFILIATION
Cherokee

PERSONAL
Born: August 2, 1941, in San Diego, California
Education:
B.A. in English literature, 1968
Certification for Alcohol/drug Counselor, 1970
Masters degree in social work, 1977
Academy of Certified Social Workers, 1979

AWARDS, HONORS
Nominee for the Lambda Literary Award, 1992; Grant from the Cottages at Hedgebrook, 1991; Grant from the Barbara Deming Memorial Fund, 1989

PUBLICATION HIGHLIGHTS
She Who Was Lost Is Remembered: Healing from Incest Through Creativity (Seattle, Wash.: The Deal Press, 1991)
Simple Songs: Stories by Vickie Sears (Ithaca, N.Y.: Firebrand Books, 1990)
A Gathering of Spirit (Rockland, Maine: Sinister Wisdom Books, 1984)
"Pow Wow," poem in *Sinister Wisdom* ([S.l.: s.n.], no. 22-23, 1984)

Sears works have also appeared in several anthologies, among them:

Talking Leaves: Contemporary Native American Short Stories, An Anthology, ed. by Craig Lesley (New York: Laurel; Dell, 1991)
Dancing on the Rim of the World: An Anthology of Contemporary Northwest Native American Writing, ed. by Andrea Lerner (Tucson: Sun Tracks; University of Arizona Press, c1990)
Spider Woman's Granddaughters: Traditional Tales and Contemporary Writing by Native American Women, ed. by Paula Gunn Allen (Boston: Beacon Press, 1989)
A Gathering of Spirit: A Collection by North American Indian Women, ed. by Beth Brant (Ithaca, N.Y.: Firebrand Books, 1988, c1984)
The Sacred Hoop: Recovering the Feminine in American Indian Traditions, by Paula Gunn Allen (Boston: Beacon Press, 1986)

NARRATIVE
Vickie Sears was born in San Diego, California, where she spent the first four years of her childhood, later moving to Washington state, where she lived in orphanages and foster homes. "Being placed in the orphanage and subsequent foster homes [had an] impact [on] all aspects of my life from racism to sexual abuse to knowing I am a strong survivor." Her one place of refuge was school. "I found school to almost always be the safest place to be and loved it. Books were friends—writers, heros and heroines. I could read about worlds of whole families and people of other cultures. Books were a wonder. I had one teacher in the eighth grade who really encouraged me to read poetry and write it. For the most part I stayed a loner. American history was a greatly difficult time when it talked about 'Manifest Destiny' because it didn't match with the positive things my father taught me and so greatly debased Native people."

One memorable writer of Sears's youth was Emily Brönte "because" she says "of my connection to her isolation and the sense I had as a child of that and kinship I wanted to be able to say it as well as she did. My own life as a child growing up in an orphanage and in foster homes kept me silent when I needed to speak, and it kept me wanting to write to speak and tell people of different ways of handling kids."

"I found graduate school very racist and spent much time in sweats to keep me sane and in a state of harmony, spiritually. There was one other Native in the Social Work department and we helped each other stay balanced also."

As Sears worked on her writing, her friends Beth Brant and Paula Gunn Allen encouraged and supported her, becoming her mentors. "Beth Brant ... first published me and kept telling me I was a good writer, and Paula Gunn Allen ... wouldn't let me give up. Both are brave women who write from their souls about what enriches or pains them." Sears says they "have taken the chance on publishing me" and kept supporting her writing because they believed in her work. She also receives encouragement from her partner "who encourages and makes space for me to write" as well as her other friends.

When asked what kinds of events changed her life Sears responded: "Having a family as an adult stretched me to allow myself to trust in love. Becoming a social worker gave me a chance to address racism, child abuse and other 'isms—has allowed me to be political. Finally becoming a Lesbian and learning to live with vision disabilities. All inform my writing and add dimension to me that just give me, hopefully, an expanded awareness of people to share."

Sears's works confront the issues of mixed-blood heritage, living as a foster child and the sense of both alienation and joy present in people's lives. She considers her strongest works to be her short stories *Grace* and *Dancer*, "because they are, I feel, real honest reflections of the lives of so many Native children who are in foster care," and her poems "Pubescence at 39," "Grandmother" and "Nagasaki Elder," because of their universality. She is also fond of one of her novels *One of Them Kids* "because I see it as a healer for myself and others."

She enjoys the works of her friends Paula Gunn Allen and Beth Brant, and Janice Gould, Diane Glancy, Anna Lee Walters, Simon Ortiz, Scott Momaday, Sue Grafton and Karen Kijeniski, P. D. James and Stephen Greenleaf. "I love mysteries and short stories." Sears has three teleplay adaptations of short stories in progress, a novel and a nonfiction work called *Moments,* which is a series of vignettes spanning several years of time in both America, England and Holland. "I write a lot about Washington state, using its flora and fauna because I know it so well for creating a scene, but I also write about the areas I have lived in as an adult. I think I probably would be considered a regional writer, though."

She has recently contributed a chapter on sexual abuse to a women's study textbook *Changing Our Power* (Kendall-Hunt, 1987), two chapters to a book about Lesbian relationships, titled *Lesbian Couples* (Seal Press, 1988) and two articles on ethics for a text to be published by members of the Feminist Therapy Institute.

Working as a Seattle-based storyteller, writer, teacher and feminist therapist, Sears says, "I enjoy being a therapist and consider it a blessing/teaching for myself. I enjoy not working a lot—just daydreaming and feeling the ground or swimming with my dog or walking or talking with my partner or friends."

NAME J, L, N, VA

Joseph E. Senungetuk

OTHER NAMES USED

Inusungaaq Sinungituq

TRIBAL AFFILIATION

Inupiaq

PERSONAL

Born: March 29, 1940, in Wales (Kingigin),
Alaska
Education:
Graduate, Nome High School, 1959
University of Alaska, Fairbanks, majored in
education, 1959–1961
Private tutelage by silversmith and wood-
worker, Ronald Senungetuk, Nome,
Alaska
One year at Indian Arts and Crafts Board
Demonstration Workshop in Sitka, Alaska
Bachelor of Fine Arts degree, majored in
printmaking, minored in sculpture, San
Francisco Art Institute,1970

PUBLICATION HIGHLIGHTS

Give or Take a Century: An Eskimo Chronicle
(San Francisco: Indian Historian Press,
[1972?]); book reviews in the *Journal of
Ethnic Studies* (Bellingham, Wash.: Western Washington State College, [n.d.]); Articles for Children in the *Weewish Tree* (San
Francisco: Indian Historian Press, [n.d.])

NARRATIVE

Senungetuk spent his childhood in the
towns of Wales and Nome. His summers
were spent hunting and fishing and working as a crewmember on his father's
skinboat (umiaq). During the school year
he learned a variety of subjects from some
multitalented instructors. "A fourth grade
teacher taught us classical music appreciation and sock darning besides the four
Rs. A high school teacher taught

Shakespearean plays and sentence dia-
gramming."

"[I] had an older brother who wrote
about a summer experience in Nome to
satisfy the English teacher and I thought
it great that school and everyday life in
Nome could be merged in that manner;
after grade school [they] primarily taught
us about fictional Dick, Jane, Sally, Spot
and so on."

After graduation from high school
Senungetuk spent two years in South
Korea serving a tour of duty for the U.S.
Army. Upon his return to Alaska, he
worked as an artist-in-residence at the
Indian Arts and Crafts Board Demonstration Workshop in Sitka, Alaska, from
1966 to 1967, and he later worked as a
writer and editor from 1968 to 1971 for
the Indian Historian Press in San Francisco. He regarded his colleague at the
Press, editor Jeannette Henry Costo, as
his mentor. "[I] liked to talk of Native
American rights at coffee breaks (french
roast coffee)." Back in Alaska, Senungetuk
worked as an instructor for the Village Art
Upgrade Program at the University of
Alaska at Fairbanks, he was the director
of the Alaskan Educational Program for
the Intercultural Communications at the
Center for Northern Educational Research, again at the University of Alaska,
Fairbanks, and he later worked as an instructor of art and anthropology at
Sheldon Jackson College, Sitka, and for
the Artists in Prisons Program at the
Hiland Mountain and Palmer Correctional Centers.

From 1980 to 1984 he held the position of cultural coordinator of the Cook
Inlet Native Association in Anchorage,
and during the years 1979 to 1984 he was
the planner for the Maritime Peoples Ex-
hibit at the Field Museum in Chicago.
From 1985 to 1988 he worked as a lecturer, artist-in-residence, teacher, guest
speaker, juror and coordinator for arts and

cultural programs for art centers, schools, conferences and workshops from Alaska to Seattle and Copenhagen. He was a columnist for the *Anchorage Daily News,* is currently a columnist for the *Anchorage Gazette* and works as a freelance artist in Anchorage. He has also been active in the community by serving on various boards dedicated to serving the needs of rural Native Alaskans.

Senungetuk writes about Native history, prehistory, art, contemporary events, sociology and anthropology, and enjoys reading the works of Herman Melville, Norman Mailer, Walt Whitman, Aldous Huxley, Truman Capote, Amy Tan, James Joyce, Leslie Silko, Joseph Bruchac, James Welch and Simon Ortiz.

When asked about his strongest work he responds: "Whatever I finish last, be it sculpture, writing or teaching, because I try to find a continuing, progression of learning and teaching. That way I do not have to choose a best of favorite work which would tend to make one complacent with past works." His latest writing project is a continuation of his previous publication. "I'm writing a sort of a sequel to my only published book—give or take a century, but am trying to fictionalize it. Having a hard time converting from historical prose to fiction." When he is not writing, Senungetuk is busy carving marble or hardwoods, making tools and reading.

❖❖❖

NAME   F, N, P
Leslie Marmon Silko

OTHER NAMES USED
Leslie M. Silko

TRIBAL AFFILIATION
Laguna Pueblo

PERSONAL
Born: March 5, 1948, in Albuquerque, New Mexico

Education: B.A. from the University of New Mexico, Albuquerque; coursework at the University of New Mexico, American Indian Law program, Albuquerque, New Mexico

AWARDS, HONORS
John D. and Catherine T. MacArthur Foundation Grant for *The Almanac of the Dead,* 1983; National Endowment Fellowship, 1974; *Chicago Review* Poetry Award, 1974

PUBLICATION HIGHLIGHTS
Yellow Woman and a Beauty of Spirit: Essays on Native American Life Today (New York: Simon and Schuster, 1996)

My Heart Like a Fish (Tucson: Flood Plain Press, 1995)

Laguna Woman (Greenfield Center, N.Y.: Greenfield Review Press, 1974, 1994)

Sacred Water, second edition (Tucson: Flood Plain Press, 1994)

A Circle of Nations: Voices and Visions of American Indians, Leslie Silko, Michael Dorris and Joy Harjo, ed. by John Gattuso (Hillsboro, Oreg.: Beyond Words Publishing, 1993)

Yellow Woman (New Brunswick, N.J.: Rutgers University Press, 1993)

Almanac of the Dead: A Novel (New York: Simon & Schuster, c1991)

With the Delicacy and Strength of Lace: Letters Between Leslie Marmon Silko and James Wright, by Leslie Marmon Silko and James A. Wright (St. Paul, Minn.: Graywolf Press, 1985)

Storyteller (New York: Sever Books, 1981)

Ceremony (New York: Viking Press, 1977)

Silko's works have also appeared in numerous anthologies, such as:

American Visions: Multicultural Literature for Writers, by Delores La Guardia and Hans P. Guth (Mountain View, Calif.: Mayfield, 1995)

Winged Words: American Indian Writers Speak, by Laura Coltelli (Lincoln: University of Nebraska Press, 1990)

Carriers of the Dream Wheel: Contemporary Native American Poetry, ed. by Duane Niatum (New York: Harper & Row, 1975)

Voices of the Rainbow: Contemporary Poetry by American Indians, ed. by Kenneth Rosen (New York: Viking, 1975)

Come to Power: Eleven Contemporary American Indian Poets (Trumansburg, N.Y.: Crossing Press, [1974])

The Man to Send Rain Clouds: Contemporary Stories by American Indians, ed. by Kenneth Rosen (New York: Viking, 1974)

NARRATIVE

Silko was raised at the Laguna Pueblo and is of Laguna, Mexican and white ancestry. As a youth growing up at the pueblo, her grandmother and aunt taught her many stories. She attended Catholic school in Albuquerque as a young woman and later attended the University of New Mexico. After college she worked as an instructor at the Navajo Community College in Tsaile, Arizona, and then moved to Ketchikan, Alaska, with her husband and two sons. Silko returned to the Southwest after her stay in Alaska and taught at the University of New Mexico and at the University of Arizona. She currently lives and writes in Tucson, Arizona. Her writings have also appeared in the journals TriQuarterly and Artforum.

NAME   E, J, L, N

Rodney Simard

TRIBAL AFFILIATION

Cherokee Nation of Oklahoma

PERSONAL

Born: June 18, 1952, in Ft. Smith, Arkansas

Education: B.A. in English and magazine journalism, cum laude, Memphis State University, 1974; M.A. from Mississippi State University, 1976; Ph.D. from the University of Alabama, 1982

AWARDS, HONORS

Meritorious Performance and Professional Promise Award, California State College, Bakersfield, 1982–1983

PUBLICATION HIGHLIGHTS

"American Indian Literatures, Authenticity, and the Canon" in World Literature Today (Norman: University of Oklahoma Press, Spring 1992)

The Whole Writer's Catalog: An Introduction to Advanced Composition with Susan Stone (San Francisco: EMTexts-Mellen, 1992)

"Christopher Marlowe," "Joe Orton," "William Shakespeare," "Tennessee Williams" in The Encyclopedia of Homosexuality, ed. by Wayne Dynes, 2 vols. (New York: Garland, 1990)

"Teaching Argument and Persuasion: One Instructor's Comments" in The Prose Reader: Essays for Thinking, Reading and Writing, second annotated instructor's edition, by Kim Flachmann and Michael Flachmann (Englewood Cliffe, N.J.: Prentice-Hall, 1990)

"American Conservatory Theatre" in American Theatre Companies, 1931–1986, ed. by Weldon B. Durham. (New York: Greenwood, 1989)

Postmodern Drama: Contemporary Playwrights in America and Britain (Lanham, Md.: UPA-American Theatre Association, 1984)

NARRATIVE

Simard was born and raised in Ft. Smith, Arkansas, where, as a youth, he spent much of his time in solitude, roaming the deeply wooded, hilly Ozark region.

Throughout his academic career, Simard has enjoyed the entire process of learning, exploring his potential as an academic and taking part in the community of writers and scholars.

Simard had the good fortune to have a professor who recognized the talent within him, and worked to help him realize his potential as a writer. As Simard says, writing has always been in "my bone marrow." Of all the individuals Simard has had as instructors and guides in his career, however, Simard readily admits that his students have "probably had the greatest impact" on his life and work as a writer.

Simard has worked throughout the southern United States as an educator. He was a teaching assistant at Mississippi State University in Starkville, an instructor at Brewer State Junior College in Tuscaloosa, Alabama, and a teaching assistant at the University of Alabana at Tuscaloosa. He went on to work as an instructor at Birmingham-Southern College in Birmingham, Alabama, a lecturer in English and communications at California State College in Bakersfield and has been a lecturer in arts and letters at the Institute of Gay and Lesbian Education, West Hollywood, California, from 1992 to the present. Simard is currently an associate professor of English and coordinator of American studies at California State University, San Bernardino, which he adds, is interesting geographically, because southern California, and especially Hollywood, "is an unavoidable creative context."

Simard's teaching and research interests are American Indian literature and cultures, the works of William Shakespeare, theory and history of drama, modern and contemporary British and American Literature, among several other areas. He is the author of numerous professional publications on theater, literature and education, has served as editor advisor, contributing editor, consulting editor and manuscript reviewer for numerous journals and periodicals. He currently is the general editor of the *American Indian Studies* series, published in New York by Peter Lang Publishing. During the years 1988 to 1989, he was the faculty editor of the literary journal the *Pacific Review,* which was published by California State University in San Bernardino, during the years 1988 to 1989, he was the consulting editor of the national arts magazine *Elan,* which was published in Colton, California, and from 1978 to 1979, he was the editor of the literary journal the *Black Warrior Review,* published by the University of Alabama.

Since 1989 Simard has been a member of the American Indian Advisory Committee in the California State University system, and is a resource consultant on Native American issues for the National Council of Teachers of English. Through his academic career, Simard has also frequently served as a conference presenter and has had an active role in academic committees and community service activities. Simard's works in progress include an anthology and introduction to traditional and contemporary American Indian literatures, with coauthor Julie LaMay Abner, titled *Tradition and Text, Self/ Other, An Anthology and Introduction to Gender-Specific Readings for Composition,* and an anthology and introduction to multicultural readings for argument and persuasion, with coauthor Susan Stone, titled *American Ideas.* Simard's works have also appeared in many journals, such as *Theatre Journal, American Indian Quarterly* and *Theatre Research International.*

He enjoys reading a number of contemporary Native American works, but especially the fictional works of Gerald Vizenor and the literary criticism of Paula Gunn Allen.

NAME   E, P, VA
Glen Simpson

TRIBAL AFFILIATION
Tahltan and Kaska Athabaskan

PERSONAL
Born: October 9, 1941, in Atlin, British Columbia
Education: M.F.A. in metals from the R.I.T. School of American Craftsmen, 1969

PUBLICATION HIGHLIGHTS
"Night Without Dawn," "Tahltan Country," "Traveling in the Land of the Native Art Historians," "Front Street," poems in *Alaska Quarterly Review* (Anchorage: College of Arts and Sciences, University of Alaska, vol. 4, nos. 3 and 4, 1986)

Simpson's works have also appeared in the following anthologies:

Raven Tells Stories: An Anthology of Alaskan Native Writing, first edition, ed. by Joseph Bruchac (Greenfield Center, N.Y.: Greenfield Review Press, 1991)
Dancing on the Rim of the World: An Anthology of Contemporary Northwest Native American Writing, ed. by Andrea Lerner (Tucson: Sun Tracks; University of Arizona Press, c1990)
Studies in American Indian Literatures: Series 2 New Native American Writing (New York: Association for Study of American Indian Literatures, vol. 2, Summer 1990)

NARRATIVE
Simpson is of Scottish, Kansa and Irish descent and is the son of a gold miner. He was raised near Whitehorse during the Second World War. As a youth his family moved closer to the Alaska Highway, where they ran a roadhouse for thirty years. Simpson was sent to a boarding school in Victoria, British Columbia, and later studied at the Unviversity of Alaska at Fairbanks. Simpson now teaches at the University of Alaska at Fairbanks, where he has been a member of the faculty for more than twenty years.

NAME   F, N, P, VA, M
Michael W. Simpson

OTHER NAMES USED
Blue Fox Man

TRIBAL AFFILIATION
Tsalagi/Yakonan

PERSONAL
Born: November 9, 1951, Lebanon, Oregon
Education:
High school diploma, 1968
A.A., 1972
Bachelors degree in general studies, 1974
M.F.A., 1983
Ph.D., 1990

AWARDS, HONORS
NWIAS Grant, 1991; East-West Scholarship, 1985; Kenny Moore Creative Writing Scholarship, 1983

PUBLICATION HIGHLIGHTS
The Making of Native American Pottery (Happy Camp, Calif.: Naturegraph, 1991)

Dreams of a Rainbow, a Book of Poems, English text by Kauraka Kauraka, ed. by Michael W. Simpson and John Unterecker (Suava, Fiji: University of South Pacific Press, 1987)

On the Landing (Muscogee, Okla.: Indian University Press, Bacone College, 1984)

"Native American Church Comes to the Oregon Coast" in *Accent Magazine* (Coos Bay, Oreg.: [s.n.], July 1, 1980)

"Sweat Lodge Custom Still Alive Today" in the *Bay Reporter* (Empire, Oreg.: [s.n.], September 19, 1979)

"Ancient Rites Revived in Indian Wedding" in the *Bay Reporter* (Empire, Oreg.: [s.n.], August 29, 1979)

Simpson's works have also appeared in: *Returning the Gift: Poetry and Prose from the First North American Native Writers' Festival,* ed. by Joseph Bruchac with the support of the Association for the Study of American Indian Literatures (Tucson: University of Arizona, 1994).

NARRATIVE

Simpson was raised throughout the Pacific Northwest region, including Northern California, Oregon and Washington. He began writing at an early age, and he recalls a memorable experience while he was in the sixth grade in which he had written a story for a little girl and she became his girlfriend. In the eleventh grade his English teacher encouraged him to write poems and enter them in a statewide writing contest.

Several people have inspired and guided Simpson, including his grandmothers, who were poets; his mother, because of her common sense; his elder brother who is an actor; his father, who is a painter and a hunter and teachers such as scholar Floyd Matson, poet Ralph Salisbury and poet and novelist James Dickey. It was Dickey, who Simpson said "taught me to perfect form and use the

image coupled with deeply felt rhythms, to articulate and express mystical feelings evident in the life experience." Two events determined the direction his life was to take; one was the experience of discrimination and racial prejudice he encountered as a teenager, and the other was his award of the East-West Center Scholarship to work on his Ph.D.

Simpson's favorite poets are Hart Crane, Walt Whitman, Joy Harjo and Emily Dickinson. Simpson's current projects include several books of poems, nonfiction works, environmental essays and various articles on Native American literature. Simpson considers his strongest works to be *On the Landing,* which shows his promise as a poet, and *Making Native American Pottery,* because "it is a good example of cultural preservation in popular rather than an academic format." Simpson is also a painter, carver and musician, and creates beadwork and leatherwork.

❖❖❖

NAME   E, F, L, N, P, PL, S, VA

Victor Alan Blanchard Singing Eagle

OTHER NAMES USED

V. Blanchard Singing Eagle

TRIBAL AFFILIATION

Potawatomi, Chitimacha, Creek

PERSONAL

Born: July 8, 1965, in Pomona, California

Education: A.A. from the College of the Siskiyous, Weed, California, 1983; B.A. in English and anthropology from the University of California, Santa Barbara, 1990; M.F.A. from Eastern Washington University, Cheney, Washington, 1992

AWARDS, HONORS

W.E.B. (William Edward Burghardt) DuBois Poetry, First Prize, 1990; University of California Award of Distinction, 1990; W.E.B. DuBois Poetry, Honorable Mention, 1989

PUBLICATION HIGHLIGHTS

"Christmas Morning," poem in *Expressions* (Santa Barbara: University of California at Santa Barbara Press, 1990)

"The Story of Devil's Tower" poem in *Bright Honor Path* (Santa Barbara: University of California at Santa Barbara Press, 1990)

"The Pow-wow," poem in *Expressions* (Santa Barbara: University of California at Santa Barbara Press, 1989)

NARRATIVE

Singing Eagle was raised by his grandmother on the Morongo Indian Reservation near Banning, California. He had a memorable teacher named Pat Estrada while he was a young man in parochial school. "You see, back at Saint Philomena Elementary School, I was a bit of a brat. In fact, the very name 'Victor' struck terror in the hearts of nuns and priests alike. Well, one day, Sister Mary Elizabeth spied me all hunched over some writing instead of paying attention, so she did what every other red-blooded American nun would've: she snatched it up and proceeded to read it out aloud before the entire class. To make a long story short, there were nuns running around all over the school reciting my poetry when along came my 'lay' English teacher who had the gall to ask: 'what are you reciting?' It was she who thrust me into my career. She was a very honorable, brave and sometimes outspoken Indian educator ... she was the first to teach us be proud that we're Indians."

He served in the U.S. Coast Guard, at Astoria, Oregon, for two years and re-ceived an honorable discharge due to a service-related injury.

Singing Eagle writes works of fiction, controversial nonfiction and is a storyteller for several Spokane elementary schools. He enjoyed writing his upcoming poetry book *Coyote's Little Brother: Poems That Got Him into Trouble* "because it's a jolly and irreverent romp through (and on top of) the Hallowed Halls of Academia."

Several instructors and friends have been influential in Singing Eagle's writing career over the years, among them are Professor Susanna S. Shreeve, Professor Michael W. Simpson, Professor Pauline Flett and Sherman Alexi. He enjoys reading works by "Leslie Marmon Silko, N. Scott Momaday, Ray Young Bear, Marge Piercy, Toni Morrison, Sherman Alexi, Johnathan Swift, Alexander Pope, John Dryden, John Wilmot (second Earl of Rochester) and Shakespeare—yes, they have influenced my work!"

When he is not writing, he participates in sweats, does beadwork and quillwork, drawings, paintings, carvings and featherwork, makes obsidian arrowheads and gardens at his home on the slope of Mt. Shasta.

He is currently a college English and Indian studies instructor.

NAME   E, L, P, S

Eleonore Tecumseh Sioui

TRIBAL AFFILIATION

Huron Wyandot

PERSONAL

Born: May 20
Education:
B.P.E. from Laval University, 1972
Special diploma from the University of Ottawa, 1978

Coursework from Trent University, 1980
M.A. from the University of Miami
Ph.D from the Union for Experimenting
Colleges and Universities, 1989

PUBLICATION HIGHLIGHTS

Andatha (Quebec: Collection Bribes
d'Univers, 1985); *Femme de l'isle* (Rillieux,
France: Sur le Dos de la Tortue, [n.d.]);
Corps a coeur eperdus (Quebec: Editions
d'Ici d'Ailleurs, [n.d.])

NAME   J, N, S

Grace Slwooko

OTHER NAMES USED

Grace Kulukhon Slwooko

TRIBAL AFFILIATION

Siberian Yupik

PERSONAL

Born: October 22, 1921
Education: High school graduate; college
coursework by correspondence

PUBLICATION HIGHLIGHTS

Eskimo Boy and the Giant (Anchorage: Uni-
versity of Alaska, 1978)
St. Lawrence Island Legends, 1 (Anchorage:
University of Alaska, 1977)
St. Lawrence Island Legends, 2 (Anchorage:
University of Alaska, 1977)
*Yuggaankuk Mayeraaghpagenkuk (Eskimo
Man and the Giant),* by G. Slwooko, M.
Poage, M. Apatiki (Nome, Alaska:
Ulimakat Nome Agency M., 1976)
*Ayumiim Ungipaghaa Tangi (Stories of Long
Ago),* by G. Slwooko, R. Kuluknon
(Fairbanks: University of Alaska, 1975)
Sanighmelnguut (Switzerland: Nicholas
Lotscher, [n.d.])

NARRATIVE

Grace Slwooko grew up on St. Lawrence
Island, where her childhood memories
include writing in her diary, and the help
she and her classmates received from their
teachers, back in the 1930s. Her tribe
came from Siberia some 150 years ago.
"Now, I'm seventy-one years old and my
parents were the first children to go to
school (missionary school). Their parents
were adult already, but some went to
school ... I [would] like to thank the white
man for bringing this wonderful happening, writing. Now I can write, I even wrote
legends and Eskimo stories, they mean a
lot to us, they have meaning. ... I also
have a song about this wonderful writing.
Eskimos have sayings and songs, too. One
saying is that songs float up on you from
the bottom of the sea. [If] there is one that
float[s] up on me, I just sing it out."

Slwooko writes about Eskimo stories
and news (which she considers to be both
fun and good examples of life), people and
places in history and her own life. She is
now working on writing books, one of
which is titled *Treasures in the Pages.*

Slwooko works on sewing when she
is not writing, and is currently busy taking care of children at home.

NAME   F, L, N, P

Virginia Sneve

OTHER NAMES USED

Virginia Driving Hawk Sneve

TRIBAL AFFILIATION

Rosebud Sioux

PERSONAL

Born: February 21, 1934, in Rosebud, South
Dakota

Education: B.S. from South Dakota State University, 1954; M.Ed. from South Dakota State University, 1969

AWARDS, HONORS

Distinguished Native American Alumnus, South Dakota State University, 1992

Native American Press Award, University of Nebraska Press, 1992

Outstanding Instructor, Oglala Lakota College, 1986 and 1993

Writer of the Year, South Dakota Hall of Fame, 1984

Distinguished Contributor to South Dakota History, South Dakota Historical Conference, 1982

Special Contribution to Education, South Dakota Indian Education Association, 1975

Woman of Achievement, National Federation of Press Women, 1975

Distinguished Alumnus, South Dakota State University, 1974

Woman of Achievement, South Dakota Press Women, 1974

Best Work of the Year in the American Indian category by the Interracial Council for Minority Books for Children for the book *Jimmy Yellow Hawk*, 1971

Western Writers of America Award for *Betrayed*

PUBLICATION HIGHLIGHTS

Completing the Circle (Lincoln: University of Nebraska, 1995)

High Elk's Treasure (Boston: Houghton Mifflin, 1995)

The Hopi (New York: Holiday House, 1995)

The Iroquois (New York: Holiday House, 1995)

The Nez Perce (New York: Holiday House, 1994)

The Seminoles (New York: Holiday House, 1994)

When Thunder Spoke (Lincoln: University of Nebraska, 1994)

The Chichi HooHoo Bogeyman (New York: Holiday House, 1993)

The Navajos (New York: Holiday House, 1993)

The Sioux (New York: Holiday House, 1993)

When Thunders Spoke (New York: Holiday House, 1993)

Everyone Has a Name (New York: Lee and Low Books, 1992)

Dancing Teepees, selected by Virginia Driving Hawk Sneve (New York: Holiday House, 1989)

"Grandmother" I, II, III in *Wanbli Ho Journal/Eagles Voice* (Mission, S. Dak.: Sinte Gleska College, 1988)

"Grandpa Was a Cowboy and an Indian" in *Dakota West* ([S.l.: s.n.], April 1985)

"Story Tellers" in *Plainswoman* (Grand Forks, N. Dak.: Plainswoman, September 1984)

That They May Have Life: The Episcopal Church in South Dakota, 1859–1976 (New York: Seabury Press, 1977)

The Dakota Heritage (Sioux Falls, S. Dak.: Brevet, 1975)

They Led a Nation (Sioux Falls, S. Dak.: Brevet, 1975)

Betrayed (New York: Holiday House, 1974)

South Dakota Geographic Names, ed. by Virginia Driving Hawk Sneve (Sioux Falls, S. Dak.: Brevet Press, 1973)

Jimmy Yellow Hawk (New York: Holiday House, 1972)

High Elk's Treasure (New York: Holiday House, 1972)

NARRATIVE

Virginia Sneve was born and raised on the Rosebud Reservation in South Dakota, where as a child she attended a Bureau of Indian Affairs elementary school. As she remembers, she was encouraged to advance her reading skills beyond the expected curriculum level by a third grade teacher who gave her extra books to take home and read. She attended an Episcopal

High School for Indian Girls, where she was again encouraged to excel by her teachers, who "expect[ed] only the best from the students." As a young woman, academic scholarship was reinforced by a supportive family, particularly her father who was an Episcopalian priest and "stressed the importance of education."

While she was a college student, an English instructor encouraged her to try her hand at writing. As she was learning her art, Sneve had another individual in her life who served as a mentor, writer "Evelyn Sibley Lampman, children's fiction and nonfiction author, now deceased, encouraged, criticized and gave helpful writing and personal advice." Her interest in juvenile literature was piqued when her daughter began to read. "My daugher, when in elementary school, bringing her reading books home. I saw there was little about Native Americans and nothing authorized by a Native writer. I began reading children's literature which led to my writing for children." Since that time she has written a number of books for children, and she enjoys the genre and its rewards. When asked which are her strongest works, she responds, "My fiction for children, because children from all over the U.S. and Canada have written to tell me how they like/dislike the characters, setting, plot—which shows that my writing has made them think."

Sneve writes about Native Americans, not only in the genre of juvenile literature, but also in historical and nonfiction works, poetry and works for television productions. "I write about this land and its people that I've known all of my life."

In addition to her children's books and monographs, Sneve has had short stories published in several journals, such as *Image* and *Boys' Life*, over a dozen articles and essays published in various journals

and monographs, such as the *Historical Magazine of the Episcopal Church, Country Living,* the *Rapid City Journal, South Dakota Heritage,* the *Indian Historian* and in the *Dakota State History Conference Collection* (1985), the *Ethnic American Woman* (1978) and *Maka Sica: Photographs of the South Dakota Badlands* (1989) and she has written twelve articles for the Dakota Territory Centennial Project, which was in turn published in various North and South Dakota newspapers from 1988 to 1989.

In her television experience, Sneve worked as a writer and talent for a program on the South Dakota bicentennial, which was produced by South Dakota Public Television in 1976, she dramatized the book *The Chichi Hoohoo Bogeyman* for the Public Broadcasting System program *Vegetable Soup Children's Series* in 1977 and she was a writer for the South Dakota History Series programs 1, 14 and 19, all produced by South Dakota Instructional Television in 1980. Sneve wrote a pilot script for the Native American Consortium for the Corporation for Public Broadcasting titled *I Am Different from My Brother* and has worked as a writer for the program "South Dakota Centennial Minutes," produced by South Dakota Public Television in 1989.

She has been the editor of Brevet Press of Sioux Falls, South Dakota, and is a member of the National League of American Pen Women and of the South Dakota Press Women. She is a member of the Rosebud Tribe and has served as a member of the board of directors for the United Sioux Tribes Cultural Arts Council.

She married Vance Sneve in 1955. In her spare time, Sneve enjoys reading "Michael Dorris's and Louise Erdrich's collaborative fiction and Jo Harjo and Roberta Hill Whitman's poetry." She has recently been a high school counselor in the Rapid City Central High Schools and

Associate Instructor at the Oglala Lakota College, Rapid City Extension. She retired in 1995. During her leisure time, Sneve works in her garden, reads, plays the piano and organ and enjoys spending time with her grandchildren.

NAME E, N
Darlene Speidel

TRIBAL AFFILIATION
Lakota

PERSONAL
Born: March 5, 1952, on the Standing Rock Reservation
Education: Bachelors degree in secondary education, Black Hills State University; masters degree in secondary school administration, South Dakota State University

PUBLICATION HIGHLIGHTS
Tukted Unsti Mapi (Prince Albert, Sask.: Dakota Nations of Canada, 1991)
Heyaka Wecun (Prince Albert, Sask.: Dakota Nations of Canada, 1991)
Wanyanka Owakihi (Prince Albert, Sask.: Dakota Nations of Canada, 1991)
Nahon Owakihi (Prince Albert, Sask.: Dakota Nations of Canada, 1991)
The Hunter and the Wolf (Prince Albert, Sask.: Dakota Nations of Canada, 1990)
The Rabbit and the Bear with the Flint Body (Prince Albert, Sask.: Dakota Nations of Canada, 1989)
Pet Donkey (Prince Albert, Sask.: Dakota Nations of Canada, 1989)
Unci Stories (four books) (Rapid City, S. Dak.: Rapid City Area Schools, 1982)
Friendship (Rapid City, S. Dak.: Rapid City Area Schools, 1982)
Chief Fools Crows (Rapid City, S. Dak.: Rapid City Area Schools, 1982)
The Eva Nichols Story (Rapid City, S. Dak.: Rapid City Area Schools, 1982)

NARRATIVE
Speidel was born and raised on the Standing Rock Reservation and attended a predominately Indian school in Fort Yates, North Dakota, where she recalls with relish the superior athletes and teams the school produced. She says the sports teams were "a force that the non-Indian schools did not want to reckon with!"

Speidel's many works in the fields of education and writing are a result of the support provided her by her elders who encouraged her to accurately record, preserve and teach the traditional teachings of her people. As Speidel adds, her career focus developed by "recognizing the need to develop materials so that our children and future generations can retain what is ours and assert our inherent rights." Among those who also served as advisors to her in her writing career are friend Sonny Lurvie and the many chiefs of the Dakota Nations of Canada.

When asked if her geographic surroundings play a significant role in her writings, Speidel responded, "Yes, they do, the need to make people understand that the Dakota/Lakota people in Canada are not 'refugees from the States,' is a real driving force along the the intent of drawing recognition to the Canadian Dakota/Lakota/Nakota." Speidel has also recently relocated, moving away from an environment which was "dominantly Dakota/Lakota/Nakota to work in a center which serves other Indian language/culture groups."

When not writing, Speidel works on research in various disciplines, in particularly with the Elders, going to Dakota/Lakota pow-wows, teaching about her language, culture and history and working on self-government projects for the Dakota

Nations of Canada. "I find it a real challenge."

Her current projects include a five-dialect dictionary that will compare variants of the Dakota, Nakota, Lakota languages, a Dakota studies teachers' resource guide, thirty units, each of Dakota and Nakota for beginners, which include teachers' guide and support materials. She is also writing a K-3 Nakota studies teachers' guide, book *Practicing the Law of Circular Interaction: First Nations Environment and Conservation Principles,* an environmental curriculum package, *Nursery to Grade 12 Curriculum Guide for the Instruction of Dakota/Lakota/Nakota Language, Dakota/Nakota/Lakota Bilingual/bicultural Education Curriculum Guide Nursery to grade 12* and *Kehte-Ayak Masinahikan.* She is working on the Dakota/Nakota stories project, which is to be a collection of fifty-three stories, and she is also conducting a series of interviews with women elders from across Saskatchewan, representative of the seventy-four first nations in the province of Sasketchewan.

Speidel is also working on a sociolinguistic survey video, which will be a research study on the current status of Indian language in Saskatchewan, and she is also writing an accompanying report to the video titled *On the Critical List.* Speidel is currently the managing editor of the publications division of the Sasketchewan Indian Cultural Center in Saskatoon, Saskatchewan, where she also works as the editor for all materials published by her Center, including the journal *The Arrow.*

NAME E, F, N, P

Jean Starr

TRIBAL AFFILIATION

Cherokee

PERSONAL

Born: July 6, 1935, in Alexandria, Virginia
Education: B.A. in history and journalism, Franklin College, Granklin, Indiana; M.A. in English, University of Nevada at Reno

AWARDS, HONORS

Human and Civil Rights Advocate Award, Capital Service Center, California Teachers Association, 1992

PUBLICATION HIGHLIGHTS

Tales from the Cherokee Hills (Winston-Salem, N.C.: John Blair, 1988)
Songs of Power (Sacramento: Little Sister Pub., 1988)
"Toronogashi Festival, Sacramento California, August 21, 1988: An Elegy for B." in *Tea leaves, An Asian-American Arts Magazine* (Berkeley: Fall 1988, vol. 14)
"At the Euchee-Creek Ribbon-Dance" in *Tamaqua* (Champaign, Ill.: Parkland College, [n.d.])

Starr's works also appear in *Returning the Gift: Poetry and Prose from the First North American Native Writers' Festival,* ed. by Joseph Bruchac with the support of the Assoication for the Study of American Indian Literatures (Tucson: University of Arizona, 1994).

NARRATIVE

Educator Jean Starr grew up in several states, including Virginia, Kentucky, Florida and Indiana. Among the people who influenced her life were her father, through his storytelling and "examples in daily life," Dr. Harvey Jacobs, editor of the *Indianapolis News,* Starr's journalism professor at Franklin, who taught her "to be painstakingly accurate, to be ethical, to be true to ourselves," and Walter Van Tilburg Clark, a professor at the University of Nevada who decided Starr was going to be a poet and taught her how to write poetry.

Starr currently teaches English at the American Legion High School in Sacramento. She was director of the first American Indian Education Program for Sacramento City Unified School District. In this arena, she had the chance to teach Indian Studies to American Indian Students "who had, for the most part, been raised in cities, had trouble understanding traditional stories. In trying to communicate with them, I wrote poems that showed my my own poetic voice, gave me a standard by which I could evaluate my work. It was like reaching solid ground. From there on, I could build on what I had done and try new things." She has also taught primary, junior high school and has directed student publications. Starr is active in presenting her work through readings, at various locations in the Northern California region. Because of these activities, she was elected to the board of the Sacramento Arts Council.

Starr enjoys reading W. H. Auden, Dickinson, Whitman, Yeats, Dylan Thomas, G. M. Hopkins, Margery Allingham, Carson McCullars, Walter Clark, Robert J. Conley, Joe Bruchac, Joy Harjo, Rayna Green, N. Scott Momaday and Leslie Marmon Silko. She is currently working on a novel, a number of short stories and two groups of poems: one is a collection about American Indian themes, and the other is a collection about themes in everyday life. Her works have also been published in the journal *Callaloo*.

NAME   P
James Thomas Stevens

OTHER NAMES USED
Aronhiotas

TRIBAL AFFILIATION
Akwesasne Mohawk

PERSONAL
Born: June 26, 1966 in Niagara Falls, New York
Education: A.F.A. Institute of American Indian Arts, Santa Fe, New Mexico; M.F.A. candidate in creative writing, Brown University, Providence, Rhode Island

AWARDS, HONORS
Gerald Red Elk Scholarship to study at the Naropa Institute, 1990; Full Fellowship to Brown University's Graduate Writing Program

PUBLICATION HIGHLIGHTS
Tokinish (Staten Island; Toronto: First Intensity; Shuffaloff, 1994)
"Three Songs of the Medicine Bundle," poem in *Blue Mesa Review* (Albuquerque: University of New Mexico Press, no. 2, Spring 1990)
Desire and Time, poem (Ann Arbor, Mich.: NcNaughton & Gunn, 1990)
"Learning Not to Sew," poem in *Clerestory Journal* ([Dexter, Mich.]: Thomas-Shore, vol. 8, issue 3)

NARRATIVE
James Thomas Stevens was raised just north of the Niagara Falls–Buffalo area, on the mouth of Lake Ontario. Stevens now lives on Narragansett Bay, in Providence, Rhode Island, where he is close to the sea. "Being around water is incredibly important to me, having grown up on the Great Lakes." His work and perspective have been shaped by his Mohawk heritage and by the geology of the Niagara Gorge that he lived near and explored as a young man.

While a student at the Institute of American Indian Arts, Stevens had the opportunity to meet poet Arthur Sze.

"Arthur Sze was my mentor. He is an Asian-American poet who is head of the Creative Writing Department at the Institute of American Indian Arts. ... He taught me that being a poet gives you the gift of being able to 'orchestrate your silences.'" Stevens also was deeply impressed by another poet, Michael Palmer. "I once attended a reading by California poet Michael Palmer in Santa Fe. After hearing his work, I knew what I wanted to do."

Deemed a "visionary geologist" by a graduate professor, Stevens writes poems about one's "personal geology" and the science of living. He considers one of his strongest works to be his poem "Camera Orchestral" for its blend of sound and vision, ceremony and science. Other writers who Stevens enjoys reading are Mei-Mei Bersssenbrugge, Michael Palmer, Clark Coolidge, George Oppen, Jeanette Winterson, Arthur Sze and Christopher Dewdney. "They influence me in the way they see the world around them."

Formerly a visual artist, Stevens is now an M.F.A. student at Brown University and is working on translating the poetry of Jean Genet, a long poem of his own and putting his graduate thesis together for publication. In his spare time, Stevens works on sculptures and painting.

NAME   N, P
Hyemeyohsts Storm

OTHER NAMES USED
Golden Silver
Charles Storm

TRIBAL AFFILIATION
Northern Cheyenne

PERSONAL
Born: 1935 on the Lame Deer Agency, Montana

Education: Coursework at Oakland City College, California; coursework at Eastern Montana College, Billings, Montana

PUBLICATION HIGHLIGHTS
Lightning Bolt (New York: Ballantine, 1994); *The Song of Heyoehkah* (New York: Harper & Row, 1981); *Seven Arrows* (New York: Harper & Row, 1972)

Storm's works have also appeared in the following anthologies:

Native American Literature, by Andrew Wiget (Boston: Twayne, 1985)
Native American Renaissance, by Kenneth Lincoln (Berkeley: University of California Press, c1983)
Literature of the American Indians: Views and Interpretations: A Gathering of Indian Memories, Symbolic Contexts and Literary Criticism, ed. by Abraham Chapman (New York: New American Library, 1975)

NARRATIVE
Born and raised on the Lame Deer Agency in Montana until he reached the age of 21, Storm was moved to Oakland, California, as part of the federal Indian Relocation policy of the 1950s. While living in California, Storm studied at Oakland City College but later returned to the reservation in Montana. He continued his studies at Eastern Montana College and also worked as an oil rigger for a time. His book *Seven Arrows* has generated heated debate among Native Americans because of its content and form. Storm is married and has three children.

NAME   P
Robert A. Swanson

TRIBAL AFFILIATION
Ojibwe

PERSONAL
Born: 1946 in Minnesota

PUBLICATION HIGHLIGHTS
Breaking Stereotypes (Poland: [s.n.], 1986); *Solemn Spirits,* poems ([S.l.: s.n., n.d.]); *Little Warrior,* poems ([S.l.: s.n., n.d.])

Swanson's works have appeared in these anthologies:

Dancing on the Rim of the World: An Anthology of Contemporary Northwest Native American Writing, ed. by Andrea Lerner (Tucson: Sun Tracks; University of Arizona Press, c1990)
Native American Reader: Stories, Speeches and Poems, ed. by Jerry D. Blanche (Juneau: Denali Press, c1990)
The Remembered Earth: An Anthology of Contemporary Native American Literature, ed. by Geary Hobson (Albuquerque: Red Earth Press, 1979)

NARRATIVE
From the Grand Portage Reservation in Minnesota, poet Swanson now lives in Washington state. His works have also appeared in the journals *Many Smokes, Phantasm* and *Akwesasne Notes.*

NAME   P, N
Denise Sweet

TRIBAL AFFILIATION
White Earth Anishinabe

PUBLICATION HIGHLIGHTS
Days of Obsidian, Days of Grace: Selected Poetry and Prose by Four Native American Writers, Adrian C. Louis et al. (Poetry Harbor, 1994)
Know by Heart (Eau Claire, Wisc.: Rhiannon, 1992)
"Winter Farm Auction," poem in *Northeast Indian Quarterly* (Ithaca, N.Y.: American Indian Program at Cornell University, vol. 8, no. 3, Fall 1990)
"Prayer for Women Filled with Grace," poem in *Upriver: Wisconsin Poetry and Prose* ([S.l.: s.n.], 1990)
"Mission at White Earth," poem in *Transactions: A Journal of the Wisconsin Academy of Arts, Sciences and Letters* ([S.l.: s.n.], 1990)

Sweet's works have also appeared in *Returning the Gift: Poetry and Prose from the First North American Native Writers' Festival,* ed. by Joseph Bruchac with the support of the Association for the Study of American Indian Literatures (Tucson: University of Arizona, 1994).

NARRATIVE
Sweet currently teaches at the University of Wisconsin at Green Bay and is working on a play for the Newage Social Action Theatre. She is the mother of two sons.

T

NAME
Terry Tafoya

E, F, J, L, N, P, PA, PL
P, PA, PL, S, SC, V

TRIBAL AFFILIATION
Taos Pueblo and Warm Springs Apache

PERSONAL
Born: March 25, 1952, in Trinidad, Colorado
Education:
B.A. in English/psychology, University of
South Florida, 1973
M.Ed. in higher education, University of
Washington, 1974
M.C. in communications, University of
Washington, 1975
Ph.D. educational psychology, University of
Washington, 1985

AWARDS, HONORS
Multiculturalism Award, University of Minnesota at Morris, 1992
Invited to give address for Divisions 44 and
45, American Psychological Association
Annual Conference 1991
Community Partnership Award, Black Coalition on AIDS, 1990
Distinguished Visiting Professor, University
of California at Chico, 1987
Educator of the Year, Mokakit Indian Research Association, 1986
NW Nominee for the *Esquire Magazine
Directory* of "Under-40 Leaders of the
National Impact," 1985
National Humanities Scholar by the National Endowment for the Humanities,
named as one of the five "Indians of the
1980s," 1984

PUBLICATION HIGHLIGHTS
*David Gilhooly, Kenneth Baker, Tony Will-
iams, and Terry A. Tafoya* ([S.l.]: John
Natsoulas Gallery, 1992)
"Singing Your Own Song: Adapting Existing AIDS Curriculum for Bilingual/Bicultural Use," by Terry Tafoya and D.
Wirth, in *Getting the Word Out: A Practical Guide to AIDS Materials Development*,
A. C. Matiella, ed. (Santa Cruz, CA: Network Publications, 1990)
"Circles and Cedar: Native Americans and
Family Therapy" in *Minorities and Family Therapy*, ed. by G. Saba, B. M. Karrer
and K. V. Hardy (New York: Haworth
Press, 1989)
"Case Histories—Nicholas: A Heterosexual
Alcoholic" in *Face to Face: A Guide to AIDS
Counseling*, ed. by J. W. Dilley, C. Pies, and
M. Helquist (San Francisco: Celestial Arts
for the University of California, 1989)
"Pulling Coyote's Tale: Native American
Sexuality and AIDS" in *Primary Prevention of AIDS*, ed. by V. Mays, G. Albee
and S. Schneider (Newbury Park, Calif.:
Sage Publications, 1989)

NARRATIVE
Tafoya grew up in the American Southwest, spending his high school years in
Oklahoma. In his youth Tafoya was surrounded by relatives, grandparents and
parents who taught him to value, respect
and pay attention to "all sorts of people."
As a child Tafoya enjoyed writing. "I had
to write, so I did, from the time I could
hold a pencil." And when he was eight
years old Tafoya wrote a letter to science
writer Isaac Asimov, asking "him how he
became an expert on so many subjects—
he sent back a postcard, and replied 'I'm
not an expert—I just sound like one.' I
was thrilled such a famous and important
writer/scientist responded to a little kid."

Tafoya recalls a moment in his career as a student: "I've won a number of awards—but what sticks is when I was in graduate school, an advisor told me that if I insisted on continuing to publish both fiction and scholarly material, I had to do so under different names, because academics wouldn't trust someone who worked in more than one field."

Tafoya is inspired by Marion Zimmer Bradley, who became an editor of his short stories, and Ursula LaGuin, an old friend who was a "real approachable person with humor. These were people I knew long before I encountered Leslie Silko, or Paula Allen—James Welch was just getting recognized when I met him at the University of Washington."

Tafoya writes about "things that make people think. I always try to start with a traditional Native story that serves as a touchstone for what I explore. Since I constantly travel, I would say it [geography] all plays a significant role—e.g., my work with Eskimo and Inuit people in Alaska and the Northwest Territories gave me the background for my short story, *Tupilak.* People inspire me more than geography." Tafoya enjoys the works of writers James Branch Cabell, Tanith Lee, Sheri Tepper—"all combine myth with prose that constantly erupts into poetry, but always has a sense of humor. The essays of Ursula Le Guin, of Paula Gunn Allen, the short stories of Leslie Silko."

Tafoya is currently writing the curriculum for a National Native American Substance Abuse Prevention project, and he is completing a National AIDS curriculum for training psychologists for the American Psychological Association. "I'd like to have some time off to go back to doing more fictional based work—plays, seems like there's no time to do a novel. Maybe one day."

Tafoya works as a consulting psychologist, traveling to universities, tribes, social service organizations, schools and businesses and participates in countless conferences throughout the United States and other countries to train all ethnic groups to "learn to see through different eyes in an attempt to achieve harmony" using traditional Native American stories. He is currently the executive director of Tamanawit, Unlimited, San Francisco, California, which is an International consulting firm on multiculturalism, bilingual education and transcultural issues of mental health, providing training and technical assistance to local, state, tribal and federal agencies, universities, school districts and private industries. He has been providing services to the American Psychological Association, U.S. Office of Substance Abuse Prevention and Indian Health Services since 1989. Tafoya has also illustrated children's books for the *Indian Readers* series of the Northwest Regional Education Laboratories. He has also worked as the director of training for the National Native American AIDS Prevention Center, Oakland, California from 1988 to 1989, he was professor of psychology at Evergreen State College, Olympia, Washington from 1985 to 1990 and he was a member of the clinical faculty, Interpersonal Psychotherapy Clinic, Harborview Community Mental Health Center, Seattle, Washington, from 1981 to 1988.

When Tafoya is not writing, he is: "Living—guess that's research. I remember as a college student, I decided one wrote poems, or lived them. My first professional job at 18 was as a graphic artist—I miss doing visual art."

NAME   J, N

Henry Tall Bull

TRIBAL AFFILIATION

Cheyenne

PUBLICATION HIGHLIGHTS

Cheyenne Warriors, by H. Tall Bull and T. Weist (Billings, Mont.: Council for Indian Education, 1983, 1971)

Northern Cheyenne Forest Fighters, by H. Tall Bull and T. Weist (Billings: Montana Indian Publications, 1979, 1970)

Cheyenne Fire Fighters (Billings: Montana Indian Publications, 1971)

The Winter Hunt, by H. Tall Bull and T. Weist (Billings: Montana Reading Publishers, 1971)

The Spotted Horse, by H. Tall Bull, T. Weist and B. Bearchum (Billings: Montana Council for Indian Education, 1971)

Grandfather and the Popping Machine, by H. Tall Bull and T. Weist (Billings: Montana Reading Publishers, 1970)

NARRATIVE

Tall Bull was a writer of weekly columns for the Browning, Montana, newspaper, *Glacier Reporter,* in the 1950s, and was also the author of numerous juvenile literature works. He is now deceased.

NAME   F, N, P, S

Mary Tall Mountain

OTHER NAMES USED

Mary L. Randle

TRIBAL AFFILIATION

Athabascan of Alaska

PERSONAL

Born: June 19, 1918, in Nuleto, Alaska
Education: High school graduate

AWARDS, HONORS

Pushcart Prize for *There Is No Word for Good-bye,* 1982–1983

PUBLICATION HIGHLIGHTS

A Quick Brush of Wings (San Francisco: Red Star Black Rose Press, 1991)

The Light on the Tent Wall, A Bridging (Los Angeles: University of California at Los Angeles Press, 1990)

Listen to the Night (Berkeley: Heyday Books, 1990)

Matrilineal Cycle (Oakland, Calif.: Red Star Black Rose Printing, 1990; reprinted from the Open Heart Press publication, 1988)

There Is No Word for Good-bye: Poems by Mary Tall Mountain (Oakland, Calif.: Red Star Black Rose Printing, 1990; reprinted from Open Heart Press, 1988)

Continuum (Marvin, S. Dak.: Blue Cloud Quarterly Press, 1988)

Green March Moons (Berkeley: New Seed Press, 1987)

Good Grease (New York: Strawberry Press, 1978)

Nine Poems (San Francisco: Friars Press, 1977)

Tall Mountain's works have appeared in several anthologies:

Braided Lives: An Anthology of Multicultural American Writing, by the Minnesota Humanities Commission and the Minnesota Council of Teachers of English (St. Paul: The Commission, 1991)

Circle of Motion: Arizona Anthology of Contemporary American Indian Literature, ed. by Kathleen Mullen Sands (Tempe: Arizona Historical Society, 1990)

Season of Dead Water, ed. by Helen Frost (Portland, Oreg: Breitenbush Books, 1990)

Spider Woman's Granddaughters: Traditional Tales and Contemporary Writing by Native American Women, ed. by Paula Gunn Allen (Boston: Beacon Press, 1989)

Living the Spirit: A Gay American Indian Anthology, by Will Roscoe (New York: St. Martins, 1988)

I Tell You Now: Autobiographical Essays by

Native American Writers, ed. by Brian Swann and Arnold Krupat (Lincoln: University of Nebraska Press, 1987)

The Sacred Hoop: Recovering the Feminine in American Indian Traditions, by Paula Gunn Allen (Boston: Beacon, 1986)

Earth Power Coming: Short Fiction in Native American Literature, ed. by Simon J. Ortiz (Tsaile, Ariz.: Navajo Community College Press, 1983)

The Remembered Earth: An Anthology of Contemporary Native American Literature, ed. by Geary Hobson (Albuquerque: Red Earth Press, 1979)

NARRATIVE

Tall Mountain was born in Nuleto, Alaska, on the Yukon River and raised in Oregon and California. Of Russian Scots-Irish and Athabascan descent, she was separated from her family by adoption in 1924 and raised by Agnes Randle, an Alaskan teacher who started her daughter reading and writing at an early age. Through the years Randle had lost touch with her parents, but searched for them until she located her eighty-six-year-old father, over fifty years after their separation. He was retired from the air force and living in Arizona and spent his last two years with her before he passed away at the age of 88.

In 1970 Tall Mountain began writing under the tutelage of author and friend Paula Gunn Allen, who, along with Agnes Randle, became one of her mentors. "These two women taught and advised me."

A long-time resident of San Francisco, and now living in Petaluma, California, Tall Mountain writes about people, animals and the environment. She has published several books of her poetry and has appeared in numerous anthologies and periodicals such as *Animals Agenda, Alaska Quarterly, Poetry Northwest, Shantih: Na-*tive American Issue, Pacific Vision,* the *Wicazo Sa Review,* the *Wooster Review, Sunbury* and *Mountain View Digest.* Her book of poetry *There Is No Word for Goodbye* won a Pushcart Prize in 1981, and since November 1970 she has written a column entitled "Meditations for Wayfarers" for the journal *Way of St. Francis,* a Catholic Franciscan publication. She has also appeared on the Bill Moyers poetry series, *Power of the Word.*

Tall Mountain enjoys the works of many writers, such as Dylan Thomas, Walker Percy, Emily Dickinson, Thackeray, Louise Erdrich and Hawthorne. Though retired, she is working on one long-term and two or three short term projects, and she enjoys reading "to myself and in company."

NAME   E, P
Luci Tapahonso

TRIBAL AFFILIATION
Navajo

PERSONAL
Born: 1951, another source says 1953
Education: Bachelors degree from the University of New Mexico, Albuquerque; graduate coursework at the University of New Mexico, Albuquerque

PUBLICATION HIGHLIGHTS
Navajo ABC: A Dine Alphabet Book, Eleanor Schick and Luci Tapahonso (New York: Simon & Schuster, 1995)

This Is How They Were Placed for Us: A Poem, Lucy Tapahonso, ed. by Gloria V. Hickok ([S.l.]: Helicon Nine Editions, 1994)

Saanii Dah Hataal (The Women Are Singing) (Tucson: University of Arizona Press, 1993)

A Breeze Swept Through (Albuquerque: West End Press, c1987)
Seasonal Woman (Corrales, N. Mex.: Tooth of Time Books, 1982)
One More Shiprock Night: Poems and Stories (Corrales, N. Mex.: Tooth of Time Books, 1982)

Tapahonso's works have also appeared in the following anthologies:

Returning the Gift: Poetry and Prose from the First North American Native Writers' Festival, ed. by Joseph Bruchac with the support of the Association for the Study of American Indian Literatures (Tucson: University of Arizona, 1994)
A Gathering of Spirit: A Collection by North American Indian Women, ed. by Beth Brant (Degonwadonti) (Ithaca, N.Y.: Firebrand Books, 1988, c1984)
Survival This Way: Interviews with Native American Poets, by Joseph Bruchac (Tucson: Sun Tracks; University of Arizona Press, 1987)
Earth Power Coming: Short Fiction in Native American Literature, ed. by Simon J. Ortiz (Tsaile, Ariz.: Navajo Community College Press, c1983)
The Remembered Earth: An Anthology of Contemporary Native American Literature, ed. by Geary Hobson (Albuquerque: Red Earth Press, 1979)

NARRATIVE

Born and raised in Shiprock, New Mexico, Tapahonso was one of eleven children who spoke Navajo as their first language and who were raised in the traditional Navajo ways. Tapahonso learned English as her second language from her parents before she started attending school at the Navajo Methodist Mission in Farmington, New Mexico. After college Tapahonso joined the faculty of the University of New Mexico, where she became an assistant professor of English, women's studies and American Indian studies.

Currently Tapahonso is an assistant professor of English at the University of Kansas at Lawrence. Her husband, Bob Martin, is the president of the Haskell Indian Junior College, also in Lawrence. They have two daughters.

NAME F, J, N, PL
Drew Hayden Taylor

TRIBAL AFFILIATION
Ojibway

PERSONAL
Born: July 1, 1962, in Curve Lake, Ontario, Canada
Education: Honors diploma in radio/television broadcasting

AWARDS, HONORS
Canadian Authors Association Literary Award for Best Drama for the play *The Bootlegger Blues;* Chalmer's Canadian Play Award Best Play for Young Audiences for the play *Toronto at Dreamers Rock*

PUBLICATION HIGHLIGHTS
Someday: A Play (Saskatoon, Sask.: Fifth House, 1993)
Voices: Being Native in Canada, D. H. Taylor and L. Jaine (Saskatoon, Sask.: University of Saskatchewan, 1992)
The Bootlegger Blues: A Play (Saskatoon, Sask.: Fifth House, 1991)
"Pretty Like a White Boy," essay in *This Magazine* (Toronto: Red Maple, August 1991)
Toronto at Dreamers Rock and Education Is Our Right, Two One-act Plays (Saskatoon, Sask.: Fifth House Pub., 1990)
"Someday," short story in *Globe and Mail* (Toronto: Globe and Mail, Division of Canadian Newspapers, December 24, 1990)

Taylor's works also appear in: *Returning the Gift: Poetry and Prose from the First North American Native Writers' Festival*, ed. by Joseph Bruchac with the support of the Association for the Study of American Indian Literatures (Tucson: University of Arizona, 1994).

NARRATIVE

Drew Hayden Taylor grew up on the Curve Lake Reserve, where he lived with his mother until he reached the age of 18. "Even though I have lived in the city for the past twelve years, most of my stories take place on the reserve." As a child in school, Taylor was shy and hated writing, until he discovered the library. "And I haven't turned back since."

Tayor is also active in film documentary production as an editor and consultant/researcher, and he is also a facilitator in writing, performing arts, film and video and scriptwriting workshops. In 1988, Taylor helped coordinate and facilitate the Native ballet, *In the Land of Spirits*, produced by John Kim Bell, with the Canadian Native Arts Foundation. He has sat on various juries for the Gemini Awards and the Ontario Arts Council, and he has delivered a paper in Italy on Native theater in Canada, sponsored by New York University and the Rockefeller Foundation.

He enjoys the works of writers Tomson Highway "since he has broken the ground and laid the path for Native playwrights. I also enjoy Anne Rice, Kurt Vonnegut, Stephen King, H. G. Wells." Taylor is now working on four plays, two or three possible books, a number of short stories and a made-for-television movie. He writes full-time and often works as a scriptwriting workshop leader and facilitator.

NAME P

Earle Thompson

TRIBAL AFFILIATION

Yakima

PERSONAL

Born: March 15, 1950, in Nespelem, Washington

AWARDS, HONORS

Bumbershoot Literary Arts Festival Award for Writing Arts for *The Juniper Moon Pulls at My Bones*, Seattle, Washington, 1985

PUBLICATION HIGHLIGHTS

The Juniper Moon Pulls at My Bones, poems (Marvin, S. Dak.: Blue Cloud Quarterly, 1985; published as the *Quarterly's* publication vol. 32, no. 2)

Thompson's works have appeared in these anthologies:

Returning the Gift: Poetry and Prose from the First North American Native Writers' Festival, ed. by Joseph Bruchac with the support of the Association for the Study of American Indian Literatures (Tucson: University of Arizona, 1994)

Dancing on the Rim of the World: An Anthology of Contemporary Northwest Native American Writing, ed. by Andrea Lerner (Tucson: Sun Tracks; University of Arizona Press, 1990)

Harper's Anthology of Twentieth-Century Native American Poetry, first edition (San Francisco: Harper & Row, 1988)

Songs from This Earth on Turtle's Back, first edition, ed. by Joseph Bruchac (Greenfield Center, N.Y.: Greenfield Review Press, 1983)

Anthology of Third World Writing (Youngstown, Ohio: Pig Iron Press, [n.d.])

NARRATIVE

Thompson was raised on the Yakima Indian Reservation and was close to his grandfather during his youth. Thompson's works reflect the oral traditions he learned from his elders.

His works have been published in several journals, such as the *Pacific Review, Contact II,* the *Wooster Review, Wicazo Sa Review, Poetry East* and the *Greenfield Review,* among many others.

NAME   E, P, PL, S

Dorothy Thorsen

OTHER NAMES USED

Serena Lee

TRIBAL AFFILIATION

Metis

PERSONAL

Born: October 6, 1946, in Saskatoon, Saskatchewan

Education: Masters degree in business education from the University of Alaska

AWARDS, HONORS

Advanced Arts Award from the Yukon Territorial Government, 1992; Canada Council Explorations Program, 1992

PUBLICATION HIGHLIGHTS

"Eagle," "Sunrise," "Voices," poems in *Shakat Journal* ([S.l.: s.n.], Summer 1990)

"The Party of Despair," poem in *Dannzha* (Whitehorse, Yukon: Ye Sa To Communications Society, August/September 1990)

"Nightmare," poem in *Dannzha* (Whitehorse, Yukon: Ye Sa To Communications Society, October/November 1990)

"In Memory—A Tribute to Archie Charlie," *Dannzha* (Whitehorse, Yukon: Ye Sa To Communications Society, April/May 1990)

NARRATIVE

Raised by a poor Irish family in the town of Prince Albert, Dorothy Thorsen spent time as a child with a neighbor named Grandma Spencer, who taught her Cree stories and legends. While in school Thorsen received a recognition award as a public speaker. She raised a family of four daughters while moving throughout Canada and working a variety of occupations: in a meat market, shoe store and ten years in the banking business. Raised to identify herself as a non-Native, a turning point in her life was finding her Cree birth family. For the past twenty years, she has been living in the Yukon, writing and working in a group named the Women's Refuge Theatre Collective. She is also a lecturer and teacher in the areas of race relations, cross-cultural communications, and participates in volunteer services for her community and territory. An early mentor in Thorsen's career was Audry McLaughlin, member of Parliament for the Yukon and national leader of the New Democratic Party, who provided her with a great deal of encouragement and support. Writers Thorsen enjoys include Maria Campbell, Lee Maracle, Chrystos, Beth Brant and Bernie Culleton. Thorsen is working on several long-term projects, including an autobiography in the form of letters to a younger woman, a story about a give-away child looking for her family and her identity and a story about the mainstream invasion of northern Canada over the past fifty years.

NAME   E, M, N, P

Laura Tohe

TRIBAL AFFILIATION

Navajo

PERSONAL

Born: October 5, 1952, at Fort Defiance, Arizona

Education: B.A. in psychology from the University of New Mexico, Albuquerque, 1975; M.A. in English from the University of Nebraska, Lincoln, 1985; Ph.D. in English from University of Nebraska, Lincoln, 1993

AWARDS, HONORS

University of Nebraska Minority Fellowship, 1990–1991; Prize winner for poetry from the *Blue Mesa Review,* University of New Mexico, 1990; Outstanding Young Woman of America, 1980; Tohe has also received several assistantships and regents tuition fellowships.

PUBLICATION HIGHLIGHTS

"Joe Babes" in *Callaloo,* January 1994

"The Sacrament," poem in *Platte Valley Review* (Kearney, Nebr.: Kearney State College, vol. 19, no. 1, 1991)

"Restoring the Creative Voice Through Landscape," essay in *Nebraska Humanities* ([S.l.: s.n.], vol. 1, no. 1, 1991)

"Body Identified," poem in *Blue Mesa Review* ([S.l.: s.n.], no. 2, 1990)

Making Friends with Water, poems (Omaha, Nebr.: Nosila Press, 1986)

"Woolworths," poem in *Wanbli Ho/Eagle Voice* (Mission, S. Dak.: Sinte Gleska College, 1986)

Tohe's works have also appeared in *Returning the Gift: Poetry and Prose from the First North American Native Writers' Festival,* ed. by Joseph Bruchac with the support of the Association for the Study of American Indian Literatures (Tucson: University of Arizona, 1994) and *Braided Lives: An Anthology of Multicultural American Writing,* by the Minnesota Humanities Commission and the Minnesota Council of Teachers of English (St. Paul: The Commission, 1991).

NARRATIVE

Laura Tohe was raised in Arizona and New Mexico on the Navajo Reservation. In first grade Tohe was one of the few Navajo students who was bilingual, so she interpreted for the other Navajo students in her classes who didn't speak English. "Mostly I felt that things were being taken away from us and what was given in its place felt foreign and uncomfortable."

Tohe had always loved books and reading. "At some point in my childhood I had thought of becoming a writer, but I don't know where I got that idea, perhaps from my love of reading, or because my family didn't own a TV and we lived in an isolated community where our only link to the outside world was a dirt road and books."

Tohe's endeavors as a writer were supported by several people. "Rudy Anaya and Simon Ortiz encouraged and supported my first attempts at writing. My family, especially my mother, always told me stories as a child which I have used in my writing. The oral culture of the Navajo also played an important role. The major influence in my writing would have to be Rudy Anaya's class. Rudy Anaya encouraged my writing when I enrolled in his creative writing class. He had faith in my writing and supported my early attempt at storytelling. Luci Tapahonso, who was also a beginning writer when I was, encouraged and supported by work. Simon Ortiz's instruction and guidance, and his work influenced me as well. ... When I first began writing I read many of the Native writers from the Southwest. Leslie Silko's work as well as Simon Ortiz influenced my work. I tried to imitate them. The writers that I read are always influencing my work. Some of these are

Pablo Neruda, Joy Harjo, Sharon Olds, Louise Erdrich and Sandra Cisneros."

"Being part of the Southwest landscape, in particular the Navajo Reservation, has also influenced me as it still does. Belonging to a place continues to influence and inform much of my writing. This Nebraska landscape is foreign to me even after ten years. Mostly my writing comes out of the Southwest landscape, the people, the culture and the stories. I feel separated from the center of my familiar existence. Writing is a way for me to connect to my home, my center."

Tohe enjoys participating in many activities, among them traveling, music, watching movies. "I love to see movies." She also participates in physical activities, sports, aerobics and body sculpting. She is currently a member of the English department at the University of Arizona.

NAME   P
James Tollerud

OTHER NAMES USED
Jim Tollerud

TRIBAL AFFILIATION
Makah

PERSONAL
Born: 1954 in Port Angeles, Washington

PUBLICATION HIGHLIGHTS
Tollerud's works have appeared in the following anthologies: *The Remembered Earth: An Anthology of Contemporary Native American Literature,* ed. by Geary Hobson (Albuquerque: Red Earth Press, 1979); *Voices of the Rainbow: Contemporary Poetry by American Indians,* ed. by Kenneth Rosen (New York: Viking,

1975); *The First Skin Around Me: Contemporary American Tribal Poetry,* ed. by James L. White (Moorehead, Minn.: Territorial Press, 1976)

NARRATIVE
His works have also appeared in *Akwesasne Notes, Quetzal* and *Seattle Indian News.*

NAME   E, L, N
Haunani-Kay Trask

TRIBAL AFFILIATION
Hawaiian

PERSONAL
Born: October 3, 1949, in San Francisco, California

Education: B.A. in political science, University of Wisconsin, Madison; M.A. in political science, University of Wisconsin, Madison; Ph.D. in political science, University of Wisconsin, Madison

PUBLICATION HIGHLIGHTS
Eros and Power: The Promise of Feminist Theory (Philadelphia: University of Pennsylvania Press, c1986)

Fighting the Battle of Double Colonization: The View of a Hawaiian Feminist (East Lansing, Mich.: [Office of Women in International Development], c1984)

Hawaiian Sovereignty and Self Determination, videorecording, by U. H. Manoa, H. Trask et al. (Honolulu: Native Hawaiian Sovereignty Conference, 1988)

Hawaiians, American Colonization, and the Quest for Independence ([S.l.: s.n.], 1984)

Hawaiians, Self-determination and Ethno Development, by Haunani-Kay Trask and Mililani B. Trask ([S.l: s.n.],1988)

Hawaiians, the United Nations, and Human Rights ([S.l.: s.n.], 1984)

The Native Hawaiians Study Commission Report ([Honolulu: s.n.], 1982)
Native Nationalism: The Struggle for Hawaiian Independence ([S.l.: s.n., 1985])
The Question of Archaeological Privacy, videorecording (Honolulu: KHET, 1983)
Seminar of Hawaiian Sovereignty, videorecording ([Honolulu]: Na Maka o ka Aina, 1988)
A Talk with Haunani Kay Trask, audio recording (Arlington, Va.: Mutual Broadcasting System, 1986)

NARRATIVE

Haunani-Kay Trask was raised in Hawaii. She is Haunaniokawekiuo Haleakala, descendant of the Pi'ilani line of Maui and the Kahakumakaliua line of Kaua'i.

"I attended an all-Hawaiian high school and so was surrounded by my own Native people."

Her writings reflect her interest in Native politics, Native land, tourism, Native sovereignty and Native collaboration with colonization. Trask considers her best works to be her long poems on Hawai'i. She enjoys the works of writers "Linda Hogan, Joy Harjo, Leslie Silko, Kerek Walcott, Eugenio Montale, Adrienne Rich, Gail Tremblay, Tess Gallagher, Antonio Machado, Pablo Neruda, Garcia Lorca, Audre Lorde and many, many more." Trask is now a professor of Hawaiian Studies at the University of Hawai'i-Manoa, Honolulu. Her works have also appeared in the journals *Bamboo Rider: The Hawaii Writers' Quarterly, Hawaii Review* and *Literary Arts Hawaii: A Publication of the Hawaii Literary Arts Council,* among others.

NAME   P

Gail Tremblay

TRIBAL AFFILIATION

Onondaga and Micmac

PERSONAL

Born: December 15, 1945, in Buffalo, New York
Education: B.A. in drama, University of New Hampshire, 1967; M.F.A. in English, University of Oregon, 1969

AWARDS, HONORS

Alfred E. Richards Poetry Prize, 1967

PUBLICATION HIGHLIGHTS

Night Gives Woman the Word, R. Hickman, G. Tremblay (Omaha, Nebr.: [Omaha Printing], 1979)

Tremblay's works have appeared in the following anthologies:

Returning the Gift: Poetry and Prose from the First North American Native Writers' Festival, ed. by Joseph Bruchac with the support of the Association for the Study of American Indian Literatures (Tucson: University of Arizona, 1994)
Indian Singing in 20th-Century America (Corvallis, Oreg.: Calyx Press, 1990)
New Voices from the Longhouse: An Anthology of Contemporary Iroquois Writing, ed. by Joseph Bruchac (Greenfield, N.Y.: Greenfield Review Press, 1990)
Harper's Anthology of Twentieth-Century Native American Poetry (New York: Harper & Row, 1989)
Close to Home: Poems, by G. Tremblay et. al. ([Omaha]: University of Nebraska at Omaha Creative Writing Program, 1981)

NARRATIVE

Pauline Johnson is a person who has inspired Tremblay and moved her to write. One of Tremblay's most treasured memories is of her grandfather giving her a copy of a book by Pauline Johnson to show her that Indians could write. The inspiration she found in Johnson's words moved her to try writing herself. Tom Williams, John Haislip and Dick Hugo to those of N. Scott Momaday and Duane Niatum also stimulated her creative works. "Living on this confused planet and growing up in a world where Native traditions are important and endangered has influenced my writing."

Tremblay was raised in New York, New Hampshire and Maine. She enjoys the works of Joy Harjo, Luille Clifton, N. Scott Momaday and Simon Ortiz. Of her own work she considers her poems in *Indian Singing in the 20th Century* to be her strongest works because they reflect a mature voice and style. Tremblay is currently at work on a volume of poetry.

❖❖❖

NAME A, E, L, N, M, P, S, VA
Lincoln Tritt

TRIBAL AFFILIATION
Gwich'in Athabaskan

PERSONAL
Born: October 18, 1946, in Salmon River, Alaska
Education: Coursework at the University of Alaska at Fairbanks

PUBLICATION HIGHLIGHTS
Tritt's works have appeared in: *Raven Tells Stories: An Anthology of Alaskan Native Writing,* ed. by Joseph Bruchac (Greenfield Center, N.Y.: Greenfield Review Press, 1991).

NARRATIVE
Tritt was the son of a minister and spent part of his childhood in Arctic Village, "where people at that time still spent a lot of the time in the forest." He also spent much of this childhood in Ft. Yukon, Alaska. "At 13 I was sent to boarding school for the next six years." He later spent three and a half years serving in the U.S. Navy with a tour in Southeast Asia. He was discharged at the age of 23 and moved back to Arctic Village.

Tritt writes about Native history and values and their relationship to today's world. He is currently translating his grandfather's and father's journals into English, as he explains: "My grandfather and father kept a journal that dates back to 1880. In our area that is practically back to before and during the contact period with the whites." He adds that he may begin writing his own journal after the translating is done "to ultimately bring the whole thing into perspective, so people today can understand what happened to the human race." Tritt enjoys reading the works of John D. McDonald because of his "ability to make stories come alive" and more recently Richard Bach, because of his "observations that most people tend to miss."

Tritt is also active as a lecturer and writes articles for his local newspaper's weekly magazine. In 1992 Tritt recorded a sound cassette titled *Oil Development of Sacred Ground,* which was part of the University Lecture Series at Iowa State University.

❖❖❖

NAME F, J, N, P, PA, PL
Ed Donald Two-Rivers Broeffle

OTHER NAMES USED
Ed Two-Rivers

TRIBAL AFFILIATION
Seine River Band of Ojibwa of Ontario—Treaty #3

PERSONAL

Born: June 29, 1945, in Emo, Ontario, Canada

Education: One and one-half years of college

AWARDS, HONORS

Iron Eyes Cody Peace Medal, 1991

PUBLICATION HIGHLIGHTS

A Dozen Cold Ones, poems (Chicago: March/ABRAZO Press, 1992)

"I Ain't No Tonto," poem in *In the Company of Poets Magazine* (Oakland, Calif.: JACAL Publications, 1991)

"Queen of Scriptures," poem in *Howling Dog* (Detroit: Parkville Publishers, 1991)

A Symbol of Hope (Chicago: *AIM,* vol. 16, no. 2, 1989)

NARRATIVE

Two-Rivers Broeffle was raised in the Atikokan, Ontario, vicinity and later moved to Chicago when he was sixteen years old. While he was growing up Two-Rivers Broeffle was close to his step-father and later, while serving a prison sentence as a young man, met an individual who helped him refocus his energies, writer and prison GED instructor Paul Crump, author of *Burn Killer, Burn.* "A prison sentence turned me around as a writer. I began writing poetry there." Two-Rivers Broeffle writes about Native Americans, homelessness and the environment. "I write about Indians in an urban setting." He considers his best work to be a play titled *Act Dead—Indian,* because, he says, "humor is the best way to get some messages across." Two-Rivers Broeffle is now working on a collection of short stories, a book of poetry and three plays. He is also teaching a course called "Writing from the Source." He works as a machinist and enjoys cooking and working with automobiles.

U

NAME   F, N

Paula Underwood

OTHER NAMES USED

Paula Underwood Spencer
Turtle Woman Singing

TRIBAL AFFILIATION

Iroquois

PERSONAL

Born: 1930
Education: Masters degree from George
Washington University, Washington,
D.C.

PUBLICATION HIGHLIGHTS

*The Walking People: A Native American Oral
History,* first edition (San Anselmo, Ca-
lif.: Sausalito, Calif.: Tribe of Two Press;
Institute of Noetic Sciences, 1993)
*Who Speaks for Wolf: A Native American
Learning Story,* second edition (San
Anselmo, Calif.: Tribe of Two Press, 1991)

*Three Strands in the Braid: A Guide for
Enablers of Learning,* second edition (San
Anselmo, Calif.: Tribe of Two Press, 1991)
*Who Speaks for Wolf: A Native American Learn-
ing Story as Told to Turtle Woman Singing by
Her Father, Sharp-eyed Hawk,* first edition
(Austin, Tex.: Tribe of Two Press, 1983)

NARRATIVE

Paula Underwood is of Iroquois, Irish,
English and Welsh descent. Her first career was in government and international
affairs. After earning her masters degree
from George Washington University, she
worked for the Senate Foreign Relations
Subcommittee on Disarmament and was
a Foreign Affairs Assistant to House Foreign Affairs Committee member Robert
R. Barry during the early 1960s.
Underwood later worked for twelve years
at the Overseas Education Fund, acting
as the president of the Fund's Asian Program for a portion of her tenure.
Underwood now writes the stories that
she learned from her father and his elders.

V

NAME   F, N, P
Alma Luz Villanueva

TRIBAL AFFILIATION
Yaqui

PERSONAL
Born: October 4, 1944, in Lompoc, California

Education: Coursework from Norwich University; M.F.A. from Vermont College, 1984

AWARDS, HONORS
American Book Award for *The Ultraviolet Sky*, 1989; Third Chicano Literary Prize, University of California, Irvine, first prize for *Poems*, 1977

PUBLICATION HIGHLIGHTS
Naked Ladies (Tempe, Ariz.: Bilingual Press/Editoriale Bilingue, 1994)

Weeping Woman: La Llorona and Other Stories (Tempe, Ariz.: Bilingual Press, 1994)

Golden Glass (Binghamton, N.Y.: State University of New York at Binghamton, Graduate School, 1981, 1993)

Planet, with Mother May I? (Tempe, Ariz.: Bilingual Press/Editoriale Bilingue, 1993)

The Ultraviolet Sky (Tempe, Ariz.: Bilingual Review/Press, 1988)

La Chingada (Tempe, Ariz.: Bilingual Review/Press, 1985)

Life Span (Austin, Texas: Place of Herons Press, 1984)

Mother, May I? (Pittsburgh, Penn.: Motheroot Publications, 1978)

Bloodroot (Austin, Tex.: Place of Herons Press, 1977)

Villanueva's works have also appeared in numerous anthologies:

She Rises Like the Sun (Freedom, Calif.: Crossing Press, 1989)

Quarry West (Santa Cruz, Calif.: University of California Press, 1989)

Contemporary Chicana Poetry: A Critical Approach to an Emerging Literature (Berkeley: University of California Press, 1985)

Women Poets of the World (New York: Macmillan, 1983)

Stanford's Women Writing Poetry in America (Stanford, Calif.: Stanford University Press, 1982)

I Sing a Song to Myself, ed. by David Kherdian (New York: Morrow, 1978)

The Next World, ed. by Joseph Bruchac (Freedom, Calif.: Crossing Press, 1978)

NARRATIVE
A poet and novelist, Villanueva has also written juvenile literature and short stories for numerous journals, such as *Somos, Ms.* and *American Poetry Review*. Villanueva's works have been taped by the New Radio and Performing Arts in New York City and by the Poetry Center at San Francisco State University as part of their Poetry archives series. She has three children.

NAME   E, F, N, P
Gerald Robert Vizenor

TRIBAL AFFILIATION
Chippewa

PERSONAL
Born: October 22, 1934, in Minneapolis, Minnesota

Education:
Coursework at New York University, 1955 to 1956
B.A. from the University of Minnesota, 1960
Graduate coursework from the University of Minnesota, 1962–1965
Graduate coursework at Harvard University

PUBLICATION HIGHLIGHTS

Empty Savings (Nodin Press, [n.d.])

Interior Landscapes: Autobiographical Myths and Metaphors (Minneapolis: University of Minnesota Press, c1995)

Native American Literature: A Brief Introduction and Anthology (New York: HarperCollins, 1995)

Dead Voices: Natural Agonies in the New World, first paperback edition (Norman: University of Oklahoma Press, 1994)

Shadow Distance: A Gerald Vizenor Reader (Hanover, N.H.: University Press of New England for Weslyan University Press, 1994)

Touchwood: A Collection of Ojibway Prose, ed. by Gerald Vizenor (Minneapolis: New Rivers Press, 1994)

Manifest Manners: Postindian Warriors of Survivance (Hanover: University Press of New England, 1994)

Anishinaabe Lyric Poems and Stories, new edition (Norman: University of Oklahoma, 1993)

Narrative Chance: Postmodern Discourse on Native American Indian Literatures, ed. by Gerald Vizenor (Norman: University of Oklahoma, 1993)

Summer in the Spring: Anishinaabe Lyric Poems and Stories, ed. by Gerald Vizenor (Norman: University of Oklahoma, 1993)

Heirs of Columbus (Middletown, Conn.: Wesleyan University Press: Hanover, N.H.: University Press of New England, c1991)

Landfill Meditation: Crossblood Stories (Hanover, N.H.: University Press of New England, 1991)

Bearheart: The Heirship Chronicles (Minneapolis: University of Minnesota Press, c1990), previously published as *Darkness in Saint Louis Bearheart*

Crossbloods: Bone Cours, Bingo, and Other Reports (Minneapolis: University of Minnesota Press, 1990)

The Trickster of Liberty: Tribal Heirs to a Wild Baronage (Minneapolis: University of Minnesota Press, 1988)

Darkness in Saint Louis Bearheart ([S.l.]: Truck Press, 1973), later published as *Bearheart: The Heirship Chronicles*

Griever: An American Monkey King in China (Normal: Illinois State University; Fiction Collective, 1987)

Matsushima: Pine Islands (Minneapolis: Nodin, 1984)

Earthdivers: Tribal Narratives on Mixed Descent (Minneapolis: University of Minnesota Press, 1984)

The People Named the Chippewa: Narrative Histories (Minneapolis: University of Minnesota Press, 1984)

Earthdrivers: Tribal Narratives on Mixed Descent (Minneapolis: University of Minnesota Press, 1981)

Summer in the Spring: Ojibwa Songs and Stories (Minneapolis: Nodin, 1981)

Wordarrows: Indians and Whites in the New Fur Trade (Minneapolis: University of Minnesota Press, 1978)

Anishinabe Nagomon: Songs of the Ojibwa (Minneapolis: Nodin, 1974)

Anishinabe Adisokan: Stories of the Ojibwa (Minneapolis: Nodin, 1974)

The Everlasting Sky (New York: Crowell, 1972)

Thomas James White Hawk (New York: Four Winds, 1968)

Seveneen Chirps (Minneapolis: Nodin, 1967)

Raising the Moon Vines: Original Haiku in English (Minneapolis: Callimachus, 1964)

South of the Painted Stone ([S.l.]: Obercraft, 1963)

The Old Park Sleepers ([S.l.]: Obercraft, 1961)

Empty Swings (Minneapolis: Nodin Press, n.d.)

Vizenor's works have also appeared in many anthologies:

The Lightning Within: An Anthology of Contemporary American Indian Fiction, ed. by Alan Velie (Lincoln: University of Nebraska Press, 1991)

I Tell You Now: Autobiographical Essays by Native American Writers, ed. by Brian Swann and Arnold Krupat (Lincoln: University of Nebraska Press, c1987)

The Sacred Hoop: Recovering the Feminine in American Indian Traditions, by Paula Gunn Allen (Boston: Beacon Press, 1986)

Earth Power Coming: Short Fiction in Native American Literature, ed. by Simon J. Ortiz (Tsaile, Ariz.: Navajo Community College Press, c1983)

Four American Indian Literary Masters, by A. R. (Alan) Velie (Norman: University of Oklahoma Press, 1982)

NARRATIVE

Vizenor is of French and Chippewa descent. Vizenor was a youth when his father was murdered, and the criminal responsible was never found. As a young man he joined the Minnesota National Guard and later the U.S. Army, where he served in Japan from 1952 until 1955. While he attended the University of Minnesota, Vizenor was a group worker for the Ramsey County Corrections Authority in St. Paul until 1958. He was also employed as a corrections agent for the Minnesota State Reformatory in St. Cloud until 1961. Changing directions, Vizenor next joined the *Minneapolis Tribune* newspaper as a staff writer until 1970, then switched careers and became a teacher trainer at the Park Rapids Public Schools in Park Rapids, Minnesota. Between the years 1971 to 1973 Vizenor worked as an instructor at Lake Forest College in Lake

Forest, Illinois, and at Bemidji State University in Bemidji, Minnesota.

Vizenor moved to California, where he worked as a lecturer for the University of California at Berkeley from 1976 to 1980. In 1980 be returned to the University of Minnesota in Minneapolis as a professor of American Indian studies. He also worked at the University of Oklahoma during the 1990–1991 academic year. Back in California since 1991, he is currently a professor of Native American studies at the University of California at Berkeley. Vizenor's poems and stories have been widely published in anthologies and collections and have appeared in publications, such as *American Studies, Chicago Review, American Indian Quarterly, Boundary2.*

NAME
E, F, N, P, PL

Judith Mountain Leaf Volborth

TRIBAL AFFILIATION
Blackfoot/Comanche

PERSONAL

Born: October 23, 1950, in New York City
Education: Coursework at Pierce College and University of California at Los Angeles

AWARDS, HONORS

The Carol Elzer Prize for Poetry, 1986
The Ina Coolbrith Memorial Prize, 1985
May Merrill Miller Award for Poetry, 1985
Academy of American Poets Award, 1984
Shirle Dorothy Robbins Creative Writing Award, 1977

PUBLICATION HIGHLIGHTS

"Self-portrait," "Vihio Images," "A Time of Turquoise" and other poems in *That's*

What She Said: Contemporary Poetry and Fiction by Native American Women, ed. by Rayna Green (Bloomington, Ind.: Indiana University Press, 1984); *Thunder-root: Traditional and Contemporary Native American Verse* (Los Angeles: American Indian Studies Center, University of California, 1978) Native American Series

NARRATIVE

Volborth moved away from New York City when she turned 18. Her school years were difficult for her "… due to discrimination—I was denied the right to both a junior high school and high school education."

Volborth remembers she had always experienced the urge to create with words and images. "I do remember wanting to be an artist (oil painter) and writer since early childhood. I do look forward to some day being able to get back to painting." In her writing Volborth believes that "… writing is a heartseed, a giftseed where even the darkest part or deepest suffering is mingled with affirmation; it is a celebration of the Great Mystery. I spent many years growing up in a brutal institution for misplaced children. It was one of the darkest times of my life, but those years taught me to use the seeds of the 'word bundle' through writing. Writing or carrying a word bundle has helped me to reclaim and celebrate both a spiritual and a cultural dignity as well as to acknowledge and give thanks to ancestral roots, which both nourishes and pollinates my heart."

She has had many of her writings published in numerous anthologies and has worked as an instructor in art and music, and has also worked in social services and emergency medical care. When not writing Volborth teaches classes in American Indian studies, poetry, music, music appreciation, ethnic studies and mask making. She also works with mentally ill people, most of whom are homeless. She enjoys music, especially classical and Celtic, gardening and studying medicine, especially emergency medicine. Because of her interest in medicine and people Volborth became a certified emergency medical technician "and so I could help people more."

Volborth enjoys reading the works of Linda Hogan, Ann Cameron, Beth Brant, Jamaica Kincade, Roberta Hill Whiteman, Joseph Bruchac, Wendy Rose, Dylan Thomas, Yukio Mishima and Alice Walker, among many others. She is now working on four separate collections of poetry, which includes a collection of coyote poems, a collection of free verse, haiku and a collection of Lesbian erotica. Volborth is also working on a journal of hunger and homelessness titled *The Hunger Journal,* and is also involved in performance poetry.

Volborth has three children, Striperdy (Petey), Mousie and Raso Genet. "They are my close family of heartseeds." She is very close with Robin Cartwright Enwright, who, she says, "… has been a loving role model and inspiration to me, I am a very lucky person having so much love in my life!"

NAME   E, F, N, S
Anna Walters

OTHER NAMES USED
Anna Lee Walters

TRIBAL AFFILIATION
Pawnee and Otoe-Missouria

PERSONAL
Born: September 9, 1946, in Pawnee, Oklahoma

Education: B.A. in creative writing; M.F.A. in creative writing

PUBLICATION HIGHLIGHTS
Ghost Singer: A Novel (Flagstaff, Ariz.: Northland, 1994)

Neon Pow Wow: New Native American Voices of the Southwest, first edition, ed. by Anna Lee Walters (Flagstaff, Ariz.: Northland, 1993)

The Two-legged Creature: An Otoe Story, first edition (Flagstaff: Northland, 1993)

Talking Indian: Reflections on Survival and Writing (Ithaca, N.Y.: Firebrand Books, 1992)

The Sacred: Ways of Knowledge, Sources of Life, redesigned edition, by Anna Lee Walters, Peggy V. Beck, Nia Francisco (chapter 12) (Tsaile, Ariz.: Navajo Community College Press; Flagstaff: Northland, 1990, 1977)

The Spirit of Native America: Beauty and Mysticism in American Indian Art (San Francisco: Chronicle Books, 1989)

The Sun Is Not Merciful: Short Stories (Ithaca, N.Y.: Firebrand Books, 1985)

Haz Agii Botto Aah: The Learning of That Which Pertains to the Home, by Chester Hubbard, ed. by Anna L. Walters (Tsaile, Ariz.: Navajo Community College Press, 1977)

Navajo Weaving: From Spider Woman to Synthetic Rugs, ed. by Anna L. Walters (Tsaile, Ariz.: Navajo Community College Press, 1977)

Walter's works have also appeared in numerous anthologies:

Talking Leaves: Contemporary Native American Short Stories, An Anthology, ed. by Craig Lesley (New York: Laurel; Dell, 1991)

Spider Woman's Granddaughters: Traditional Tales and Contemporary Writing by Native American Women, ed. by Paula Gunn Allen (Boston: Beacon Press, 1989)

Coyote Was Here: Essays on Contemporary Native American Literary and Political Mobilization, ed. by Bo Scholer (Aarhaus, Denmark: SEKLOS, 1984)

Earth Power Coming: Short Fiction in Native American Literature, ed. by Simon J. Ortiz (Tsaile, Ariz.: Navajo Community College Press, 1983)

The Remembered Earth: An Anthology of Contemporary Native American Literature, ed. by Geary Hobson (Albuquerque: Red Earth Press, 1979)

The Third Woman, ed. by D. Fisher (Boston: Houghton & Mifflin, 1978)

Warriors of the Rainbow, ed. by K. Rosen (New York: Viking Press, 1975)

Voices of the Rainbow: Contemporary Poetry by American Indians, ed. by Kenneth Rosen (New York: Viking Press, 1975)

The Man to Send Rainclouds: Contemporary Stories by American Indians, ed. by K. Rosen (New York: Viking Press, 1974)

NARRATIVE

Anna Walters was raised by her grandparents until she reached school age, when she went to live with her parents. Walters is the oldest of three sisters. Her childhood memories are filled with fond remembrances of her grandparents, all of whom she was close to while growing up in Oklahoma, and she was also quite close to her mother. When Walters and her sisters were around the ages of 7 or 8 they were placed in a government boarding school for two years. Walters later attended public schools from grades 5 through 11. At the age of 16 her family left Oklahoma and moved to Santa Fe, New Mexico, where she completed her high school education at the Institute of American Indian Arts. While a student at the Institute, Walters met and married a fellow student, museum curator and Navajo artist Harry Walters (Na-ton-sa-ka). They have two sons.

Walters has worked at the Institute of American Indian Arts in Santa Fe, New Mexico, and was a library technician between the years 1968–1974. She worked as a technical writer in 1975 at the Dineh Cooperatives in Chinle, Arizona, and joined the faculty of the Navajo Community College in Tsaile, Arizona, as an instructor. At the same institution she became the director of the Navajo Community College Press and worked as a technical writer for curriculum development. She is currently an instructor at the Navajo Community College and lectures on the subjects of contemporary American Indian life and American Indian literature, among many other topics.

Walters writes about the Native American experience, and two of her favorite works are *The Sun Is Not Merciful* and *Talking Indian* "for many reasons, too many to list here." Her work is represented in more than forty-five publications in the United States and Europe, including anthologies, scholarly journals, periodicals and news magazines, such as *American Indian Historian, Shantih* and *Chouteau Review.* In addressing her writing and the creative process, Walters says, "I have been involved in several kinds of writing. I find I am more inclined to be a creative writer than a technical writer. I write daily and do not wait for 'inspiration,' although it, of course, adds significantly to the content of material when 'inspiration' is there. I write about things I know, people I know. I write because of my need to write. It is my 'true love.'" (*Contemporary Authors* vol. 73–76 [Detroit: Gale, 1991])

Walters also enjoys painting and visual arts in addition to writing: "I like to paint as well as write. Both allow consistent examination and evaluation of oneself. In all the world, only this is important. But I cannot speak for anyone else, only myself." (*Contemporary Authors* vol. 73–76 [Detroit: Gale, 1991])

NAME P

Vincent Wannassay

TRIBAL AFFILIATION

Umatilla

PERSONAL

Born: Pendleton, Oregon
Education: Associate of Fine Arts degree from the Institute of American Indian Arts, Santa Fe, New Mexico; B.A. from the College of Santa Fe, Santa Fe, New Mexico

PUBLICATION HIGHLIGHTS

Wannassay's works have appeared in: *Dancing on the Rim of the World: An Anthology of Contemporary Northwest Native*

American Writing, ed. by Andrea Lerner (Tucson: Sun Tracks; University of Arizona Press, c1990); *Rolling Thunder: Voice of the People* (Santa Fe: Institute of American Indian Arts, Press, [n.d.]) and *Northwest Native American Writers* ([S.l.]: Firecreek Press, [n.d.]).

NARRATIVE

While a student at the Institute, Wannassay studied under writer Joy Harjo and worked as an editor for the school paper, *Spearhead Press.* Wannassay was one of the founding members of the Northwest Native Writers Group. He now lives in Oregon.

❖❖❖

NAME   F, P, S

Emma Lee Warrior

OTHER NAMES USED

Ipisowahs ("Ipisowahs name means wet hanging jerky, or more precisely, meat stripped from buffalo legs that is grisly and will make jerky that is thick and chewy, suitable for taking on long journeys, also the name of the Sun and Moons son, commonly referred to as the Morning Star.")

TRIBAL AFFILIATION

Peigan

PERSONAL

Born: January 10, 1941, on Peigan Reserve, Alberta, Canada

Education:

Bachelor of education, University of Calgary, Alberta

Masters degree in English and creative writing, University of Washington, Seattle, Washington

Master of education in guidance and counseling, Heritage College, Toppenish, Washington

AWARDS, HONORS

Invitation to Native Writers Festival, Duck Lake, Saskatchewan 1992; Invitation to Returning the Gift Conference, Norman, Oklahoma, 1992

PUBLICATION HIGHLIGHTS

"How I Came to Have a Man's Name," "Reginald Pugh, the Man Who Came from the Army," "The Enemy's Eyes," "New Indian Medicine," poems in *Wicaza Sa Review* (Cheney, Wash.: Indian Studies, Eastern Washington University, vol. 1, no. 2, Fall 1985); "Compatriots," short story in *Canadian Native Literature in English* (Don Mills, Ont.: Oxford University Press, Canada, [n.d.])

Warrior's poems have also appeared in *Harper's Anthology of Twentieth-Century Native American Poetry,* first edition, ed. by Duane Niatum (San Francisco: Harper & Row, 1988)

NARRATIVE

Emma Lee Warrior was born and raised in Brocket, Alberta, Canada, on the Peigan Reserve, and spent ten years in the Reserve's boarding school as a child. As she remembers, her school years were sad ones. "I suppose the main thing that happened was the joint experience of incarceration bonded our [students] spirits to help us survive that time."

Warrior's creative works deal with the of loss or retention of culture, values and "beliefs in this technological world." She has had the encouragement of many people in the course of her writing career. As she explains, "Elizabeth Cook-Lynn has been a role model for me. Knowing Elizabeth Cook-Lynn gave me encouragement and support I needed. She was so gracious and knowledgeable. She helped me find self-respect. She has encouraged me. Also Roberta Wilson, Kathleen Hill,

Gail Tremblay and James McAuley. Their support has given me belief in myself. I must not forget Robert Watson. Professor Robert Watson at the University of Calgary was the first person who described my writing as creative and poetic. He, I guess, turned the lock that opened the door to possibilities. Professor Watson and later Elizabeth Cook-Lynn and James McAuley, a professor at Eastern Washington University. I didn't know a thing about poetry until I studied it under his guidance. He showed me the beauty of poetry."

One of her favorite works is the popular short story about culture theft titled *Compatriots*, though, she says, "Personally I like *How I Came to Have a Man's Name* because it was (still is) a strong tie to the skies. Now *Indian Medicine* is also popular; [it's] about new-age sweat lodgers/shamans." Among the works of the many writers who Warrior enjoys reading, those of her friend Elizabeth Cook-Lynn are especially esteemed. "Of course I enjoy Elizabeth Cook-Lynn's writing. I like her descriptions of the land, and her journeys into the past via mythology and serve to stir childhood stories that lay dormant within my memory. I also like Roxy Gordon, Judith Minty, Earle Thompson, Lee Ann Howe for 'Roxy's Bead Mountain,' Minty's bear story, Thompson's spirit poems and Lee Anne's humor."

Having lived in several locations, Warrior feels closest to the landscape of the Rocky Mountains and northern Plains. "I cherish the landscape: the Rocky Mountains, the lush foothills, the Old Man River Valley and the prairies. I feel gifted in having known such a variety of landscapes. There are places of spiritual significance and mythological happenings." Warrior currently works as an educator and counselor within her community in the Peigan Reserve, where she serves a broad constituency by merging the two disciplines. "I am a student in guidance and counseling and am bent on healing the Indian spirit. I care for my child and grandchildren as well as being a role model in my community. I tutor youth at our budding youth center where our goal is to make better, healthy Peigans. I am teaching part-time as an English instructor for adult students [and] I hope to become employed on the Reserve as a therapist to address the serious mental health problems Peigans experience." She is working on a novel about an Indian activist "who is really a bad spirit."

NAME   J, L, N
Robert Allen Warrior

TRIBAL AFFILIATION
Osage Nation, Pawhuska, Oklahoma

PERSONAL
Born: July 25, 1963, in Marion County, Kansas

Education: B.A. in speech communication, Pepperdine University, *summa cum laude*, Anaheim, California, 1985; M.A. in religion, Yale University Divinity School, New Haven, Connecticut, 1988; Ph.D., Union Theological Seminary, 1992

AWARDS, HONORS
Native American Journalists Association First Place Award, General Media Article, 1992; Daniel Day Williams Fellowship, Union Theological Seminary, New York City, 1991; Dwight-Hooker Prize for Excellence, Yale Divinity School, New Haven, Connecticut, 1988

PUBLICATION HIGHLIGHTS
Tribal Secrets: Recovering American Indian Intellectual Traditions (Minneapolis: University of Minnesota, 1995)

"Canaanites, Cowboys and Indians: Deliverance, Conquest and Liberation Theology Today" in *C&C 49*, 11 September 1989, reprinted in *Ethics in the Present Tense: Readings from Christianity and Crisis 1966–1991*, ed. by Leon Howell and Vivian Lindermayer (New York: Friendship Press, 1991) and in *Voices from the Margin: Interpreting the Bible in the Third World*, ed. by R. S. Sugirtharajah (Maryknoll, N.Y.: Orbis Books, 1991)

NARRATIVE

Robert Allen Warrior was raised "on the streets of Wichita, Kansas." He remembers that he was one of the minority students in the 1970s. He worked as a YMCA director in New Haven, Connecticut, as a freelance journalist and as the New York corespondent for the *Lakota Times* from 1988 through 1990. He worked in television for the Children's Television Workshop in New York City and for the Independent Television Service in Minneapolis. He is the author of numerous articles, interviews and essays, and presenter of numerous papers. He is also a reviewer for several publications on the subjects of contemporary Indian culture, literature and politics. His works have appeared in the publications *Christianity and Crisis, Native Nations*, the *Village Voice, Sojourner, Utne Reader* and *Journal of American History.*

Warrior has always been close to his extended Osage family over the years, particularly his brother, David, who recently contracted and died from the AIDS virus. After his death, Warrior wrote one of his most powerful works, titled *In Memorial: David Brian Warrior (June 12, 1960–September 26, 1992) Dances with Ghosts.*

Warrior enjoys the works of writers Vine Deloria, N. Scott Momaday, Joy Harjo, John Joseph Mathews, Hunter S. Thompson, Joan Didion, Alex Haley, Charles Dickens, Hemingway, Steven Ray Smith, T. A. Ward. He is now working on two books under contract.

Warrior is currently an assistant professor of English, American Indian literature and intellectual history at Stanford University. He is a contributing editor to *C&C* and had been a contributing editor and editorial board member of *Native Nations Magazine* between 1990 and 1991. Since 1991 he has been on the board of governors of the Native American International Prize in Literature based in Norman Oklahoma.

NAME   P
Archie Washburn

TRIBAL AFFILIATION
Navajo

PERSONAL
Born: Shiprock, New Mexico

PUBLICATION HIGHLIGHTS

Washburn's works have appeared in the following anthologies:

New and Old Voices of Wah'Kon-Tah, third edition, ed. by Robert K. Dodge and Joseph B. McCullough (New York: International Publishers, c1985)
Voices from Wah'Kon-Tah: Contemporary Poetry of Native Americans, first edition, ed. by Robert K. Dodge and Joseph B. McCullough (New York: International Publishers, [1974])
American Indian II, comp. by John R. Milton (Vermillion: University of South Dakota, 1971)

NARRATIVE

Washburn's works have also appeared in the journals *Akwesasne Notes* and the *South Dakota Review.*

NAME   F, M, P

Ron Welburn

OTHER NAMES USED

Ronald Garfield Welburn

TRIBAL AFFILIATION

Eastern Cherokee and Conoy

PERSONAL

Born: April 30, 1944, in Berwyn, Pennsylvania

Education: B.A., Lincoln University, Lincoln, Pennsylvania, 1968; M.A., University of Arizona, Tucson, 1970; Ph.D., New York University, New York City, 1983

AWARDS, HONORS

Smithsonian Institute and Music Critics Association Fellowship, 1975; Edward S. Silvera Poetry Award from Lincoln University, Lincoln, Pennsylvania, 1962 and 1968

PUBLICATION HIGHLIGHTS

Full Circle: The Jottings of a Scarborian (Scarborough: Newby, 1992)

Council Decisions: Selected Poems (Little Rock: University of Arkansas Press, 1991)

"Into the Helderbergs" and "Mohawk Memory," poems in *North Country: An Anthology of Contemporary Writing from the Adirondacks and the Upper Hudson Valley* (Greenfield Center, N.Y.: Greenfield Review Press, 1986)

Heartland: Selected Poems (Detroit: Lotus, 1981)

"Brownup" and Other Poems (Greenfield Center, N.Y.: Greenfield Review Press, c1977)

Peripheries: Selected Poems (Greenfield Center, N.Y.: Greenfield Review Press, c1972)

Welburn's works also appear in: *Returning the Gift: Poetry and Prose from the First North American Native Writers' Festival,* ed. by Joseph Bruchac with the support of the Association for the Study of American Indian Literatures (Tucson: University of Arizona, 1994).

NARRATIVE

Welburn grew up in Berwyn and Philadelphia. His family lived in west Philadelphia in a Black neighborhood "with many Native and Native-derived families. We tended to lead secret lives. On my block alone were people of Cherokee, Pueblo, Mattaponi, Choctaw and Seminole descent, but I also visited family in rural Pennsylvania and walked the woods there as a youngster and teenager. I grew up in an environment and family where people did not speak of being Native but as being 'colored' or Americans. Yet I learned as much about Native people from about fourth grade as I could. There was no reinforcement. Once I began attending pow-wows in the Northeast in the mid-1970s, I knew where I belonged."

During his school years he had several memorable instructors, among them history teacher Louis Tuppeny, who taught his students how a society crumbles from within, and his English teachers Richard Caccione and Eileen Moran. His friend Wilmer F. Lucas Jr. inadvertently attracted him to a career in writing by advising him "against a literary career, which I took as a challenge." Lucas also encouraged Welburn to read every writer whose books he could find, and with such advice served as a mentor to Welburn early in his career. Several members of his family were storytellers, including his mother, her brother and his paternal grandmother.

Welburn enjoys reading Leslie Marmon Silko, N. Scott Momaday, Henry James, William Faulkner, V. S. Naipaul, George Luis Borges, Ivan Arguelles, Maurice Kenny and Toni

Morrison. He is working on a sixth collection of poetry, and a short-story group that focuses on Native Americans living in African-American neighborhoods.

Welburn is the author of book and music reviews, has produced over five books of poetry and has numerous poems published in a variety of publications. He is also the publisher and cofounding editor of the journal *The Grackle*, which focuses on "improvised music in transition." Welburn now lives in an open wooded area close to the University of Massachusetts at Amherst, where he composes and plays music on the saxophones, flutes and trumpets when he is not writing. He is presently an associate professor of English at the University of Massachusetts at Amherst.

NAME   E, F, N
James Welch

TRIBAL AFFILIATION
Blackfeet and Gros Ventre

PERSONAL
Born: November 1940 in Browning, Montana
Education: B.A. from the University of Montana; coursework at Northern Montana College

AWARDS, HONORS
National Endowment for the Arts Grant, 1969; Los Angeles Times Award for Best Novel for *Fools Crow*

PUBLICATION HIGHLIGHTS
Killing Custer: The Battle of the Little Bighorn and the Fate of the Plains Indians (New York: W. W. Norton, 1994, 1995)
Tribes, ed. by James Welch (Boston: Ploughshares, 1994)

The Indian Lawyer (New York: W. W. Norton, c1990)
Fools Crow: A Novel (New York: Viking, 1986)
James Welch, James Welch et al. (Lewiston, Idaho, 1986)
The Real West Marginal Way: A Poet's Autobiography, Richard Hugo, ed. by James Welch (N.Y.: W. W. Norton & Company, 1986)
The Death of Jim Loney (New York: Harper & Row, 1979)
Winter in the Blood (New York: Harper & Row, 1974)
Riding the Earthboy 40: Poems (New York: Harper & Row, 1976)

Welch's works have appeared in numerous anthologies:

Forked Tongues: Speech, Writing and Representation in North American Indian Texts, by David Murray (Bloomington: Indiana University Press, 1991)
The Lightning Within: An Anthology of Contemporary American Indian Fiction, ed. by Alan Velie (Lincoln: University of Nebraska Press, 1991)
Winged Words: American Indian Writers Speak, by Laura Coltelli (Lincoln: University of Nebraska Press, 1990)
Survival This Way: Interviews with Native American Poets, by Joseph Bruchac (Tucson: Sun Tracks; University of Arizona Press, 1987)
The Sacred Hoop: Recovering the Feminine in American Indian Traditions, by Paula Gunn Allen (Boston: Beacon Press, 1986)
Four American Indian Literary Masters, by A. R. (Alan) Velie (Norman: University of Oklahoma Press, 1982)
The American Indian Speaks, ed. by John R. Milton (Vermillion: Dakota Press; University of South Dakota, 1969)

NARRATIVE
Welch's mother is Gros Venture and his father Blackfeet. As a young man Welch

attended schools on the Blackfeet and Fort Belknap Reservations, and also attended schools in other locations throughout the Northwest region.

Now a full-time writer, Welch has had a variety of jobs throughout his life. He worked as a laborer, a forest service employee and firefighter, and he was employed as a counselor for the Upward Bound program at the University of Montana. Besides his work as a writer, Welch occasionally teaches classes in American Indian literature at the University of Washington and at Cornell University.

Welch's works have appeared in many anthologies and collections, and have appeared many journals such as *Poetry Northwest*, the *New Yorker*, the *South Dakota Review*, *New American Review* and *Harper's Bazaar*. He is married and lives in Montana.

❖❖❖

NAME

Don Whiteside

OTHER NAMES USED

Sin a paw

TRIBAL AFFILIATION

Creek

PERSONAL

Born: May 9, 1931, in New York City
Education: B.S. from Wisconsin State University, 1958; M.S. from University of Wisconsin, 1960; Ph.D. from Stanford University, Stanford, California, 1967

AWARDS, HONORS

Stanford University Fellowship, 1963–1964; National Science Foundation Fellowship, 1963

PUBLICATION HIGHLIGHTS

A Look into Indian History ([S.l.]: Aboriginal Institute of Canada, 1983)

Indians in Upper Canada Through 1945: The Circle Being Threatened, with Scott D. Whiteside (Ottawa, Ont.: Aboriginal Institute of Canada, February, 1979)

Indians in Upper Canada 1846 Through 1885: The Circle Is Broken, with Scott D. Whiteside (Ottawa, Ont.: Aboriginal Institute of Canada, March 1979)

"We Are the People and You Are Our Heart" in *Nesida* (Vancouver, B.C.: [s.n.], October–December 1976)

"A Good Blanket Has Four Corners: A Comparison of Aboriginal Administration in Canada and the United States" in *Sociology Canada: Readings*, ed. by Christopher Beattie and Stuart Crysdale (Toronto: Butterworths, 1974)

Aboriginal People: A Selected Bibliography Concerning Canada's First People (Ottawa: National Indian Brotherhood, 1973)

Indians, Indians, Indians ([S.l.: s.n., n.d.])

NARRATIVE

Don Whiteside was raised in the borough of Brooklyn until the age of 16. He was not a reader as a child: "Only when I was older did I know people wrote. I cannot even remember reading a newspaper when I was young (or comic books)." He was introduced to the joys of reading by a Sunday school teacher who "... gave me Jules Verne's *20,000 Leagues Under the Sea* to read when I was about ten years old. I think this was the first book that I ever read and it developed into a love of reading and history." After high school, Whiteside joined the merchant marines in 1947, and in 1948 joined the U.S. Army, where he remained until 1954. While serving in the Army, Whiteside's appetite for reading grew even more: "When in the military I spent a lot of time in hospitals. They would bring around books on a cart and that is when I started to read with a passion."

As an academic he has taught at several institutions throughout the years, beginning in 1964 when he was an assistant professor at North Carolina State University at Raleigh. Since then he has worked at the University of Tennessee at Knoxville and at the University of Alberta at Edmonton. He has worked as a consultant for the government of Canada and was the research director for the National Indian Brotherhood in Ottawa from 1972 to 1973. Whiteside then returned to academia as a professor at Manitou College in LaMacaza, Quebec, from 1973 to 1975. He has been the owner of Whiteside and Associates since 1979.

Whiteside has been active in his community, serving as the president of the Alberta Human Rights Association from 1969 to 1970. He was president of the Civil Liberties Association's National Capital Region for the years 1970–1971, 1973, 1974 and 1977–1989, and he served in two offices of the Canadian Rights and Liberties Federation—first as secretary/treasurer from 1972 to 1974, and then as president from 1974 to 1977, and again in 1983 to 1986. He has been president of the Aboriginal Institute of Canada since 1973 and president of the Ontario Civil Liberties Association since 1989.

Whiteside writes about history, considering his best work to be *A Good Blanket Has Four Corners* "because it paints a picture of aboriginal administration in broad strokes on a wide canvas." He adds, "I want to get back to writing. It matters little about what the subject or topic will be (although it will be about my favorite topic, Indian history)."

He has noticed his reading habits and preferences changing as the years pass by. "Now that I am older I seem to read less. Perhaps it is the eyes, but sometimes I think it is because 'I have read this somewhere before.' It may be there are a limited number of ways to say the same thing." He enjoys doing genealogical research and working in the areas of civil liberties. Though he is currently retired, he still works as a consultant in the area of social development.

NAME P

Donna Whitewing

TRIBAL AFFILIATION

Sioux-Winnebago

PERSONAL

Born: Sutherland, Nebraska

PUBLICATION HIGHLIGHTS

Whitewing's works have appeared in the following anthologies:

Returning the Gift: Poetry and Prose from the First North American Native Writers' Festival, ed. by Joseph Bruchac with the support of the Association for the Study of American Indian Literatures (Tucson: University of Arizona, 1994)

New and Old Voices of Wah'Kon-Tah, third edition, ed. by Robert K. Dodge and Joseph B. McCullough (New York: International Publishers, c1985)

Voices from Wah'KonTah: Contemporary Poetry of Native Americans, first edition, ed. by Robert K. Dodge and Joseph B. McCullough (New York: International Publishers, [1974])

The Whispering Wind: Poetry by Young American Indians, ed. by Terry Allen (Garden City, N.J.: Doubleday, 1972)

The American Indian Speaks, comp. by John R. Milton (Vermillion: University of South Dakota, 1969)

NARRATIVE

Whitewing's parents were migrant workers who followed jobs throughout South Dakota and Nebraska. Whitewing attended St. Augustine's Indian Mission in Winnebago, Nebraska.

NAME   L, M, N, S, VA

Theodore C. Williams

OTHER NAMES USED

Ted C. Williams

TRIBAL AFFILIATION

Tuscarora

PERSONAL

Born: April 6, 1930, in Tuscarora Indian Reservation, Niagara Falls, New York
Education: High school graduate

PUBLICATION HIGHLIGHTS

The Reservation (Syracuse, N.Y.: Syracuse University Press, 1976)

Williams's works have also appeared in: *American Indian Literatures: An Introduction, Bibliographic Review and Selected Bibliography* (New York: Modern Language Association, 1990); *Iroquois Writing*, first edition, ed. by Joseph Bruchac (Greenfield Center, N.Y.: Greenfield Review Press, 1989) and *New Voices from the Longhouse: An Anthology of Contemporary Iroquois Writing*, first edition, ed. by Joseph Bruchac (Greenfield Center, N.Y.: Greenfield Review Press, 1989).

NARRATIVE

Theodore C. Williams was born and raised on the Tuscarora Indian Reservation, near Niagara Falls, New York. As he explains, one thing led to another in his early career as a writer: "I was courting Lorraine Frost Cross and pretended to be a writer, ended up with a wife and a book." A medicine man who is well-respected among his people, Williams writes on the subjects of Indian medicine, healing and spirituality.

Although he is now retired, Williams is working on a collection of spiritual and extrasensory perception stories, and experiences that have occurred among the Iroquois. In addition to his writing, he also works as a speaker and storyteller, talking to groups and individuals about Indian medicine ways, healing and the spiritual experiences of his Indian acquaintances.

NAME   E, F, N, L, P, S

Darryl Babe Wilson

TRIBAL AFFILIATION

A-juma-we/Atsuge-we (Pit River-Northeastern California)

PERSONAL

Born: November 21, 1939, in Fall River Mills, California
Education:
Coursework at the University of California, Davis
Presently in M.F.A. program in American Indian Studies at the University of Arizona, Tucson
Seeking Ph.D. in culture and literature (English)

AWARDS, HONORS

President's Undergraduate Fellowship for Poetry

PUBLICATION HIGHLIGHTS

"Diamond Island: Alcatraz," in *Talking Leaves: Contemporary Native American*

Short Stories, An Anthology, ed. by Craig Lesley (New York: Laurel, 1991)

"Dancing," "Gedin-ch-lum-na" in *Fiction International*, no. 20 (San Diego: San Diego State University, Fall 1991)

"Jema-web-ti-wi-ji" in *American Indian Quarterly* (University of California Berkeley, Fall 1989)

NARRATIVE

Darryl Babe Wilson was born and raised in Northern California. As a young man he joined the armed forces, becoming a marine. After his time in the service, he worked as a logger. He is now writing and working as a full-time student and has been active in many Native American rights issues. As a full-time graduate student at the University of Arizona in Tucson Wilson works on the Sun Tracks series of Native American publications published at the university. He has participated in the Minorities Undergraduate Research Apprenticeship in Letters and Science for two years.

The death of his mother was a tremendous blow. "The morning the sun went down." As was the death of his wife, Danell, the mother of their twin boys. "The morning the sun did not rise ... After the death of Danell, I thought the best way to live was in the seclusion of the mountains. But looking into the bright innocent eyes of her children, knowing that their future may be decided by my present accomplishments, I returned to college and into the world of writers, publishers, editors, dreamers." He has received support in his educational endeavors from his father, "... who said he hoped there would be an artist in the family," his people, "who encourage one to continue the process of education," and also from his children, "who constantly inspire me."

Wilson's writings focus on nature and Native people, narratives, lessons, legends and the spiritual world. Many people who served as guides and mentors to him, among them is R. Joseph Lowery, an English teacher, "who encouraged us to write (express)," and Mr. Hal Gossen, also an English teacher, "who saw 'substance' in my efforts to write, not only errors." He also mentioned the works of author Robert Service. "Once the only reading material I had while in jail was *The Complete Works of Robert Service!* In my thirty-day incarceration I memorized much of Service." He enjoys reading the writings of Native American children and, as he says, "is influenced every time I read or hear their work." Commenting on his own work, Wilson says, "My best work is emerging quickly. It is a story of my life among my people, upon our land. The trials, the pain, the joy."

Long-term projects include a book of poems and an autobiographical work and a book about the struggle of Native Americans in northeast California. Wilson's short-term work includes his ongoing writings for several quarterlies and journals, such as *News from Native California* (Berkeley), *American Indian Culture and Research Journal* (UCLA), *American Indian Quarterly* (Berkeley) and *Anthropology and Humanism Quarterly.*

When not writing he is busy helping his children with their projects, building things out of wood and nails, traveling, camping and talking with ancient people about future events.

NAME E, P
Ramona Wilson

TRIBAL AFFILIATION
Colville

PERSONAL
Born: Nespelem, Washington

Education: B.A. in education from Eastern Washington University at Cheney; post-graduate coursework in English, humanities and education from Northern Virginia University at Fairfax, the University of California at Berkeley and California State University at Hayward

PUBLICATION HIGHLIGHTS

Wilson's works have appeared in the following anthologies:

Returning the Gift: Poetry and Prose from the First North American Native Writers' Festival, ed. by Joseph Bruchac with the support of the Association for the Study of American Indian Literatures (Tucson: University of Arizona, 1994)

Dancing on the Rim of the World: An Anthology of Contemporary Northwest Native American Writing, ed. by Andrea Lerner (Tucson: Sun Tracks; University of Arizona Press, c1990)

"Field Trip," poem in *Wicazo Sa Review* (Cheney, Wash.: Indian Studies Department, Eastern Washington University, vol. 3, no. 1, Spring 1987)

Voices of the Rainbow: Contemporary Poetry by American Indians, ed. by Kenneth Rosen (New York: Viking, 1975)

NARRATIVE

Wilson attended school in Brewster and Bridgeport, Washington. She was raised close to the Columbia River, but left the region at the age of 17 to attend high school at the Institute of American Indian Arts in Santa Fe, New Mexico.

Now living and working in Oakland, California, Wilson works as the project director for the American Indian Bilingual Project in the Oakland Public Schools. She is married and has two children.

NAME   F, J, M, N, P, PL
Shirlee Winder

TRIBAL AFFILIATION
Seneca and Oneida

PERSONAL
Born: Sept. 17, 1951, in Penn Yan, New York
Education: Associate of Fine Arts, Creative Writing degree, Institute of American Indian Arts, Santa Fe, New Mexico, 1982; currently pursuing Associate degree in applied science/computer technology in management at the State University of New York, Morrisville, New York

PUBLICATION HIGHLIGHTS
"The Clouds Threw This Light," poem in *Contemporary Native American Poetry* (Santa Fe: Institute of American Indian Arts Press, 1983)

"Critique of Bruce King's 'Dustoff,'" "Dinner for Two Please," fiction and "Rain," poem in *Akwegon* (Hogansburg, N.Y.: *Akwasasne Notes,* 1983)

"Valdez Is Coming," play in "Have You Hugged Your Indian Today" in *Spawning the Medicine River* (Santa Fe: Institute of American Indian Arts Press, Spring 1981)

NARRATIVE
Shirlee Winder grew up in Victor, New York, which was the location of an ancient Seneca village named Gonondagon, and is now a well-known museum. Winder has always enjoyed close ties to her parents and siblings. "My family has been encouraging, especially my sister, Sandy. Many close relatives, especially Aunts, have been emotionally, spiritually and sometimes financially supportive ... I live among Indian people, a small, close-knit community that adds much to the

flavor of my life." Winder also has two daughters, Summer Star and Laurah Morningstar, and a granddaughter, Amber Dawn.

Winder's writings focus on the subjects of abuse, alcohol, love, hurt, spouse and child abuse and homelessness. She is working on several projects, long, short and "in-between," and has recently had a play of hers produced titled *Valdez Is Coming*. She is now writing a play about Columbus, which will involve the children living on the Oneida Nation Territory.

Phil Foss Jr., Joy Harjo, Leslie Silko and N. Scott Momaday are among her favorite writers, and she also enjoys the works of Simon Ortiz, Liz Woody and Ted Williams.

Winder is now a full-time student at the State University of New York at Morrisville and works full-time in Oneida Nation Smokeshop. When she is not working at school or her full-time job, she enjoys playing with her VCR, beadwork, skiing and working on cars.

NAME E, F, N, S

Craig S. Womack

OTHER NAMES USED

Craig Steven Womack

TRIBAL AFFILIATION

Creek and Cherokee

PERSONAL

Born: February 19, 1960, in San Pablo, California

Education: M.A. in English from South Dakota State University, 1991; Ph.D. candidate in English at the University of Oklahoma, Norman

PUBLICATION HIGHLIGHTS

"Seek the Word" in *Evergreen Chronicles* (Minneapolis: *Evergreen Chronicles,* Summer 1992)

"Medicine River," "Carroll Arnett's Night Perimeter" in *American Indian Culture and Research Journal* (Los Angeles: University of California, American Indian Culture and Resource Center, Summer 1992)

NARRATIVE

Womack grew up in the San Francisco Bay Area and in the Sacramento Valley with, as he adds, "physical and imaginative journeys to eastern Oklahoma." He explains his long-held fascination with the state of Oklahoma. "I grew up in California, and Oklahoma was a place in my imagination, a place in my grandparents' stories. Now, I live here and both geographies—the physical and imaginative one interplay in creative ways." Womack was influenced by two of his female relatives as a young man, his great aunt Barbara Coachman "who taught me much of what I know about Creek identity and my grandmother Velma Jones, a wonderful storyteller with a keen sense of irony and understatement."

Womack says he writes about "the kind of mixed-blood identity that my grandparents passed on to me; the experience of being both Indian and poor white, of knowing something about Native culture and being outside it. Many of my characters are further materialized because of their gay or Lesbian identities, but eventually they learn that they can only understand their tribal identities in terms of their gayness and vice versa. My writing attempts to explore my sense of Indian identity and gay identity in a way that confronts the silence yet remains respectful to my Native community."

He enjoys the works of authors Flannery O'Connor "because of her understanding of the spirit world, William Faulkner because of his storytelling characters, numerous Native poets (impossible to name them all) because they write about things that matter—survival, the magic of words." He is currently working on a novel titled *Dancing Around the Fire*. His works have also appeared in numerous publications, such as the *James White Review, Callaloo, American Indian Quarterly* and *Christopher Street*. He now teaches in the University of Nebraska at Omaha, English Department.

NAME F, L, N, P, VA

Elizabeth Woody

TRIBAL AFFILIATION(S)

Warm Springs, Yakima, Wasco, Cascades and Navajo

PERSONAL

Born: December 26, 1959, in Ganado, Arizona

Education: Institute of American Indian Arts, 1980–1983; Portland State University; B.A. in humanities, Evergreen State College, 1991

AWARDS, HONORS

American Book Award from the Before Columbus Foundation for *Hand Into Stone*, 1990; Brandywine Fellowship in Printmaking, 1988

PUBLICATION HIGHLIGHTS

Seven Hands, Seven Hearts (Portland, Oreg.: Eighth Mountain, 1994)

Luminaries of the Humble (Tucson: University of Arizona, 1994)

"Homecooking" in *Talking Leaves* (New York: Dell; Laurel, 1991)

"Warm Springs" in *Native America* (Singapore: APA Insight Guides, 1991)

Hand into Stone, poems (New York: Contact II Publications, 1988)

Woody's works also appear in the following anthologies:

Returning the Gift: Poetry and Prose from the First North American Native Writers' Festival, ed. by Joseph Bruchac with the support of the Association for the Study of American Indian Literatures (Tucson: University of Arizona, 1994)

The Clouds Threw This Light: Contemporary Native American Poetry, first edition, ed. by Phillip Foss (Santa Fe: Institute of American Indian Arts Press, 1983)

A Gathering of Spirit: A Collection by North American Indian Women, ed. by Beth Brant (Degonwadonti) (Ithaca, N.Y.: Firebrand Books, 1988)

Songs from This Earth on Turtle's Back, first edition, ed. by Joseph Bruchac (Greenfield Center, N.Y.: Greenfield Review Press, 1983)

NARRATIVE

Elizabeth Woody was raised in Madras, Oregon, until 1973; her family then moved to Warm Springs, Oregon, until 1980. She was close to many of her family members: her grandparents Lewis Pitt Sr. and Elizabeth Thompson Pitt, her aunt and uncle Lillian and Lewis Pitt, Lewis Pitt and her mother Charlotte Pitt. "They always had time to talk and teach me." Later, as a high school student Woody was sent to Onomichi, Japan, as an exchange student in 1977, and in 1978 she was selected as one of the twelve high school writers in the Young Writers of Oregon program to study with writers Sandra McPherson and James Welch. She enjoyed photography and art in high school, her classes in English and the helpful company of her school librarian. She majored in creative writing at the Institute of American Indian Arts and worked under the tutelage of writer Phillip Foss Jr. "He taught me craft and discipline, [and] quality of work would be the only things that will matter to me. ... Poetry is not an instant gratification business." Her years as a student at the AIAI were to provide her with the impetus to continue writing. She adds that while she was there "I was inspired by the other writing students and visiting authors." Woody writes about the land, the sense of place and family. "The land is important, because I loved taking drives, walking, taking photographs."

Her first volume of poetry, *Hand Into Stone,* was published in 1988 (and won an American Book Award from the Before Columbus Foundation). Her poems have also appeared in the journals *Bear-ing Witness/Sobreviviendo,* the *Native American Today, Fireweed, Tyuonyi, Akewon, Contact II, Greenfield Review* and *Sur Le Dos la Torture: Revue Bilingue de Literature Amerindienne* (France). In 1985 she won a poetry contest and was published along with seventeen other poets in *Image,* a project of the Seattle Arts Commission. Her work was juried into the literary readings series of the National Women's Studies Conference at the University of Washington.

Woody now lives in Portland, Oregon, and is an independent contractor and consultant in the areas of art and literature. When not writing, Woody works on "My art, painting, multi-media, traditional art, my plants, my animals, and traveling. I also like to 'junk around' at flea markets, second-hand stores and [do] beadwork."

Y

NAME   PL

William S. Yellow Robe Jr.

TRIBAL AFFILIATION

Assiniboine

PERSONAL

Born: February 1960 in Poplar, Montana

Education: High school diploma; four years of college coursework

AWARDS, HONORS

National Endowment for the Arts Playwright Fellowship, 1991; Princess Grace Fellowship, 1989; Jerome Fellowship, 1988

PUBLICATION HIGHLIGHTS

The Council, play (Honolulu Theatre for Youth, Honolulu, 1992)

The Council, play (Seattle Children's Theatre, Seattle, Wash., 1991)

"Sneaky" in *Slant Six* (Minneapolis: New Rivers Press and Minneapolis Playwrights' Center, 1990)

"The Burning of Uncle" in *Dancing on the Rim of the World: An Anthology of Contemporary Northwest Native American Writing,* ed. by Andrea Lerner (Tucson: University of Arizona Press; Sun Tracks, 1990)

The Independence of Eddie Rose, play (Seattle Group Theatre, Seattle, Wash., 1990)

Wink-Dah, play (Ensemble Studio Theatre, in "Marathon of One Acts" New York, 1989)

Wink-Dah, play (American Conservatory Theatre (ACT) "Plays in Progress" series, San Francisco, 1988)

NARRATIVE

Considering his most effective works to be plays because "it's a better way of sharing stories," writer and playwright William S. Yellow Robe Jr. sets the majority of his plays on his home reservation of Fort Peck at Wolf Point, Montana. He based his early plays on his personal experiences, but later his works evolved to include his family and friends, now including acquaintances as well. One of his earliest works, *Sneaky,* was written after the death of his grandmother, and it was this event and consequent play that proved to be a catalyst for his writing career. He regards James Welch to be an early literary guide, describing his novel *Winter in the Blood* as the catalyst that moved him to write. He also considers the playwright Eugene O'Neil to be a literary mentor, because O'Neil and Welch, both "have a great ear for life." Yellow Robe also teaches. "I want to share what I've learned."

NAME   F, N, P

Ray A. Young Bear

TRIBAL AFFILIATION

Mesquakie

PERSONAL

Born: November 12, 1950, in Tama, Iowa

Education: Coursework at the University of Northern Iowa at Cedar Falls

PUBLICATION HIGHLIGHTS

Remnants of the First Earth (New York: Grove Atlantic, 1996)

Black Eagle Child: The Face Paint Narratives (Iowa City: University of Iowa Press, 1992)

The Invisible Musician: Poems (Duluth, Minn.: Holy Cow! Press, 1990)

Winter of the Salamander: The Keeper of Importance (New York: Harper & Row, 1980)

Waiting to Be Fed (Port Townsend, Wash.: Gray Wolf, 1975)

Young Bear's works have appeared in many anthologies:

Harper's Anthology of Twentieth-Century Native American Poetry, first edition (San Francisco: Harper & Row, 1988)

Survival This Way: Interviews with Native American Poets, by Joseph Bruchac (Tucson: Sun Tracks; University of Arizona Press, 1987)

The Sacred Hoop: Recovering the Feminine in American Indian Traditions, by Paula Gunn Allen (Boston: Beacon Press, 1986)

The Remembered Earth: An Anthology of Contemporary Native American Literature, ed. by Geary Hobson (Albuquerque: Red Earth Press, 1979)

Carriers of the Dream Wheel: Contemporary Native American Poetry, ed. by Duane Niatum (New York: Harper & Row, 1975)

Voices of the Rainbow: Contemporary Poetry by American Indians, ed. by Kenneth Rosen (New York: Viking, 1975)

Come to Power: Eleven Contemporary American Indian Poets (Trumansburg, N.Y.: Crossing Press, 1974)

From the Belly of the Shark: A New Anthology of Native Americans, ed. by Walter Lowenfels (New York: Vantage, 1974)

NARRATIVE

Young Bear is of Mesquakie heritage, formerly known as Sauk and Fox. Young Bear's works have also been published in the journals *Seneca Review,* the *Phoenix,*

Ploughshares, the *Georgia Review,* the *Kenyon Review,* the *Virginia Quarterly Review, Callaloo, South Dakota Review, American Poetry Review* and *Pembroke* magazine. He is married and lives in Tama, Iowa.

NAME   L, N, P
Greg Young-Ing

TRIBAL AFFILIATION
Cree

PERSONAL
Born: March 18, 1961, in Halifax, Nova Scotia

Education: B.A. from Carleton University, Ottawa, Ontario; M.A. from Carleton University, Ottawa, Ontario

PUBLICATION HIGHLIGHTS

Gatherings Volume III—Mother Earth Perspectives: Preservation Through Words, ed. by Greg Young-Ing (Penticton, B.C.: Theytus, 1992)

Mother Earth Perspectives: Preservation Through Words, by G. Young-Ing and D. Suzuki (Penticton, B.C.: Theytus, 1992)

Gatherings Volume II, Poems (Penticton, B.C.: Theytus Books, 1991)

Gatherings Volume I, Poems (Penticton, B.C.: Theytus Books, 1990)

Seventh Generation, Poems (Penticton, B.C.: Theytus Books, 1989)

Young-Ing's works also appear in: *Returning the Gift: Poetry and Prose from the First North American Native Writers' Festival,* ed. by Joseph Bruchac with the support of the Association for the Study of American Indian Literatures (Tucson: University of Arizona, 1994) and *Looking at the Words of our People, First Nations Analysis of Literature,* ed. by Jeannette Armstrong (Penticton, B.C.: Theytus, 1993).

NARRATIVE

Young-Ing's grandfather John Young was one of the greatest influences in his life. When Young-Ing was a young writer, Jeannette Armstrong was one of his teachers and mentor. One of the most significant times in his life was "Oka in the summer of 1991 (the 'Mohawk crisis')." Young-Ing is currently the manager of Theytus Books in Penticton, British Columbia.

NAME   N, VA

Alfred Young Man

TRIBAL AFFILIATION

Chippewa and Cree-Rocky Boy Indian Reservation, Montana

PERSONAL

Born: April 12, 1948, in Browning, Montana

Education:

High school graduate, Institute of American Indian Arts, Santa Fe, New Mexico, 1966

Post-graduate diploma, Institute of American Indian Arts, Santa Fe, New Mexico, 1968

B.A. in fine art, Slade School of Fine Arts, University College, London, England, 1972

M.A. from the University of Montana, Missoula, Montana, 1973

Teachers Certificate, Northern Montana College, Havre, Montana, 1975

Television specialist training, Total Community Education, Flathead Valley Community College, Kalispell, Montana, 1977

Doctoral candidate in anthropology, Rutgers University, New Brunswick, New Jersey, 1989–present

AWARDS, HONORS

Grants from various agencies to hold the conference National Native Indian Arts Symposium IV at the University of Lethbridge, 1987

Grant from Canada Council to publish *Networking: Proceedings from the National Native Indian Artists Symposium IV,* 1987

Grant from the Northwest Area Foundation in Minneapolis for the Community Education Program at Flathead Valley Community College, Kalispell, Montana, 1976

University of Montana Scholarship to study Indian art in the Graduate Program of American Indian Art, 1972–1974

Bureau of Indian Affairs Scholarship to the Slade School of Fine Arts, University College, London, 1968–1972

PUBLICATION HIGHLIGHTS

Kiskayetum: Allen Sapp, a Retrospective (Kiskayetum: Allen Sapp, une Retrospective), by A. Young-Man and B. Boyer (Regina: MacKenzie Art Gallery, 1994)

"On a Contemporary Ecological Anthropology" in *Newsletter* (Native Art Studies Association of Canada) (Canada: Native Art Studies Association of Canada, vol. 4, no. 2, Summer 1990)

A Dominican Experience: Three Aboriginal Artists of Canada in the Dominican Republic, ed. by Alfred Young Man ([S.l.]: Om Niiak Native Arts Group, 1989)

"Token and Taboo: Academia versus Native Art" in *FUSE* magazine (Toronto, Ont.: Arton's Cultural Affairs Society and Pub., vol. 11, no. 6, July 1988)

"Issues and Trends in Contemporary Native Art" in *Paralellogramme* (Vancouver, B.C.: Canadian Association of Non-profit Artist Centres, vol. 13, no. 3, February/March 1988)

Networking: National Native Indian Artists Symposium IV, ed. by Alfred Young Man (Lethbridge, Alberta: Graphicom, 1987)

Young Man's works also appear in: *Visions of Power: Contemporary Art by First Nations, Inuit and Japanese Canadians* (Toronto: Earth Spirit Festival, 1991).

NARRATIVE

Alfred Young Man was raised east of Glacier National Park on the Blackfeet Indian Reservation. He was sent to the Bureau of Indian Affairs Boarding School on the Reservation as a child. Young Man is now an associate professor on North American Indian art history and studio art at the University of Lethbridge, Lethbridge, Alberta, Canada.

Young Man has had many of his articles, essays and book reviews published in a number of journals, periodicals and exhibition catalogs on the subject of Native American art. His art work has also been shown in many galleries, and has been reproduced and critiqued in several journals. Young Man is also active in video production and filmmaking, as a producer, director, interviewer and subject. He enjoys the works of writers Vine Deloria Jr., Jimmie Durham and Clifford Geertz.

Z

NAME   E, F, N, P
Ofelia Zepeda

TRIBAL AFFILIATION
Tohono O'odham

PERSONAL
Born: March 24, 1954 in Stanfield, Arizona
Education:
A.A. from Central Arizona College, 1974
B.A. from the University of Arizona, Tucson
M.A. from the University of Arizona, Tucson
Ph.D. from the University of Arizona, Tucson, 1984

PUBLICATION HIGHLIGHTS
Home Places: Contemporary Native Writing from Suntracks, by O. Zepeda and L. Evers (Tucson: University of Arizona, 1995)
Ocean Power: Poems from the Desert (Tucson: University of Arizona, 1995)
When It Rains, Papago and Pima Poetry (Mat Hekid o ju, 'O'odham Na-cejitodag), ed. by Ofelia Zepeda (Tucson: Sun Tracks: University of Arizona Press, 1982)

The Sand Papago Oral History Project (Tucson: National Park Service, Division of Archeology, Westerern Archeological and Conservation Center, 1985)
A Papago Grammar (Tucson: University of Arizona Press, 1983)

Zepeda's works have appeared in: *Returning the Gift: Poetry and Prose from the First North American Native Writers' Festival,* ed. by Joseph Bruchac with the support of the Association for the Sudy of American Indian Literatures (Tucson: University of Arizona, 1994) and *South Corner of Time: Hopi, Navajo, Papago, Yaqui Tribal Literature,* ed. by Larry Evers et al. (Tucson: University of Arizona, 1980).

NARRATIVE
Zepeda is the daughter of a farmer. Currently an instructor of linguistics at the University of Arizona, Zepeda also teaches in the summers at Arizona State University at Tempe and works as a consultant to the Tohono O'odham and Pima Tribes.

APPENDIX:
LIST OF ADDITIONAL WRITERS

The following is a compilation of names of writers whom the authors had found and identified but were unable to include biographical entries for. Some of the authors published materials that were older than the time frame we had established, many had published only a few writings and we were assured that many were writers yet we could not locate citations for their works. Another reason many names are on this list is that we became aware of some of the writers too late in the compilation process, and a few had chosen to be excluded from the main text. It is our intention to be inclusive and not exclusive in this publication, and we sincerely apologize to those writers who should have had a full biographical entry but did not. We encourage the writers to contact Fulcrum Publishing if they are interested in becoming part of another edition of this work.

A

Abeita, Pablo
Ackley, Randall
Acoose, Janice
Adams, Barbara Means
Adams, Howard
Adams, Jane H.
Adams, Margaret
Adams, Randy
Ahtone, Heather
Aiken, Martha N.
Ak'abal, Humberto
Akelkok, Brenda
Albert, Rose
Allen, Elsie
Anderson, Vicki
Angellan, Max
Annharte
Antelop, Beryls
Antone, Barbara A.
Anungazuk, Herbert
Anungazuk, Ralph
Apatiki, Dennis
Apatiki, Shelley
Archambault, Avis
Arthur, Donald
Arviso, Rachael

Atcitty, Marlene
Austin, Martha
Azbill, Henry

B

Bahe, Elizabeth
Bahe, LaVern
Baker, Marie Annharte
Bass, Vincent
Bautista, Mario P. T.
Bavilla, Vernon
Beach, Marion
Beach, Robert
Bear, Shirley
Beardy, Jackson
Beeler, Joe
Begay, Blanche Bizahaloni
Begay, Eleanor
Begay, Lorene
Begay, Loretta
Begay, Shirley
Belin, Esther G.
Bell, Juanita
Belone, Nora
Beltz, Markey Albert
Benally, Louise
Bighorse, Tiana
Bird, Dolly
Bird, Harold
Blackhorse, Bernice
Blackmon, Thomas W.
Blue Clark, C.
Blue Eagle, Acee
Boulanger, Tom
Bowers, Sharon A.
Bowman, Beulah
Boyd, Nora
Bray, William
Brean, Alice
Broker, Ignacia
Brown, William
Burns, Wanda
Bush, Bobbie

C

Caldwell, E. K.
Cardinal, Harold

Charging Eagle, Tom
Charles, Vangie
Chester, Bruce
Chief Meyers
Chute, Robert
Clements, Susan
Cohoe, William
Coke, A. A. Hedge
Cornall, Robert
Crank, Dan L.
Crofoot, Ricky
Cronin, Patricia
Cuero, Delphina
Curley, Eleanora
Curley, Marie

D

Davidson, Florence
Deacon, Belle
Degrote, Nella
Deloria Sr., Vine
Diaz, Rosemary
Dick, Galena
Dick, Lynda
Dockstader, John
Dotson, Rebecca
Dubois, Rochelle Holt
Dugaqua, Gilbert E.
Dull, Vicki L.
Dumont, Marilyn

E

Eben, Owen
Esmailka, Laurie Jay

F

Fasthorse, Rose
Fawcett, Melissa
Fleet, Chris
Frank, Jeanette
Fredricks, Oswald White Bear
Frenzl, Cecelia J.

G

Gabourie, Fred Whitedeer
Galaktionoff, Robert
George, Gene A.

Goodbird, Edward
Gregory, George Ann
Grey, Herman
Greyhawk, Greg

H

Hagen, Richard D.
Hane'ibyjim
Harvey, Arthur J.
Harvey, Violet
Hayward, Russell
Hershman, John
Hilbert, Vi
Hobson, Dottie
Honie, Lorraine
Hudson, Clarissa
Humishima
Huntington, James

I

Irving, Patricia

J

Jackson, Edgar
Jay, Ralph Johnson
Joe, Roberta D.
Johnson, Sandra
Joseph, Reggie
Josie, Edith
Jumbo, Della
Jumbo, Paul P.
Jumper, Moses

K

Kahn, Annie
Kalerak, Ruth
Kalloch, Gina
Kanentiio, Doug George
Kavena, Juanita Tiger
Kaywaykla, James
Kenick, Leora
Kennedy, Dan
Kimball, Yeffe
Konupeok, Vernon Bob T.
Koschmann, John W.
Koutchak, Polly

L

LaFlesche, Francis
Lake Sr., David
Lambert, Frances
Lame Deer, Archie
Little, Joseph
Logan, Adelphena
Lone Dog, Louise
Lowe, Bertha
Lowry, Annie
Lucero, Evelina Zuni
Lucero-Giaccardo, Felice

M

Mackey, Mary
Mankiller, Wilma
Manyarrows, Victoria Lena
Many Goats, Betty
Martin, Judy
Maryboy, Nancy C.
Masters, Nicholas J.
Mateo, Jose Balvino C.
Mather, Elsie
Mayokok, Robert
McCarthy, James
McCarty, Darlene
McCloud, Lise
McIntosh, Chief Dode
Medicine Crow, Joseph
Medicine Story
Meyette, Terri
Midge, Tiffany
Miebs, Sheila
Mitchell, Frank
Modesto, Ruby
Molina, Felipe
Montana, David
Moore, Sharon
Morales, Rosalio
Morrison, Joan
Mountain Chief
Mountain Wolf Woman
Mulluk, Robert Jr.
Murray, Ida L.

N

Nasnaga
Nequatewa, Edmund

Newell, William
Ningeulook, Albert
Nowell, Charles
Nuligak (Nalungiaq)

O

Oakes, Abel
Okpealuk, Stanley L.
Okpealuk, Vincent S.
Oliver, Betty
Oquilhuk, William
Ortiz, Bev
Ortiz, Margaret
Otto, Simon

P

Pachanco, Jane (Willis)
Palmer, Gus
Parker, Chief Everett
Paschem, Elise
Patencio, Chief Francisco
Perkins, Ellovina Tsosie
Peters, Russell
Peterson, Mary Jane
Pitseolak
Plain, Ferguson
Poitras, Jane Ash
Pope, Melissa A.
Popkes, Stephen
Potts, Marie
Pratt, Vince E.
Presley, John Woodrow

R

Rafael, Simon
Red Hawk
Red Hawk, Richard
Red Horse Owner
Redsky, James
Reid, Bill
Ridley, Ruth S.
Robinson, Harry
Roessel, Ruth

S

Sacoman, Beverly

Salabiye, Velma
Sanchez, Walter
Sark, John Joe
Saubel, Katherine Siva
Savala, Refugio
Savino, Patroclus Eugene
Scribe, Murdo
Sebwenna, Magdelene L.
Seeganna, Margaret
Seelatsee, Julia
Sekaquaptewa, Emery
Sekaquaptewa, Helen
Sewid, James
Shaw, Anna Moore
Shegonee, Loyal
Sheppard, Susan
Sherry, Robin
Shoppert, Robert James
Silas, Ray P.
Silentman, Irene
Simeonoff, June
Singer, Linda
Skin, Ray P.
Smith, Barbara
Smith, George
Smith, Ray
Spitler, Sherry C.
Stands in Timber, John
Stanley, Julie
Starr, Winn (Oliver)
Stewart, Irene
Stickman, Eileen
Storm Horse
Strete, Craig
Strong, Karen
Strong, Wally
Stump, Sarain
Sumdum, Sherman J.
Sundgren, Billie
Swan, Madonna
Sweezy, Carl

T

Tawa, Mana
Tetso, John
Thomas, Robert K.
Thompson, Luci

Threepersons, Lorene
Toadlena, Brant
Toineeta, Joy Yellowtail
Trahant, Mark
Traveller Bird (Tsisghwanai)
Tsinajinnie, Stella
Tsinnie, Lolita
Tsonakwa
Tucker, James
Tullie, Verna
Tyman, James

V

Van Dyke, Helen
Vaudrin, Bill
Velarde, Pablita
Velarde, Stacey
Villasenor, David
Vinventi, Carlson

W

Wade, Patricia
Wallis, Velma
Walters, Gertrude
War Cloud, Paul
Warren, William
Waters, Ann
Waubageshig (Harvey McCue)
Wauneka, Annie
Webb, Eddie
Weeks, Rupert
Wheeler, Jordan
White Bull, Chief Joseph
Whitehead, Annie
Whitehead, Baida
Whitewolf, Jim
Whitstone, Dean
Willetto, Carla
William, Gerry
Willis, Anna
Willoya, William
Winnie, Lucille "Jerry" (Sah-gan-de-oh)
Wolf, Helen Pease
Wolfe, Alexander
Wood, Margaret
Wright, Muriel Hazel

Wuttunee, William I. C.
Wynecoop, David C.

Y

Yazzie, Dolly
Yazzie, Emma Jean
Yazzie, Ethelou
Yazzie, Etta
Yazzie, Nora
Yazzie-Shaw, Carole
Yellow Robe, Rosebud
Yellow Wolf

BIBLIOGRAPHY

American Indian 1492–1976: A Chronology and Fact Book, second edition, comp. and ed. by Henry C. Dennis, foreword by Robert L. Bennett (Dobbs Ferry, N.Y.: Oceana Publishers, 1977)

American Indian and Eskimo Authors: A Comprehensive Bibliography, comp. by Arlene B. Hirschfelder (New York: Association for American Indian Affairs, [c1973])

An American Indian Anthology, by Tuedten Benet (Marvin, S. Dak.: Blue Cloud Abbey, 1971)

American Indian Authors: A Representative Bibliography, comp. by Arlene B. Hirschfelder (New York: Association on American Indian Affairs, [1970])

American Indian Authors for Young Readers: A Selected Bibliography, comp. by Mary Gloyne Byler (New York: Association on American Indian Affairs, [1973])

American Indian Fiction, first edition, by Charles R. Larson (Albuquerque: University of New Mexico Press, c1978)

American Indian II, ed. by John R. Milton (Vermillion, S. Dak.: Dakota Press; University of South Dakota, 1971)

The American Indian in Short Fiction: An Annotated Bibliography, Peter Beidler and Marion Egge (Metuchen, N.J.: Scarecrow Press, 1979)

The American Indian Language and Literature, comp. by Jack W. Marken (Arlington Heights, Ill.: AHM Publishing, c1978)

American Indian Literature: An Anthology, ed. by Alan Velie (Norman: University of Oklahoma Press, 1991)

American Indian Literatures: An Introduction, Bibliographic Review and Selected Bibliography, by A. LaVonne Brown Ruoff (New York: Modern Language Association, 1990)

American Indian Novelists: An Annotated Critical Bibliography, by Tom Colonnese and Louis Owens (New York: Garland Publishing, 1985)

American Indian Periodicals in the Princeton University Library, by Alfred L. Bush and Robert S. Fraser (Princeton, N.J.: Princeton University Press, 1970)

American Indian Poetry, by Helen Addison Howard (Boston: Twayne, 1979)

American Indian Prose and Poetry: An Anthology, ed. with an introductory essay by Margot Luise Therese Astrov (Gloucester, Mass.: P. Smith, 1970, [1946])

American Indian Prose and Poetry: We Wait in Darkness, ed. with an introduction by Gloria Levitas (New York: Putnam, 1974)

The American Indian Reader, ed. by Jeanette Henry (San Francisco: Indian Historian Press, 1972–1977)

The American Indian Speaks, ed. by John R. Milton (Vermillion: Dakota Press; University of South Dakota, 1969)

American Indian Women: A Guide to Research, by Gretchen M. Bataille and Kathleen M. Sands (New York: Garland Publishing, 1991)

American Indian Women: Telling Their Lives, by Gretchen M. Bataille and Kathleen Mullen Sands (Lincoln: University of Nebraska Press, 1984)

American Indians: An Annotated Bibliography of Selected Library Resources, by Will Antell, Lee Antell (Minneapolis: University of Minnesota Library Services Institute for Minnesota Indians, 1970)

American Visions: Multicultural Literature for Writers, by Delores La Guardia and Hans P. Guth (Mountain View, Calif.: Mayfield Publishing, 1995)

Ancestral Voice: Conversations with N. Scott Momaday, by Charles L. Woodard (Lincoln: University of Nebraska, c1989)

An Annotated Bibliography of American Indian and Eskimo Autobiographies, by David H. Brumble III (Lincoln: University of Nebraska, c1981)

Annotated Bibliography of the Literature on American Indians Published in State Historical Society Publications: New England and Middle Atlantic States, by Arlene Hirschfelder (Millwood, N.Y.: Kraus International Publications, 1982)

Arrows Four: Prose and Poetry by Young American Indians, ed. by T. D. Allen. (New York: Washington Square Press, c1974)

Association for the Study of American Indian Literatures Notes Journal (Las Cruces, N. Mex.: Department of English, New Mexico State University, 1984)

A Biobibliography of Native American Writers 1772–1924, by Daniel F. Littlefield Jr. and James W. Parins (Metuchen N.J. : Scarecrow Press, 1981)

A Biobibliography of Native American Writers 1771–1924, a supplement by Daniel F. Littlefield Jr. and James W. Parins (Metuchen N.J.: Scarerow Press, 1985)

Biographical Dictionary of Indians of the Americas, two vols., ed. and published, by CISCO; associate editor Gail Hamlin-Wilson (Newport Beach, Calif.: American Indian Publishers, 1991)

Braided Lives: An Anthology of Multicultural American Writing, first edition, by the Minnesota Humanities Commission and the Minnesota Council of Teachers of English (St. Paul: The Commission, 1991)

Carriers of the Dream Wheel: Contemporary Native American Poetry, first edition, ed. by Duane Niatum (New York: Harper & Row, 1975)

Circle of Motion: Arizona Anthology of Contemporary American Indian Literature, ed. by Kathleen Mullen Sands (Tempe: Arizona Historical Foundation, c1990)

The Clouds Threw This Light: Contemporary Native American Poetry, first edition, ed. by Phillip Foss (Santa Fe: Institute of American Indian Arts Press, 1983)

Come to Power: Eleven Contemporary American Indian Poets, by Dick Lourie, with an introduction by Joseph Bruchac (Trumansburg, N.Y.: Crossing Press, 1974)

Contemporary Authors (Detroit: Gale Research, 1981)

Contemporary Native American Literature: A Selected and Partially Annotated Bibliography, comp. by Angeline Jacobson (Metuchen, N.J.: Scarecrow Press, 1977)

Coyote's Journal, first edition, ed. by James Koller et al. (Berkeley: Wingbow Press, 1982)

Coyote the Trickster: Legends of North American Indians, retold by Gail Robinson and Douglas Hill (New York: Crane Russak, c1976)

Coyote Was Going There: Indian Literature of the Oregon Country, ed. and comp. by Jarold Ramsay (Seattle: University of Washington Press, c1977)

Coyote Was Here: Essays on Contemporary Native American Literary and Political Mobilization, ed. by Bo Scholer (Aarhaus, Denmark: SEKLOS, 1984)

Dancing on the Rim of the World: An Anthology of Contemporary Northwest Native American Writing, ed. by Andrea Lerner (Tucson: Sun Tracks; University of Arizona, c1990)

Dena'ina Sukdu'a (Taina Stories), by Kathleen Trefon, Joan M. Tenebaum (Fairbanks: Alaska Native Language Center, University of Alaska, 1976)

Dictionary of Native American Literature, ed. by Andrew Wiget (New York: Garland Publishing, 1994)

Earth Power Coming: Short Fiction in Native American Literature, ed. by Simon J. Ortiz (Tsaile, Ariz.: Navajo Community College Press, c1983)

Eskimo Poems from Canada and Greenland, trans. by Tom Lowenstein from material originally collected by Knud Rasmussen (Pittsburgh: University of Pittsburg Press, [1973])

Ethnohistorical Bibliography of the Ute Indians of Colorado, by Omer C. Stewart (Boulder: University of Colorado Press, 1971)

Fifty Western Writers: A Bio-bibliographical Sourcebook, ed. by Fred Erisman and Richard W. Etulain (Westport, Conn.: Greenwood Press, 1982)

First People, First Voices, ed. by Penny Petrone (Toronto; Buffalo: University of Toronto Press, c1983)

Folklore of the North American Indians: An Annotated Bibliography, comp. by Judith C. Ullom (Washington, D.C.: Library of Congress, 1969)

For Every North American Indian Who Begins to Disappear, I Also Begin to Disappear, by Willfred Pelletier (Agincourt, Ont.: Book Society of Canada, 1980)

For Those Who Come After: A Study of Native American Autobiography, by Arnold Krupat (Berkeley: University of California Press, 1985)

Forever There: Race and Gender in Contemporary Native American Fiction, by Elizabeth I. Hanson (New York: P. Lang, c1989)

Forked Tongues: Speech, Writing and Representation in North American Indian Texts, by David Murray (Bloomington: Indiana University Press, 1991)

Four American Indian Literary Masters: N. Scott Momaday, James Welch, Leslie Marmon Silko, and Gerald Vizenor, by Alan Velie (Norman: University of Oklahoma Press, c1982)

Four Corners of the Sky: Poems Chants and Oratory, first edition, selected by Theodore Clymer (Boston: Little, Brown, [1975])

Four Indian Poets, ed. by John R. Milton (Vermilion, S. Dak.: Dakota Press, 1974)

From the Belly of the Shark: A New Anthology of Native Americans, ed. by Walter Lowenfels (New York: Vantage, 1974)

A Gathering of Spirit: A Collection by North American Indian Women, ed. by Beth Brant (Degonwadonti) (Ithaca, N.Y. : Firebrand Books, 1988)

Guide to Research on North American Indians, by Arlene B. Hirschfelder, Mary Gloyne Byler, Michael A. Dorris (Chicago: American Library Association, 1983)

Harper's Anthology of Twentieth-Century Native American Poetry, first edition, ed. by Duane Niatum (San Francisco: Harper & Row, 1988)

I Am an Indian, ed. by Kent Gooderham (New York: Dent, 1969)

I Am the Fire of Time: The Voices of Native American Women, first edition, ed. by Jane B. Katz (New York: Dutton, 1977)

I Breathe a New Song: Poems of the Eskimo, by Richard Lewis with an introduction by Edmund Carpenter (New York: Simon & Schuster, 1971)

I Tell You Now: Autobiographical Essays by Native American Writers, ed. by Brian Swann and Arnold Krupat (Lincoln: University of Nebraska, c1987)

Image of the New World: The American Continent Portrayed in Native Texts, comp. by Gordon Brotherston, translations prepared in collaboration with Ed Dorn (London: Thames & Hudson, 1979)

In the Trail of the Wind: American Indian Poems and Ritual Orations, first edition, ed. by John Bierhorst (New York: Farrar, Straus and Giroux, 1971)

"In Vain I Tried to Tell You": Essays in Native American Ethnopoetics, by Dell H. Hymes (Philadelphia: University of Pennsylvania, 1981)

Index to Literature on the American Indian, journal (San Francisco: Indian Historian Press, 1970–1973)

Indian Lives, by Nancy Oestreich Lurie (Milwaukee: Milwaukee Public Museum, 1985)

Indian Voices: The First Convocation of American Indian Scholars (San Francisco: Indian Historian Press, c1970)

Indians of North and South America: A Bibliography Based on the Collection at the Willard E. Yager Library-Museum, Hartwick College, Oneonta, New York, supplement, by C. E. Wolf and N. S. Chang (Metuchen, N.J.: Scarecrow Press, 1988)

Indians of the United States and Canada: A Bibliography, ed. by Dwight L. Smith (Santa Barbara: ABC-CLIO, 1974)

Indians of Today, fourth edition, ed. and comp. by Marion F. Gridley ([S.l.]: I.C.F.P., 1971)

INAD Literary Journal (Albuquerque: Institute for Native American Development, Native American Studies, University of New Mexico, 1980)

Interpreting the Indian: Twentieth-Century Poets and the Native American, first edition, Michael Castro (Albuquerque: University of New Mexico Press, c1983)

Inventing the Indian: White Images, Native Oral Literature and Contemporary Native Writers, microfilm, by Thomas Hunt King (Ph.D. Thesis, University of Utah, 1986)

Keepers of the Earth: Native American Stories and Environmental Activities for Children, by Michael J. Caduto and Joseph Bruchac, foreword by N. Scott Momaday (Golden, Colo.: Fulcrum, c1988 [paperback, 1997])

The Lightning Within: An Anthology of Contemporary American Indian Fiction, ed. with an introduction by Alan Velie (Lincoln: University of Nebraska Press, c1991)

Literature by and about the American Indian: An Annotated Bibliography for Junior and Senior High School Students, by Anna Lee Stensland (Urbana, Ill.: National Council for Teachers of English, 1973)

Literature of the American Indian, comp. by Thomas Sanders and William Peek (Beverly Hills: Glencoe Press, [1973])

Literature of the American Indians: Views and Interpretations; a Gathering of Indian Memories, Symbolic Contexts and Literary Criticism, ed. with an introduction and notes by Abraham Chapman (New York: New American Library, 1975)

Living the Spirit: A Gay American Indian Anthology, comp. by Gay American Indians, co-ordinating editor Will Roscoe (New York: St. Martin's Press, c1988)

Looking at the Words of Our People: First Nations Analysis of Literature, ed. by Jeannette Armstrong (Penticton, B.C.: Theytus Books, 1993)

The Man to Send Rain Clouds: Contemporary Stories by American Indians, ed. with an introduction by Kenneth Rosen (New York: Viking Press, [1974])

Manohar Malgonkar, by G. S. Amur (New York: Humanities Press, [1973])

Narrative Chance: Postmodern Discourse on Native American Indian Literatures, ed. by Gerald Vizenor (Albuquerque: University of New Mexico Press, 1989)

A Nation Within: Contemporary Native American Writing, selected by Ralph Salisbury (Hamilton, New Zealand: Outrigger Publishers, 1983)

Native American Discourse: Poetics and Rhetoric, ed. by Joel Sherzer and Anthony C. Woodbury (Cambridge: Cambridge University Press, 1987)

The Native American in American Literature: A Selectively Annotated Bibliography, comp. by Roger O. Rock (Westport, Conn.: Greenwood Press, 1985)

Native American Literature, by Andrew Wiget (Boston: Twayne, 1985)

Native American Literature: A Guide to Native American Literature in the NAU [Northern Arizona University] Libraries, Vicky Granada and the editors of *Discovery* ([Flagstaff]: Northern Arizona University Libraries, 1981)

Native American Reader: Stories, Speeches and Poems, ed. and commentary by Jerry D. Blanche (Juneau: Denali Press, c1990)

Native American Renaissance, by Kenneth Lincoln (Berkeley: University of California Press, c1983)

Native North American Literature: Biographical and Critical Information on Native Writers and Orators from the United States and Canada from Historical Times to the Present,

Janet Witalec, editor; Jefferey Chapman, Christopher Giroux, associated editors (New York: Gale Research, c1994)

Native Writers and Canadian Writing, ed. by William H. New (Vancouver, B.C.: University of British Columbia Press, 1990)

Navajo Bibliography, David N. Brugge, J. Lee Connell and Edith Watson (Window Rock, Ariz.: Navajo Tribal Museum, 1967)

Navajo Folk Tales, by Franc Johndson Newcomb, foreword by Paul Zolbrod (Albuquerque: University of New Mexico Press, 1990, 1967)

Neon Pow-wow: New Native American Voices of the Southwest, first edition, ed. by Anna Lee Walters (Flagstaff: Northland, c1993)

New and Old Voices of Wah'Kon-Tah, third edition, ed. by Robert K. Dodge and Joseph B. McCollugh with a foreword by Vine Deloria Jr. (New York: International Publishers, c1985)

New Voices from the Longhouse: An Anthology of Contemporary Iroquois Writing, first edition, ed. by Joseph Bruhac; contributing editors, Maurice Kenny, Karonia Ktatie (Greenfield Center, NY: Greenfield Review Press, c1989)

The Only Good Indian: Essays by Canadian Indians, revised edition, H. A. McCue (Don Mills, Ont.: New Press, 1974, 1970)

Plains Indian Autobiographies, Lynn Woods O'Brien (Boise: Boise State College, [1973])

Portable North American Indian Reader, ed. by Frederick W. Turner III (New York: Viking Press, [1974])

Raven Tells Stories: An Anthology of Alaskan Native Writing, ed. by Joseph Bruchac (Greenfield Center, N.Y.: Greenfield Review Press, c1991)

Reading the Fire: Essays in the Traditional Indian Literatures of the Far West, by Jarold Ramsay (Lincoln: University of Nebraska Press, 1983)

Recovering the Word: Essays on Native American Literature, ed. by Brian Swann and Arnold Krupat (Berkeley: University of California Press, c1987)

Reference Encyclopedia of the American Indian, sixth edition, ed. by Barry T. Klein (West Nyak, N.Y.: Todd Publications, c1993)

The Remembered Earth: An Anthology of Contemporary Native American Literature, ed. by Geary Hobson (Albuquerque: Red Earth Press, 1979)

Returning the Gift: Poetry and Prose from the First North American Native Writers' Festival, ed. by Joseph Bruchac with the support of the Association for the Study of American Indian Literatures (Tucson: University of Arizona, c1994)

The Sacred Hoop: Recovering the Feminine in American Indian Traditions, by Paula Gunn Allen (Boston: Beacon Press, 1986)

Shaking the Pumpkin: Traditional Poetry of the Indian North Americas, revised edition, comp. by Jerome Rothenberg (Albuquerque: University of New Mexico, 1991)

The Sky Clears: Poetry of the American Indians, by A. Grove Day (Lincoln: University of Nebraska Press, [1964, c1951])

Songs of the Dream People: Chants and Images from the Indians and Eskimos of North America, ed. by James A. Houston (Don Mills, Ont.: Longman Canada, 1972)

Songs of This Earth on Turtle's Back, first edition, ed. by Joseph Bruchac (Greenfield Center, N.Y.: Greenfield Review Press, 1983)

The South Corner of Time: Hopi, Navajo, Papago, Yaqui Tribal Literature, ed. by Larry Evers et al. (Tucson: University of Arizona, 1980)

Southern Writers: A Biographical Dictionary, ed. by Robert Bain, Josephe M. Flora, and Louis D. Rubin Jr. (Baton Rouge: Louisiana State University Press, 1979)

Southwest Heritage: A Literary History with Bibliographies, third edition, revised and enlarged, by Mabel Major and T. M. Pearce (Albuquerque: University of New Mexico Press, [1972])

Spider Woman's Granddaughters: Traditional Tales and Contemporary Writing by Native American Women, ed. by Paula Gunn Allen (Boston: Beacon Press, 1989)

Stories of Native Alaskans, by the Alaska Library Association (Fairbanks: University of Alaska Press, 1977)

Studies in American Indian Literature: Critical Essays and Course Designs, ed. by Paula Gunn Allen (New York: Modern Languages Association, c1983)

Studies in American Indian Literatures: Newsletter of the Association for the Study of American Indian Literatures, series 2, vol. 2, no. 2 (New York: The Association, Summer 1990)

Sun Tracks, journal (Tucson, Ariz.: Sun Tracks, vols. 1–6, 1971–1980)

Survival This Way: Interviews with Native American Poets, by Joseph Bruhac (Tucson: Sun Tracks; University of Arizona Press, c1987)

Talking Leaves: Contemporary Native American Short Stories, An Anthology, introduced and ed. by Craig Lesley, associate editor Katheryn Stavrakis (New York: Laurel; Dell, 1991).

That's What She Said: Contemporary Poetry and Fiction by Native American Women, ed. by Rayna Green (Bloomington: Indiana University Press, c1984)

To Be an Indian: An Oral History, ed. by Joseph H. Cash and Herbert T. Hoover (New York: Holt, 1971)

To Carry Forth the Vine: An Anthology of Native North American Poetry, Alfonso Ortiz and Margaret D. Ortiz (New York: Columbia University, 1974)

Traditional Literatures of the American Indian: Texts and Interpretation, comp. and ed. by Karl Kroeber (Lincoln: University of Nebraska Press, 1981)

Twentieth-Century Western Writers, preface by C. L. Sonnichsen; ed. by James Vinson; associate editor D. L. Kirkpatrick (Detroit: Gale, 1982)

Voices from Wah'Kon-Tah, ed. by Robert K. Dodge and Joseph B. McCullough (New York: International Publishers, 1974)

Voices of the Rainbow: Contemporary Poetry by American Indians, ed. by Kenneth Rosen (New York: Viking Press, 1975)

The Way: An Anthology of American Indian Literature, ed. by Shirley Witt and Stan Steiner (New York: Vantage, [1972])

The Whispering Wind: Poetry by Young American Indians, first edition, ed. by Terry Allen with an introduction by Mae J. Durham (Garden City, N.Y.: Doubleday, [1972])

White on Red: Images of the American Indian, ed. by Nancy B. Black and Bette S. Weidman (Port Washington, N.Y.: Kennikat Press, 1976)

Windigo: An Anthology of Fact and Fantastic Fiction, ed. by John Robert Colombo (Saskatoon, Sask.: Western Producer Prairie Books, 1982)

Winged Words: American Indian Writers Speak, reported by Laura Coltelli (Lincoln: University of Nebraska Press, 1990)

Words in the Blood: Contemporary Indian Writers of North and South America, ed. with an introduction and notes by Jamaike Highwater (New York: New American Library, 1984)

Yaqui Deer Songs, Maso Bwikam: A Native American Poetry, by Larry Evers and Felipe S. Molina (Tucson: Sun Tracks: University of Arizona Press, c1987)

ABOUT THE AUTHORS

Kay Juricek was born and raised in Crete, Nebraska. She received a B.F.A. from the University of Nebraska and was awarded the Hollingsworth Scholarship to attend Columbia University where she earned her M.S. from the School of Library Service in 1984. Juricek worked as an assistant professor at the University of Wyoming Library and also at the Colorado School of Mines in Golden. She has published in the journal *College and Research Libraries* and is presently the librarian at the Department of Public Health and Environment Library in Denver.

Kelly J. Morgan was born on Blackfeet Indian Reservation in Montana and was raised in Standing Rock Reservation in North and South Dakota. After receiving B.A. and M.A. degrees at the University of North Dakota at Grand Forks, she was awarded a Centennial Research Assistantship in the English department from the University of Oklahoma.

DATE DUE

PRINTED IN U.S.A.